Women

OF THE BIBLE

THE LIFE AND TIMES
OF EVERY WOMAN IN THE BIBLE

THOMAS NELSON
Since 1798

NASHVILLE DALLAS MEXICO CITY RIO DE JANEIRO BEIJING

Women of the Bible

© 2003 by Sue Poorman Richards and Lawrence O. Richards

Published in Nashville, Tennessee, by Thomas Nelson, Inc.
P.O. Box 14100, Nashville, Tennessee 37214.

Library of Congress Cataloging-in-Publication Data is available.

Richards, Sue Poorman
Women of the Bible
(Formerly Every Woman in the Bible / Sue and Larry Richards; illustrated by Paul Richards.)

Includes indexes.

ISBN 10-0-7852-5148-0
ISBN 13-978-0-7852-5148-4

23 24 25 26 27 LBC 23 22 21 20 19

Dedication

This book is dedicated to our mothers, C. Gertrude Cunningham Poorman, and in memory of Charlotte Mable Zeluff Richards; to our sisters, Eunice Richards Cresswell, Jeane Poorman Ripley, and JoAnn Gilson Poorman. And in memory of Sue's sister, Judith Margaret Poorman Zylstra, who passed away suddenly at age 52 during the writing of the first edition of this book. Judie's life modeled how we are to "love one another." She is sadly missed, yet we thank God we do not grieve as those who have no hope. And lastly, we dedicate this book to our daughters, Joy Grace Richards, Sarah Janine Duffitt, and in memory of Jennifer Lauretta Duffitt, and Sue's grandmother, Winnie Tippi Haughtelling.

—Larry and Sue

Contents

Introduction

Welcome to *Women of the Bible*. Women have played exciting roles as the drama of redemption has unfolded across the centuries. For a number of reasons, many people are more familiar with the roles played by men. In this book, however, you will meet the women whom God used to forge His plan of salvation and learn from their lives.

Several features make this book unique among books on Bible women. First, you will notice that every woman, named and unnamed, is listed in alphabetical order. A handy index in the back of the book will help you further to find the information you need. Following the A to Z® listing, you will find several appendices. These appendices are rich with cultural and historical data—from an in-depth study of the Proverbs 31 woman, to Jesus' relationships with women. Again, the index will help you find the information you seek.

Whether you use this book as a resource for Bible or character study, or as a daily devotional, years of enjoyment are at your fingertips. As a supplement to your library, we have also published the men's companion piece, *Men of the Bible*.

Now, turn the pages and go back in time to experience the life and times of *Women of the Bible*.

Abigail

Scripture References: *1 Samuel 25:3–42; 27:3; 30:5;*
2 Samuel 2:2; 3:2; 1 Chronicles 3:1

When They Lived: *About 1000 B.C.*

Name: *Abigail [AB-uh-gail:"father rejoices"]*

Historical Significance: *Abigail prevented David from shedding the blood of God's people and so impressed David that he later married her.*

HER ROLE IN SCRIPTURE

*A**bigail's story*. Abigail was married to a man named Nabal ["fool"], a wealthy rancher. During his outlaw years David and his followers had been camped near Nabal's lands. Rather than raid Nabal's flocks, David's men helped his shepherds protect the sheep.

When sheep shearing time arrived, David sent some of his men to Nabal, asking for appropriate remuneration. Nabal, despite the testimony of his herdsmen and shepherds, refused their request and insulted David. When David heard, he was furious, and he immediately set out with his men to wipe out Nabal and his whole household.

Meanwhile, the herdsmen, shocked by Nabal's response and terrified at what David might do, went to Abigail. She immediately assembled foodstuffs and set out to intercept David. First Samuel 25:23–31 tells us:

> Now when Abigail saw David, she dismounted quickly from the donkey, fell on her face before David, and bowed down to the ground. So she fell at his feet and said: "On me, my LORD, on me let this iniquity be! And please let your maidservant speak in your ears, and hear the words of your maidservant. Please, let not my LORD regard this scoundrel Nabal. For as his name is, so is he: Nabal is his name, and folly is with him! But I, your maidservant, did not see the young men of my lord whom you sent. Now therefore, my lord, as the LORD lives and as your soul lives, since the LORD has held

you back from coming to bloodshed and from avenging yourself with your own hand, now then, let your enemies and those who seek harm for my lord be as Nabal. And now this present, which your maidservant has brought to my lord, let it be given to the young men who follow my lord. Please forgive the trespass of your maidservant. For the LORD will certainly make for my lord an enduring house, because my lord fights the battles of the LORD, and evil is not found in you throughout your days.

Yet a man has risen to pursue you and seek your life, but the life of my lord shall be bound in the bundle of the living with the LORD your God; and the lives of your enemies He shall sling out, as from the pocket of a sling. And it shall come to pass, when the LORD has done for my lord according to all the good that He has spoken concerning you, and has appointed you ruler over Israel, that this will be no grief to you, nor offense of heart to my lord, either that you have shed blood without cause, or that my lord has avenged himself. But when the LORD has dealt well with my lord, then remember your maidservant.

Abigail's quick action and her words reveal both a special intelligence and wisdom. She succeeded in turning David from his plan and so impressed him that when Nabal died of a stroke a few days later, David married Abigail.

Abigail's strategy. An analysis of Abigail's appeal to David indicates she was wise and politically astute.

Abigail sided with David. Abigail agreed that the way David had been treated by her husband was evil (v. 25), and even though no one had told her of the young men's request, Abigail counted her failure to respond to their request as a trespass (v. 28). In acknowledging that David had been in the right, Abigail dealt with the personal affront that had so angered David.

Abigail met David's request. The food Abigail brought with her showed she agreed that David's original request was justified. She did not rely on words alone to convey her agreement but added actions to her words.

Abigail emphasized her positive view of David's character. Abigail was careful to convey an appropriate image of David. People often act out our expectations. In speaking of David, Abigail emphasized those character traits that contrasted with David's angry intent to take revenge. Abigail reminded David that he was the kind of person who "fights the battles of the LORD, and evil is not found in you throughout your days" (v. 28).

Abigail appealed to David to identify with those he had intended to kill. Abigail reminded David that Saul had "risen to pursue you and seek your life" while God had bound him "in the bundle of the living" (v. 29). Nabal might deserve death for insulting David, but to kill all the males in Nabal's household, as David had vowed, would be to treat them as Saul had treated him.

Abigail reminded David of his own values. David felt that unnecessary bloodshed was wrong. A person who avenged himself with his own hand violated God's commandment against murder (v. 26). Abigail invited David to see her own appearance as a sign that "the LORD has held you back" from such sinful actions.

Abigail also suggested that killing Nabal would be politically unwise. Abigail invited David to look ahead to the time when the Lord would make David "ruler over Israel" (v. 30). She urged him to hold back now so that then "this will be no grief" to him. If David were to rule a united Israel, how foolish it would be to alienate one of the tribes of Israel by murdering one of its members!

David's response. Abigail's speech, although brief, is filled with subtle argument, the wisdom of which David immediately recognized. His response to Abigail was, "Blessed is the LORD God of Israel, who sent you this day to meet me!" (v. 32).

Abigail truly was God's messenger to David, and even more, David's counselor. David, a strong man, was not offended by the words of this wise woman. He recognized her strengths and deeply appreciated them.

As noted, when Nabal died a few days later from a stroke (1 Sam. 25:38), David "sent and proposed to Abigail, to take her as his wife" (v. 40). Abigail eagerly accepted David's proposal and she "became his wife" (v. 42).

BIBLE BACKGROUND: "WITH YOUR OWN HAND"

Two Hebrew words are translated as "kill" and "murder." One of the words simply describes a killing, without making a moral judgment. This word is used when killing in warfare or judicial execution is involved. The other Hebrew word is found in the Ten Commandments, and should be translated "you shall not murder" rather than "you shall not kill." What the word translated "murder" implies is a *personal killing*. That is, one person takes the life of another for a personal reason, not as an impersonal act in warfare, and not as a judicial, governmental act.

Both Abigail and David knew that a person who "avenges himself with his own hand" commits murder, for this was definitely a personal killing.

A CLOSE-UP

All we know of Abigail is summed up in the passage that describes her brief but intense meeting with David. Yet she comes through as one of the most notable women of the Old Testament. Abigail was wise, decisive, and yet sensitive. She clearly had great interpersonal skills, and was not only able to diffuse David's anger, but also was able to help him think through the consequences of his hastily conceived intentions. She enabled David to retain his self-respect and the respect of his men. Abigail seemed intuitively able to realize that David was a complex individual, and she shaped her appeal to fit not only David's political goals but also his moral commitments. Abigail appealed to what was best in David's character. She helped him choose to act out of those basic values.

The brief glimpse of Abigail that the Bible gives us shows a strong and independent woman. Those in Nabal's household, who hurried to Abigail when their master acted foolishly, recognized these qualities in her. Abigail was a person on whom all around her could and did depend.

David's brief encounter with Abigail so impressed him that when Nabal died a few days later, David was eager to take Abigail as his wife. David clearly saw Abigail as a person who could complement his own strengths and balance his weaknesses. Like other men who are secure in themselves, David found himself attracted by Abigail's obvious strengths. Only weak and insecure men are frightened of strong women. Women who have some of Abigail's qualities do themselves a disservice if they try to hide their strengths out of fear of frightening away men.

AN EXAMPLE FOR TODAY

- ◆ Abigail provides us with a pattern for successful confrontation.
- ◆ Couples today should emulate the exchange between Abigail and David. Abigail offered advice, but in a wise and gracious way. David did not let his ego deter him from heeding what she said.
- ◆ Abigail reminds us that women should not hide their strengths in an effort to be acceptable to men. Many weak men want women who are less intelligent and less confident than themselves. In hiding their strengths for fear they will put off potential dates or marriage, many women disguise the very qualities that might make them attractive to stronger, confident godly men.

~ Achsah ~

Caleb's Daughter

Scripture References: *Joshua 15:13–19*
When They Lived: *About 1400 B.C.*
Name: *Achsah [ACK-sah]*

HER ROLE IN SCRIPTURE

Achsah was the daughter of Caleb, one of the two spies who, forty years earlier, had urged the Israelites to trust God and invade Canaan (Num. 13). Only Caleb and his companion, Joshua, survived the thirty-eight years of wandering in the wilderness. Caleb, as filled with faith in his old age as he had been four decades earlier, attacked the Canaanite strongholds on the lands that were to be his portion after the conquest. Eager to have son's-in-law as courageous and faith-filled as himself, Caleb promised his daughter Achsah to the man who would attack and take Kirjath Sepher.

Othniel, Caleb's nephew, accepted the challenge and won Achsah's hand. While Achsah had no legal right to hold land in her own name, her influence with her husband and father was critical in providing for her family.

EXPLORING HER RELATIONSHIPS

Achsah's relationship with her father. Caleb must have thought that his daughter, Achsah, was special, since he offered her to the man who would conquer Kirjath Sepher. It is doubtful that a man would go to battle to win the hand of a woman if he did not think she was special. With two good men from different generations thinking Aschsah was so remarkable, she probably was.

Achsah must have also felt especially close to her father. She felt comfortable enough to tell her husband to ask for land from her father, and after he had given them land, she felt secure enough to pay a call on him and ask to be blessed with some land with springs as well. If this father and daughter didn't have a good rapport and trust, she probably would not have felt free to make these requests.

A CLOSE-UP

Achsah was an assertive young woman with some definite ideas about what she wanted. How important it is when we read about women of the Old Testament to remember an important reality. Whatever position society may assign an individual, that person's personality will have a tremendous impact on his or her future. Achsah was clearly able to persuade her husband and to appeal effectively to her father and gain what she wanted.

Who we are and how we behave within our circumstances will likely have a greater impact on our experience than the limits society seeks to impose on us.

AN EXAMPLE FOR TODAY

Achsah reminds us of the time James said, "You do not have because you do not ask [God]" (James 4:2). Achsah told her husband to ask her father for land. Then she personally asked for springs of water and Caleb gave her what she wanted. Sometimes communicating with God or even other people is the most direct way of having our needs met, yet often we are unwilling to ask.

Adah & Zillah

Lamech's Two Wives

Scripture References: *Genesis 4:19–24*
Names: *Adah [AY-duh, "adorned"]*
Zillah [ZIL-uh, "shadow protection"]

THEIR ROLE IN SCRIPTURE

Lamech was a descendant of Cain. He is the first recorded person to have two wives. This clearly was not God's desire. As we have seen, Scripture's ideal is that "a man shall leave his father and mother and be joined to his wife, and they shall become one flesh" (Gen. 2:24). With Lamech's choice we begin the erosion of God's ideal of lifelong bonding between one woman and one man.

The two women are significant as the mothers of sons who mark the rise of an advanced civilization. Adah's son, Jabal, was "the father of those who dwell in tents and have livestock" (Gen. 4:20), and her son Jubal was the father of "all those who play the harp and flute" (Gen. 4:21). Zillah's son, Tubal-Cain, became an instructor of craftsmen in bronze and iron.

With these three individuals, pre-Flood society moves beyond a subsistence level economy to become a tool-making society able to support individual devotion to the arts.

EXPLORING THEIR RELATIONSHIPS

We know little about their relationship with their husband or children. We do know that they were willing to live outside God's will in a polygamist situation. Despite the creature comforts suggested in their sons' achievements, these women must have had empty lives.

EXAMPLES FOR TODAY

How important is a person's ability to provide creature comforts? What are we willing to sacrifice to marry a man or woman who is well off? The brief portrait of the two wives of Lamech reminds us that we should not be willing to surrender our self-respect, or trade ourselves for the things a wealthy spouse might be able to provide. And we surely must not be willing to surrender doing God's will—the one true guide to blessing in this life and in the world to come.

The Adulteress

Scripture References: *John 8:3–11*

HER ROLE IN SCRIPTURE

The situation. One day some scribes and Pharisees brought to Jesus a woman who had been caught in adultery, "in the very act" (John 8:4). They quoted Moses' Law, which called for stoning, and asked Jesus, "'But what do You say?'"

Several things make this approach to Jesus unusual:

◆ The woman was caught "in the very act." Where was the man with whom she was caught?
◆ Where would a person go to catch someone "in the very act?" How would the Pharisees, noted for their claim to holiness, have known where to go?

◆ While Mosaic Law prescribed stoning for adultery, this penalty was not imposed in the first century. Rabbinic courts rigorously avoided imposing the death penalty.

◆ A panel of rabbis, not an individual, would deal with such a case. Besides, the scribes and Pharisees did not recognize Jesus' authority.

These facts make it clear that the delegation was not seeking a legal opinion, nor were they concerned with punishing the woman. They wanted to discredit Jesus. If He called for stoning, He would alienate the people. If He failed to call for stoning, they could accuse Him of denying the authority of the Law.

Rather than answer their question, Jesus simply said, "He who is without sin among you, let him throw a stone at her first" (John 8:7). Jesus then stooped and wrote on the ground. One by one, the woman's accusers slipped away, leaving Jesus and the adulteress alone. No one was left to condemn her, and Jesus said, "'Neither do I condemn you; go and sin no more'" (John 8:11).

Jesus' response to the challenge not only avoided the trap; it also radically changed the status of the woman. Before Christ spoke, the woman had been nothing more than an abstract test case, a disposable object to be used against Jesus. But Jesus would not deal with her in the abstract. Jesus treated her and her accusers as human beings. In insisting that one without sin cast the first stone, Jesus forced each opponent to examine his own conscience and to deal with his own humanity rather than with legal theory.

Then Jesus spoke to the woman. While Jesus assured the woman that He did not condemn her, He let her know that He was fully aware of her guilt. He told her to go, but He also told her to sin no more. Jesus treated her as a person responsible for her own actions. She had the ability to make choices—even to make choices that reversed the course of her former life.

The woman. While we do not know this woman's name, we know more about her than a brief reading of the text might suggest. We know she was an adulteress. That she was taken "in the very act" suggests that she may have been a prostitute, whose venue was well known. We know from ancient literature that prostitutes lived in Jerusalem in the first century, so this is not unlikely. Surely a "professional" would have been easy to locate and to catch "in the very act."

First-century rabbinic writings portray loose women as bold and brazen. However, women who engaged in prostitution were likely driven to that life by grim necessity. They faced ostracism by respectable citizens and were viewed with utter contempt by the more religious people. Such women certainly did not possess a positive self-image, nor were they the temptresses portrayed in rabbinic writings. They would have been as much victims as victimizers.

Yet there is no doubt this woman was a sinner. Ironically, the response of her accusers when Jesus challenged them showed that they were sinners, too. Guilty men brought a guilty woman before the One Person who knew the hearts of all: the One Person who had entered the world not to condemn sinners but to save them.

In this, we sense there is hope for the woman and for all of us. "'Neither do I condemn you,'" Jesus said. "'Go, and sin no more'" (v. 11).

Jesus did not dismiss her sin; He granted her a reprieve, gave her the freedom to go, and He implicitly recognized that the choices she had yet to make would determine the shape of her future. In telling her to "'sin no more,'" Jesus reminded the woman that the choice was hers. She had known what was right in the past and had made the wrong choice. Would she make a better choice tomorrow?

When Jesus asked who would accuse her, the woman replied, "'No one, LORD'" (8:11). Did she recognize Jesus as LORD and commit herself to obey Him? Wasn't her future secure? No, for the Greek word translated "lord" was also used simply to express respect. Her words might better be rendered, "No one, *sir*."

In this passage, we meet a woman who was used by Jesus' enemies, whose humanity and value Jesus reaffirmed, but whose future remained in doubt. Would she return to her past life, or would she accept the responsibility for herself that Jesus offered? Would she return to her past life, or would she go and sin no more?

AN EXAMPLE FOR TODAY

◆ It's so easy to condemn others for their sins, or to use their sins to justify our own. ("At least I've never done *that!*") Thankfully, our Savior is more gracious than we are.

◆ This woman's story provides us with a beautiful example of how Christians can display Christ's graciousness toward others. We are not to excuse sin, but we are not to condemn the sinner. Rather, we point others to Jesus. He forgives sin and provides the power needed to "'go, and sin no more.'"

~ *Ahinoam* ~

The Wife of Saul

Scripture References: *1 Samuel 14:50*
When They Lived: *About 1025 B.C.*
Name: *Ahinoam [uh-HIN-oh-am:"brother is delight"]*

HER ROLE IN SCRIPTURE

The Ahinoam to whom Saul was married is mentioned only one time in the Old Testament: "Saul's wife was Ahinoam the daughter of Ahimaaz." David married a woman of the same name, of whom we also know little except that she gave David his firstborn son, Amnon. Yet David's Ahinoam is mentioned no less than six times in Scripture.

We might account for the difference by the fact that David is far more significant in sacred history than Saul. Yet the single brief mention of Saul's Ahinoam seems somehow suggestive. Her name is never associated with the names of Saul's sons or daughters, although, as Saul's sole wife, she must have borne them. It is almost as if Ahinoam were a ghost, so insubstantial a presence in the royal household that no one took notice of her.

This impression is strengthened when we recall the experience of Michal, Saul's daughter. Where was Ahinoam when Saul chose to use Michal's innocent love to ensnare David? Where was Ahinoam when Saul tried to kill David, and Michal bravely stood by her husband? Where was Ahinoam when Saul denounced the marriage of Michal and David and gave his daughter to another man? Perhaps Ahinoam had died by then. Or, perhaps, Ahinoam was one of those well-meaning but ineffective individuals who wanted the best for her daughter, but was too fearful to intercede on her behalf.

How many women enter marriage with such a strong desire to please their husbands that their own identity gradually slips away? How many women, after years of marriage, know only the things their husbands like or dislike, and no longer have tastes or opinions of their own? And how many women become so insubstantial that, when their children most need their support, they simply have nothing to give?

We cannot know if Ahinoam was one of these women. But if Ahinoam still lived when controversy swirled around David, Saul, and Michal, the Bible's silence about her may be significant indeed.

AN EXAMPLE FOR TODAY

- ◆ While it is easier for some people to be assertive, we all have a responsibility to confront others. This is especially true for the married. When we see a spouse using poor judgment, or not looking at all the options, or doing wrong (to name a few), we need to speak up.
- ◆ When a spouse points something out to us, we should carefully weigh the message and its implications. After all, husbands are to love their wives sacrificially as Christ loved the church. And true love—whether from a husband or a wife—doesn't ignore or become hostile.

The Anointing Sinner

Scripture References: *Luke 7:36–50*
See also page 299.

This is another of the anonymous women of the Gospels. We are never told her name, although some have erroneously identified her with other women who also anointed Jesus with oil or perfume. This woman, unlike the others, performed her act of love early in Jesus' ministry while she was in the home of a Pharisee who despised her.

The following chart suggests three distinct women who anointed Jesus. While there are a number of similarities between the incidents, there are also enough differences to enable us to distinguish between them. That three women performed this act suggests that such an act, while uncommon, was a culturally understood way of expressing devotion.

	The first woman Luke 7:36–50	The second woman John 12:1–8	The third woman Matthew 26:1–5; Mark 14:3
Location	Jerusalem	Bethany	Bethany
Place	Home of Simon a Pharisee	Home of Lazarus	House of Simon the leper
Date		Six days before Passover	Two days before Passover
Material	Alabaster jar of ointment	Pound of perfume made of nard	Alabaster jar of ointment of nard
Action	Bathed feet with tears, kissed feet, anointed them	Anointed feet and wiped with hair	Poured ointment on head
Response by	The Pharisee	Judas/the disciples	Some who were there
Response	"If this man were a prophet."	Why wasn't money given to the poor?	Why wasn't money given to the poor?

Jesus	Taught Simon	"Leave the woman alone." "Always have the poor with you."	"Leave the woman alone." "The poor always with you."
Jesus' remarks to the woman	"Your sins are forgiven."	"For the day of my burial."	"Prepared me for burial." "What she has done will be told in remembrance of her."

HER ROLE IN SCRIPTURE

What we know about the woman's past (Luke 7:37). The text tells us she was "a sinner." While the Pharisees tended to look down on those not of their own order, Luke's usage of the phrase "a sinner" and the Pharisee's horror at the sight of her touching Jesus indicates she was a prostitute. As the Pharisee would have considered himself ceremonially unclean if such a woman touched him, the Pharisee immediately concluded that Jesus could not be a prophet or He would "know who and what manner of woman this is who is touching Him, for she is a sinner" (Luke 7:39).

What we know about the woman's future (Luke 7:39, 50). The Pharisee's reaction tells us much about the woman's prospects for the future. Her past actions had so defined her in the eyes of decent society that there was no hope for redemption. She had been labeled a "sinner." Nothing the woman could do in the future would remove the label as far as the Pharisee and his like were concerned.

At this point, Jesus asked the Pharisee to solve a simple riddle. If a creditor were to forgive two debtors, one who owed ten times as much as the other, which would love the creditor more? The answer was obvious, but Christ's point was profound. The Pharisee, who assumed he had not sinned, served God but did not love God. The woman, who knew the depths of her degradation and who had sensed Jesus' forgiving love, had been transformed within and now loved God supremely.

Knowing this, Jesus told the woman, "'Your sins are forgiven,'" and added, "Your faith has saved you. Go in peace" (7:48, 50). By these words, the woman and her future were transformed, her past was wiped out, and she was granted God's own peace—a peace that would sustain her through the rest of her days on earth and into eternity.

BIBLE BACKGROUND: ANOINTING WOMEN

The chart on pages 13–14 helps us distinguish between three women who anointed Jesus. While there are a number of similarities between the incidents, there are also enough differences to enable us to distinguish between them. That three women performed this act suggests that such an act, while uncommon, was a culturally understood way of expressing devotion.

AN EXAMPLE FOR TODAY

◆ Our past is not as important as our present. The woman who came to Jesus had a past that she regretted. Yet society, represented by the Pharisee, would always identify her by what she had been and had done. How wonderful that Jesus is able to transform our hearts. What we were, we no longer need be. In time, even society will recognize our new identity and take notice that we have been with Jesus.

◆ Similarly, our past does not determine our future. Jesus accepted and appreciated the ministry of this woman who had been a sinner—even when His own disciples stood in judgment. Today, some seek to hinder others who are eager to serve for reasons that are no longer relevant in Christ. We need to listen to Him as we set out to minister in His name.

The Anointing Woman

at Simon the Leper's House

Scripture References: Matthew 26:1, 2, 6–13; Mark 14:3–9

HER ROLE IN SCRIPTURE

As the chart on pages 13–14 points out, there were three occasions on which women displayed their love for Jesus by anointing him with precious perfumes. This woman is unnamed, but her act is memorialized.

She anointed Jesus just two days before His crucifixion. Unlike the other anointing women, she poured it on Christ's head rather than His feet. Again there were objections. Wouldn't it have been better to sell the ointment and give the money to the poor? Jesus responded:

"Why do you trouble the woman? For she has done a good work for Me. For you have the poor with you always, but Me you do not have always. For in pouring this fragrant oil on My body, she did it for My burial. Assuredly, I say to you, wherever this gospel is preached in the whole world, what this woman has done will also be told as a memorial to her" (Matt. 26:10–13).

Jesus' words bring the woman's action into focus. He said, "'She did it for My burial'" (Matt. 26:12). We do not know whether the woman understood the significance of her action, but Matthew 26:1 tells us that Jesus had just told "His disciples" that He was about to be crucified. Since women were among His disciples, it is possible that she knew exactly what she was doing. Hers was undoubtedly an act of love, but it may well have signaled an understanding of what Jesus faced that the male disciples lacked.

This anointing—and that of the other anointing women—was destined to be the only anointing Jesus' body would receive. Before the women who planned to anoint His dead body returned to the tomb where Jesus was laid, He had risen from the dead.

No wonder that the retelling of this incident is a "memorial to her" (Matt. 26:13). It was this woman—and quite possibly Mary of Bethany—who alone was sensitive to the suffering Jesus would soon face. In anointing Him, the anointing women showed that they shared His pain.

~ *Athaliah* ~

Scripture References: *2 Kings 8:26; 11:1–20;*
2 Chronicles 22; 23; 24:7

When They Lived: Date: *640* B.C.

Name: *Athaliah [ath-uh-LIE-ah:"Yahweh is great"]*

Historical Significance: *She was the only woman to rule Judah in her own right.*

HER ROLE IN SCRIPTURE

Athaliah was the daughter of Ahab and Jezebel of Israel and the wife of Jehoram, Judah's king. She followed the path set by her parents and influenced her husband to walk "in the way of the kings of Israel" (2 Kin. 8:18) and worship Baal.

Jehoram ruled for only eight years, but during this time "the sons of Athaliah, that wicked woman…had presented all the dedicated things of the house of the Lord to the Baals" (2 Chr. 24:7). When Jehoram died, his son Ahaziah succeeded him. But Ahaziah was killed during his first year as king. When Athaliah learned that her son was dead, she acted quickly to destroy all the royal heirs (2 Kin. 11:1). With the royal family apparently wiped out, Athaliah took the throne and ruled as queen for six years.

But one of the king's sons survived and was hidden during this time by God's high priest. When the boy, Joash (Jehoash), was seven years old, the high priest organized a coup. Athaliah was executed immediately and to great rejoicing. The text says:

And all the people of the land went to the temple of Baal, and tore it down. They thoroughly broke in pieces its altars and images, and killed Mattan the priest of Baal before the altars…So all the people of the land rejoiced; and the city was quiet, for they had slain Athaliah with the sword in the king's house (2 Kin. 11:18, 20).

EXPLORING HER RELATIONSHIPS

Athaliah's relationship with her parents. Athaliah proved to be as dedicated to paganism as her mother had been. She also turned the hearts of her husband and sons away from the Lord. The existence of a temple to Baal in Jerusalem suggests that she may have been as intent as Jezebel to wipe out worship of the Lord and replace it with Baal worship. While some children seem intent on rejecting the values of their parents, Athaliah was dedicated to imposing her parents' values on her husband and her adopted country, Judah.

Athaliah's relationship with Jehoram and Ahaziah. The text makes it clear that Athaliah was a powerful influence on her husband and her sons. They enthusiastically adopted her faith and her wicked ways.

What is striking is that Jehoram was the son of Jehoshaphat, and Jehoshaphat was a godly king who "did not turn aside from…doing what was right in the eyes of the LORD" (1 Kin. 22:43). However, Jehoshaphat made one disastrous mistake: he made peace with Ahab of Israel and married his son Jehoram to Athaliah. In so doing, Jehoshaphat welcomed a poisonous viper into his family and exposed his son to a woman dedicated to doing evil.

Athaliah's commitment to her parents' wicked ways reminds us that parents can often set the course of their children's lives. But Jehoram's abandonment of his father's commitment to God and to good reminds us that parents cannot guarantee that their children will follow in their footsteps. The story also reminds us that it is important to limit our children's exposure to evil as much as we possibly can.

Athaliah's relationship with the citizens of Judah. The people greeted Athaliah's death with national rejoicing. Athaliah had apparently been an unpopular and brutal ruler, intent on enforcing her views on a nation unwilling to accept them. Ironically, the people's hostility to Athaliah may have made them more eager to return to the Lord than they would have been had Athaliah not been so intent on forcing her opinion on them.

A CLOSE-UP

Athaliah appears to have been a self-centered individual. Like her mother, Jezebel, she was a strong personality who was able to dominate her husband and son. But Athaliah apparently wanted more than to be the power behind the throne. When her son was killed, Athaliah jumped at the chance to rule in her own right.

In the ancient world it was common practice to appoint a regent to rule on behalf of an underage heir to the throne. Athaliah might have claimed that right and ruled on behalf of one of her grandsons. Instead, Athaliah chose to murder all the royal heirs so she might grasp absolute power. This action reveals the utter selfishness and wickedness that characterized this evil queen. Athaliah discovered a reality that still influences us: our lives reflect the character of the God we worship. Athaliah worshiped deities known for their brutality and bloodlust. It should not surprise us that she acted as she did.

AN EXAMPLE FOR TODAY

- Ambition can be a positive thing, but Athaliah is an example of selfish ambition run riot. Whenever we consider doing wrong to achieve a personal goal, we need to remember this wicked queen's fate.
- God used this wicked person as an instrument to bring His people back to Him. God can and does use the worst circumstances and the worst people to accomplish His purposes.

Bathsheba

Scripture References: *2 Samuel 11:1–27; 12:1–24, 28–31;*
1 Kings 1:21; 2:13–25

When They Lived: *About 990 B.C.*

Name: *Bathsheba [Bath-SHEE-bah:"daughter of an oath"]*

Historical Significance: *Bathsheba was the mother of Solomon, who succeeded David as king of the united Hebrew kingdom.*

HER ROLE IN SCRIPTURE

Bathsheba's early life. As a young woman, Bathsheba was married to Uriah, a Hittite who served as an officer in David's army and is listed among the thirty-seven top-ranking heroes—David's "mighty men" (2 Sam. 23:39). While the biblical text does not say so, the fact that Uriah had a house in Jerusalem near the palace may suggest that, when the nation was not at war, he served in David's palace guard.

Aside from this basic information, we know little of Bathsheba's early life. We do know, however, that she was "very beautiful." The Hebrew text has two words that are typically used to describe personal appearance. One, *yapeh*, is rather mild and means, "good looking." The other, *tob*, when applied to women's looks, conveys sensual appeal. This type of woman is so beautiful that she arouses the desire of men who see her. Bathsheba was "very beautiful" in this second sense, and it was her beauty that would betray her.

Bathsheba's seduction by David. One night when Uriah was away campaigning with the army, David saw Bathsheba bathing in her courtyard and he was aroused. He sent servants to get her, had sex with her, and sent her home. But Bathsheba became pregnant. So David recalled Uriah, expecting him to sleep with his wife so the infant could be passed off as premature. But Uriah, feeling dutybound to share his army companions' hardships, would not go home. In a panic, David sent instructions to his commanding general to expose Uriah to danger. The general did, and Uriah was killed. When David learned of his death, he sent for Bathsheba and married her.

Many commentators on this critical incident have cast Bathsheba as a seductress, and blamed her for David's sin. But the biblical text describes her differently.

Bathsheba's innocence. Several details in the biblical account that tell how David saw and took Bathsheba make it clear that Bathsheba was an innocent victim.

- "It happened in the spring of the year, at the time when kings go out to battle" (2 Sam. 11:1). David should have been leading his troops, but instead he stayed in Jerusalem.
- "Then it happened one evening that David arose from his bed" (v. 2). Bathsheba was bathing at night, when she might have expected others were sleeping.
- "And from the roof he saw a woman bathing" (v. 2). Bathsheba was bathing in the courtyard of her own house, where she could expect privacy.
- "He saw a woman bathing, and the woman was very beautiful to behold" (v. 2). David could have turned away and respected Bathsheba's privacy. But he reacted in a different way indeed!
- "So David sent and inquired about the woman" (v. 3). David took the initiative to find out about the woman he had seen. What David learned was that her name was Bathsheba and she was married to Uriah the Hittite.
- "Then David sent messengers, and took her" (v. 4). Bathsheba was a woman alone, with her husband away at war. David was the king. When David's men came to fetch her, she was unable to refuse.
- "She came to him, and he lay with her" (v. 4). Again, David is cast as the actor, Bathsheba as the one acted upon. In saying "he lay with her" the inspired author makes it clear that the initiative came from David. What took place was, in essence, rape.

The text of Scripture makes it clear that we must view Bathsheba as a victim of David's lust, not the seductress as she is sometimes portrayed. The

Scripture's portrait is clearly more in keeping with the reality of the power of ancient kings and the relative powerlessness of women of the royal court.

Bathsheba's life with David. It is striking, in view of the way the marriage was launched, to discover that David and Bathsheba had four sons, whose names are listed in 1 Chronicles 3:5.

It is also impressive to see David portrayed in 2 Samuel 12:24 comforting Bathsheba after the death of the child she had conceived. Something must have occured before or during the stillbirth that would allow her to accept David as a comforter.

Even more impressive is the story told in 1 Kings 2 and 3. There, we see an aged and indecisive king who is about to die. Sensing his father's weakness, one of his sons, Adonijah, proclaimed himself king. Nathan, the prophet, enlisted Bathsheba's help to appeal to David. David had promised that their son Solomon would succeed him. Bathsheba reminded David that unless he acted, both Solomon's life and her own life would be in danger. David was moved by the danger to Bathsheba, and roused himself enough to publicly anoint Solomon and thus save Bathsheba.

Clearly, a relationship that began as an act of lust and the victimization of a woman by a man with power had become a loving, caring marriage.

EXPLORING HER RELATIONSHIPS

Bathsheba's relationship with David. Bathsheba's relationship with David was one of the most significant described in Scripture.

Bathsheba's violation (2 Sam. 11). Bathsheba's first experience with David was a brutal and demeaning one: she was seen, desired, and taken— she was violated and treated as an object, not as a person of worth and value. David's initial plan to bring Uriah home so the child he fathered could be passed off as her husband's showed how little David regarded Bathsheba as a person. Only fear of exposure led David to think of marrying the object of his lust.

Bathsheba's deliverance (1 Kin. 2). At the end of David's life, Bathsheba was not only close to David, but David also loved her. The two had had four sons together, and David promised that their son, Solomon, would succeed him. Nathan, the prophet, realized that concern for Bathsheba's welfare might be the only thing capable of stirring the dying David to take action. So Nathan urged Bathsheba to beg the king to keep his promise concerning Solomon, pleading that, without David's help, his rival would kill both her and Solomon. David truly cared for Bathsheba, and responded to her appeal.

The transformation of the relationship (2 Sam. 12; Ps. 32 and 51). What effected the radical change in the relationship between David and Bathsheba? At issue is not only what changed David's attitude toward her, but also what enabled Bathsheba to forgive this man who treated her so brutally and to forge a loving, lasting marriage with him.

Second Samuel 12 relates the first step in the transformation. It took place when Nathan, the prophet, confronted David, accusing him of taking another man's wife and then killing Uriah. David's actions were totally "evil in His [God's] sight" (2 Sam. 12:9). David's response was to confess that "I have sinned against the LORD." While Nathan announced that David's sin would have unavoidable consequences, God declared to David: I have "put away your sin; you shall not die" (2 Sam. 12:13).

Psalm 32:3–5, although not specifically linked to David's sin with Bathsheba, reveals the inner turmoil sin creates in a basically decent person. It goes on to describe the relief that comes with confession and salvation. David wrote:

> *When I kept silent, my bones grew old*
> *Through my groaning all the day long.*
> *For day and night Your hand was heavy upon me;*
> *My vitality was turned into the drought of summer.*
> *I acknowledged my sin to You,*
> *And my iniquity I have not hidden.*
> *I said, "I will confess my transgressions to the LORD,"*
> *And You forgave the iniquity of my sin.*

This act of confession not only brought David peace, but also must have reoriented his relationship with Bathsheba. He had acted as he did because he viewed her as an object to possess rather than as a person of worth and value. In acknowledging his sin, David implicitly acknowledged that his way of relating to Bathsheba was flawed from the first.

While David's confession to Nathan and to God began the process of transforming his attitude toward Bathsheba, something else was required if Bathsheba's attitude toward David was to be transformed.

While Scripture is silent on this matter, the experience of other women who have been victimized as Bathsheba is suggestive. After being raped, women typically feel shame. Even when totally innocent of any responsibility for their mistreatment, victims typically feel guilty, and much of their anger is directed against themselves as well as their attacker. Victims of spouse abuse feel the same emotions. Many women feel that somehow they were to blame for their partner's brutalizing them. The only way for a relationship involving such actions to be salvaged is for the man to take full, public responsibility for his actions. Confession and forgiveness then can lead to a healing of a violated relationship, and to the building of a happy, healthy marriage.

Strikingly, this is exactly the action that David took. The superscription of Psalm 51 tells us that David wrote this psalm and delivered it to the chief musician to be used in public worship. That superscription indicates the specific occasion on which the psalm was written: "when Nathan the prophet went to him, after he had gone in to Bathsheba." In this psalm, David took full responsibility for what he had done, publicly confessing the sin he had committed in private.

David's public confession was a first and necessary step in freeing Bathsheba to forgive him. It laid the foundation on which a strong, loving, and lasting marriage could be built. The account of Solomon's coronation and the interaction between Bathsheba and David reported there indicates that the two did build such a marriage.

Bathsheba's relationship with God. The Bible does not mention Bathsheba's relationship with God. That she ultimately forgave David and bonded to him shows a grace on her part that suggests personal experience with the God of all grace.

Bathsheba's relationship with Solomon (1 Kin. 1; 2). It is clear from the scene portrayed in 1 Kings 2 that Bathsheba had lobbied on behalf of her son, Solomon, and had been promised by David that Solomon would succeed him (1 Kin. 2:17). History illustrates that the several wives of kings in every ancient society actively competed and plotted to gain the throne for their own son when their royal husband died. We can assume something similar took place in ancient Israel. From the promise that David made to Bathsheba, we can conclude that Bathsheba was David's favorite. We do not know why Solomon was her favorite of her four sons, but clearly he was.

Two things suggest that Bathsheba also had influence with Solomon. The first is an unsubstantiated tradition that holds that Solomon wrote Proverbs 31 in honor of his mother, Bathsheba. The second is that after Solomon was crowned king, his rival, Adonijah, asked Bathsheba to intercede for him with Solomon, to ask permission to marry Abishag, a young woman who had cared for the dying David. Adonijah clearly felt that his best chance to gain Solomon's agreement was to approach him through his mother.

It is clear, then, that Bathsheba had a closer relationship with Solomon than with any of her other sons, and that the perception within the royal court was that Solomon was close to his mother and likely to grant her any request.

A CLOSE-UP

Bathsheba filled many roles during her lifetime. She was the wife of one of David's key military officers. She was a victim of the king's unbridled lust. She was a wife who found grace to forgive her royal husband his horrible sins against her. She was a woman who had the strength to put the past behind her and build a strong marriage on one of the shakiest foundations imaginable. In the end, she won her husband's love, respect, and concern.

Bathsheba, as a mother, was a strong advocate for her son, Solomon. She won David's promise that Solomon would succeed him, and she acted courageously on Solomon's behalf when it seemed another would claim the throne.

The final incident involving Bathsheba, however, suggests that she was either politically naive or politically acute. After Solomon was established as king, his older brother and rival, Adonijah, asked Bathsheba to intercede with Solomon and permit him to marry Abishag, a young woman who had nursed David through his final months and weeks. When Bathsheba conveyed this request to Solomon, Solomon immediately saw it as an attempt by Adonijah to strengthen his claim of a right to Israel's throne. While David had not had sex with Abishag, she had warmed the bed of the aged and chilled David, and was technically his concubine. Solomon responded by condemning Adonijah to death, not for his previous attempt to gain the throne, but for what Solomon recognized as a treasonous act indicating that Adonijah intended to lead a rebellion in the future.

When Bathsheba agreed to convey Adonijah's request, did she act as a kind but politically näive person? Or was she fully aware of the implications of Adonijah's request and agreed to convey it to Solomon to give him a reason for removing a future rival? While this issue may be in doubt, Bathsheba's position as David's favorite wife may suggest that she was far from naïve.

Whatever else we can say about Bathsheba, we have to admire her strength and the grace she showed in building a lasting relationship with David. In essence, David was a godly man whose sin with Bathsheba reminds us that we are all vulnerable to temptation. Bathsheba was able not only to forgive David but also to discern his positive qualities. Unlike Michal, who became bitter and was unable to sense God's grace because of the mistreatment she had suffered at the hands of her father and David, Bathsheba did sense God's grace despite her violation. She went on to win David's love and her son's gratitude.

AN EXAMPLE FOR TODAY

- Bathsheba is an example of how God's grace can heal the severely wounded, keeping bitterness from paralyzing the spirit.
- Bathsheba models the courage and grace needed after the loss of a child. Bathsheba was blessed with four other children, among them a king. The

loss of a child, however agonizing, need not make us lose hope for the future.

◆ Bathsheba's experience reminds us that people, like relationships, are redeemable. Her experience also warns us that unless those who wrong us accept responsibility for their actions, as David did, no reconciliation is possible.

Bernice

Scripture References: *Acts 25:13, 23; 26:30*

HER ROLE IN SCRIPTURE

Bernice was another woman who wore royal robes. She was much like Drusilla, although the two women disliked each other intensely. They shared a family heritage. Bernice was actually Drusilla's sister, the granddaughter of Herod the Great and the daughter of Herod Antipas.

They shared a reputation for immorality. While Drusilla had abandoned her husband to bigamously wed the Roman governor of Judea, Bernice was reputed to have had an incestuous relationship with her brother, Agrippa. Bernice had married a man named Marcus, then her uncle Herod, who was king of Chalcis. She was then consort to her own brother for some years, after which time she married Ptolemy, king of Cilicia. Later, she returned to her brother, and after that became the mistress, first of Vespasian, and then of his son, Titus, both of whom would become emperors of Rome.

The two women also shared a gift—God's gift of a wonderful opportunity to hear the gospel. Drusilla heard the gospel from the apostle Paul when her husband, Felix, governed Judea. When Felix's successor, Festus, became governor, King Agrippa and his sister Bernice visited him. Agrippa eagerly accepted the invitation to hear the prisoner Paul tell his story. Paul presented the gospel before the new Roman governor, Agrippa, Bernice, and all their entourage.

During the brief time Paul spoke, all the listeners made choices on which hinged the direction of their earthly lives as well as their eternal destiny. Festus left, thinking that Paul was mad. Agrippa left, after making a joke about being "almost persuaded." And Bernice left to continue on a path of immorality that scandalized even the pagans in the Roman Empire.

AN EXAMPLE FOR TODAY

◆ The lineage of Christ contains a prostitute. Unlike Bernice, when Rahab heard God's message, she committed herself to Him and to His people. She became a new creation. But Bernice hardened her heart and continued in sin. How good it is to know that God will change our hearts and our lives if we only allow Him to.

◆ Shame, as well as hardness of heart, has kept many from the Savior. And far too many of us are burdened by a past of which we are ashamed. Christ welcomes us as we are, and His forgiveness wipes out our past as well as transforming our future.

~ *Bilhah & Zilpah* ~

Scripture References: *Genesis 29—30; 35:22—25*
When They Lived: *About 1875 B.C.*
Names: *Bilhah [BILL-hah: meaning uncertain]*
Zilpah [ZILL-pah: meaning uncertain]
Historical Significance: *Each bore two sons who became the forefathers of Israelite tribes.*

THEIR ROLE IN SCRIPTURE

These two women were slaves, bound to Rachel and Leah respectively. While their lives were interwoven with those of their mistresses, and while each had a vital role in shaping the Jewish people, little is known of them as individuals—not even the meaning of their names.

Bilhah and Zilpah's life stories (Gen. 29; 30) Bilhah and Zilpah were slaves in Laban's household before either Rachel or Leah was married (see Gen. 29:24, 29). This may suggest that the two were older than their mistresses. While wealthy city dwellers often purchased children to be companions for their young sons and daughters, Laban worked a ranch. The fact that even beautiful Rachel was pressed into service as a shepherdess makes it likely the two slaves were set to work.

Bilhah and Zilpah had been Laban's slaves and were his wedding gifts to his two daughters. The transfer of ownership may not have made much difference to the two slave women. After all, they were still slaves, bound to obey whoever owned them. Yet in that day, slave women owned by men were often used as sexual partners by their masters or casually given to their owners' sons or to friends as sex partners. Bilhah and Zilpah may have actually felt safer with women as their owners. No man could touch them without their mistresses' permission.

If they did feel safer, they did not count on the intense rivalry that developed between the two sisters who owned them. Both sisters were married to the same man, Jacob. As Rachel watched her sister produce son after son for their husband, she became more and more frustrated and jealous. Following a custom explained earlier, Rachel gave her maid Bilhah to Jacob as a surrogate.

We have no indication in the biblical text of how Bilhah felt about this, or even what Jacob felt. Rachel commanded; Bilhah obeyed. By custom the sons born to the slave women belonged to the wife, a fact underlined by the Genesis report that Rachel was the one who named each boy. One she named Dan, and the other Naphtali.

When Bilhah had produced two sons for Jacob, Leah felt compelled to respond. She gave Zilpah to Jacob, and he fathered two more sons through her. Leah claimed them as her own and named these two Gad and Asher.

Those who have found the direction of their life set by others and have been forced to cope with situations growing out of decisions in which they had no part can empathize with Bilhah and Zilpah. Nothing about their lives was under their control. They lived—and died—as slaves. Yet together they produced four sons who were destined to father a third of Israel's twelve tribes and to be celebrated forever by God's Old Testament people.

EXPLORING THEIR RELATIONSHIPS

The two servants were given to Jacob as concubines. Each woman bore him two sons. These women, unlike Hagar, could adjust to their roles without showing animosity toward their mistresses. Indeed, relationships among the four women and their many children seem to have been amicable.

Only one problematic incident is recorded. Reuben, Jacob and Leah's oldest son, "went and lay with Bilhah his father's concubine; and Israel heard about it" (Gen. 35:22). Later in Genesis, when Jacob lay dying, he blessed his sons, but said of Reuben, "Unstable as water, you shall not excel, because you went up to your father's bed; then you defiled it" (Gen. 49:4).

The Bride of Cana

Scripture References: John 2:1–11

HER ROLE IN SCRIPTURE

During Jewish wedding celebrations, the bride was queen, and the groom, king. Festivities might last several days or even a week. Her wedding was truly the highlight of many a woman's life.

It's no wonder that Mary, a sensitive and caring person, was upset when she became aware that the wine had run out at the wedding feast. This bride's wedding might not be remembered as a joyous occasion but recalled as the wedding at which the hosts scrimped on the wine.

We have no idea whether the bride was aware that the wine had run out. Likely, she did not know, for that was a matter for the master of the feast. We do know that Jesus, in turning water into wine, saved the young bride and her groom from social disaster.

The story reminds us that Christ is at work behind the scenes for us as well. Only when we arrive in heaven will we know how often His intervention saved us from disasters of which we were totally unaware.

BIBLE BACKGROUND: WINE

In Bible times, fermented wine contained 7 to 10 percent alcohol. Rabbinic literature prescribes the dilution of wine with three to five parts of water for every part of wine. The drink served at Cana was far from modern wine, which often contains 10 to 13.5 percent alcohol and is undiluted.

Actually, the Old Testament attitude toward wine is ambivalent. *The Expository Dictionary of Bible Words* says:

Fermented wines were drunk at feasts, given as gifts (1 Sam. 25:18; 2 Sam. 16:1), and used in offerings to God (Ex. 29:40; Lev. 23:13; Num. 15:7). Yet the OT calls for moderation and rejects both drunkenness and a love for drink (Prov. 20:1; 21:17; 23:20). The two sides of the use of wine—abuse and proper use—are seen in Amos. God's people were condemned for sins associated with wine (Amos 2:8, 12; 5:11; 6:6) and, in the later chapters which are filled with promise of restoration, they were promised "the mountain shall drip with sweet wine" (Amos 9:13) and that they would "plant vineyards and drink wine" (Amos 9:14).

—Page 628

Caiaphas's Servant Girls

Scripture References: *Matthew 26:69–71; Mark 14:66–69; Luke 22:56–60*

THEIR ROLE IN SCRIPTURE

The night before the crucifixion, the soldiers took Jesus to the house of Caiaphas, the high priest. While Jesus was being interrogated inside, Peter remained out in the courtyard, trying to be as inconspicuous as possible. One of the servant girls of the high priest confronted Peter, saying, "You also were with Jesus of Galilee" (Matt. 26:69). Peter loudly denied any connection with Jesus, and the girl went away. Later the first girl returned (Mark 14:69), or another girl (Matt. 26:71) approached him, and questioned Peter again. The third questioner was apparently a man (John 18:26). Each time Peter swore that he had nothing to do with Jesus of Nazareth.

Typically we focus our attention on Peter and his denials, but here we're concerned with the servant girls. They were women of especially low status, with no claim to any authority. Yet they took pride in being in the high priest's household. That they were slaves was less important than that they were *his* slaves. They not only took pride in being members of the high priest's household; they also identified themselves with him. Jesus was their master's enemy, so He was their enemy as well. Even though slaves, they felt bold enough to confront a man whom they thought might be their master's enemy.

AN EXAMPLE FOR TODAY

The servant girls, slaves of Jerusalem's high priest, have a lesson to teach us. We, too, are slaves, slaves of Jesus Christ (see Rom. 1:1). As Jesus' bondservants,

◆ We take pride in being members of God's household. Our true identity is rooted in our relationship to Him—not in who we are in ourselves.

- We are to identify ourselves with our Lord and with His purposes. We are to value what He values, love those whom He loves, and reject everything that He rejects.
- We are to struggle against every evil He condemns, seek to right everything He sees as wrong, and take a stand against all that He labels sin.
- We are to be bold in the power of His name, remembering that when we are weak, He is strong.
- We are to act resolutely, confident of His empowerment, aware that God is at work in us to do His good will.

Cain's Wife

Scripture References: *Genesis 4:1–18*

HER ROLE IN SCRIPTURE

One of the first questions scoffers are likely to ask young Christians is, "Where did Cain get his wife?" The answer is found in Genesis 5:3: "After Seth was born, Adam lived 800 years and had other sons and daughters." Cain married one of his sisters.

This troubles some, as marriage between brothers and sisters is forbidden in Moses' law (Lev. 18:9). But that law was millenniums away, and the period following creation was certainly unique.

For one thing, the human gene pool was pure. After the Fall, genes began to mutate. While the mutation has been gradual, medical science today traces many of the diseases that distress humankind to flaws in the genetic code. Marriage between brothers and sisters can lead to serious problems for their offspring, as any flaws in the family genetic code would be magnified. History has many examples of the dangers of intra-family marriages. The Caesars had a genetic propensity for epilepsy; the Hapsburgs, for hemophilia.

I once purchased a videotape of my daughter's dance recital. The one mother who'd been given permission to tape the recital and sell tapes made a copy of a copy of a copy—and I must have purchased a twenty-fifth generation copy. We can hardly pick out our daughter. Had the mother run each copy from the original, we could still be enjoying our little ballerina on tape. Adam and Eve's children were copies of the original, and the purity of God's creation protected the first humans from the damage inter marriage would cause later on.

It is important to note one more point. Genesis 2:24 states that a "man shall leave his father and mother and be joined to his wife." While Adam's sons and daughters wed, the first pair did not have children with their own offspring.

EXPLORING HER RELATIONSHIPS

We do not know the name of Cain's wife. She is the first woman mentioned after Eve. Yet we know her only through her relationship with Cain, and that relationship shaped her life.

Genesis 4 tells us that Cain slew his brother, Abel. As punishment Cain was sent away from the family to live as a "fugitive and vagabond" (4:12).

Cain said to the Lord, "My punishment is greater than I can bear! Surely You have driven me out this day from the face of the ground; I shall be hidden from your face; I shall be a fugitive and a vagabond on the earth, and it will happen that anyone who finds me will kill me." Then Cain went out from the presence of the Lord and dwelt in the land of Nod on the east of Eden. And Cain knew his wife, and she conceived.

From this text we conclude that Cain was already married when he killed his brother. His wife went into exile with him, for no other reason than that she had married Cain.

From the day that Cain was banished from Eden, his wife never saw her parents, brothers, sisters, nieces, nephews, or any other family members for the rest of her life. What a terrible price this woman paid for the sin of her husband, evidently through no fault of her own.

While there is no record of conversations between Cain and his wife, it would be hard to imagine that this situation failed to cause serious problems. Cain himself said that his punishment was more than he could bear, and he was the guilty party. How much worse it must have been for his wife!

Cain's wife must have suffered many hardships from the exile imposed upon her because of her husband. She may have resented him for loss of family support. Her parents wouldn't even see her children. Her mother wouldn't be there to help when it came time to give birth. Did Cain's wife find strength in the Lord? Was her faith increased by hardship, as the apostle Paul's was later? Or did she become bitter and spiteful? From what little we know of this woman, we can't even make an educated guess. We can, however, say that the exile impacted her life in significant ways.

AN EXAMPLE FOR TODAY

Cain's wife provides a clear example of how innocent people may face lifelong consequences due to another's sins. When this happens, we must recognize that our response is our own choosing. We can follow the example of the apostle Paul, who suffered unjustly many times and became one of the giants of the faith, or we can make other choices that may bring even more hardships into our lives.

Cozbi

Scripture References: *Numbers 25; 31:15, 16*
When They Lived: *About 1410 B.C.*
Name: *Cozbi [KOZ-bih:"voluptuousness"]*
Historical Significance: *Her attempt to corrupt the Israelites failed.*

HER ROLE IN SCRIPTURE

When the Israelites approached the land of the Midianites on their way to Canaan, the Midianite ruler was frightened. He called for Balaam, a man reputed to have influence over supernatural powers, to curse Israel for him. But God intervened, and each time Balaam attempted to curse God's people, he was forced to utter a blessing instead.

Still eager to please his employer, Balaam suggested that the Midianites attempt to get the Lord to curse His people for them. Balaam reasoned that if young Midianite women were sent to the outskirts of the Israelite camp, they would be able first to seduce Israelite men, and then persuade them to worship their idols (cf. Num. 31:15, 16). Balaam reasoned that God would then turn against His unfaithful people, and the threat to Midian would be removed.

The king of Midian immediately initiated Balaam's plan. It succeeded, and a number of Israelites fornicated with the women of Moab. These invited the Israelites to sacrifice to their gods, "and the people ate and bowed down to their gods" (Num. 25:1, 2). This chapter identifies Cozbi as the daughter of an influential Midianite. She was so wanton that at the moment Moses was rebuking the Israelites, Cozbi entered the tent of an Israelite man "in the sight of Moses and in the sight of all the congregation of Israel" (Num. 25:6).

The Midianite plot aroused God's wrath, but Balaam had not understood God's grace, justice, and commitment to His covenant people. The guilty were punished, and the community purified. God's commitment to bless Israel was unshaken. Those who plotted against Israel only turned

God's wrath against them. In the end it was the Midianites and Balaam who lost their lands and their lives.

EXPLORING THEIR RELATIONSHIPS

Cozbi's relationships with men. Cozbi, one of the wanton Midianite women, was happy to try to get Israel's God to destroy His own people. Her relationships with men resemble those of the prostitute described in Proverbs 7.

> *With the attire of a harlot and a crafty heart.*
> *She was loud and rebellious,*
> *Her feet would not stay at home...*
> *With her enticing speech she caused him to yield,*
> *With her flattering lips she seduced him.*
> *Immediately he went after her, as an ox goes to the slaughter...*
> *He did not know it would cost his life.*
>
> —Prov. 7:10, 11, 21–23

Cozbi was delighted to help Balaam carry out his plan to seduce the Israelite men and then get them to worship their gods. Even these pagans knew that God would not stand by while His people were sexually promiscuous and bowed down to other gods. But she wasn't counting on godly men doing what was right. Phinehas, grandson of Aaron, "took a javelin in his hand; and he went after the man of Israel into the tent and thrust both of them through, the man of Israel, and the woman through her body. So the plague was stopped among the children of Israel" (Num. 25:7, 8).

AN EXAMPLE FOR TODAY

- God does not want His people to be seduced away from Him by illicit sexual behavior or any other sinful behavior.
- God does not want us to fall into the role of Cozbi and seduce others into sin with us.

- Our culture tells us that if it feels good, do it. But God tells us that if we are obedient to Him, He will bless us.
- Cozbi was beautiful and felt her sexuality gave her power over men. Christian women must be careful not to be pulled into this mentality that dominates our culture.

A Crippled Woman

Scripture References: *Luke 13:10–17*
See also page 301.

HER ROLE IN SCRIPTURE

The story of the crippled woman is told in just four verses—but it takes many more verses to develop its implications.

Now He was teaching in one of the synagogues on the Sabbath. And behold, there was a woman who had a spirit of infirmity eighteen years, and was bent over and could in no way raise herself up. But when Jesus saw her, He called her to Him and said to her, "Woman, you are loosed from your infirmity." And He laid His hands on her, and immediately she was made straight, and glorified God (Luke 13:10–13).

As far as the woman was concerned, God had met her needs and she praised Him. But the ruler of the synagogue was indignant because Jesus had healed on the Sabbath when people were not to work.

Jesus was scandalized by this man's insensitivity. He called the man a hypocrite, saying, "'Ought not this woman, being a daughter of Abraham, whom Satan has bound; think of it; for eighteen years, be loosed from this bond on the Sabbath?'" (Luke 13:16).

The Lord's contention with the synagogue official reminds all of us to keep human need in clear focus. The sufferer

- was a woman, a human being
- was a daughter of Abraham, an object of God's love
- was a victim of Satan, who hates humankind
- had suffered for eighteen long years

It was only right that God should act to free her from her bondage.

Christ's opponents "were put to shame" (Luke 13:17). The phrase doesn't mean that *they were ashamed* but that Jesus had publicly exposed their indifference to people in need. Their response did not reflect God's command to love one's neighbor (Lev. 19:18). They had used their public commitment to keep every detail of the Law as a cloak to disguise their spiritual emptiness, and Jesus had exposed them. The crowds had seen the Jews' legalism—their true nature—contrasted with Christ's compassion for this suffering woman.

AN EXAMPLE FOR TODAY

- Grace is God's bottom line, and compassion is its hallmark. Let's be careful lest we become so righteous that we no longer care for sinners.
- How good it is to know that we can rely on God's grace. Like the healed woman, we are freed by Christ to glorify God.

David's Ten Concubines

Scripture References: *2 Samuel 16:21–23; 20:3*

THEIR ROLE IN SCRIPTURE

When David was forced to flee Jerusalem during Absalom's rebellion, he left ten of his concubines behind to take care of the palace. When Absalom's forces entered Jerusalem, Absalom was advised to publicly have sex with several of them. For this purpose, a tent was set up on the roof of David's palace.

The action was symbolic, demonstrating that Absalom had supplanted his father as king. Clearly, it was another example of women being used as objects, with no regard for them as persons. It also demonstrated that Absalom intended to replace David or give up his own life, for the insult implied to all Israel that Absalom and David could never reconcile.

The Daughters of Men

Scripture References: Genesis 6:1–5

THEIR ROLE IN SCRIPTURE

The phrase "daughters of men," from Genesis 6:2, is easy to overlook but fascinating to study. The Genesis text says,

> Now it came to pass, when men began to multiply on the face of the earth, and daughters were born to them, that the sons of God saw the daughters of men, that they were beautiful; and they took wives for themselves of all whom they chose. ...There were giants on the earth in those days, and also afterward, when the sons of God came in to the daughters of men and they bore children to them. Those were the mighty men who were of old, men of renown.
>
> Then the LORD saw that the wickedness of man was great in the earth, and that every intent of the thoughts of his heart was only evil continually.

The central issue in this passage is the identity of "the daughters of men" and of the "sons of God." Some scholars have assumed that the passage describes intermarriage between the godly line of Seth and the line of Cain. There are, however, problems with this interpretation.

First, why use the phrase "sons of God" for Seth's line, which, like Cain's line, has been corrupted by the Fall?

Second, how would this union have produced "giants" (Gen. 6:4)? Strikingly, the word translated "giants" here is *nephalim*. While the exact meaning is uncertain, the term implies a marked physical distinction from ordinary human beings.

Third, the phrase "sons of God" in other Old Testament Scriptures need not refer to humans at all!

The Hebrew phrase that is translated as "sons of God" [*ben Elohim*] is found in Deuteronomy 14:1 and 32:5, in Psalm 73:125, and Hosea 1:18. The first three passages are references not to males, but to all Israel as God's covenant people. The usual translation is "children of God." The Hosea passage, translated "sons of the living God," again speaks of God's covenant people.

But when the phrase *ben Elohim* is used in Job 1:6 and 2:1, the reference is clearly to angelic beings, not humans and not men. In these passages the Hebrew *ben* ["son"] is used in another of its common senses, to identify angels *as the direct creation of*, and thus, metaphorically, the "sons" of God.

The question becomes for us whether we are to understand "sons of God" in Genesis 6 as a reference to fallen angels or to human males. This question is discussed thoroughly in another book in this series, *Every Good and Evil Angel*. For our purposes the following passage from the New Testament Book of Jude supports the view that the "sons of God" are fallen angels:

And the angels who *did not keep their proper domain, but left their own abode*, He has reserved in everlasting chains under darkness for the judgment of the great day; as Sodom and Gomorrah, and the cities around them *in a similar manner to these, having given themselves over to sexual immorality and gone after strange flesh*, are set forth as an example, suffering the vengeance of eternal fire. Likewise also these dreamers defile the flesh, reject authority, and speak evil of dignitaries. (italics mine)

Should these passages suggest an unnatural union of women with fallen angels, the role of these women was significant indeed. For this strange practice is closely associated with the Flood, which shortly afterward destroyed life on earth.

EXPLORING THEIR RELATIONSHIPS

One phrase in Genesis 6 seems to exonerate the women involved in this practice. The text says that the sons of God "took wives for themselves of all whom they chose" (Gen. 6:2). Women did not initiate this relationship. If we can find any parallels in Greek and Roman myths of deities' involvement with human women, we can be confident that the "taking" was often accomplished by rape, sometimes by deceit—never to the advantage of the women involved.

The women portrayed in Genesis 6 were victims, not partners, in the betrayal of their race, for the beings who "took" them so wickedly were far more powerful than any human.

EXAMPLES FOR TODAY

In a society that places so much emphasis on physical beauty, it's important to be aware of certain dangers associated with beauty. It was the beauty of the "daughters of men" that first drew the "sons of God." When we dress to emphasize sexual attractiveness, we are more likely to attract the wrong men.

Deborah

Scripture References: *Judges 4; 5*
When They Lived: *About 1300 B.C.*
Name: *Deborah [DEB-uh-rah, "honey bee"]*
Historical Significance: *She led Israel as a prophetess and judge. The battle with the Canaanites in Deborah's time took place here, and involved only a few of Israel's twelve tribes.*

HER ROLE IN SCRIPTURE

The age of the judges was marked by repeated cycles of national sin, servitude, supplication, and salvation. When the Israelites turned aside to worship pagan deities, God permitted them to be oppressed by foreign powers until their distress became so intense that they turned back to Him and prayed for relief. When God's people did return to Him, the Lord raised up a judge, who not only overcame the oppressors but typically continued to lead His people and keep them faithful to Him. Deborah was one of these unusual, charismatic leaders who emerged in a time of great distress to lead God's people spiritually and politically.

In Deborah's time, the king of Hazor oppressed the tribes of northern Israel. (Josh. 11:1–11). A century earlier, Joshua had destroyed Hazor but the Canaanites had rebuilt the city and were once again the dominant local power. Sisera, the military commander under the Jabin [king] of Hazor, commanded 900 chariots of iron. Until David's time, the Israelites lacked knowledge of iron technology; thus their enemies like the Philistines, who had mastered ironworking, dominated them. Yet in response to a word from God, Deborah called out to the Israelites to do battle. She was held in such respect that the reluctant Israelites complied, and 10,000 men assembled to confront the enemy.

The story of Deborah focuses on a critical battle that took place on the flatlands near the Kishon River. Military strategists who have studied the geography and the reference in Judges 5:4 to the clouds pouring water have explained how God enabled the relatively small Israelite force to defeat, such a powerful enemy. To reach the battlefield, the Canaanites would have had to dismantle their chariots and reassemble them on the flat plain. The heavy rains not only made reassembly difficult, but also so thoroughly soaked the ground that the heavy chariots bogged down in the mud.

The Canaanites were defeated, and their commander was killed when he took refuge in a Kenite tent. The defeat was so decisive that within a few years Hazor itself was destroyed and the northern Israelite tribes enjoyed forty years of relative peace.

EXPLORING HER RELATIONSHIPS

Deborah is introduced in Judges as "a prophetess, the wife of Lapidoth, [who] was judging Israel at that time" (Judg. 4:4). These significant relationships help us understand this vital and unusual woman.

Deborah's relationship with God (Judg. 4:4). Deborah is introduced as a prophetess. Prophets were significant persons in Old Testament times. God chose these men and women to communicate His will to His people.

Deuteronomy 18 reminds us that all the peoples of the ancient world sensed a need for supernatural guidance when circumstances forced them to make critical choices. The people of Canaan looked to mediums and spiritists. All these occult avenues were defined in Deuteronomy as "detestable to the LORD." And so God promised to raise up individuals, prophets, from among His own people, through whom He would speak and provide the guidance needed. God called men and women to be His spokespersons.

Unlike other roles in the religion of Israel, this was not a cultic position—such as priest or Levite—and it was not hereditary. God called whomever He wished to be His spokesperson, and those He called He confirmed as prophets and prophetesses in the eyes of the people.

The first thing we learn about Deborah is that she had a special relationship with God. She had been called by Him and commissioned to speak in His name. All Israel recognized that special relationship.

In the words of Deborah's song, this prophetess loved God, and as a result, seemed "like the sun, when it comes out in full strength" (Judg. 5:31).

Deborah's relationship with her husband (Judg. 4:4). It may seem strange to us that, while Deborah's husband is identified, he played no role in the story of the victory over the Canaanites. Since Israel was a patriarchal society, it is not surprising that Deborah should be defined as "the wife of Lepidoth." Women throughout the Old Testament era were identified by the men in whose households they lived, whether their father's or their husband's. The family "belonged" to the man; the woman "belonged" to the household.

Some have felt that Deborah's position precluded her being so defined by her husband. They translate the Hebrew phrase as "a woman of valor" rather than "the wife of Lepidoth." Yet the traditional translation is most likely, and important. While Deborah was clearly an unusual woman, we need to remember—and the text emphasizes the fact—that Deborah's special role in Scripture is not viewed as a challenge to the natural order of Old Testament society. She was a prophetess and a "leader in Israel." But Deborah was also a wife, a member of Lepidoth's household. There was no conflict between being a wife in a patriarchal age and being a spiritual leader.

While the biblical text casts Deborah in a strongly positive light, the later rabbis, whose negative view of women is explored in chapter 1, were disturbed by the Old Testament's portrait of Deborah. They developed a play on Deborah's name, "honey bee," rendering it "hornet" in an attempt to ridicule her as a woman who overstepped her bounds. Despite the respect clearly showed for Deborah in Judges, the rabbis implied that she was an arrogant woman who stung rather than providing good things for her people.

The reference to Lepidoth may well be included to suggest that while Deborah as a woman may have walked a social tightrope, she did so without behaving inappropriately. She lived as a godly woman, a special woman. At the same time, she was a wife whose virtue won the community's respect for her husband.

Deborah's relationships with the Israelites (Judg. 4:4). The Hebrew word for "judging" implies more than a judicial function. The judges were in fact spiritual, political, judicial, and in most cases, military leaders. During their lives they functioned as the government of the tribes they led, much as kings functioned in the following era.

Deborah both fit and did not fit the pattern we see in the male judges. Deborah fit the pattern in that the people recognized her as the tribe's judicial/political authority. Judges 4:5 tells us that she held court "under the palm tree of Deborah between Ramah and Bethel in the mountains of Ephraim." Her duty involved settling disputes the Israelites were unable to resolve locally. Moses had fulfilled this role before her, as had the other judges. The kings that followed her era also performed these functions. Clearly, Deborah was the acknowledged leader of the Israelite tribes. It is appropriate to say that during her time Deborah was leading Israel.

Two things, however, set Deborah apart from other judges. First, she was a prophetess. None of the other judges aside from Samuel, who was a priest as well as prophet, are so identified. We can assume that Deborah was first recognized as a prophetess, and that this special relationship with God preceded her recognition by the Israelites as a judge.

Second, she was *not* a military leader. When Deborah was about to call on her people to fight the Canaanites of Hazor, she first summoned Barak, a military man, in the name of the Lord. She then passed on the instructions from God, which Barak was to follow.

Strikingly, other judges were established as leaders in the sight of the people because they demonstrated military might, winning victories over God's enemies. Not so for Deborah. Exercising her prophetic gift, she appointed a man to command Israel's army.

We can conclude from this that God did not want Deborah in the role of military leader. God had appointed Deborah as prophetess and judge and had communicated His intention to commission Barak to lead the battle.

Deborah's relationship with Barak (Judg. 4:8, 9). Barak responded to Deborah's call and accepted the commission as army commander. But Barak placed a condition on his acceptance: "If you go with me, I will go, but if you don't go with me, I won't go." This reaction suggests the extent of Deborah's credibility as God's spokesperson and as Israel's leader. Barak felt inadequate; he was willing to fight only if Deborah were present at the battle.

Deborah accepted the condition, but rebuked Barak. God had called Barak and promised him victory (Judg. 4:6, 7). Barak should have placed his faith in God's word. Yet Barak's reaction suggests how deeply the Israelites respected Deborah and her relationship with God. Barak viewed Deborah as a talisman, a symbol of the divine presence with His people.

Deborah recognized Israel's need to see Barak as the military leader placing herself in the background. Even when writing the victory poem we have in Judges 5, Deborah attempted to give Barak credit for the "song." But while the verse credited Barak by name, the Hebrew has a feminine singular verb, *vatashar*, literally "and *she* sang."

This interplay suggests that while Deborah's special relationship with God made her the acknowledged leader of the Israelite tribes, her gender defined those roles of leadership in which she could function with God's blessing.

A CLOSE-UP

Deborah was a woman whose confidence was rooted in a close personal relationship with God and in her awareness that God had chosen to use her to guide His people. It is certainly true that Deborah's role was not typical for a woman in a strongly patriarchal society. Yet Deborah clearly did not draw back, concerned about what others might think. Deborah had heard God speaking to her, and she was willing to put herself forward only because she knew that God had also chosen to speak through her.

At the same time, Deborah was sensitive to the limitations of her sex. Deborah would settle disputes, as any other judge would, but she would not lead the army. The military role was one God chose to give to Barak, and Deborah clearly concurred. In fact, Deborah was not even comfortable with the role Barak insisted she fulfill. She would have preferred it if Barak had simply trusted God and gone off to battle without her. Deborah neither needed nor wanted any credit for the victory.

What an unusual combination of traits Deborah displayed! She was self-confident and assertive, yet modest and self-effacing. She was bold enough to step out of the shadows in which most women of her time lived, yet she was unassuming enough to avoid the spotlight in a military campaign whose results would define her own leadership.

In displaying these qualities, Deborah stands as a timeless example for spiritual leaders of either sex.

AN EXAMPLE FOR TODAY

◆ Deborah reminds us that God does gift women for spiritual leadership. We do violence to Scripture if we rule women out of leadership solely on the basis of gender. At the same time, God's choice of Barak as military commander may indicate that not every leadership role is appropriate for women.

◆ Deborah was an obedient servant of the Lord, and He blessed her with spiritual discernment. Certainly the roles of prophet and judge were more significant in Israel than the role of military commander. We must make sure that godly women have the opportunity to exercise the gifts given to them by the Spirit.

◆ Deborah was a woman who balanced her many roles in life. She was a wife, possibly a mother, a prophetess, and a judge. In each capacity the Lord gave her, she served Him competently. It is not always easy to balance our roles in life. Let's be sure that we seek God's guidance and, like Deborah, serve Him in each of our callings.

Delilah

Scripture References: *Judges 16*
When They Lived: *About 1175 B.C.*
Name: *Delilah [duh-LI-luh:"small," "dainty"]*
Historical Significance: *She tricked Samson into revealing the secret of his strength to his enemies.*

HER ROLE IN SCRIPTURE

Samson had shown himself to be an implacable enemy of the Philistines. Although he had not led any organized Israelite resistance against the Philistines who dominated them at the time, Samson himself had fought and killed hundreds of Philistines. Because of Samson's great physical strength, a gift from God, no Philistine force had been able to defeat him.

But Samson was morally weak, a victim of his passion for women. Today we would call Samson sexually addicted, a person unable and unwilling to exercise self-control.

When Samson began an affair with Delilah, the Philistines seized the opportunity to learn the secret of Samson's strength. They offered her a fortune to discover his secret and betray it to them. Delilah, eager to gain the promised wealth, complied.

At first Samson put Delilah off with lies, telling her that fresh thongs or new ropes or braiding his hair would weaken him. Three times when Samson slept, Delilah tied him down and then awoke him with a cry that the Philistines were upon him. Each time Samson easily broke free, ready to fight.

But with each fresh lie, Delilah complained, insisting that if Samson truly loved her he would confide in her. Finally, Samson gave in to her constant urging and told her the truth. The secret of his strength lay in the fact that as a Nazirite his braided hair had never been cut. This time while Samson slept, Delilah let a man slip in and cut off his braids. Samson lost his strength, his freedom and his eyesight.

A CLOSE-UP

The biblical text gives us a clear picture of Delilah. She was a calculating woman. She was aware of her sexual power and quick to use it for personal gain. While Samson had fallen in love with Delilah, she only pretended affection for him. Delilah was more than willing to let Samson use her body, for she was using him to become rich.

How Samson failed to see what was happening we cannot imagine. Her repeated efforts to get him to betray the secret of his strength seem transparent. But Samson was blinded by his passion and easily manipulated. Her pretended doubt of his love, and her appeal to prove his love by revealing his secret finally wore Samson down.

Delilah was determined to get ahead, and chose to use sex to advance herself. In so doing Delilah betrayed not only her lover but also herself. Sex is a gift from God given to bind a married couple together in ever-deepening commitment. When a man or woman engages in sex outside of that context, and especially in a calculated way, then he or she is as much a victim as the sexual partner.

AN EXAMPLE FOR TODAY

◆ Delilah hounded Samson for the secret of his strength. If someone hounds us to do or say something we know we shouldn't, it's time to make adamantly clear that the issue is not negotiable. The other person needs to drop it or risk the loss of the relationship.

◆ The story of Samson and Delilah serves as a warning. We will all lose God's empowerment should we step out of fellowship with Him.

◆ Delilah reminds us that fleshly weakness can topple even the most powerful person.

◆ Keeping ourselves sexually pure and equally yoked protects us from people like Delilah and is vital for empowering God's people.

Dinah

Scripture References: *Genesis 30:21; 34; 46:15*
When They Lived: *About 1850 B.C.*
Name: *Dinah [DIE-nah; "justice"]*

HER ROLE IN SCRIPTURE

Dinah was the daughter of Leah, born after her six brothers. Perhaps she was spoiled by them, as little sisters often are. When Dinah was raped, her brothers were incensed and demanded not the justice implied in her name, but revenge.

Dinah's life story (Gen. 34; 46:15). Dinah was still a young girl when Jacob's family returned to Canaan. She likely was just reaching marriageable age, then thirteen or fourteen years old. When the family stopped for a time near the city of Shechem, Dinah went looking for other girls to talk with.

The rabbis later implied that Dinah was looking for sex, building their case against Dinah on the supposed implications of the Hebrew word translated, "went out" (Gen. 34:1). This view tells us more about the rabbis' attitude toward women (see page 67) than it does about Dinah. It is far more likely that Dinah, like young girls everywhere, was eager to find friends her own age that she could talk with.

Tragically, as she approached the city a young man saw her and raped her. While we are used to hearing of rape as epidemic in our society, we need to remember that male predators have preyed on women from the beginning of history. Rape was an ever-present danger in the ancient world too, and God's Law specifically teaches that women like Dinah are to be held guiltless if they are attacked. Deuteronomy 22 states that if a young woman is forced in the countryside, "you shall do nothing to the young woman," for even if she cried out "there was no one to save her" (Deut. 22:25–27).

This law, given centuries after Dinah's experience, would have been small comfort to her. But it reminds us not to blame Dinah or any of her sisters who are violated by men.

In this unusual case Shechem, after raping Dinah, fell in love with her. He took her to his home and urged his father to begin negotiations with Jacob to make her his bride.

For Dinah, the few days in which this incident played itself out *did* constitute her life. Beyond this chapter the only other mention of Dinah in the Old Testament sees her, many years later, accompanying her father and brothers to Egypt—still an unmarried woman.

The family's reaction (Gen. 34:5–7). Dinah's rape caused both grief and anger. We can assume that the grief was for Dinah, their little sister. But the anger was for the insult done to the family. Shechem had done "a disgraceful thing in Israel ... a thing which ought not to be done."

It is apparent that what followed dealt with the family's anger, but not with Dinah's grief.

The brothers' revenge (Gen. 34:8–31). When Jacob heard what had happened to his daughter, he said nothing until his sons were available. By that time Hamor, the father of Shechem, was ready to approach Jacob with his request. He made it clear that Shechem loved Dinah and wanted to marry her and was willing to pay any price for that privilege. In this Hamor and Shechem were acting morally according to the customs of their time.

But Hamor was dealing with Dinah's brothers, not Jacob. The brother pretended to agree, but demanded that all the men of Shechem be circumcised if the two peoples were to merge, as Hamor offered. Then, after the operation was carried out and the men were incapacitated, Simeon and Levi, two of Dinah's brothers, went boldly into Shechem and killed every man. They took Dinah from Shechem's home and returned with her and much bounty to Jacob's camp.

Terrified that neighboring peoples would wipe out his little family because of his sons' violent actions, Jacob gathered his herds and hurried away with his family.

EXPLORING HER RELATIONSHIPS

Dinah's relationships are difficult to describe because so little is said of them. Yet the silence itself is significant. When the sons of Leah bargained with Hamor, Shechem's father, they never spoke to their sister to solicit her opinions or to see if she wanted the kind of justice they had in mind. Dinah's brothers seem more concerned with their honor, and perhaps with plunder, than with their sister's feelings.

Over twenty years later Dinah's name is included on the list of those who traveled to Egypt where her half-brother Joseph was vizier. Genesis 46 lists all sixty-six people who made that journey. Dinah, among them, is still alone and childless. It would seem that the young woman whose name meant "justice" received little of it in her life on earth.

AN EXAMPLE FOR TODAY

Dinah's tragic life is a reminder that we may fall victim to cruel events far beyond our ability to control. These experiences may be made even worse by the ignorant yet well-meant responses of those who love us. We may even mature into adulthood with old wounds that have never healed.

But unlike Dinah, who may never have had help coping with her pain, we can seek help. We may find it from friends, from gifted counselors God has provided for His people, and most importantly in a growing, intimate relationship with the Lord.

Dorcas (Tabitha)

Scripture References: *Acts 9:36–43*
When They Lived: A.D. *35*
Name: *Dorcas [Tabitha] [DOR-cuss:"gazelle"]*
Historical Significance: *Beloved for her concern for the poor, Dorcas was brought back to life by Peter.*

HER ROLE IN SCRIPTURE

Dorcas was dearly loved in her church. She wasn't famous as a prophetess; neither was she a preacher. Instead she was a woman full of good works and charitable deeds. The people loved Dorcas because she cared for others and demonstrated her caring in practical ways.

When she became sick, her fellow believers were deeply concerned and sent for Peter, who was then in Joppa. When Peter arrived he found that Dorcas had died. Even in their grief, her friends wanted Peter to know what a wonderful woman Dorcas had been. Acts says "all the widows stood by him weeping, showing the tunics and garments which Dorcas had made while she was with them" (9:39).

Peter was moved enough to pray for her restoration. When he rose from prayer, he called to her; she opened here eyes, and sat up.

The miracle was widely reported, and many who heard about it came to faith in Christ.

EXPLORING HER RELATIONSHIPS

Dorcas's relationship with her husband. When we are introduced to Dorcas she was a woman who had lost her husband. We don't know how long ago this had happened, but from the number of people for whom Dorcas had made clothing, we can perhaps assume he had died some years before. Dorcas had not stopped living because her husband was gone. Instead she reached out to other believers and found a meaningful and happy life in serving them.

Dorcas's relationship with other believers. It's clear that Dorcas was deeply involved in the lives of the members of her congregation. Although a widow herself, she had made "tunics and garments" for the other widows in the church and undoubtedly for other needy folk as well.

Dorcas is the only named woman in Scripture who is specifically called a "disciple" (9:36). Some have taken this to suggest that Dorcas held the office of deaconess. Certainly her focus on providing practical help to other believers fits the kind of ministry first-century deacons performed (see Acts 6:1–8).

But ministry involves more than distributing clothing. Those Dorcas served truly loved her. She must have been so caring, so involved in the lives of those she helped, that her giving was never perceived as demeaning or as charity. Dorcas had the gift of giving herself even as she gave the clothing she made for others.

A CLOSE-UP

From the brief comments in Acts about Dorcas, she seems to have been a truly nice person. Perhaps the word "neighbor" or "neighborly" is appropriate. Like a good neighbor, Dorcas was always there for others. And people loved her for herself, not just for what she did for them.

AN EXAMPLE FOR TODAY

◆ Her simple concern for others rather than powerful speech or a great singing voice won Dorcas the love of her friends and neighbors. Sometimes in our desire for a more public ministry we forget that the greatest in God's kingdom are called to be servants, and servants are called to care for those they serve.

♦ Serving others wins a great reward here as well as hereafter. Look how those Dorcas cared for loved her. We get so caught up in accumulating things that we seem to have no time to love one another. Yet loving relationships fill the heart as no possessions can.

Drusilla

Scripture References: *Acts 24:24*

HER ROLE IN SCRIPTURE

Drusilla is mentioned only in this verse. She was the Jewish wife of Felix, the Roman governor of Judea. History, however, tells us more about her.

Drusilla was the granddaughter of Herod the Great. Just before Herod died, he ordered the death of boy children near Bethlehem in an attempt to rid himself of a child born "king of the Jews" (Matt. 2:16–18). Her father, Herod Antipas, had ordered the execution of John the Baptist. So while a Jew, her family had an unbroken record of hostility toward God.

Drusilla herself had married King Aziz of Emesa at age fifteen. Later she left him to marry Felix, without bothering to obtain a divorce. While King Aziz had been forced to convert to Judaism to wed Drusilla, no such conversion was asked of Felix. Felix himself was an ex-slave, whom the Roman historian Tacitus condemned as a brutal man bent primarily on extorting a fortune from those he governed.

When Paul was tried before Felix at Caesarea after a riot in Jerusalem, Drusilla was about twenty years old. Rather than settle the case, Felix put a decision off, at least in part because Felix "hoped that money would be given him by Paul, that he might release him" (24:26).

However, the time Paul was forced to spend in Caesarea not only gave Luke time to locate the eye-witnesses who provided the details of the account of Christ's life recorded in Luke's Gospel, but also gave Paul the opportunity to witness to Felix and Drusilla. Luke tells us that he "reasoned [with them] about righteousness, self-control, and the judgment to come" (Acts 24:25).

What an opportunity for the young Drusilla, already steeped in the guilt of her sins. Yet, Drusilla gave no indication that she felt anything but hostility toward Paul, and she rejected the forgiveness offered in the gospel. Drusilla seems to have been like so many people. She was guilty enough not to want to be confronted about righteousness, young enough not to be concerned about the judgment to come.

While we do not know what happened to Felix, history tells us that some twenty years after listening to Paul, Drusilla was near Pompeii when Mount Vesuvius erupted. It was too late when she tried to flee that great catastrophe, and too late to escape the judgment of which Paul had warned her two decades earlier.

AN EXAMPLE FOR TODAY

◆ Rather than becoming defensive when we are confronted concerning our sins, we need to humble ourselves in the sight of the Lord.

◆ We do not know how much time we have on this earth. Some will continue to be caught with a hard heart as Drusilla was. The choice is ours.

Elizabeth

Scripture References: *Luke 1:5–7, 36–45, 57–61*

When They Lived: *5 B.C.*

Name: *Elizabeth [ee-LIZ-uh-buth:"God is my oath"].*

Historical Significance: *She gave birth to John the Baptist, whose prophetic ministry prepared for Jesus' appearance.*

HER ROLE IN SCRIPTURE

Elizabeth was the wife of a priest named Zacharias. She was selected by God to give birth to John the Baptist whom Jesus called the greatest of the Old Testament prophets. John met the conditions necessary to be identified as the prophet whose appearance preceded the establishment of God's earthly kingdom (Mal. 4:5, 6).

EXPLORING HER RELATIONSHIPS

Elizabeth's relationship with God (Luke 1:5, 6). Luke gives Elizabeth's lineage. Like her husband Zacharias, Elizabeth was a member of a priestly family. Luke took care to describe not only Zacharias's character but also Elizabeth's: "They were both righteous before God, walking in all the commandments and ordinances of the LORD blameless" (v. 6). This description does not imply sinlessness; it is a common formula that indicates a true heart-dedication to God.

This is clearly implied in Luke's later description of Elizabeth's filling with the Holy Spirit when her relative, Mary, visited (1:41). Elizabeth was open to the Lord and sensitive to the revelation that Mary was to be the mother of a child who was Elizabeth's Lord.

Elizabeth's relationship with her husband (Luke 1:13, 57–61). Elizabeth and Zacharias had a warm and loving relationship. They were old and childless. If Zacharias had not loved his wife, her childlessness would have been grounds for divorce and a remarriage. Yet, through many long years the two had clung together.

We are told that the angel said to Zacharias, "'Your prayer is heard'" (1:13). Despite the couple's age Zacharias had not ceased praying for a child, which was so important to every Jewish woman. Zacharias's continuing prayer indicates not only his love for Elizabeth but also the couple's continuing trust in God.

A final indication of the nature of Elizabeth's relationship with Zacharias is found in verses 59–64. Elizabeth announced that her newborn child's name was to be John. The surprise of the guests at the circumcision reflects that most children were named after a relative. Elizabeth's confirmation of the name announced for the infant by the angel (1:13) simply reflects that this couple lived in complete harmony.

Elizabeth's relationship with Mary (Luke 1:36–45). Mary and Elizabeth were relatives, quite possibly cousins. It was not unusual for the younger Mary to visit Elizabeth and stay with her for weeks or months. It is quite likely that Elizabeth had a mentoring relationship with Mary.

Yet when Mary visited Elizabeth during the sixth month of Elizabeth's pregnancy, Elizabeth realized that Mary had been chosen to give birth to the Messiah. Rather than exhibit jealousy at this role reversal, Elizabeth rejoiced at Mary's calling. Such selfless action is an exhibition of a special grace.

A CLOSE-UP

In Elizabeth we see a mature believer whose years of disappointment deepened rather than destroyed her faith. Elizabeth was able to maintain both a close walk with God through many years despite unanswered prayer and also a close relationship with her husband. Her maturity was also displayed in her relationship with Mary, her much younger relative. When God revealed to Elizabeth the role for which Mary had been chosen, Elizabeth simply rejoiced with her, humbled at the privilege of being visited by the mother of One she recognized as her Lord. In each mention of Elizabeth, her maturity shone through.

An Example for Today

◆ Elizabeth had a vital relationship with God. When the Holy Spirit filled her (Luke 1:41), she did not doubt the insights He imparted. Today we have the benefit of the New Testament that teaches us such ministries of the Holy Spirit as testifying about Jesus (John 15:26), and telling us things to come (John 16:13). We need to pray that our hearts will be as open to the Spirit's ministry and as obedient to Him as was Elizabeth's heart.

◆ From the account of Mary's visit to Elizabeth, it is clear that the babe in her womb was filled with the Spirit even before Elizabeth was. The NKJV says, "'He will also be filled with the Holy Spirit, even from his mother's womb'" (Luke 1:15). That "from" here means *while in* is proven by verse Luke 1:41. The NIV translates this "from birth." While subtle, the difference in meaning is important. It affirms the individual personhood of the unborn. God would hardly fill a mass of living tissue that is "part of the mother's body" with the Holy Spirit. John was John, an individual with his own identity, even while in the womb.

Esther

Scripture References: *The Book of Esther*
When They Lived: *About 475 B.C.*
Name: *Esther [ESS-ter: "star"]*
Historical Significance: *As queen of Persia she thwarted a plot to exterminate all Jews in the Persian Empire.*

Her Role in Scripture

Esther was the niece of Mordecai, a Jewish official in the royal court. Mordecai aroused the hostility of Haman, a higher official. Haman determined to take revenge, but he was not satisfied with engineering

Mordecai's death. Instead Haman determined to wipe out Mordecai's whole race.

Haman was successful in winning permission for this early holocaust from the king and began to throw dice to determine the propitious moment to carry out his plan.

In the meantime, Queen Vashti was deposed, and Esther was selected to be queen.

Through a series of God-ordained events, King Ahasuerus discovered that Mordecai had once saved his life. When Queen Esther exposed "this wicked Haman" (Esth. 7:6), the king ordered Haman's execution on the very gallows Haman had erected to hang Mordecai.

Together Mordecai and Esther created a decree that not only saved the Jewish people, but also rid the Jews of their most virulent enemies.

EXPLORING HER RELATIONSHIPS

Esther's relationship with God. One of the unique features of the book of Esther is that it contains no mention of God. Yet it is clear that Esther and her uncle had a deep and abiding faith in Him.

Esther's faith expressed in fasting (Esth. 4:16). Esther asked Mordecai to "gather all the Jews" and fast for three days and nights. She and her maids would do the same. In the *Expository Dictionary of Bible Words* (1985), Larry Richards identifies four reasons given in the Old Testament for fasting. The fast Esther requested was that "undertaken in times of deep trouble and underlined the seriousness of personal and national appeals to God" (p. 265). Without doubt prayer accompanied such fasting.

Mordecai urged Esther's faith-response. Mordecai warned Esther: "If you remain completely silent at this time, relief and deliverance will arise for the Jews from another place" (Esth. 4:14). This confident assertion could only be made by one who was fully aware of God's covenant commitment to Abraham and his descendants (Gen. 12:1–3) and whose trust in God was complete. Clearly Mordecai expected Esther to share these convictions and act on them.

Esther's relationship with Mordecai. Mordecai was a surrogate father to Esther, and Esther showed him the respect that Scripture teaches a child should show to a parent. Esther looked to Mordecai for advice, and so respected his opinion that she overcame her fear and took the initiative to approach the king.

It would be wrong, however, to see Esther as a person unable to make decisions. Rather, in a time of crisis Esther relied on a wise parent who had proved his love for her over the years and whose judgment she had come to respect.

Esther stepped out in faith (4:16). Esther determined to do as Mordecai asked, and she approached her husband. Her statement, "If I perish, I perish," is not fatalistic abandonment but a conscious trusting of herself into God's hands. Whatever happened, God would be with her, and He would welcome her into His presence. Her faith was not unlike that of Abraham who trusted God with the life of his son Isaac. Her choice prefigures Jesus' remark to His disciples, "Greater love has no one than this, than to lay down one's life for his friends" (John 15:13).

Esther honored Mordecai by accepting his guidance. Mordecai saw the call for beautiful young virgins to vie to become queen as an opportunity for Esther. She did as Mordecai suggested and ultimately became queen.

Esther honored Mordecai by following his advice. Esther did not reveal her race before or after she became queen. In those times as well as throughout much of history, significant anti-Jewish prejudice existed.

Esther honored Mordecai by remaining in contact with him. Even as queen, Esther's maids passed messages between Esther and Mordecai. This enabled Esther to warn the king of a plot that Mordecai uncovered against the king's life.

When her maids reported that Mordecai was seated in sackcloth and ashes—a sign of mourning—Esther immediately sent to find out what was wrong. The messages sent between the two show that they were quite close and that Esther deeply respected her uncle and his advice.

Esther's relationship with King Ahasuerus [Xerxes I]. Esther's husband was an absolute ruler, but there is good reason to believe that he was also slightly mad. He launched a number of campaigns against the Greeks, suffering successive defeats. On one occasion when a storm destroyed a pontoon bridge over which he expected his troops to pass, he ordered soldiers into the water to beat the waves with whips.

Xerxes' erratic decision-making was illustrated in his treatment of Vashti (1:10–17). When his beautiful queen refused to be put on display for the king's drunken guests, he quickly deposed her. It did not pay to embarrass the king!

Xerxes' brutality is illustrated in his ready agreement to Haman's plan to wipe out an entire race of people in his empire (3:8–11). While he called on his counsel to advise him concerning Vashti, he felt no need to consult with them concerning the planned holocaust.

Xerxes' unpredictability was illustrated by his inaccessibility (4:11). People were not allowed to approach the king unless he sent for them. Anyone who did so was to be put to death—unless the king raised his golden scepter and pointed to that person. Even Esther, who had not been called by the king for thirty days, was terrified at the thought of going to him.

If ever a woman had a difficult marriage it was Esther!

A CLOSE-UP

When we first meet Esther she is a young girl of marriageable age living in Mordecai's household. She is selected as one of the empire's beauties, to be considered by the king as a possible queen. It is significant that when Esther was chosen and placed in the royal women's quarters to undergo a year of training and beauty treatments she quickly won the allegiance of Hegai, the custodian of the women. Esther's sweet spirit and personality matched her physical attractiveness.

Even when Esther had been selected by the king to become his queen, Esther maintained contact with Mordecai and sought his advice. When Mordecai uncovered a plot to murder the king, Esther passed the information on to Ahasuerus, giving credit to her source.

When Mordecai informed Esther of the danger Haman posed to the Jewish people and urged her to intercede with the king, Esther was afraid. The king had not called for her in over a month, and if she should go to him uninvited, he might be angered and have her executed. After consideration, Esther asked Mordecai to gather all the Jews in the capital city to fast for three days. The implication is that the fasting was intended to enable the Jews to concentrate in their prayers, asking God to act for them. Esther and her maids fasted also. Only when Esther was sure that God's help had been sought earnestly did she risk approaching the king.

In the end Esther found in her faith the courage to approach the king and appeal to him. Her appeal was successful. Because of the great deliverance she won for the Jewish people, her courage is commemorated in an annual celebration called the Feast of Purim, and Jewish women's groups everywhere have adopted Esther's Jewish name, Hadassah.

AN EXAMPLE FOR TODAY

- Mordecai reminded Esther that perhaps God had made her queen to meet the challenge that Haman posed to her people. Perhaps we have come to our own "kingdom" for God's special purpose through us.
- Esther showed wisdom and patience in a terrible situation while dealing with a difficult husband. She operated within God's will in the situation and used every gift He had given her. We too are to do what is right. But let's do it wisely, using our God-given gifts.
- Esther was a model adult daughter. While she was free to act as she chose, she carefully weighed Mordecai's advice.
- Mordecai is a good example of a wise parent of an adult child. He gave wise advice but let the child make up her own mind.

Euodia & Syntyche

Scripture References: *Philippians 4:2*

THEIR ROLE IN SCRIPTURE

It's ironic. These two women in the church of Philippi had a hard time getting along, yet they are forever bound together in Paul's letter to the Philippians and in our thoughts.

What was the disagreement that divided them? What triggered the hard feelings? Why didn't the two deal with the problem and work toward reconciliation? They were both believers, and they were both well known in the Philippian church. But something had driven a wedge between them and destroyed the love and harmony that is the mark of Jesus' living presence in His church (see John 13:34, 35).

We cannot answer these questions about the dispute that divided these two women. But Paul's mention of their dispute is a warning to us. Although we are saints, we remain sinners. We are each vulnerable to the passions that stir in our sin nature. It takes constant reliance on God's grace, and unfailing love for one another, to maintain that unity in the Spirit that marks Christ's brethren.

Eve

Scripture References: *Genesis 3; 4; 2 Corinthians 11:3;*
1 Timothy 2:13
Name: *Eve means "life giver"*
Historical Significance: *The mother of all people except Adam*
The serpent deceived Eve by leading her to question God's Word.

HER ROLE IN SCRIPTURE

Eve's role in Scripture has been discussed thoroughly in chapter 1. So we begin this chapter exploring Eve's relationships.

EXPLORING HER RELATIONSHIPS

Eve's Relationship with God

Eve had a relationship with God both before and after the Fall. That relationship goes back to her creation by the Lord.

The basis of Eve's relationship with God (Gen. 1:27). In God's revelation of Creation to Moses, the Lord made it clear that Eve had been created in God's image, just as Adam had. Genesis 1:27 states, "So God created man in His own image; in the image of God He created him; male and female He created them."

As the creation story continues, God declared, "It is not good that man should be alone; I will make him a helper comparable to him" (Gen. 2:18). But before Eve was formed, God took the beasts and birds to Adam so he could name them, "but for Adam there was not found a helper comparable to him" (Gen. 2:20). Evidently God wanted Adam to understand on his own that in all of creation, there was not another who shared in God's image.

It was not until Adam had named the other creatures, recognizing his own uniqueness, that God "caused a deep sleep to fall on Adam, and he slept; and He took one of his ribs, and closed up the flesh in its place" (Gen. 2:21).

From the living tissue of Adam, God formed Eve. He wanted Adam to see that Eve was of the same essence as he.

While Adam had been formed from dust and God had "breathed into his nostrils the breath of life" (Gen 2:7), we are told that Eve was formed from man (Gen. 2:22). When God brought Eve to Adam, Adam recognized her immediately. "This is now bone of my bones and flesh of my flesh" (Gen. 2:23). Adam had not seen his nature in the animals God brought to him. But Adam immediately saw his nature in Eve. "She shall be called Woman because she was taken out of Man" (Gen. 2:23b).

The special nature of Eve's relationship with God. In spiritual essence Adam and Eve were the same; both were created in the image of God. But in all creation, Eve alone was created from what God had already refined. Adam and all the rest were made from the earth; Eve alone was fashioned by the hand of God from the living tissue of Adam.

Perhaps God reveals more of Himself in Eve's special creation. In spiritual essence and in personhood, Adam and Eve are equals. Adam reflected his Creator in part. Together, Adam and Eve give an even more complete representation of our magnificent Father in heaven.

Anyone familiar with concepts in *Men Are from Mars, Women Are from Venus* would probably agree that there are differences between men and women that go beyond the biological. (Actually, most of my friends have known for decades of this "Martian connection." Sometimes it does seem the only plausible explanation!) Most of us can laugh at this, but even admitting that some see significant differences between men and women has led to ugly battles. Any woman who has watched TV with a man in possession of the remote control knows in her heart that differences exist. This is not to suggest that one sex is inferior to the other. We know from Scripture that the reason this issue is so hotly debated is because of the distortion of relationships between men and women which occurred at the Fall (Gen. 3:16c).

Both Adam and Eve were special to God, for God shared with each His image and likeness, making them truly persons. Each had been given the capacity to think, to plan, to remember, to appreciate beauty, to establish priorities, to distinguish right from wrong, to make decisions and carry them out. This unique gift is the basis of each human being's capacity to relate to each other and to God.

Expressions of Eve's relationship with God before the Fall. We know that "God [walked] in the garden in the cool of the day" (Gen. 3:8). We can only begin to imagine what communing with God was like as the three shared an afternoon stroll through paradise. But Eve and Adam *knew*. And while there is no record of the conversations that God had with Eve, as there is of conversations He had with Adam (Gen. 2:16, 17), we can assume that the two did commune and communicate. God created Eve in His image; He loved her, and had given her the capacity to love and share in return. How precious those intimate times must have been to our first mother.

The breakdown of Eve's relationship with God. When the serpent came on the scene and spoke to Eve, he planted a seed of doubt in her heart. "You will not surely die," the serpent told her, contradicting God's words to Adam. "For God knows that in the day you eat of it [the tree of the knowledge of good and evil], your eyes will be opened, and you will be like God, knowing good and evil" (Gen. 3:4, 5). The fruit appealed to Eve's sense of beauty, and the serpent told her it would give her wisdom. As today, Satan was twisting things around until wrong seemed right. No wonder Paul wrote, "But I fear, lest somehow, as the serpent deceived Eve by his craftiness, so your minds may be corrupted from the simplicity that is in Christ" (2 Cor. 11:3).

BIBLE BACKGROUND: RABBINICAL EMPHASES

The sayings of the rabbis who lived during and after the time of Christ emphasize the "otherness" of women. The supposition was that women were essentially different from men. Rabbinic sages even offered a different explanation of Eve's Hebrew name, linking it to the Aramaic word for "serpent." As a result, many midrashic stories related about Eve portray her either as a dangerously evil character or as a silly and childish female who was approached by the serpent because she was "light-minded" and vulnerable to his cunning. How different the Eve of the rabbis is from the Eve portrayed in Scripture who, although deceived, was neither evil nor silly.

How striking that stereotypes promoted by men tend to emphasize real or imagined differences between men and women while God's Word in Genesis emphasizes their essential equality.

Eve succumbed. After the Fall, when God came to walk in the garden, Adam and Eve tried to hide not only from Him but from each other, for they were ashamed of their nakedness (Gen. 3:8–18). Sin had introduced a barrier between Eve and the Lord where before there had been none.

It was then that history's first blood sacrifice was offered, to cover the sins of Adam and Eve (Gen. 3:21). God also covered them physically with the skins of the animals which had died, and banished them from the garden. Eve would still remember her Creator, but the intimacy of the relationship they had enjoyed was gone for the rest of her earthly life.

The impact of Eve's personhood on her relationship with God. Twice we have listed some of the traits of personhood that the first couple shared with the Creator. Let's examine how certain critical capacities affected the relationship Eve had with God.

◆ Eve had the capacity to think. As the serpent tempted Eve, she reasoned that if the fruit of the forbidden tree made one wise, it must be good. But disobedience to any of God's commands, even for a "good" cause, is still sin. No wonder the Lord tells us in Proverbs 3:5, "Lean not on your own understanding." Eve's choice was not the right one, but we do see her think about it. We also see Eve's thought processes reflected as she names both Cain (Gen. 4:1) and Abel (Gen. 4:25).

◆ Eve had the capacity to remember and reflect. We see Eve remembering Abel in Genesis 4:25. Even more importantly we see Eve remembering and reflecting on God: "For God has appointed another seed for me instead of Abel, whom Cain killed." Eve sees God's hand in the gift of a new son. She is banished from the garden, but she has not forgotten the love, compassion, or garden walks with her Creator. And she remembers His words to Satan, "He shall bruise your head, and you shall bruise His heel" (Gen. 3:15c). Eve did not know that Seth was not the promised one, but from Seth's line would come the perfect sacrifice not only for her sin, but for every sin.

◆ Eve was able to distinguish right from wrong, for she told the serpent, "God has said, 'You shall not eat it, nor shall you touch it, lest you die'" (Gen. 3:3). But the capacity to tell the difference was not enough to protect her.

◆ Eve made decisions and acted on them. And Eve was aware that she was fully responsible for what she chose to do. "The serpent deceived me, and I ate" (Gen. 3:13).

God gave Eve and Adam traits of personhood that the animals did not share. With the critical gifts of judgment and of free choice came an awesome responsibility. Eve's free choices affected not only her relationship with God but every human relationship that followed.

Eve's Relationship with Adam

Eve's relationship with Adam before the Fall. Before the Fall, what must it have been like for Adam and Eve? The relationship must have been so blissful it would have been boring if it hadn't been perfect. Was it marriage without discord? Adam didn't have to work late. Eve didn't get headaches. Financial, communication, and sexual problems simply did not exist. There were no divorces, no attorneys, no broken homes, no latch-key kids, no domestic violence, no child abuse. There was no cancer, no thigh bulge, no medical insurance payments. No baggage from the past came between the partners; no obstacles lay between the first couple and God. No stress! Just trying to imagine what this relationship must have been like causes me to lose focus on what I'm doing.

Then up slithered Satan as his favorite serpent. He deceived Eve. She ate the forbidden fruit, and like all good wives, wanted to share with her husband. Too bad he didn't follow today's slogan and "just say no." Instead he thought it over, and knowing full well what he was doing, chose to eat the forbidden fruit.

Eve's relationships with Adam after the Fall (Gen. 3). The Genesis text gives immediate insight into the relational impact of the first couple's sin, as the harmonious relationship between Adam and Eve breaks down in several ways.

The first hint is found in Genesis 3:7: "Then the eyes of both of them were opened, and they knew that they were naked; and they sewed fig leaves together and made themselves coverings." What had once been a good and natural way to live now caused Adam and Eve shame.

We don't know whether their feelings of shame affected them sexually at first. It is certainly possible, since shame over one's nakedness can be a factor in sexual dysfunction. We do know that after this Adam and Eve had three sons named in Scripture as well as other sons and daughters (Gen. 5:4b).

But there was another, obvious breakdown in what had been a harmonious loving relationship. When God called out in the garden, Adam said that he hid because he was naked. "Who told you that you were naked?" God replied. "Have you eaten from the tree of which I commanded that you should not eat?" Adam's response was to blame God for giving him the woman, and then to blame Eve for offering him the fruit. "The woman whom You gave to be with me, she gave me of the tree, and I ate" (Gen. 3:11, 12).

Any time a person blames a spouse for something of significance, there will be problems in the relationship. We can only guess at some of the later conversation that Adam and Eve might have had.

BIBLE BACKGROUND: DOES GENESIS 3 IMPLY MALE DOMINATION?

Rabbi Nathan M. Sarna, in his commentary on Genesis (1989), agrees with many Christian commentators when he writes: "It is quite clear from 2:18, 23 that the ideal society, which hitherto existed, affirmed the absolute equality of the sexes. The new state of male domination is regarded as a deterioration of the human condition that resulted from defiance of the divine will."

But the critical question is, does "he shall rule over you" express *God's will* for male-female relationships, or does it simply describe *the distortion of God's will which sin introduced* into our race? If the latter, the many expressions of male domination in our own and other societies are clearly *wrongs* perpetrated against women by men.

Eve: "You never have time for me or the kids any more" (see Gen. 3:16b).

Adam: "Whose fault is that? I wouldn't be out here living by the sweat of my brow if you hadn't taken up with that serpent!" (see Gen. 3:17c)

Eve: "Don't tell me about the sweat of your brow! You don't have monthly cramps. You didn't suffer labor pains for 24 hours giving birth! (see Gen. 3:16). You're not getting up for the 2 a.m. feedings!"

Adam: "Like I said, whose fault is that?" (see Gen. 3:17).

If any of this sounds even vaguely familiar, remember that the troubles between men and women have their roots in the Garden of Eden. And they continue to destroy record numbers of marriages and families each year.

Eve's Relationship with Her Children

There are no recorded dialogs between Eve and her offspring. But after the Fall, the first couple produced the first dysfunctional family. Only one generation from Eden, Cain slew Abel (Gen. 4:8). We can assume that Adam and Eve loved and nurtured their children to the best of their ability and instructed them in the ways of God. God's reminder to Cain, "If you do well, will you not be accepted?" (Gen. 4:7) clearly implies that Adam and Eve had instructed Cain to offer a blood sacrifice as Abel had, rather than a sacrifice of crops. But just as Adam and Eve had chosen wrongly, so did their son, Cain.

It's helpful here to remember that Scripture does not blame parents for all the choices of their children. After all, God was a perfect parent, yet

Adam and Eve went wrong. At the same time we need to remember that because of the Fall, all human relationships have been tainted by sin.

A CLOSE-UP

It has been suggested by many that Eve was probably the most beautiful woman who ever lived. As she was literally fashioned by the hand and mind of God, it seems only logical. How could sinful people in a corrupted universe have offspring more beautiful than what God Himself had formed? So we can assume that Eve was physically flawless. How stunning she must have looked to Adam the first time he saw her!

But even more significantly, the initial relationship between Adam and Eve must have been perfect. There was no competition between the sexes, no sense of need to establish superiority, no conflict over whose needs should be given priority. But then came the Fall, and as we've seen, the unity of the two was shattered. Eve blamed the serpent. Adam blamed Eve. And an element of conflict was introduced into a relationship that previously had known none, but which would forever after corrupt our best efforts to maintain intimacy.

One can sense Eve's sorrow at what her choice cost her. Her relationship with Adam was distorted. Eve could recall the good old days when things were different between them. She could remember a time when the Lord Himself came and walked in the garden with them—how real that remembered experience must have been. Just imagine that you were the one who took Satan's bait. Imagine knowing that life would never again be the same because of your choice. Imagine you were the one to pass sin on to your children. What a burden of guilt Eve must have borne.

But we know that Eve never lost hope. When she bore her first son Eve said, "I have acquired a man from the LORD" (Gen. 4:1), a verse many say should be rendered, "I have acquired *the* man from the Lord." Her heart and mind were not far from God's at that moment, as she looked at her newborn son and imagined that he would be the promised Redeemer.

But it was not to be—not yet.

So we can imagine the dashing of Eve's hopes when Cain brutally murdered Abel, and we can imagine her grief. It takes little imagination to sense the anguish and despair of a mother who not only loses her son, but loses him at the hand of his own brother—remembering all the time that she was the one who had taken the bait and urged her husband to eat. One wonders if the burden was ever lifted from her heart.

When I look at Eve close-up, I can hardly bear to see where she began and what became of her. Yet, courageously, Eve continued on. The last mention of Eve in the Book of Genesis comes just after her third son, Seth, is born. "God has appointed another seed for me instead of Abel, whom Cain killed" (Gen. 4:25). Eve, like other mothers who have lost children, never forgot Abel, or even Cain. But she never lost hope. In this verse we realize that God is still on Eve's mind too—that she still views Him as close to her, loving her, and graciously giving her another son.

AN EXAMPLE FOR TODAY

What lessons are we to learn from Scripture's portrait of Eve? Several.

- Relationships between men and women have been terribly distorted as a consequence of the Fall. The distortion cannot be dismissed as reflecting God's desire for us today. The story of the Fall reminds us that marriages need to be worked on in a climate of commitment which ends only at death.
- Like Eve, we are likely to sin and will have to face consequences of our choices. Yet we can look to Eve's example of continuing to cling to God and going on with life.
- Like Eve, when we sin we will need ultimately to accept responsibility for our actions. Yes, Eve complained that the serpent deceived her. But in the end she also admitted, "and *I* ate."
- Those of us who are parents have been given an example of forgiving. After all, God forgave Adam and Eve after their fall and continued to be with them. We need to forgive when our children sin and continue to be there for them.

◆ I believe that Eve must have forgiven herself in time. Without forgiveness, how could she have found the strength to continue on with the many burdens she had to bear? If Eve could forgive herself, then any of us can and should forgive ourselves for what we have done.

◆ Let's remember that God promised Adam and Eve a Savior. Even though Eve mistook His timing, it was faith in God's promise that brought the first pair the forgiveness promised to us in Christ. The Savior Eve yearned for has come, and no matter what we have done, faith in the Son of God will save us as well.

◆ How strange to think that the Fall in Eden contributed to the joy we feel today at the triumph of our risen Lord. Despite the flaws we share with Eve, Christ will never leave us or forsake us.

Gifted Artisans

Scripture References: *Exodus 35:22–29*
When They Lived: *About 1445 B.C.*
Major Contribution: *These women used their talents as well as their treasures to beautify the tablernacle.*

THEIR ROLE IN SCRIPTURE

At Sinai God gave the Israelites His Law; He also gave them the blueprints of a portable worship center. Men and women quickly contributed the wood, cloth, gold, silver, and precious stones required. The text then tells us that "all the women who were gifted artisans" (Ex. 35:25) spun the yarn to be used in construction.

All too often in our day we limit the idea of "spiritual gifts" to "spiritual" ministries. But any gift or ability God provides can be dedicated to God.

EXAMPLES FOR TODAY

◆ The Lord spoke to Moses and told him to have those with a willing heart to bring offerings of jewelry and other valuables such as gold, onyx, silver, bronze, thread of fine linen and goats' hair in blue, purple and scarlet, ram skins dyed red, badger skins, acacia wood, oil for the light, spices, and incense. These would all be used by artisans with willing hearts to build the tabernacle of meeting, including its tent, its covering, its clasps, its boards, its bars, its pillars, its sockets, the ark with the mercy seat and its poles, and the veil of the covering as well as all the accoutrements (Ex. 35:5–18).

◆ Exodus 35 reminds us that women and men with willing hearts are to use their gifts and their wealth to glorify God (Ex. 35:25, 26, 29).

◆ These artisans contributed to all elements of the tabernacle. Though we are not all artistic, all believers have gifts to be used for the edification of the body.

Hagar

Scripture References: *Genesis 16:1–8, 15, 16; 21:9–17; 25:12; Galatians 4:24, 25*

When They Lived: *About 2075 B.C.*

Name: *Hagar [HAY-gahr: "light"]*

Historical Significance: *Hagar was the mother of the Arab peoples. The first appearance of the Angel of the Lord was to Hagar, Sarah's despairing Egyptian slave.*

HER ROLE IN SCRIPTURE

While the NKJV describes Hagar, as an "Egyptian maidservant" the blunt fact is that Hagar was a slave. Slavery in the ancient world did not involve the oppression of one race by another. But by its nature slavery involved the ownership of one person by another and thus the loss of the slave's right to make personal choices.

Hagar's life story. We don't know how Hagar entered Abram's household. She may have been sold by poverty-stricken parents to traders as a child and purchased later by Abram for his wife Sarai. She may have been captured after an incursion into Egypt by raiders from the north and sold as booty. But at least she was Sarai's slave, not Abram's. Unlike many women sold into slavery she was not purchased to be sexually available to a man or his sons. Hagar was not a concubine: she was a household slave. It seems possible that at first she and Sarai had a relatively pleasant relationship—until, that is, the barren Sarai became determined to follow custom and gave Hagar to Abram that Sarai might obtain a child for Abram through a surrogate. Hagar is introduced at this point in Scripture. It is at this point that this Egyptian slave diverts the flow of history and sets something new in motion.

Sarai's choice (Gen. 16:1–6). When Sarai decided to give her husband Abram a child through Hagar, everything changed for the slave woman. Hagar of course had no choice in the matter, and we have no insight into her feelings about her mistress's decision. What we do know is that Hagar quickly became pregnant. With her pregnancy Hagar's attitude toward Sarai changed, and Sarai "became despised in her eyes." The word "despised" suggests a natural reaction. Hagar felt contempt for her mistress. All those years of childlessness clearly were not due to Abram's sterility. Sarai was "less of a woman" than her slave was!

When Hagar failed to disguise her feelings Sarai became angry and complained to her husband. Abram simply reminded Sarai of her legal rights: "Your maid is in your hand." You may "do to her as you please" (Gen. 16:6). And what Sarai pleased was to make Hagar pay for her disrespect! In fact, Sarai treated Hagar so harshly that finally her slave ran away.

Hagar's first encounter with God (Gen. 16:7–15). Sarai's treatment of Hagar was so harsh that within weeks Hagar simply ran away. She headed south, trudging toward Egypt through the desert region, which we know today as the Negev. There, as she sat despondently by a spring of water, "the Angel of the LORD" found her.

While there is debate about the identity of the Angel of the Lord, the evidence suggests that the title indicates an appearance of God Himself. It is particularly significant that this is the first record of God's appearance in this guise in Scripture. Think of it! God did not come as the Angel of the Lord to Adam, or Noah, or Abraham, or any of the great men of early Genesis. Instead He came to a woman, an Egyptian woman, and a slave at that.

The Angel of the Lord told Hagar to return to her mistress and to submit to her. And the Angel of the Lord promised, "I will multiply your descendants exceedingly, so that they shall not be counted for multitude" (Gen. 16:10). So Hagar, clutching God's promise, obeyed, even as Abram had clutched another of God's promises and obeyed God's voice before her. Hagar returned to Sarai's tent, and there she bore Abram a son named Ishmael.

Hagar's second encounter with God (Gen. 21:8–21). We know little of Hagar's next sixteen years. Despite Abram's deep affection for his son Ishmael (see Gen. 17:18), Hagar remained nothing more than Sarai's slave. Apparently there was little improvement in the relationship between the two women. Even after Sarah bore her own son, the miracle child Isaac, the relationship seems to have remained strained. The only time Sarah spoke of her slave, she did not even call her name. She simply called her "this bond-woman" (Gen. 21:10).

During the happy celebration of Isaac's weaning, when Isaac was three or four, and Ishmael sixteen or seventeen years old, Ishmael was teasing his little half-brother. The Hebrew word does not tell us whether the teasing was good-natured or an expression of an underlying jealousy. But we do know that Sarah exploded and demanded that both Hagar and Ishmael be sent away immediately.

This time Abraham didn't agree. The text tells us that Abraham was "very displeased" at Sarah's demand—"because of his son." [See the discussion of this incident in the commentary on Sarah, page 216]. Then God intervened, and told Abraham that it was His will too that Hagar and Ishmael go.

Abraham obeyed God's voice, and "early in the morning" he supplied Hagar and Ishmael with food and water and sent them away. They wandered in the desert until the water was gone. Then, in despair, she left her exhausted son in the shade of a low bush and dragged herself some distance away, weeping broken-heartedly. There, a second time, the Angel of the Lord spoke to Hagar. He repeated His promise to make Ishmael a great nation, and the Lord opened Hagar's eyes "and she saw a well of water" (Gen. 21:19)—a well that, like God Himself, had been there all along.

The last mention of Hagar in the Old Testament reminds us of God's faithfulness to the oppressed. God's words are about the future, not the past. "So God was with the lad; and he grew and dwelt in the wilderness, and became an archer. He dwelt in the Wilderness of Paran; and his mother took a wife for him from the land of Egypt" (Gen. 21:20, 21).

Hagar in the New Testament (Gal. 4:22–31). The Old Testament gives us insight into Hagar as a person. In the New Testament Book of Galatians Paul treats Hagar as a symbol. Looking back the apostle Paul views Sarai's intent to have a child through her maidservant as human self-effort, in contrast to a trusting reliance on God's supernatural intervention symbolized in the birth of Isaac long after Sarai ceased menstruating. In Paul's analogy Hagar stands for the view of law held in first-century Judaism, while Sarah stands for Christianity founded on total reliance on God's grace. The analogy is a telling one. Yet it is important to remember that in drawing his analogy the apostle is making no statement about Hagar as a person. To understand Hagar the woman we must return to Genesis, to see her fleshed out, to sense the pain she felt as well as the joy she found in a son she bore for another, yet who in the end became hers alone.

Most significantly, we must see her as a person for whom God cared. Hagar was the first person to encounter God in His guise as the Angel of the Lord. She responded obediently to Him and found her fulfillment in promises God made to her alone.

EXPLORING HER RELATIONSHIPS

Hagar's relationship with Sarah. From the Genesis account, there seems to have been no animosity between Hagar and Sarah before Sarah gave her slave to Abraham. Hagar, as a slave, had no choice in the way she was being used. Today this appalls us. But in that time, slavery seemed a normal state, as did the assignment of a female slave as a surrogate for a childless woman. The only choice Hagar had was to decide how she would act under the circumstances in which she found herself. What Hagar chose to do was openly despise her mistress, who then felt justified in treating Hagar harshly. Soon Hagar preferred to take her chances in the desert rather than stay and bear the treatment she was receiving.

Some seventeen years later Ishmael's teasing of his younger brother led to Hagar's expulsion from Abraham's household. Sarah had reached her limit; she demanded that Abraham get rid of the bondwoman and her son. We cannot know if Hagar was to blame in any way. When God had told Hagar to return after running away so many years before, the Lord had told Hagar to submit to her mistress. Under the circumstances, submission really called for a change of attitude. But was Hagar's attitude really changed? Did she infect her son with animosity toward Sarah and his younger rival Isaac?

In any case, anyone having raised a teenage son should feel tremendous empathy for Hagar at this point. Hagar hadn't chosen to be a slave, and she had not chosen to give birth to an old man's son. She had apparently been obedient when God told her to return to Sarah and submit to her mistress. For her trouble, she and her son were put out into the wilderness, where Hagar fully expected they would die. The relationship between Hagar and Sarah reminds us that life certainly can be unfair.

Hagar's relationship with God. Hagar was an Egyptian. We don't know if she grew up worshiping pagan deities or if she had been exposed to Abraham's God at an early age. We do know that God appeared to her as the Angel of the Lord and made promises to her. We know that God cared for Hagar, for the Lord heard her affliction (Gen. 16:11).

Just as important as God's appearance to Hagar was her response to Him. God told her, "Return to your mistress, and submit yourself under her hand...I will multiply your descendants exceedingly, so that they shall not be counted for multitude" (Gen. 16:9, 10). The text says that "then she called the name of the LORD who spoke to her, You-Are-the-God-Who-Sees" (Gen. 16:13), and that she obeyed the Word of the Lord and returned to her mistress.

Hagar responded to God, believing He would do as He had said. She returned in faith and for the next sixteen or seventeen years tried to make the best of the situation. Through all those years, she continued to be Sarah's slave and, of course, Ishmael's mother.

Yet we see another aspect of Hagar's relationship with God in the account of His next appearance to her. Hagar:

> *...lifted her voice and wept. And God heard the voice of the lad. Then the angel of God called to Hagar out of heaven, and said to her, "What ails you, Hagar? Fear not, for God has heard the voice of the lad where he is. Arise, lift up the lad and hold him with your hand, for I will make him a great nation." Then God opened her eyes, and she saw a well of water. And she went and filled the skin with water, and gave the lad a drink. So God was with the lad; and he grew and dwelt in the wilderness, and became an archer.*
>
> —Gen. 21:16–20

Hagar had responded in faith and obeyed God, and when the time came God saved her and her son as He had promised. Yet, from the biblical record, there is no suggestion of Hagar praying or of any growth in the relationship between Hagar and God. Even when she and Ishmael faced death in the desert, she merely lifted her voice and wept. The lad called out to God, and God heard his voice.

Hagar's relationship with Abraham. Hagar was Sarah's slave. Sarah presented her to Abraham as a surrogate. Abraham impregnated Hagar, and that is all we know of any relationship between Abraham and Hagar.

When Hagar was insolent to Sarah, Abraham told his wife, "Your maid is in your hand; do to her as you please" (Gen. 16:6). Abraham saw Hagar as property, belonging to Sarah and not to him. His response indicates no compassion, affection, or even concern for Hagar's welfare.

When Sarah demanded Abraham send Ishmael and Hagar away, the "matter was very displeasing in Abraham's sight *because of his son*" (Gen. 21:11). Clearly Abraham had no feelings for Hagar.

Hagar's relationship with Ishmael. While Hagar despised her mistress and had no personal relationship with Abraham, she appears to have been a good and loving mother. This is evident in the way she tried to protect him from the sun after they had been thrown out and in the fact she could not bear to see him die. As any loving mother, she was overcome with grief when she felt her son's death was imminent.

A CLOSE-UP

Hagar was a victim of circumstances beyond her control. She was away from her homeland and family. She had no one on her side. She had no choice in being used by an old man to produce an heir. She had nowhere to turn for refuge from her harsh and jealous mistress. While Hagar's attitude certainly contributed to her harsh treatment, one wonders whether Hagar would have been treated any better even if she had felt honored to be a surrogate for Sarah.

In spite of all the factors which robbed Hagar of control of her own life, and there were many, Hagar did respond in faith and with obedience to God.

AN EXAMPLE FOR TODAY

Like many women today, Hagar had few personal resources. But she did the best she could with what she had and trusted God to protect her.

Hagar found herself in a situation over which she had no control. Modern women often feel this same frustration. Like Hagar, however, we can remain faithful to God.

Hagar's life illustrates how unfair, difficult, and unglamorous this life can be. Yet she somehow maintained her dignity. Her obedience to and faith in God helped her to survive. She found solace in knowing that her son would be blessed. In even the darkest of times, there is hope for the future.

~ *Hannah* ~

Scripture References: *1 Samuel 1; 2*
When They Lived: *About 1125 B.C.*
Name: *Hannah [HAN-nuh: "grace"]*
Historical Significance: *Hannah became the mother of Samuel, Israel's last judge. Hannah's desperate prayer at the tabernacle led to the birth of her son, whom she brought before Eli, the priest.*

HER ROLE IN SCRIPTURE

When Hannah lived, their more powerful neighbors, the Philistines, oppressed the Israelite tribes. Hannah was far more concerned with her own personal tragedy than with the political oppression. She was childless, and she yearned to give her husband a son. The pressure she felt was even greater because her husband's other wife had borne him children, and she was quick to ridicule the childless Hannah.

The Bible takes up her story when the family came to the tabernacle at Shiloh to worship and offer sacrifices. When night fell Hannah crept off to the tabernacle and "in bitterness of soul" prayed to the Lord for a son. As she prayed she vowed to dedicate the son God would give her to serve Him.

Hannah's prayer was answered. She bore a son and named him Samuel. She cared for Samuel for three or four years until he was weaned. Then Hannah brought Samuel to the tabernacle and left him with the high priest, Eli, to serve God there. Hannah's son Samuel was soon recognized as a prophet; later he became Israel's last judge. Near the end of Samuel's life he anointed first Saul, and then David, to become king of Israel.

EXPLORING HER RELATIONSHIPS

Hannah's relationship with her husband (1 Sam. 1:5, 8, 23). Hannah's husband Elkanah clearly loved Hannah very much and showed her favoritism by giving her twice as much as his other wife. While Elkanah's actions undoubtedly promoted rivalry between the two women, they do make it clear that Hannah was secure in her relationship with him.

Hannah's problem was that Elkanah was not enough. She was desperate to have a son. Elkanah likely did not understand the depths of his wife's feelings, for he asked her, "Hannah, why do you weep? Why do you not eat? And why is your heart grieved? Am I not better to you than ten sons?" (1 Sam. 1:8). Even though he tried to be supportive, he did not understand and could not enter into her despair.

After Samuel's birth, Hannah must have explained her vow. At this point, according to the Law, Elkanah could have voided her vow. Numbers 30:6–8 says:

> *If indeed she takes a husband, while bound by her vows or by a rash utterance from her lips by which she bound herself, and her husband hears it, and makes no response to her on the day that he hears, then her vows shall stand, and her agreements by which she bound herself shall stand. But if her husband overrules her on the day that he hears it, he shall make void her vow which she took and what she uttered with her lips, by which she bound herself, and the LORD will release her.*

Elkanah, however truly loved Hannah, and he let her vow stand. When Samuel was weaned, Hannah kept her promise to God and left him with Eli the priest.

Elkanah not only permitted her to keep her vow, but when the time came to bring the child to the tabernacle, he went with Hannah and participated in the sacrifice by which they dedicated Samuel to God.

Hannah was blessed in her husband. He loved and supported her even though he could not understand her emotions. Elkanah may not have been the most understanding of men, but he was willing to give Hannah the free-dom to follow her own heart—even though that freedom cost him a son.

Hannah's relationship with Eli (1 Sam. 1:12–17, 24–28). When Eli first saw Hannah she was in the tabernacle, praying desperately. Her prayer was so passionate that Eli assumed from her actions that she was drunk, and he rebuked her. When Hannah explained that she was praying, Eli blessed her.

The blessing was, "Go in peace, and the God of Israel grant your peti-tion which you have asked Him" (1 Sam. 1:17). The blessing quieted Hannah's heart, and she returned to her family happy and relieved. The rea-son for her relief was simple: the blessing of the high priest was considered prophetic, and so Hannah was assured that God would answer her prayer. And God did.

After Samuel was weaned, Hannah and her husband brought him to Eli. Hannah reminded Eli of the time he had seen her praying, and she present-ed the child to Eli that "as long as he lives he shall be lent to the LORD" (1:28). Eli accepted the responsibility for the child, and Samuel grew up in Shiloh where the tabernacle then stood.

Hannah's relationship with the Lord (1 Sam. 1:11; 2:1–10). Hannah's relationship with God has often been misunderstood. The misun-derstanding is derived from Hannah's vow, in 1 Samuel 1:11:

> *"O LORD of hosts, if You will indeed look on the affliction of Your maidser-vant and remember me, and not forget Your maidservant, but will give Your maidservant a male child, then I will give him to the LORD all the days of his life, and no razor shall come upon his head."*

Some have taken Hannah's vow as bargaining with God, assuming that in her heart she was offering the Lord a *quid pro quo*. The form of her vow is similar to that of a person seeking to bargain. If you do X, I will do Y. But Hannah was not making a bargain, but a vow. Four times in the Old Testament a vow made to the Lord is identified with a freewill or voluntary offering (Lev. 7:16; 22:21; Num. 15:3; Deut. 12:17).

What had happened in Hannah's heart was that she had come to the place where she was willing to give to God the one thing that had become most important to her in life: a son. Hannah's prayer was not an act of bargaining, but an act of surrender. In giving up to God the thing that was most precious to her, Hannah found inner peace.

When Samuel was born, Hannah was truly delighted and thankful. We can imagine her, bending over her son, watching him take nourishment from her breast. We can imagine her delight when he took his first steps and uttered his first words. What perhaps surprises us, however, is the sense of joy that Hannah expressed when the day came for her to keep her vow and lend Samuel to Eli and the Lord.

As we read Hannah's prayer in 1 Samuel 2 we discover that, far from being heartbroken at Samuel's surrender, Hannah was filled with joy. She said, "My heart rejoices in the LORD" (1 Sam. 2:1), and throughout her prayer of praise Hannah exalted God and all His works. In surrendering her heart's desire to God, Hannah found her heart filled, not emptied!

In surrendering our heart's desire to God, we discover joy; in truth only God can satisfy our deepest needs.

God continued to be gracious to Hannah. The text tells us that each year Hannah visited Samuel at the tabernacle, and that she "used to make him a little robe, and bring it to him year by year when she came up with her husband to offer the yearly sacrifice" (1 Sam. 2:19). Undoubtedly Hannah missed Samuel, but she was busy and fulfilled, for "the LORD visited Hannah, so that she conceived and bore three sons and two daughters" (2:21). Hannah knew that the son she had loaned to the Lord would become great, for while Samuel was still a child he began to prophesy, "and all Israel from Dan to Beersheba knew that Samuel had been established as a prophet of the LORD" (1 Sam. 3:20).

A CLOSE-UP

Hannah was a woman who for a long time could not enjoy her blessings. Her heart was so focused on having a son that nothing else seemed to matter. But life changed for Hannah when she surrendered the thing she wanted most to the Lord in a vow.

Hannah discovered a truth that Christ would teach to His disciples a millenium later. In Matthew 16 Jesus urged his disciples to deny themselves, to take up their cross, and follow Him. What, Jesus asked, can "a man give in exchange for his soul?" (Matt. 16:26). The Greek phrase in our New Testament reflects a Hebrew grammatical construction in which the *nephesh*, "soul," serves as a reflexive pronoun. What Jesus was actually asking is, what can a person give in exchange for his or her *self?*

The disciples had a choice to make. They could hang on to the old self or they could surrender all to Jesus and by following Him become the new persons God would enable them to become. In surrender, the disciples would discover not loss, but gain—as Hannah similarly discovered so long ago.

In surrendering to God the son she so desperately wanted, Hannah gained a fresh appreciation for the Lord, a deep sense of joy, and a truly satisfying life. She gained the sure knowledge that in surrendering Samuel to the Lord, she had set him on course to become one of the Old Testament's great men of faith.

AN EXAMPLE FOR TODAY

◆ Hannah's life portrays how setting our hearts on something we do not have can rob us of appreciation for the gifts God has given us. It was only when Hannah surrendered the object of her desire to God that she found release from her anguish and discovered peace.

◆ Hannah's prayer reminds us that when our motivation is right, God is more likely to say yes to our petitions.

The joy Hannah found in surrendering to God what was most important to her can be ours when we surrender all to Him.

The Hemorrhaging Woman

Scripture References: *Matthew 9:20–22; Mark 5:25–34;*
Luke 8:43–48
When They Lived: A.D. 30
Historical Significance: *Her trust in Jesus' healing powers*
was rewarded.

HER ROLE IN SCRIPTURE

We only meet the hemorrhaging woman for a few brief moments, but we know much about her. She had had an issue of blood for twelve years. That condition made her ritually unclean, so that she could not be touched by her husband or share in the annual worship celebrations so important in Judaism. She could not go into the temple court, light the Sabbath evening candles, or participate in the Passover meal. She would have hovered as a ghost in her home, there and yet not there.

The woman had tried desperately to find a cure. Mark bluntly reports that she "had suffered many things from many physicians" and "had spent all that she had and was no better, but rather grew worse" (Mark 5:26). Over and over, this woman had likely felt brief moments of hope, only to be cast deeper into despair.

Yet despite a dozen years of disappointments, she had not lost her faith in God. Undoubtedly the stories about Jesus had fanned her faith even more, for when she heard Jesus was in the city, she set out to find Him, thinking, "If only I may touch His clothes, I shall be made well" (Mark 5:28).

It's uncertain why this woman did not approach Jesus and ask for help rather than reaching out anonymously to touch Him. Perhaps she didn't feel worthy of bothering the miracle-working Teacher. Perhaps she was too ashamed of her unclean state to speak of it in public. Whatever the reason, it was not lack of faith that kept her from speaking to Jesus. This woman had far more faith than most—although hers was a private faith.

So she touched Him.

And "immediately the fountain of her blood was dried up, and she felt in her body that she was healed of the affliction" (Mark 5:29). Her private faith had prevailed. From that moment on, all that she had lost was restored. That one moment spent with Jesus changed her life forever.

The story doesn't end there. Jesus sensed that healing power had flowed from Him, and He stopped. He turned to the crowd that pressed in around Him and asked, "'Who touched My clothes?'" (Mark 5:30). Fearful and uncertain, the woman fell before Him and told her story. What relief must have flooded her soul as she heard Jesus say, "'Daughter, your faith has made you well. Go in peace, and be healed of your affliction'" (Mark 5:34).

We may wonder why Jesus stopped to call the woman before Him. On the one hand, it may be that Jesus acted for the woman's sake. Her private faith had healed her. However, only when she had spoken publicly of her need and of Christ's grace did she hear His confirming words, "'Your faith has made you well,'" and "'Go in peace.'"

Yet Jesus may have had another reason. With the telling of her story, the woman's inner healing and her faith as well left the realm of the private and personal and became a witness to the world of Jesus' power. The woman, in being blessed, became a blessing to all.

AN EXAMPLE FOR TODAY

- This woman knew in her soul that if she could just touch Jesus' garment, she would be healed. She set out to do it. Often we hear a little voice inside telling us to do or say something, or not to do or say something. Unlike this woman, we often fail to step out in faith. That voice may well be the Holy Spirit, and we are to obey.
- The story reminds us that Jesus' healing is real. In our world we're concerned with harnessing energy: hydroelectric, natural gas, nuclear. If we really want to get hooked up to the source of power, we must reach out and touch Jesus. His power truly is unlimited and is available to all who will reach out in faith.

Herodias & Her Daughter

Scripture References: *Matthew 14:1–12; Mark 6:14–29*

THEIR ROLE IN SCRIPTURE

Herodias had married Philip, and then his brother, King Herod Antipas. John the Baptist preached against this marriage, which was incestuous according to Old Testament Law. Herod had John imprisoned, but he was afraid to execute the popular prophet. Herod feared John himself, "knowing that he was a just and holy man" (Mark 6:20). Herodias however was incensed that John had publicly condemned her, and she "held it against him and wanted to kill him" (Mark 16:19).

Her chance came when Herodias's daughter danced at a feast Herod gave, and the king effusively told the young woman to name her own reward. When she looked to her mother for advice, Herodias told her to ask for John the Baptist's head.

Certainly Herodias was a grasping and self-centered woman. She abandoned Philip to marry the more important Herod, even though she knew this was condemned in God's Law. When John preached against the marriage, her pride generated murderous intent. She did not hesitate for a moment to involve her own daughter in what was nothing less than the murder of a godly man. Harsh, brittle and hardened, Herodias cared for nothing but revenge.

She won her revenge. But sacred history has marked her as the New Testament counterpart of the Old Testament's detested Jezebel.

EXAMPLES FOR TODAY

◆ John the Baptist had spoken out against Herod's decision to wed his brother's wife which was contrary to God's law. While Herod seems to have been shaken by John's preaching, Herodias became furious. She knew that what she had done was wrong, but when confronted she refused to admit and correct her fault. Anger at others is often a sign of hardness in our own hearts—a warning we need to heed.

◆ Herodias's response to godly counsel was to retaliate against the counselor. Her anger led her to a far greater sin, as she conspired to end John's life. If we harden our hearts, we make ourselves vulnerable to far greater sins.

Huldah the Prophetess

Scripture References: *2 Kings 22:13, 14;*
2 Chronicles 34:22

When They Lived: *About 625* B.C.

Name: *Huldah [HUL-duh; "weasel"(?)]*

Historical Significance: *A prophetess consulted by King Josiah when workers discovered a lost book of God's Law.*

HER ROLE IN SCRIPTURE

Huldah lived during critical years in Judah's history. For over half a century, kings with no loyalty to the Lord had ruled, and most of Judah's people had turned to paganism. Then Josiah became king and set out to lead his people back to God.

In the process of repairing the temple a lost book of God's Law, generally thought to be Deuteronomy, was discovered. When Josiah read the lost book, he was shocked and shaken. Josiah had not fully understood how guilty his people were of departing from God, nor had he known the punishments Scripture decreed for their sins. Immediately the king sent representatives to inquire about what God wanted and what He would do.

What is fascinating is that these representatives were sent to Huldah, a prophetess. Clearly, Huldah had established a reputation as God's spokesperson. We are even more impressed when we realize that the prophet Habakkuk, whose book is part of the Old Testament, was living at this time. Yet Huldah was clearly the king's first choice when seeking to know God's will.

His choice was wise, for Huldah had a word from God for the young king. God would indeed bring calamity on His sinning people. But because Josiah's heart was tender and he had responded when he heard God's Word, judgment would not fall during Josiah's reign.

EXPLORING HER RELATIONSHIPS

Each verse where Huldah's name is mentioned refers to her as a prophetess and as the wife of Shallum. It is significant that Deborah was identified in much the same way. She too was a prophetess and also a wife (Judg. 4:4).

AN EXAMPLE FOR TODAY

◆ Huldah experienced no conflict between the roles of prophetess and wife. Huldah's husband did not feel threatened by the fact that his wife had an important ministry.

◆ A woman can have a ministry and still win a reputation as a good wife. Marriage and ministry are not necessarily in conflict.

~ Jael ~

Scripture References: *Judges 4; 5*
When They Lived: *About 1300 B.C.*
Name: *Jael [JAY-el, "mountain goat"]*
Historical Significance: *Jael killed the commander of the Canaanite army that had oppressed Israel, assuring Israel's victory.*

HER ROLE IN SCRIPTURE

J ael was the wife of Heber the Kenite. The Kenites were a seminomadic tribe whose name means "metalsmith." The Kenites are mentioned in

Genesis 15:19 as residing in Canaan in Abraham's time, and in Exodus in copper-rich sections of the Sinai Peninsula.

At the time, Heber was loosely allied with the Canaanites of Hazor who oppressed the Israelites, although his clan was related to Moses. So after the defeat at the Kishon River, when the fleeing Canaanite commander, Sisera, came to the camp of Heber, he felt safe. He was invited in to rest by Jael, Heber's wife. Aware of the friendship of Heber with his king, Sisera asked for something to drink and told Jael that if anyone came looking for him she was to tell them he was not there. Sisera then fell into an exhausted sleep.

Deborah's victory song describes what happened next:

> Most blessed of women be Jael,
> the wife of Heber the Kenite,
> most blessed of tent-dwelling women.
> He asked for water, and she gave him milk;
> in a bowl fit for nobles she brought him curdled milk.
> Her hand reached for the tent peg,
> her right hand for the workman's hammer.
> She struck Sisera, she crushed his head,
> she shattered and pierced his temple.
> —Judg. 5:24–26 NIV

With the commander of the army dead, Canaanite oppression ended.

EXPLORING HER RELATIONSHIPS

Jael's actions are surprising in view of her husband's friendly relationships (Judg. 4:17) with the king of Hazor. We might have expected that Jael, as Heber's wife, would have taken her lead from him and hidden Sisera as he requested. Yet Jael did just the opposite, and when Sisera fell asleep she killed him.

We can suppose a number of possible reasons. Perhaps Jael had not agreed with her husband's policies and sympathized with the Israelites. Perhaps Jael recognized the defeat of Sisera as a political turning point and decided that her clan's best course was to ally itself with the victors. In either case Jael's willingness to act without consulting her husband is significant. It was undoubtedly the husband's role to make the kind of decision that Jael made. Yet when consultation was impossible Jael relied on her own judgment and took an action that decisively reversed her husband's policy, committing her family and clan to the Israelite cause.

For Jael to make this kind of decision she must have been very confident in her relationship with her husband. Perhaps she had been his counselor as they discussed relationships with their neighbors. Perhaps she knew that, in view of the Israelite victory, Heber would have done exactly what she did. We cannot know her reasoning. From the fact that she acted as she did, we have to conclude that Jael at least was not a mere possession of her husband but a participant with him in setting the course of the family and clan.

A CLOSE-UP

Old Testament law and custom suggest that women were locked into relationships in which they were essentially powerless and subservient. Yet in Judges 4 and 5 we meet two women who shatter this illusion. Deborah emerges as a judge in Israel. The other woman, Jael, is portrayed as a woman who acted decisively, without consulting her husband, even though the action she took reversed a long-standing clan policy and committed her family to a new alliance.

Whatever else we can say about Jael, she was a strong and decisive woman. Jael quickly evaluated the implications of the Canaanite defeat and was confident enough to act on that evaluation. She was comfortable enough in her relationship with her husband to feel free to act in his absence. She believed that he would support what she had done. Whatever we can say about women who are celebrated in Scripture, we must agree that they are celebrated for their strengths, not their weaknesses.

AN EXAMPLE FOR TODAY

◆ Jael's actions may have surprised some, but she was doing God's will. That will had been expressed by Deborah, who told Barak that "the LORD will sell Sisera into the hand of a woman." Clearly Jael had been led by the Spirit of God to act as she did.

- ◆ Jael's responsiveness to God contrasts with Barak's objections when told to lead the Israelite forces. When Barak was unwilling to obey, God raised up a woman to do the job. And it is her name that has been honored through the centuries as the one who did the Lord's bidding.

- ◆ Jael's action in setting a new direction for Heber's clan reflects a close and trusting relationship between this husband and wife. He trusted her to act when he was not present. She trusted him not to be angry or reverse her decisions. Married couples need to build this kind of trusting relationship, which develops only where there is both love and open lines of communication.

Jairus's Wife & Daughter

Scripture References: *Matthew 9:18, 23–25;*
Mark 5:22, 23, 35–42;
Luke 8:41, 42, 49–55

THEIR ROLE IN SCRIPTURE

We know little about Jairus's wife and her daughter. We know that the two women, one an adult and one a child, were members of a privileged class. Jairus's position as an important official in the synagogue indicates that the family possessed both wealth and a good reputation. Yet none of this protected them from tragedy. The daughter fell deathly ill and died. All the mother could do was to look on, helpless and heartbroken.

Then Jesus came, in response to Jairus's desperate request. Jesus brought the twelve-year-old back to life. In so doing, Jesus healed the mother's broken heart.

The story reminds us of our own vulnerability. Neither wealth nor privilege can protect us from the tragedies of life. How often we are forced to suffer in silence, unable to do anything for those we love. It must have been terrible for the girl's mother as she waited at home, forced to rely on her husband to importune Jesus, watching as each breath her daughter drew seemed more shallow—until the breathing stopped, and hope died.

Yet Jairus had prevailed on Jesus to come. With Jesus' presence, life flowed back into the little girl's body.

There's a lesson here to remember when we find ourselves in need as Jairus' daughter or as helpless as Jairus' wife. Let's send those who care about us and who know Christ to importune Him and cry out for His aid. What we cannot do, Jesus can do. Jesus still responds to the cries of those who come to Him for aid.

Jehosheba

Scripture References: *2 Kings 11:2; 2 Chronicles 22:11*
When They Lived: *About 850 B.C.*
Name: *Jehosheba [juh-HAH-shuh-buh:*
"Yahweh is abundance"]
Historical Significance: *She saved Joash's life when Athaliah attempted to murder all the heirs to Judah's throne.*

HER ROLE IN SCRIPTURE

When King Ahaziah of Judah was killed, his mother Athaliah determined to seize the throne for herself. So she ordered all the royal heirs—her own grandchildren!—executed. While Athaliah did seize the throne for herself, one of Ahaziah's infant sons, Joash, was spared.

The rescue was accomplished by Ahaziah's sister named Jehosheba [called "Jehoshabeath" in 2 Chr. 22:11]. Jehosheba, who was married to the Lord's high priest, Jehoiada, sheltered the infant in the temple itself until he reached seven years of age. Then Jehoiada organized a coup, executed Athaliah, and placed the seven-year-old Joash on Judah's throne.

EXPLORING HER RELATIONSHIPS

Jehosheba's relationship with the royal family. The Bible tells us that Jehosheba was a "daughter of the king" (2 Chr. 22:11), that is, Jehoram. Thus Jehosheba was the sister of Ahaziah and the aunt of the infant she saved.

It is significant that, although Jehosheba was part of the royal family, she was not like Athaliah or either of the two kings. Jehosheba had compassion for the infant Joash and risked her own life to hide him.

Jehosheba's relationship with Jehoiada. Jehosheba was married to God's high priest, Jehoiada. Her actions reveal that she worshiped the Lord whom her husband served. We can credit her as well as her husband with Joash's early commitment to God, expressed in the religious reforms he instituted as a young adult (cf. 2 Chr. 24:1–14).

A CLOSE-UP

Jehosheba provides a corrective to a misunderstanding shared by too many believers today. While Athaliah reminds us of the powerful influence parents have on their children, Jehosheba reminds us that every person makes his or her own choices in life. While parents do influence their children, what parents do cannot and will not determine who their children become.

Jehosheba was a member of the royal family, a sister of King Ahaziah. Yet she chose to go a different way from that taken by the others. She had married the high priest of the Lord, and in saving the infant Joash, she set herself in opposition to the power-hungry Athaliah. What motivated her was not only her compassion for the infant, but also her commitment to the Lord.

Even as Athaliah took on the worst characteristics of the god she worshiped, so Jehosheba reflected the best qualities of our God.

AN EXAMPLE FOR TODAY

◆ Sometimes doing the right thing puts us at risk. Jehosheba risked her life to save a life—and in the end saved a generation for the Lord.

◆ We must all set our sights on living godly lives—whatever those around us may do. God gave each of us the ability to make choices, and we are responsible to Him for the choices we make.

Jephthah's Daughter

Scripture References: *Judges 10; 11*

When They Lived: *About 1250 B.C.*

Historical Significance: *Jephthah's daughter illustrates the limitations on women's freedom of self-determination.*

HER ROLE IN SCRIPTURE

Jephthah was the illegitimate son of an Israelite who was expelled by his family and clan after his father's death. But Jephthah was an exceptional leader, and when the Ammonites attacked the Israelites, Jephthah was recalled to lead them in battle.

When Jephthah was about to lead the attack on the enemy forces he made a vow to the Lord, that "whatever comes out of the door of my house to meet me when I return in triumph from the Ammonites will be the Lord's, and I will sacrifice it as a burnt offering" (Judg. 11:31 NIV).

To Jephthah's dismay, his only child, a daughter, was the first to come out to meet him! Crushed and miserable, Jephthah told her of the vow "that I cannot break" (Judg. 11:35 NIV).

Many have concluded from this dialog that Jephthah did kill and burn his daughter as a sacrifice. However, this is unlikely, in view of the wider context of Scripture. What actually did happen is suggested in the following:

The Old Testament displays an absolute revulsion toward human sacrifice (Lev. 18:21; 20:2,3; Deut. 12:31; 18:10). While some argue that Jephthah must have fulfilled his vow by killing and burning his daughter, this is not required by the text or by Hebrew practices. Old Testament law introduces a principle in Exodus 28:8 and illustrates it in 1 Samuel 1:28 and Luke 2:36,37. This principle is that a person or thing dedicated to God might fulfill the vow by a lifetime of service as well as by the surrender of a life.

Indications that this is what happened in the case of Jephthah's daughter are: (1) the knowledge Jephthah had previously displayed of Old Testament history and law, as in his letter to the Ammonites (10:15–27a); (2) every sacrifice to the Lord required that a priest officiate, and no Hebrew priest would offer a human sacrifice; (3) the reaction of Jephthah's daughter who went out with friends to lament not over her imminent death but "because I will never marry" (11:37). All this leads us to the conclusion that Jephthah *did* fulfill his vow by dedicating his daughter's life to the service of the Lord (*735 Baffling Bible Questions Answered* [1997], 95).

EXPLORING HER RELATIONSHIPS

While the text tells us little about Jephthah's daughter, it does tell us much about her relationship with her father. Like other daughters in Israel, she lived under her father's authority. He had—and in this case he exercised—the right to make decisions that would set the direction of her entire life.

The fact that this was not the direction she herself would have chosen is reflected in her response to her father's revelation:

"My father, you have given your word to the Lord. Do to me just as you promised, now that the LORD has avenged you of your enemies, the Ammonites. But grant me this one request: Give me two months to roam the hills and weep with my friends, because I will never marry" (Judg. 11:36, 37 NIV).

Like other young women in Israel, Jephthah's daughter had looked forward to marrying and having a family of her own. Now this would be impossible.

Yet the young woman never questioned her father's right to dedicate her life to the service of God. She realized that her father must not break his vow, even though they were both devastated at its unexpected impact on her life.

There could hardly be a more powerful example in Scripture of a father's right in Old Testament times to exercise authority over the women in his household. At the same time, the deep emotion displayed by Jephthah and by his daughter reveals that bonds of mutual love rather than legalities motivated members of loving families. Both Jephthah and his daughter seem deeply aware of each other's pain, and both were eager to do whatever they could to alleviate that pain.

Hopefully they both came to the place where they recognized God's hand in the daughter's dedication to serve the Lord, and in time this young woman found fulfillment in her lifelong ministry of prayer.

AN EXAMPLE FOR TODAY

- Singleness is not a curse, though it may not be what we initially expected from life. Remaining single will free some to have more time to devote to the Lord.
- The experience of Jephthah's daughter illustrates how another's decisions may impact our lives and our happiness. We will not always have control over what happens to us. When this happens, may we respond with a love and grace like that displayed by this young girl.
- Jephthah's daughter's courage to go on even when her life had been irrevocably changed by the actions of others can be inspiring to us. The grace she showed in supporting her devastated father and her submission to God's will challenge us all.

Jeroboam's Wife

Scripture References: *1 Kings 14:1–13*

HER ROLE IN SCRIPTURE

After Solomon's death the united kingdom divided. In the south, Rehoboam, a descendant of David, ruled Judah from the city of Jerusalem. The first ruler of the northern Hebrew kingdom, Israel, was Jeroboam.

When the kingdom divided, Jeroboam was afraid that if his subjects went up to Jerusalem to worship God, as Old Testament Law required, that in time they would want to reunite with their brothers in the south. To avoid this, Jeroboam set up a counterfeit religious system that mimicked but also violated the practices laid down in the Old Testament. This decision of Jeroboam set the northern kingdom on the road to destruction. Not one of Israel's succeeding kings reversed this religious policy.

Some time after Jeroboam had done this his son Abijah became sick. Jeroboam sent his wife to seek help from the prophet Ahijah. Although she went in disguise, the prophet knew her and announced that Jeroboam was doomed and that his line would not only be cut off, but that his descendants would die unmourned and unburied. But Ahijah also told Jeroboam's wife:

"Arise therefore, go to your own house. When your feet enter the city, the child shall die. And all Israel shall mourn for him and bury him, for he is the only one of Jeroboam who shall come to the grave, because in him there is found something good toward the LORD God of Israel in the house of Jeroboam" (1 Kin. 14:12, 13).

We know nothing of Jeroboam's wife besides insights we can draw from this incident. From the few words recorded here we can sense her anguish and perhaps her fear. Her husband had sent her on a sensitive mission, and she would have to report back to him. Yet to return would doom her son, for the moment she entered the city, her son would die. We can perhaps measure her fear by the fact that she immediately "arose and departed." And, "when she came to the threshold of the house, the child died" (1 Kin. 14:17).

In a real sense Jeroboam's wife had no choice. Perhaps sometime in the past she might have had a choice: a choice to accept or reject the marriage negotiated by her parents. But then she may not have known what Jeroboam was like, or had any hint of what the future would hold. We can only suggest from this poor woman's experience that when we do have a choice of whom to marry, we carefully consider character. For the choice we make of a mate is likely to be the most significant choice of all.

Jezebel

Scripture References: *1 Kings 16:31; 18:1–13; 19:1, 2;*
21:1–25; 2 Kings 9:1–37;
Revelation 2:20

When They Lived: *About 875 B.C.*

Name: *Jezebel [JEZ-uh-bel: "un-exalted"]*

Historical Significance: *As King Ahab's wife, Jezebel set out to replace worship of the Lord in Israel with the worship of Baal.*

HER ROLE IN SCRIPTURE

Jezebel was the daughter of the king of Sidon, and was totally committed to the virulent form of Baal worship practiced there. Her marriage to Ahab resulted in Ahab worshiping the Sidonian deity and cooperating with Jezebel in her efforts to make Baal the god of Israel. She came close to succeeding.

First Kings 18:4 and 13 make it clear that Jezebel took the initiative in this religious crusade, for the text tells us that "Jezebel killed the prophets of the LORD." This does not mean that she personally killed God's prophets, but rather that they were killed at her command. This and other references to Jezebel in the Old Testament make it clear that she was a forceful woman.

In many ways, Jezebel dominated her husband and set the course of the kingdom.

God responded to the threat posed by Jezebel by raising up the prophet, Elijah. Elijah not only turned the hearts of the people back to the Lord, but he predicted Jezebel's death as a punishment from God.

In the end, God commissioned an army officer named Jehu to replace Ahab. Jehu fulfilled God's commission by wiping out all those in Israel who worshiped Baal and by killing every member of Ahab's household.

EXPLORING HER RELATIONSHIPS

Jezebel's relationship with God. Jezebel was a determined opponent of God, set on wiping out His prophets and purging Israel of worshipers of the Lord. She initiated a campaign to exterminate God's prophets and threatened Elijah's life.

Despite her antagonism toward the Lord, it seems significant that when Elijah challenged the 450 prophets of Baal "and the four hundred prophets of Asherah [Baal's consort goddess] who eat at Jezebel's table" to a contest, King Ahab accepted the challenge. However, Jezebel did not permit her prophets to enter the fray. Jezebel's antagonism to God may not have been rooted in disbelief as much as in a rejection of the moral standards for which the Lord stood.

Jezebel's relationship with Ahab. Jezebel exercised dominance over her royal husband. This is particularly striking because Ahab was a skilled military man and capable ruler. Twice he defeated the forces of Syria's King Benhadad II. Ahab also joined a coalition of kings that defeated the Assyrians under Shalmaneser II at Qarqar in 853 B.C., contributing more war chariots to the allied effort than any other ruler. Ahab also maintained peace with Judah, working out an alliance with King Jehoshaphat. Yet the biblical text suggests that his wife, Jezebel, dominated Ahab.

This is most clearly seen in the story of Naboth's vineyard, developed on page 292.

Jezebel's relationship with Elijah. It was only natural that Jezebel's antagonism to the Lord would make her the enemy of Elijah, God's prophet. When Elijah had defeated the prophets of Baal in a contest at Mount Carmel (1 Kin. 18), and had 450 prophets of the pagan deity put to death, Ahab seemed subdued and quiet. But when Jezebel heard, her immediate reaction was to threaten to kill Elijah. And this time it was Elijah who "arose and ran for his life" (1 Kin. 19:3).

In the end, God restored Elijah's courage, and he was the one who announced "concerning Jezebel the LORD also spoke, saying, 'The dogs shall eat Jezebel by the wall of Jezreel'" (1 Kin. 21:23). It is a testimony to the reality of God that Elijah's words rather than Jezebel's threat came true.

In the New Testament

The one reference in the New Testament to Jezebel is found in Revelation 2:20: "You allow that woman Jezebel, who calls herself a prophetess, to teach and seduce My servants to commit sexual immorality and eat things sacrificed to idols."

The name Jezebel is probably used symbolically here. Yet the stated reasons why the real woman in the church at Thyatira was identified as a "Jezebel" is significant.

◆ A Jezebel "calls herself a prophetess"—that is, presents herself as a religious leader.
◆ A Jezebel teaches and seduces God's people "to commit sexual immorality."
◆ A Jezebel teaches and seduces God's people to "eat things sacrificed to idols."

This verse in turn suggests that much of Jezebel's power over Ahab was rooted in Jezebel's sexuality. She apparently relied on her sexuality to the end. As Jehu entered Jezreel after killing Ahab's successor, "Jezebel heard of it; and she put paint on her eyes and adorned her head, and looked through a window" (2 Kin. 9:30). This last desperate act was futile, however, for at Jehu's command Jezebel was thrown through the window to her death, and dogs ate her body as Elijah had predicted.

A CLOSE-UP

Jezebel was undoubtedly a strong woman. She relied on her sexuality and the force of her character to dominate her husband, King Ahab, and to set national religious policy. It would seem that Jezebel rather than Ahab was the dominant personality in the ruling house. Jezebel never hesitated to act as if she ruled. The immediate obedience of those she commanded indicates that her power was real indeed.

The tragedy of Jezebel is that she was committed to evil rather than to God. She used her many gifts and influence to harm others rather than help them. Despite the power she exercised, Jezebel's life was meaningless and empty. Her death was a consequence of her own evil ways.

AN EXAMPLE FOR TODAY

◆ How important it is to use our gifts to serve rather than exploit others. Only in servanthood do we achieve greatness or earn lasting rewards.

◆ Today, Jezebel's name is synonymous with a woman of low moral character. We are remembered by our character.

Job's Wife

Scripture References: *Job 2:9, 10*

HER ROLE IN SCRIPTURE

Job and his wife probably lived in the age of the patriarchs, around 2000 B.C. They almost surely did not live during the age of kings, for in the entire book of Job there is no mention of the Mosaic Law and no reference to the Jewish people.

To fix a date for the timeless story of Job and the struggle to understand why bad things happen to good people is unnecessary.

Job's wife had a small role in his story and in the book. She is mentioned only after Job had lost his wealth and his children, and had been stricken with "painful boils from the sole of his foot to the crown of his head" (Job 2:7). As Job sat in ashes, exhausted and in pain, his wife spoke:

"Do you still hold fast to your integrity?
Curse God and die!"
But he said to her, "You speak as one of the foolish women speaks.
Shall we indeed accept good from God, and shall we not accept adversity?"
—Job 2:9, 10

It would be easy to misunderstand these verses and criticize Job's wife. Job did not suggest that she is one of the "foolish women." In Hebrew, the word translated "foolish" here doesn't indicate a lack of sense. Rather "foolish" is a moral term. Job's wife is not morally deficient but in giving this advice she speaks "as" a foolish woman might.

What we see here is a wife who was being torn apart by her husband's suffering. She saw the tension in his body; she heard the moans that escaped his lips when he supposed no one was listening. At last, she cried out in her own anguish, urging him to give up and die. Anything seemed better to her than to see him suffering—even his death.

But Job wouldn't listen to his wife. He was convinced that suffering and joy are both gifts distributed by God. Outwardly at least, Job welcomed suffering until God's purpose in giving it had been achieved.

It's easy to admire Job. And it should be just as easy for us to understand and to sympathize with the feelings expressed by Job's wife. How much easier it seems at times to suffer ourselves than to see a loved one in pain. Love undoubtedly moved Job's wife to release him by her words. Even though she would be left a penniless widow, at least Job's sufferings would end.

But Job did not die. In the end, Job's health and wealth were restored, and Job and his wife shared the joy bringing a new family into the world.

AN EXAMPLE FOR TODAY

◆ Job's wife was quite human, and she displayed a natural response to human suffering. But Job's response was godly and showed spiritual depth. We need to check our reactions, for they may well be carnal rather than spiritual.

◆ Job's wife's advice shows that she was truly moved by his suffering. What a tragedy it would have been if Job had listened to her and given up on life. What blessings Job would have missed if he had not waited on God!

~ *Jochebed* ~

Scripture References: *Exodus 2:1–10; 6:20;*
Numbers 26:59

When They Lived: *About 1525 B.C.*

Name: *Jochebed [JAH-kuh-bed:"Yahweh is glory"]*

Major Contribution: *The mother and nurse of Moses,*
who taught him to love God and be loyal to his own people.
Moses' mother may have intentionally placed her baby where Pharaoh's
daughter would find him when she came to the river to bathe.

HER ROLE IN SCRIPTURE

Jochebed is named only in two genealogies, where she is identified as the mother of Moses, Aaron, and Miriam. Undoubtedly her most significant role was in the early shaping of her son Moses, a dominant figure throughout the Old Testament.

Jochebed was a Hebrew woman in Egypt, a member of a slave race. When she bore Moses, Pharaoh had commanded that all boys born to Hebrews should be thrown into the Nile. When Jochebed could no longer hide her child, she made a boat of papyrus reeds and concealed him in the river where Pharaoh intended that such children would meet their doom. Jochebed set her daughter to watch the baby and see that no harm came to him.

We know the familiar story of how Moses was discovered by Pharaoh's daughter and adopted by her. Then the princess unknowingly placed Moses in the charge of his own mother to be nursed.

BIBLE BACKGROUND: PAPYRUS BOATS

Papyrus reeds grew in marshy areas and were used in constructing large boats as well as the "basket boat" in which Moses survived. Bundled together and tied, the reeds floated high in the water and were capable of bearing heavy loads.

It was common in Egypt as in most ancient societies for upper-class women to have wet nurses who would nurse their children. This relieved the mothers of a tiresome task and helped them keep their figures. So it was natural for Pharaoh's daughter to employ a Hebrew wet nurse.

In biblical times, children were not weaned until the age of three or even four. We can assume that the first three to four years of Moses' life were spent with his mother rather than with the princess (Ex. 2:9, 10), and they were among the most important of his life. Jochebed's influence during these years was critical in giving Moses a strong sense of identity with the Hebrew people, as well as a basic knowledge of the God of Abraham, Isaac, and Jacob.

EXPLORING HER RELATIONSHIPS

The relationship of Jochebed and her husband. Jochebed was of the family of Levi, the third son of Leah and Jacob. She married her brother Kohath's oldest son, Amram. They had three children, Miriam, Aaron, and Moses, all of whom distinguished themselves among God's chosen.

Jochebed's relationship with God. Jochebed, like most mothers, loved her children and did what she could to protect them. It's difficult to imagine living in a society where the government would order all boy babies to be killed. Jochebed, like the midwives Puah and Shiphrah, was a God-fearing woman who took desperate measures to protect her infant son.

Jochebed's relationship with Miriam. We don't know if Miriam was the oldest of Jochebed's children, but she may have been since she was given the important responsibility of watching over her baby brother while he floated in a basket on the Nile. Some scholars have assumed that Miriam may have been around eight to ten years of age when she watched over her baby brother. While today we might consider this child neglect, we must remember that thirteen was viewed as marriageable age in Bible times.

Miriam, whatever her age, obeyed her mother and spent her time keeping close watch over the baby. Scripture does not reveal if the baby was found the first day afloat or if days or weeks went by while Miriam acted as sentinel. However long it was, Miriam honored her mother by being a responsible daughter and sister. Jochebed must have had a strong bond of trust with her daughter to give her this important responsibility.

Jochebed's relationship with Moses. Jochebed saw that Moses was a beautiful child and hid him for three months. When she realized it would be too difficult to conceal him any longer, she devised a plan to hide him in a floating basket (Ex. 2:2, 3). It is likely she knew that Pharaoh's daughter and her handmaidens frequented a spot on the Nile. Perhaps Jochebed thought if she could just get Pharaoh's daughter to see her beautiful son, she would want to protect him, too.

Her plan succeeded and, thanks to the quick-thinking Miriam, Jochebed was able to continue nursing and nurturing her son and was even paid for it (Ex. 2:9). She was his primary caregiver and influenced Moses for the first three to four years of his life. During these years, Jochebed infused a lasting sense of identity with God's people in her son. Then she brought him to Pharaoh's daughter, and he became her son. The princess "called his name Moses, saying, 'Because I drew him out of the water'" (Ex. 2:10).

To save his life, Jochebed had to give up Moses to a foster mother. He became a murderer and a fugitive, escaping to the wilderness and away from everything familiar to him. He lived in exile for forty years before God's time to use him arrived. It is probable that Jochebed was living when Moses fled to the wilderness. If so, she waited, wondered, and prayed for her son, but never knew what special plans God had for him. Moses was eighty when

God spoke to him from the burning bush. It is almost certain that Jochebed had died before Moses came out of exile. But God, in His grace and in His time, had an intimate and special relationship with Moses, as He had him lead His people out of bondage and through the wilderness for forty years before finally bringing them to the edge of the Promised Land.

AN EXAMPLE FOR TODAY

- Jochebed's experiences show us that mothers need to be flexible and creative, especially during difficult circumstances.
- Jochebed stands as a reminder to parents never to lose faith that God will work in the lives of their children. Most parents live to see this, but some, like Jochebed don't. How wonderful it is to understand that even after we aren't here to pray for our children, God continues to answer our prayers.
- Jochebed, like many mothers today, lovingly gave her child up for another to raise. God honored her by using her son for His godly purposes. And God used all of Moses' circumstances to make him into the man He needed him to be.

Lois & Eunice

Scripture Reference: *2 Timothy 1:5*

THEIR ROLE IN SCRIPTURE

Only a single verse memorializes these two women, but for Christians they stand for faithful mothers everywhere. Paul declared that he thanked God,

> *When I call to remembrance the genuine faith that is in you, which dwelt first in your grandmother Lois and your mother Eunice, and I am persuaded is in you also.*
>
> — 2 Tim. 1:5

Lois and Eunice have rightly been honored as model mentors for rearing children. They had a genuine faith, and they passed it on to young Timothy. We can picture the mother and grandmother, holding him as a toddler on their knees while telling Bible stories. We can imagine them guiding and correcting the growing boy with precepts drawn from Scripture. We can be sure that they prayed each day that Timothy might know the Lord and choose to serve Him.

Timothy did grow up to become a second-generation leader of the early church. Lois and Eunice likely knew considerable heartbreak before Timothy made his commitment to Christ and to ministry. Just think of parents in Scripture who, like Lois and Eunice, were godly people.

- Jacob and Esau had the same parents. Yet one valued God's covenant promises, and the other despised them.
- Samson's mother and father dedicated themselves to bringing up their son, but he chose to go his own way.
- Hezekiah was a godly king, yet his son Manasseh was completely evil until converted near the end of his fifty-five year reign.
- Mary, the mother of John Mark, was an early disciple of Jesus and a key figure in the Jerusalem church. How she must have hurt when John Mark deserted from Paul's missionary team.

There are stories of "ideal" children, like Samuel who came to know God early, that seem never to have disappointed their mothers. But it is far more common for parents to experience heartache along the way as boys and girls do disappoint. We don't know what young Timothy was like. We do know that Lois and Eunice had a "genuine faith" in God, and they were faithful in sharing that faith with Timothy.

EXAMPLES FOR TODAY

- Lois and Eunice are models, not because Timothy turned out so well, but because they ministered so faithfully. Many a mother has been just as good and faithful as were Lois and Eunice and yet hurt as she saw her children make wrong and harmful choices.

◆ The genuine faith we share with our children does take root. Some faith planted in difficult soil may be slow in growing into healthy adulthood. But, watering our ministry with prayer, we can trust the God of all grace to see to it that the faith planted in children's hearts will one day flower.

Lydia

Scripture References: *Acts 16:14, 15; 40*
When They Lived: *About A.D. 50*
Name: *Lydia [LID-ih-uh: meaning unknown]*
Historical Significance: *She was Paul's first convert in Europe; the early Philippian church met in her house.*

HER ROLE IN SCRIPTURE

Lydia's role is summed up in these four verses in Acts:

And on the Sabbath day we went out of the city to the riverside, where prayer was customarily made; and we sat down and spoke to the women who met there. Now a certain woman named Lydia heard us. She was a seller of purple from the city of Thyatira, who worshiped God. The Lord opened her heart to heed the things spoken by Paul. And when she and her household were baptized, she begged us, saying, "If you have judged me to be faithful to the Lord, come to my house and stay." So she persuaded us. . . .

So they went out of the prison and entered the house of Lydia; and when they had seen the brethren, they encouraged them and departed.

—*Acts 16:13–15; 40*

EXPLORING HER RELATIONSHIPS

Despite the fact that Lydia is mentioned in only these four verses, we know quite a lot about her.

Lydia was a successful businesswoman. The Scriptures cite considerable evidence of Lydia's success.

She was in a luxury business (Acts 16:14). The purple of the first century was a color that shaded from blue to red, and was associated with high rank and great wealth. Purple dye was obtained from the shells of the murex, an ocean mollusk. Because it was difficult to produce, the dye and garments of that color were expensive. As a dealer in purple, Lydia would have made a good living.

She was the mistress of a household (Acts 16:15). The word *oikos* (household) encompassed both family and slaves. The reference to her "and her household" indicates both that Lydia was unmarried, and that she possessed a number of slaves. Scholars have debated whether she was a widow, divorced, a married woman who had her own business and property, or perhaps a freed woman [ex-slave] who had never married. At any rate, Luke makes it clear that it was "her" household.

She invited the missionary party to stay at her house (Acts 16:15). Lydia's house was large enough to put up the entire missionary party. As Paul typically traveled with a rather large team, the size of Lydia's house is another indication of her success.

Later, her home served as the meeting place for the Philippian church (Acts 16:40). When Paul was about to leave the city he met with the believers who were assembled at Lydia's house. We do not know how many converts there were in Philippi at that time, but we do know that they chose Lydia's house as their place of meeting.

Lydia was a spiritual leader. While Lydia may not have held any church office, she was a spiritual person to whom others looked for guidance.

Lydia met with other women for prayer (Acts 16:13). That there was no synagogue in Philippi meant there were few or no Jewish families in the city. However, there were women who worshiped God in Philippi, and they met for prayer on the Sabbath by the river. Lydia is the only one named; so she may have been the leader of the group.

Lydia is described as a worshiper of God (Acts 16:14). While Lydia most likely was not Jewish, Lydia knew and worshiped the God of the Old Testament. This is not surprising, as many non-Jews in the first century were attracted to the God of Judaism and to the Old Testament's high moral standards. These people, often called *God fearers*, were recognized as adherents of Judaism who had chosen not to go the route of full conversion or for some reason were prohibited from a full conversion.

Lydia was judged "faithful to the LORD" by Paul (Acts 16:15). The apostle was convinced that Lydia's faith in Christ was real and strong. He not only baptized her but accepted her hospitality.

A CLOSE-UP

Lydia was an entrepreneur. She had the knowledge and skill to build and run a successful and profitable business. She owned a large house, and undoubtedly owned slaves who worked in her business. It's clear that she was highly respected in her community. Quite possibly she would have been considered one of those "prominent women" described on page 309.

Lydia was also a committed believer. Her heart was open to the gospel and she eagerly accepted Christ. She immediately showed her commitment by publicly inviting the missionary party to her home. She showed this same bold commitment by hosting the church in her home, even after Paul and Silas had been beaten and imprisoned by the local authorities.

The Lydia we meet in Scripture comes through as a strong and competent person, yet she was warm and openhearted. She was both a follower of the Lord and a leader of His people.

AN EXAMPLE FOR TODAY

◆ Lydia was an independent, successful, and single businesswoman. She was also a key figure in the young church Paul planted at Philippi. It's good to remember Lydia when we hear some teach that the only career that is right for a woman is that of marriage and raising children. As Paul states in 1 Corinthians 7, whether we marry or remain single is a matter of gift. We need to honor single Christian women in their calling even as we honor Christian wives and mothers in theirs.

Mary & Martha

of Bethany

Scripture References: *Luke 10:38–42; John 11:1–45; 12:1–8*
See also page 299.

When They Lived: A.D. 30

Name: *Mary [MAIR-ee: "loved by Yahweh"]*

Martha [MAHR-thuh: "lady"]

Historical Significance: *These two sisters were friends of Jesus. Jesus rewarded their trust when He raised their brother Lazarus from death.*

THEIR ROLE IN SCRIPTURE

The two unmarried sisters lived with their brother, Lazarus, in Bethany, a small town just two miles east of Jerusalem. Jesus and His disciples often stayed with them when they came to the religious festivals held in Jerusalem. While the two sisters had distinctly different personalities, they were usually together when mentioned in Scripture.

How did they differ? Martha held firmly to traditional values. She saw her place as being in the kitchen. Mary was more "liberated," comfortable in the role of a disciple, and eager to learn all she could at Jesus' feet. Because Mary was willing to break the traditional mold, we know more about her than we do her sister.

Both Mary and Martha were women of faith. When their brother fell sick, the sisters immediately sent a messenger to Jesus—completely confident that

Jesus could heal him. Each expressed her faith when Jesus finally arrived, some four days after Lazarus had died and been buried. While sure that Jesus was Lord of life and would raise their brother in the final resurrection, neither imagined that Jesus could exercise His power that day to restore their brother's earthly life.

EXPLORING HER RELATIONSHIPS

Martha's relationship with Mary (Luke 10:38–42). Mary and Martha were unmarried sisters, living in the home that their brother, Lazarus, had possibly inherited from their father. The two women were close but different. Martha took the duties assigned to her gender seriously. She took pride in caring for the home and preparing meals. Mary, far more of a free spirit, irritated Martha at times. We can assume that Martha was older for she took the lead in welcoming Jesus on one of the occasions He visited them. That day, her irritation with Mary exploded into exasperation. As she worked in the kitchen to prepare a meal, Mary settled at Jesus' feet to listen to His dialogue with the disciples. It was hot in the kitchen, and Martha was harried as she struggled to do everything herself. Finally, she burst into the room where Jesus was seated, and querulously demanded that He send Mary to the kitchen to help her.

Jesus refused, gently telling Martha that Mary "has chosen that good part" (Luke 10:42). Food for the body was important, but food for the soul was more important. Martha's worry over preparing a special meal showed that her priorities were misplaced. It was not wrong to be committed to fulfilling the role society assigned to women, but it was wrong to place so much emphasis on fulfilling that role that Martha had no time for her own personal growth in faith.

Martha stands for all the individuals today who expend their energy doing good things and have no time to deepen their relationship with God.

Martha's relationship with Jesus (John 11). While Martha may have been too concerned with performing tasks, Martha did not lack faith. John notes that "Jesus loved Martha and her sister" (John 11:5)—not only naming Martha but identifying her first and by name as an object of His love.

When Lazarus died and Martha learned that Jesus was coming, she hurried to meet Him, while Mary stayed in the house. Martha expressed great faith in Christ, saying that "even now I know that whatever You ask of God, God will give You" (11:22). While Martha did not think that Jesus was about to restore her brother's life, she was certain that whatever He asked, God would surely do.

It is helpful to compare the two sisters' responses in John 11 when Jesus finally came.

When we compare the dialogue, the bulk of Jesus' recorded conversation was with Martha rather than Mary. We also see that while both expressed faith in Jesus, Martha's expressed faith went beyond that of her sister in affirming that Jesus could act "even now" (John 11:22).

Martha	Mary
20 Then Martha, as soon as she heard that Jesus was coming, went and met Him.	20 Mary was sitting in the house.
21 Then Martha said to Jesus, "Lord, if You had been here, my brother would not have died.	29 [Mary] arose quickly and came to Him...
22 But even now I know that whatever You ask of God, God will give you."	32 She fell down at His feet, saying to Him, "Lord, if You had been here, my brother would not have died."
23 Jesus said to her, "Your brother will rise again."	33 When Jesus saw her weeping...He groaned in the spirit and was troubled.
24 Martha said to Him, "I know that He will rise again in the resurrection at the last day."	
25 Jesus said to her, "I am the resurrection and the life...Do you believe this?"	
27 She said to Him, "Yes, Lord, I believe that You are the Christ, the Son of God, who is to come into the world."	

> 28 And when she had said these things,
> she went her way and secretly called
> Mary her sister, saying, "The Teacher has
> come and is calling for you."

> 39 Jesus said, "Take away the stone."
> Martha, the sister of him who was dead,
> said to Him, "Lord, by this time there
> is a stench, for he has been dead four days."

> 40 Jesus said to her, "Did I not say to
> you that if you would believe you would
> see the glory of God?"

At the same time, Martha was not fully aware of what she had affirmed. When Jesus called for the stone that blocked the entrance to Lazarus's tomb to be taken away, Martha objected. She reminded Jesus that her brother's body had started to decay.

How like Martha most of us are. We have faith in Jesus—even great faith. Yet when we are called on to exercise that faith in impossible situations, we focus on the obstacles rather than on God's unlimited ability to act.

Martha and Mary had faith enough, and Jesus had power enough; Lazarus *was* restored. What makes all the difference is not the amount of faith we have in Jesus, but the fact that our faith is *in* Jesus.

EXPLORING HER RELATIONSHIPS

Mary's relationship with Martha (Luke 10:38–42). Mary's attitude toward women's traditional roles, and especially Mary's view of "women's work," differed from that of her sister. This inevitably caused friction between the two women.

Mary and her sister lived together comfortably in their brother's house, even though the younger Mary refused to let her older sister press her into Martha's mold. Undoubtedly Mary helped around the house but not when Jesus visited. Being with Jesus was more important than housework.

Mary's relationship with Jesus (Luke 10:38–42; John 11:1–45; John 12:1–8). While John 11 highlights Martha's relationship with Jesus, both Luke 10 and John 12 highlight Mary's relationship with Him.

Luke reports Jesus' commendation of Mary for choosing "what is better" (Luke 10:42 NIV) by giving priority to listening to Him rather than being preoccupied with preparing a meal. John 12 portrays Mary's special love for and sensitivity to Jesus.

The occasion was a meal in their home. The text says that while Lazarus was seated at the table with Jesus, "Martha served" (12:2). One could always count on Martha.

On that occasion, Mary took ointment worth a year's wages, and anointed Jesus' feet and wiped them with her hair. When Judas complained that the ointment should have been sold and the money given to the poor, Jesus rebuked him. "'Let her alone,'" Jesus said. "'She has kept this for the day of My burial. For the poor you have with you always, but Me you do not have always'" (12:7, 8). Mary apparently sensed the imminent suffering and death of her Lord while the others remained unaware. She displayed a unique spiritual sensitivity. Mary's gift showed a love and appreciation for Jesus that we might well imitate. For Mary, nothing was too good for Jesus, and nothing was so precious that it should be withheld from Him.

A CLOSE-UP

Martha and Mary were very different women. Yet they were members of the same family and lived together in harmony. Their differences did lead to irritations and disputes, but they were family. They were bound together by family ties and by a common faith in and love for Jesus.

Martha was one of those dependable persons we can count on to do what's needed. We see her working in the kitchen and serving. She was a worker, and sometimes task-oriented to the extreme. Martha was a significant person in the family, and her contribution to its well-being was vital.

We must not mistake Martha's practical approach for a lack of faith. The text protects us from this misunderstanding by reporting Martha's affirmations of faith in Christ, and by making it clear that "Jesus loved Martha" (John 11:5).

Mary, on the other hand, was a freer spirit. Her first priority was spending time with Jesus—not cooking in the kitchen. Mary was spiritually sensitive, displaying an awareness of Jesus' moods that none of the disciples seemed to have. Mary was also emotionally expressive, weeping freely, and loving generously. While John wanted us to understand that Jesus loved Martha, He also loved her sister.

These two women were so different; yet they had so much in common. They remind us that whatever our personality type, we are able to love and serve Jesus in our own way and that Jesus loves and values us as well.

EXAMPLES FOR TODAY

◆ There is room for different personality types in Christ's kingdom. God made us all different with our own strengths and weaknesses. Let's be careful not to force other believers into our molds, assuming that our personality is "Christian" and theirs is not. Instead, we need to learn from one another because Christ is speaking to us through all our brothers and sisters.

◆ Mary sat at Jesus' feet. She knew that she would not always have Him nearby, but while she did, she drank in everything He had to say. It's so easy to become task-oriented in our fast-paced lives. But when our frenzied pace denies us time to draw near to Jesus, the quality and meaning of our lives begins to drain away.

◆ Mary wanted to do something special for Jesus. So she met His personal need by anointing Him. Christ tells us that when we do anything "for the least of these," we do it for Him. Jesus is not physically present with us today; yet we can help meet His needs by offering food to the hungry, drink to the thirsty, clothing for the naked, hospitality to strangers, and visiting those in prison.

Mary Magdalene

Scripture References: *Matthew 27:56, 61; 28:1–11;*
Mark 15:40, 47; 16:1, 9;
Luke 8:2, 3; 24:1–12;
John 19:25; 20:1, 2, 11–18

When They Lived: A.D. *30*

Name: *Mary [MAIR-ee: "loved by Yahweh"]*
Magdalene [mag-de-LEE-nih;
"from the town of Magdala"]

Historical Significance: *She was the first to see the risen Jesus*
on Easter morning. Mary Magdalene was granted the privilege of being the
first to see and speak with the resurrected Christ.

HER ROLE IN SCRIPTURE

Mary Magdalene is mentioned more frequently in the Gospels than any woman other than Mary, Jesus' mother. We know her as a woman Jesus had released from the domination of seven demons (Luke 8:2) and who had become one of His most devoted followers. Along with other women, among them Joanna and Susanna, Mary had provided funds to support Jesus and His disciples as they ministered (Luke 8:3). This suggests that Mary had independent means.

The Gospel writers also place Mary near the cross when Jesus was crucified, and Mary is given an extremely prominent role in the account of Jesus' last moments. Mary was present at the cross and at Jesus' burial (Matt. 27:56), and was one of the first to discover the stone had been rolled away (Matt. 28:1). Mary and the others hurried to tell Peter of the resurrection, but Peter did not believe them (Luke 24:10–12; John 20:1–3). Mary then returned to the tomb, where she became the first to see and hear the resurrected Christ (Mark 16:9).

Each reference to Mary Magdalene indicates a special relationship with Jesus and a role in the Gospel story which, sadly, most people have ignored.

Christine M. Carpenter, in her book *All the Women in the Bible* (CMC Press, 1996), makes a number of fascinating observations comparing Mary Magdalene and the Apostle Peter (see chart, p.123).

EXPLORING HER RELATIONSHIPS

Mary's relationship with seven demons (Luke 8:2). While the New Testament frequently mentioned possession or oppression by demonic beings, we are not told how demons obtain a grip on a human being. It is clear from Scripture that those who engage in occult practices are particularly vulnerable, but we are not told whether some choice of the person involved is necessary before demons can gain access to the personality.

Possibly the most suggestive New Testament passages on this theme are Matthew 12:43–45 and Luke 11:24–26. Each records Jesus' warning about unclean or evil spirits. Jesus spoke of such a spirit going out of a man and then returning to find his life "'empty, swept, and put in order'" (Matt. 12:44). The evil spirit then enters with "'seven other spirits more wicked than himself, and they enter and dwell there'" (Matt. 12:45). The key words are "'empty, swept, and put in order.'" The individual described has done his best to put his life in order, but he himself is empty. There is no presence of God to fill the inner life. Without God's presence, the individual is vulnerable to other spiritual beings.

Whatever led to Mary's demonization, when she met Jesus she was firmly in the grip of evil spirits. However, the most powerful evil spirits are powerless against the Son of God, and Jesus cast them from her.

Mary's relationship with Jesus. Once freed by Jesus, Mary no longer was an empty being. Her whole life was redirected toward Him.

Mary followed Jesus (Luke 8:1, 2). Luke notes that "He went through every city and village, preaching and bringing the glad tidings of the kingdom of God" and adds that "the twelve were with him, and certain women." Here, Luke specifically names Mary Magdalene, as well as Joanna and Susanna "and many others."

To think of women as disciples in training for leadership violated Jewish custom, but Jesus broke the mold in His relationships with women. Women most certainly were among His disciples.

Mary helped support Jesus' ministry (Matt. 27:55, 56; Luke 8:2, 3; Mark 15:40, 41). Jesus' twelve disciples had left their occupations to join Christ in His ministry. Luke tells us that it was primarily women who provided funds to buy food and other necessities. Early Jewish literature makes it clear that well-to-do women were frequent contributors to well-known rabbis and their students. Rather than being paid to teach, Jewish rabbis were often responsible to feed and house their students.

Mary Magdalene was apparently well-to-do. She was so committed to Jesus that she not only followed Him as a disciple herself, but she also helped support His other disciples.

Mary stood by Jesus during the crucifixion (Matt. 27:55, 56; Mark 15:40, 41; Luke 23:27–31, 48, 49; John 19:25). When the Gospel writers listed those who witnessed Jesus' crucifixion, the only man mentioned was John. Yet a number of women—among whom were Mary, the mother of Jesus and Mary Magdalene—were featured. The experience in the Garden had demoralized the male disciples, and they had fled from Gethsemane. The specific mention of named women reminds us that the women held fast to Jesus and would not let Him go to His death alone. Despite the pain they felt, despite their doubts and fears, Mary Magdalene and the others were there for their Lord.

Mary was commissioned as history's first witness to Jesus' resurrection (Matt. 28:1–10; Mark 16:1–11; Luke 24:1–18; John 20:1–10). Mary Magdalene was commissioned twice. First, she and the other women who came to the tomb that first Easter morning were told by angels to "go quickly and tell his disciples" (Matt. 28:7). Mary Magdalene was mentioned first when Luke listed the messengers who hurried to the apostles—and her words were dismissed as "idle tales" (Luke 24:11) by the men.

CONTRASTS IN LEADER EXPERIENCES: PETER AND MARY MAGDALENE

Peter was given a new name after meeting Jesus (Mark 3:16; Luke 6:14; John 1:42).	Mary kept the same name after meeting Jesus.
Peter saw the transfiguration of Jesus (Matt. 17:1–4; Mark 9:2–6; Luke 9:28–36).	Mary saw the crucifixion of Jesus (Matt. 27:56; Mark 15:40; John 19:25).
Peter heard God's voice from heaven proclaim His Son, Jesus (Matt. 17:5; Mark 9:7; Luke 9:35).	Mary heard Jesus' voice cry that His Father God had forsaken Him (Matt. 27:46; Mark 15:34).
Peter asked Jesus if he must forgive seven times (Matt. 18:21).	Mary was delivered of seven demons by Jesus (Luke 8:2).
Peter told Jesus he had left everything to follow Him (Matt. 19:27; Mark 10:28; Luke 18:28).	Mary provided for Jesus as she followed Him (Luke 8:1–3).
Peter slept in the Garden after Jesus asked him to watch and pray with Him (Matt. 26:37–46; Mark 14:33–42).	Mary stood in the Garden watching and weeping for Jesus without being asked (John 20:11–17; Mark 16:9).
Peter denied Jesus to strangers (Matt. 26:58–75; Mark 14:54–72; Luke 22:54–62; John 18:15–27).	Mary proclaimed Jesus risen to the disciples (Luke 23:10; John 20:18).
Peter fled from the cross (Matt. 26:56; Mark 14:27–29).	Mary remained near the cross (Matt. 27:56; Mark 15:40; John 19:25).
Peter was sent a message from Jesus (Mark 16:7).	Mary was given a message by Jesus (Luke 24:10; John 20:18).
Peter left the empty tomb without understanding (John 20:6–10).	Mary remained at the empty tomb, the last place she saw Jesus, and had an encounter with Him (John 20:11–17; Mark 16:9).

Mary Magdalene returned to the garden tomb. Both Mark and John credited Mary with being the first to see the risen Jesus (Mark 16:9; John 20:14f). Even more, Mary was the first one to give witness to the resurrection, for she "came and told the disciples that she had seen the LORD, and that He had spoken these things to her" (John 20:18).

That the disciples did not believe Mary should not be attributed to the fact that she was a woman. The disciple Thomas, nicknamed "Doubting" Thomas, did not believe the other ten male disciples when they announced that they, too, had seen Jesus after the resurrection. It was not the reliability of the witnesses that caused doubt; rather, it was the incredible nature of the news they bore.

The reaction of others to Mary Magdalene's news does nothing to change the fact that she was chosen to be among the first to hear God's good news and the very first to see and speak to the risen Lord.

Mary's relationship with other disciples. Mary Magdalene was not a "loner." With but one exception, she is always seen in company with others.

Mary and the women supporters of Jesus (Luke 8:1–3). When Luke named the women who contributed to Jesus' support, Mary and others were described as being with Jesus.

Mary and the other women at the crucifixion (Matt. 27:55; Mark 15:40; Luke 23:48, 49; John 19:25). At the crucifixion, Mary is named with other women followers of Jesus. The Gospels portray the little group of women standing hesitantly at a distance, watching (Luke 23:49), but then moving closer and closer until they stood "near the cross of Jesus" (John 19:25 NIV). We can imagine the arms of Mary and the others wrapped around the shoulders of Jesus' mother, trying to comfort her. Yet they suffered, too, as they watched the Savior die and what they supposed was the death of their hopes.

Mary at the tomb (Matt. 27:61). Matthew states that "Mary Magdalene was there and the other, sitting opposite the tomb." Mark also specifically places them there, along with other women (Mark 16:1).

Mary returns to the tomb on Easter (Matt. 28:1). Mary wasn't alone when she went to the tomb the first Easter morning. Matthew mentions "the other Mary" [who Mark identifies as the mother of James], while Mark also adds Salome to the delegation, and Luke mentions that Joanna and "other women" went with them. Clearly, Mary was one of the leaders of the little group of women disciples.

A CLOSE-UP

Mary Magdalene was a woman whose life had been transformed by Jesus. He had delivered her from seven demons that dominated her. We know from New Testament descriptions of demonization that demons frequently caused painful physical infirmities (see the study of demon possession in, *Every Good and Evil Angel of the Bible*). We can surmise the depth of her gratitude by her commitment to Jesus that she showed afterward.

Mary totally dedicated herself to Jesus and His cause. She joined the group of women who accompanied Jesus as disciples. Mary contributed funds to help Jesus continue teaching and preaching. She was mentioned first during Christ's early Galilean ministry, and she was still with Jesus at the crucifixion. While most of the men who were Jesus' followers fled after His capture on the Mount of Olives, Mary and the other women stayed close to the Savior and were with Him when He died. Despite the well-known threat of the Pharisees to expel Jesus' followers from the synagogue, and thus from any access to aid should they be in need, Mary and her friends openly identified with Jesus, standing near the cross and waiting by the garden tomb. When the holy days had passed, they brought the supplies needed to prepare His dead body. However hopeless Mary may have felt, she remained faithful to the end.

How her faith was rewarded! Mary was among the first to hear of Jesus' resurrection, and she was the first to see and speak to the risen Lord. It is forever stamped on the pages of sacred history that it was not a man, but Mary, who was granted this great privilege. We can hardly doubt that Mary Magdalene, although overlooked by many who stress the roles of Peter and John, was among the most faithful and honored disciples of Jesus Christ.

AN EXAMPLE FOR TODAY

♦ It's all too easy to be saved by Jesus and then go our own way. We're faithful when we need His help, but then our prayers lose their intensity. Mary never seemed to lose her intensity. She was healed of demon possession, and from that point on she never wavered in her commitment to

Christ. Mary loved her Lord, not with a passion that would burn out, but with unceasing intensity.

◆ It is fascinating that Jesus chose Mary to be the first to see Him after the resurrection and the first to share the good news. It's curious that if Mary Magdalene were with us today, many church pulpits would be closed to her. How wonderful that whatever hindrances to ministry may exist, no one can keep us from sharing Christ with neighbors and friends.

Mary of Nazareth

Mother of Jesus

Scripture References: *Matthew 1; 2; 12:46–50; 13:55;*
Mark 3:31–35; Luke 1; 2; 8:19, 20;
John 2:1–11; 7:5; 19:25–27;
Acts 1:14

When They Lived: *5 B.C.*

Name: *Mary [MAIR-ee:"loved by Yahweh"]*

Historical Significance: *Mary gave birth to Jesus, the Savior.*

HER ROLE IN SCRIPTURE

When Mary was a teenager betrothed to an older man named Joseph, the angel Gabriel announced to her that she had been chosen by God to give birth to the promised Messiah. Mary responded with simple faith, accepting the privileged role, despite the fact that her pregnancy would seem to Joseph to mark unfaithfulness and might mark her as a harlot in her community. God guarded Mary's reputation and sent the angel to speak to Joseph.

Mary and Joseph were wed, but they had no sexual relations before Jesus' birth in Bethlehem. Many unusual events were associated with that birth. Mary remembered and treasured these events. During the thirty years Jesus lived with the family and carried on Joseph's trade, Mary and

Joseph provided a home and a number of brothers and sisters for Jesus. While Mary had confidence in her oldest Son, when Jesus began His public ministry, Mary and the rest of her family were puzzled and uncertain. Certainly, Mary was devastated when Christ was crucified; her heart must have been broken as she stood nearby and watched His sufferings at Calvary. Yet Mary, perhaps more than any other, was thrilled at Jesus' resurrection. The last mention of Mary in the Bible pictures her with other believers. They were praying in Jerusalem after Christ's ascension, waiting for the coming of the Holy Spirit.

Some mistakenly cast Mary as the "mother of God." She was indeed the mother of Jesus, the Son of God. However, God the Son existed from eternity; Mary was the source of Jesus' human nature. Even so, it is appropriate that we honor Mary and the faith she displayed throughout her life. Mary was a truly remarkable woman; her faith and faithfulness set an example for us all.

EXPLORING HER RELATIONSHIPS

Mary's relationship with God (Luke 1:26–38, 46–55). Mary's relationship with God is beautifully portrayed in the account of Gabriel's visit to her and in Mary's psalm of praise known as the Magnificat.

Mary's humility (1:26–30). Gabriel's greeting troubled Mary. Mary was not frightened at the appearance of the mighty angel; she was troubled at the "manner of greeting" (v. 29). What Gabriel had said was, "'Rejoice, highly favored one, the LORD is with you; blessed are you among women!'" (v. 28).

Mary had never thought of herself as special. She was simply a young Jewish girl, probably about thirteen years of age—the typical age for betrothal in first-century Galilee. She worshiped God, as did her family and friends in the little town of Nazareth. But "'highly favored'" and "'blessed...among women'"? She would not have used words like that to describe herself. Like Moses, Mary could be described as "very humble" (see Num. 12:3). The humility it had taken Moses some eighty years to achieve was native to the young Jewish girl. Later, she would describe herself as the "'maidservant of the LORD'" (Luke 1:38). Mary simply saw herself as a person who loved God and who was privileged to serve Him any way she could. To her pure mind, this hardly made her special; every human being owed that to the Creator.

So, it is no wonder Mary was troubled at his greeting. What could this mighty angel mean? What could she possibly have done to have "'found favor with God'" (v. 30)?

Mary's calling (1:31–33). Gabriel explained the role that God's favor had decreed for Mary:

- She would conceive and bring forth a Son.
- She would name her Son Jesus ["Savior"].
- Her Son would be great.
- Her Son would be "'the Son of the Highest'" [that is, God].
- God would give Him the throne of David.
- Her Son would reign over Israel forever.
- Her Son's kingdom would never end.

God would grant Mary what all pious Jewish women desired: to be the mother of the promised Messiah!

Mary's question (1:34–37). We can measure the depth of Mary's faith by the question she asked—and the questions she did not ask.

The question Mary asked was a natural one. How could she have a child since she had never had sexual relations with a man? The question arose out of curiosity, not doubt. And the angel answered her:

"The Holy Spirit will come upon you, and the power of the Highest will overshadow you; therefore, also, that Holy One who is to be born will be called the Son of God."

—Luke 1:35

What is significant is not so much the question Mary asked, but the questions she didn't ask; questions like: "But, what will Joseph think?"

"What will people think of me when I'm found to be pregnant?" "But, what about the disgrace? What will happen to me?"

These questions, so natural under the circumstances, never crossed Mary's mind. Or, if they did, she quickly dismissed them and instead, accepted God's will: "'Behold the maidservant of the LORD! Let it be to me according to your word'" (1:38).

Three decades later, Mary's son, Jesus, would display that same attitude in the Garden of Gethsemane when He prayed, "'Nevertheless not My will, but Yours be done'" (Luke 22:42). For all time, Mary's simple faith and readiness to do God's will without thought of herself stands as a testimony to her faith. She is an example for all believers, men and women alike.

Mary's Magnificat (1:46–55). Luke records a magnificent praise poem that gives further insight into Mary's relationship with God. In it, we see her joy at the opportunity she had been given to magnify God's name, her recitation of praise to Him for His attributes, and His actions on Israel's behalf. Most significantly, we see her focus on the covenant God made with Abraham as the foundation of His faithfulness to His people. Mary's faith was not based on emotion but on knowledge of God's purposes and confidence in God's faithfulness. Mary not only trusted God; she knew God well.

In view of all this, we can characterize Mary's relationship with God—Mary knew, loved, trusted, and exalted God.

Mary's relationship with Joseph (Matt. 1:18–25; 13:55). We know little about Mary and Joseph's relationship. Tradition suggests that Joseph was older than Mary, and from what we know of the marriage practices in first-century Judaism, this seems likely. Quite frequently, young girls were betrothed to older men who had established themselves as able to support a family.

We also know that Joseph died before Mary, and probably before Jesus began His public ministry. Matthew 13:55 calls Jesus "'the carpenter's son,'" while Mark 6:3 quotes some of Jesus' neighbors calling Him "the carpenter, the Son of Mary." As eldest Son, Jesus would have learned His father's trade, and when Joseph died, He would have taken his place as "the carpenter."

We know other things about Joseph and Mary's relationship. Matthew tells us that when Joseph discovered Mary was pregnant, he considered a private divorce. Joseph was sensitive and fair. Although he must have been hurt by Mary's supposed unfaithfulness, Joseph was not vindictive. A quiet, private voiding of the marriage contract into which he had entered with Mary's father might offer Mary some protection from gossip and proscription. Joseph was also a man of faith. When an angel told Joseph that Mary had not been unfaithful, Joseph listened and went ahead with the wedding.

Joseph gave no thought to his personal reputation or the fact that the community might conclude that he and Mary had had sexual relations before the marriage. Joseph loved and trusted God and was willing to obey Him. In this vital quality, Joseph and Mary, despite any disparity in age, were well matched.

Their relationship produced a large number of additional children. Matthew specifically mentions four brothers—James, Joses, Simon, and Judas—and an unspecified number of sisters (Matt. 13:55; see also John 7:3–5). Mary had a healthy and normal relationship with Joseph. Together, they provided an ideal home for Jesus and their other children.

Mary's relationship with Jesus (Luke 2:33, 51; John 2:2–5; Mark 3:31–35). Despite the early evidence that Jesus was indeed special, the Gospels suggest that Christ grew up as such a "normal" child that even Mary's vision of His identity was clouded.

Early evidence of Jesus' uniqueness (Matt. 1; Luke 1; 2). So many events marked Jesus as special in Mary's mind. There was the angel's visit. The miraculous pregnancy. Joseph's confirmation of his confidence in her virgin state. When Jesus was born, shepherds appeared with their tale of angels celebrating in Bethlehem's skies. Luke 2:19 states that "Mary kept all these things and pondered them in her heart" (Luke 2:19).

Two months later, Mary and Joseph went to the temple for her purification and Jesus' presentation to the Lord. The aged Simeon and the prophetess Anna recognized the infant Jesus as the promised Messiah.

Certainly, Mary and Joseph remembered the angel's words to them. Yet the Bible says that "Joseph and His mother marveled at those things which were spoken of Him" (Luke 2:33).

Some two years later, the wise men found the little family, still in Bethlehem, and not only brought Him gifts but also worshiped Him. Guided by angels, Joseph took Mary and Jesus first to Egypt, and then back to Nazareth. During these early years, there were many reminders that Jesus was a special child indeed.

Mary's relationship with the child Jesus (Luke 2:41–51). While the apocryphal books tell imaginative tales of miracles supposedly performed by Jesus as a child, the Scriptures draw a curtain across Jesus' childhood years. Luke gives us our only glimpse into Christ's childhood. Luke relates a visit to Jerusalem when Jesus was twelve. There, the young Jesus amazed aged scholars with His insights into Scripture and was so engaged in His discussions that He missed the family caravan back to Nazareth. Later, when His parents found Him, Mary rebuked Jesus: "'Son, why have You done this to us? Look, Your father and I have sought You anxiously'" (Luke 2:48). Jesus responded, "'Did you not know that I must be about My Father's business?'" (Luke 2:49). While Jesus was aware of His identity and mission, Mary seemed unaware.

Luke concluded his remarks by saying that "then He went down with them and came to Nazareth, and was subject to them, but His mother kept all these things in her heart" (2:51). Jesus lived the life of a normal, growing boy. That Jesus was so normal a child in her large family must have led Mary to treat Jesus with the same love and discipline as her other sons and daughters.

Mary's relationship with Jesus changes (John 2:1–5). Jesus' baptism by John and His identification as God's Son initiated a significant change in Jesus' life. He had lived in Nazareth and followed Joseph's trade as a carpenter. At some point Joseph had died, and it was Jesus' responsibility—along with His brothers—to care for their widowed mother.

On the way back to Galilee after His baptism, Jesus and several friends who later became disciples stopped to share in a wedding celebration in

Cana. When the wine ran out, Mary found Jesus and reported, "'They have no wine'" (John 2:3). Jesus' responded in words that must have shocked Mary. Jesus addressed her as "'woman,'" and added the Greek phrase ÙÈ ÂÌÔÈ Î·È ÛÔÈ, that means literally "'what to me and to you.'" This is an ambiguous phrase, but one that clearly implies separation. *The Victor Bible Background Commentary, New Testament*, comments,

> *Jesus is about to perform the first of His miraculous signs; a sign that will reveal His glory and move His disciples to "put their faith in Him" (2:11). Long ago Jesus had insisted that "I had to be in My Father's house" (Luke 2:49). Yet Jesus returned to Nazareth, and lived as a child in Mary and Joseph's house. But now, at last, He is about to set out on the Father's business, even though the final hour of that service lies far off in the future. Gently Jesus rejects Mary's importunity: Woman, what to me and to you? Woman, now no earthly relationship can bind me, for at last I am setting out on My Father's business.*
>
> *Mary bows now to her son, and says to the servants, "Do whatever He tells you" (2:5). Jesus is now subject to the Father alone, and because of that, all humankind is subject to Christ as Lord.*
>
> —p. 221

Mary fails to understand (Matt. 12:46–50; Mark 3:31–35; Luke 8:19–21). Each of the synoptic Gospels notes that shortly after Jesus' opponents have charged him with being either mad or in league with Satan, "His brothers and His mother came, and standing outside they sent to Him, calling Him" (Mark 3:31). Clearly, this was a family delegation, coming with the intent not of listening to Jesus but of speaking *to* Him. The context is important, for they came at the moment when opposition to Jesus was becoming open. It is also important to remember that long after this time "even His brothers did not believe in Him" (John 7:5).

Why had the family delegation come? They had come to counsel this Son and Brother who was stirring up the countryside. They had come to try to calm Jesus—to urge Him to be less controversial!

Jesus' response clearly fits this interpretation and makes an important point. Jesus did not go out to meet with His family. Instead, He asked, "'Who is My mother, or My brothers?'" (Mark 3:33). Looking at those around Him, Jesus then answered His own question: "'Here are My mother and My brothers! For whoever does the will of God is My brother and My sister and mother'" (Mark 3:34, 35). Any human being can have a family relationship with Jesus, but that relationship can only be established by putting that trust in the Savior that God requires.

As sensitive and responsive to God as Mary was, she was puzzled by Jesus' ministry and uncertain about what He was doing. Mary's confusion was not due to any lack of faith. Mary, like so many others, simply was waiting to see how God's purpose in Jesus would unfold.

Mary among the disciples (John 19:25–27; Acts 1:14). We next meet Mary standing near the cross with women friends and John the disciple. We cannot imagine Mary's pain during those bitter hours. What happened reveals Jesus' special concern for His mother.

As he hung on the cross, Jesus took note of Mary and John. Fixing his gaze on Mary, Jesus nodded toward John and said, "'Woman, behold your son'" (John 19:26). And then gazing at John, he nodded toward Mary, saying, "'Behold your mother!'" John understood Jesus' request, and "from that hour that disciple took her to his own home" (John 19:27). Despite Christ's earlier statement about family relationships, Mary held a special place in His heart.

Only after the resurrection shed its light on Jesus' mission and His essential nature as God's Son did Mary fully and completely believe in her Son. The last mention of Mary in the New Testament pictures "Mary the mother of Jesus" with His brothers (Acts 1:14) meeting with the disciples, praying to the One with whom they had been so familiar but never truly known.

The relationship between Mary and Jesus was complicated by the fact that although Jesus was God the Son, He lived in this world as a true human being. He grew up as a child subject to His parents. At thirty, He set out on a course the direction of which neither Mary nor Jesus' brothers could understand. Only after His death and resurrection did the family finally understand that the Son and Brother who had lived among them was indeed God incarnate. Then, and only then, did all become clear, and Jesus' earthly family worshiped Him.

A Close-Up

Even as a young girl, Mary showed herself to have great faith. Her response to God was immediate and selfless, and her words of praise reveal an appealing simplicity. Quite possibly no other Bible person so clearly displays the truth of Augustine's observation: love God, and do as you please. Mary did love God, and what pleased her was to do God's will.

At the same time, Mary was human. As her family grew, Mary loved her husband and mothered her boys and girls. She must have thought often of the strange events that marked her oldest, Jesus, as special. Yet she mothered Him as she did the others, and He submitted to her parental authority. Mary's days were filled with the typical task of first-century housewives: grinding grain, cooking meals, weaving cloth, directing her children's activities, talking with her husband. In this, she was indistinguishable from other women in her village. She was undoubtedly known as warm and friendly, a good friend and a caring person. Even Jesus seemed no different than others during those years.

When Jesus began His public ministry, Mary seems to have been puzzled. She was as amazed as others were at His teaching and healings. Knowing her innate humility, we can be sure Mary never postured or bragged of being the mother of the Man all Israel was talking about. In the end, after Jesus rose and His identity as God's Son was no longer in any doubt, Mary took her place with the others who believed in Him. And that place was on her knees.

Here, as in every glimpse of Mary that Scripture provides, we see her as a model believer. The Mary of Scripture is an example of faith in God. Mary is a sister in Christ to be admired, appreciated, and honored. Mary is a woman whose example all are privileged to follow.

AN EXAMPLE FOR TODAY

◆ Every believer should have a faith similar to Mary's. Each day we should pray, "'Behold the [servant] of the LORD! Let it be to me according to your word'" (Luke 1:38). This is a simple prayer of faith and submission to God's will.

◆ Mary valued her commitment to God far above others' opinions. Rather than hesitate to accept the angel's commission because of what others might think, she chose God's will. It is not what people think of us that counts but God's assessment.

◆ Even Mary did not understand fully the import of Jesus' teachings. She had been inseminated by the Holy Spirit and visited by an angel telling her to name her son "Jesus" (Savior). She had also been told that the "Holy One who is to be born will be called the Son of God" (Luke 1:35). So it shouldn't surprise us if we don't understand the plan God has for our children and us.

◆ Mary's life reveals meditative wisdom. Mary remembered the wise men's words and "pondered them in her heart" (Luke 2:19). After finding the boy Jesus in the temple debating with the sages, Mary "kept all these things in her heart" (v. 51). There are special incidents that we may not fully understand, but, like Mary, we should store them in our hearts until God provides further insights.

◆ Mary kept herself sexually pure. Before marriage, in fact until after the birth of Jesus, Mary had no sexual relations with her husband. She continued to be a faithful wife to Joseph and a celibate widow after her husband's death. God's best for every man and woman is to live a sexually pure life.

~ Mary ~

Mother of James & Joses

Scripture References: *Matthew 27:56, 61; 28:1–11;
Mark 15:40, 47; Luke 24:10*

HER ROLE IN SCRIPTURE

Mary was a common name in the first century—shared by many of the women Jesus knew. This Mary was one in the group of faithful female disciples led by Mary Magdalene who was present at the crucifixion, who prepared spices to bind to Jesus' body, and who first heard from the angels at the garden tomb that Christ had been raised from the dead.

It is likely that she was the same Mary identified in John 19:25 as the wife of Clopas.

~ Mary ~

Mother of John Mark

Scripture References: *Acts 12:12*
When They Lived: *A.D. 35*
Name: *Mary [MAIR-ee: "loved by Yahweh"]*
Historical Significance: *She opened her home to leaders of the early church for prayer.*

HER ROLE IN SCRIPTURE

Mary's home was a gathering place for one of the many smaller groups that made up the Jerusalem church. We know that Mary must have been well to do, for her home must have been relatively large to hold the "many" who gathered there when Peter was imprisoned. The fact that Peter went immediately to her home when an angel released him from prison indicates that she was close to the leaders of the church and an important member of the local body.

Mary is identified in the text as "the mother of John Mark," a young man who traveled briefly with Paul and later with Barnabas on missionary journeys. He became a second-generation leader in the church.

EXPLORING HER RELATIONSHIPS

Mary's relationship with church leaders. Mary was a confidante of the apostles and other leaders of the Jerusalem church. Her home was used for worship and prayer.

Mary's relationship with other believers. In the early church, believers met in homes, not church buildings. Most homes in Jerusalem were small and could hold only a small group of worshipers. Acts tells us that Mary's house held "many" (12:12). A relatively large group of believers, possibly a hundred or more, would meet there regularly for prayer and worship. Mary graciously opened her home for this purpose.

Mary's relationship with her son, John Mark. John Mark is one of the most interesting secondary characters in the New Testament. As a boy, he must have participated in worship at Mary's home, and undoubtedly came to know Peter and other church leaders well.

While still young, John Mark set out on the apostle Paul's first missionary journey (Acts 12:25). The trip was not the grand adventure John Mark thought it might be, and he left the party at Pamphylia and returned to Jerusalem (Acts 13:13). Later, when John Mark sought to accompany Paul and Barnabas on another missionary journey, Paul was unwilling to take the "deserter" with him (Acts 15:37). Barnabas, however, saw John Mark's potential. Paul and Barnabas's disagreement became so heated that the two companions separated. Barnabas took Mark with him on a missionary trip that is not reported in Acts.

Events proved Barnabas's assessment of Mark's potential to be correct. Even the apostle Paul later asked that Mark be sent to him in prison, "for he is profitable to me" (2 Tim. 4:11 KJV). Tradition tells us that John Mark later traveled with Peter. Mark wrote his Gospel as he traveled with Peter and recorded Peter's memories and teachings.

How fascinating to speculate on Mary's feelings about her son. He must have seemed so promising in the early years as her child sat wide-eyed in church meetings, and ventured to pray aloud in the company of the apostles themselves. But how disappointed Mary must have felt when young John Mark deserted his missionary companions and came home. Paul's devastating assessment of John Mark as a worthless companion, whom he refused to take along again, must have hurt her.

A CLOSE-UP

We hardly know enough to gain an accurate picture of Mary as a person. We do know that she was well-to-do, yet willing to link herself to a movement led by poor and "uneducated" men. Mary chose to become totally involved in the Christian community. She opened her home for worship and prayer. She encouraged her son to join older men in sharing the gospel of Christ. Perhaps this is enough to know about Mary to see her as a woman who was fully dedicated to Jesus and His cause.

AN EXAMPLE FOR TODAY

◆ How thrilled Mary must have been when Barnabas showed himself willing to give her son a second chance; a chance which proved to be her son's making and the doorway to a ministry of lasting significance to all Christ's church. Mary's joy reminds us that we should never give up on wayward children; God doesn't.

◆ Hospitality is a spiritual gift we are to exercise. The welcome Mary gave to fellow believers enriched her life and helped to shape her son's life as well.

Michal

Saul's Daughter

Scripture References: *1 Samuel 14:49; 18:17–28;*
19:10–17; 25:44; 2 Samuel 3:13, 14;
6:16–23; 1 Chronicles 15:25–29
Note: 2 Chronicles 21:8 refers to Mirab,
not Michal.

When They Lived: *About 1025 B.C.*

Name: *Michal [MI-kuhl:"who is like God?"]*

Historical Significance: *David's first wife, she sided with him*
against her father Saul and helped save his life.

HER ROLE IN SCRIPTURE

Michal fell in love with David as a young girl. Her father, Saul, hoped to use her love to get rid of David. When Saul's plot failed, he married the young couple. Later, when Saul could no longer disguise his hatred of David, Saul openly tried to kill David. Michal helped David escape, but she was left behind. Her father declared Michal's marriage to the outlawed David over and gave her in marriage to another man.

Years later, after Saul's death, and with David about to become king of a united Israel, David demanded Michal be returned to him. David's motive was political, for marriage to Saul's daughter strengthened his claim to be Saul's successor. Michal was torn from her second husband and returned to David. We see Michal's bitterness in the final scene in which she appears. As David brought the ark of the covenant to Jerusalem, he led the procession, dancing and singing ecstatically. Michal, watching, was overcome with contempt and "despised him in her heart" (1 Chr. 15:29). When David entered his palace, Michal met him and spewed out her loathing. David coldly dismissed her and cut off all relations with her. The text simply says, "therefore

Michal the daughter of Saul had no children to the day of her death" (2 Sam. 6:23).

EXPLORING HER RELATIONSHIPS

For a detailed overview, see page 290.

A CLOSE-UP

Michal is as much a victim of men as any woman in Scripture. And the men who used and discarded Michal were the very men in whom she should have been most able to trust.

Michal's first betrayer was her father, Saul. Rather than seek the happiness of his daughter, Saul was quick to use her love for David as a snare to get rid of him. He was utterly insensitive to the pain David's death would have caused Michal. After David was forced outside the law by the king, Saul again ignored his daughter's feelings and married her to another man. Rather than value his daughter as a person and show concern for her, Saul used her as a pawn to gain his own private ends.

Michal's second betrayer was her first love, David. Despite the loyalty Michal had shown toward David and the risks she had taken for him, there is no record that David tried to retrieve his young bride after their separation. Instead, David married other women during his outlaw years. It was not until after Saul's death, after negotiations had begun to make David ruler of all Israel, that David remembered Michal. Then, he demanded that she be taken from her second husband, to whom she had been married for at least ten years, and returned to him.

Like Saul, David showed an utter disregard from Michal's feelings or desires. David did not consult her when he demanded she be returned to him. David, motivated by a calculated assessment of the political situation rather than love, showed that he was just as willing to use Michal as her father had been.

How terrible for Michal and how betrayed she must have felt, to be treated as an object by both her father and her first love. How helpless she must have felt. She had no control over her own life and no trust in the men who had showed themselves so willing to misuse her. We can understand the bitterness so clearly expressed when Michal confronted David after the ark of the covenant had been brought to Jerusalem. David might make a show of worshiping God, but Michal must have thought him the world's greatest hypocrite. How could a person who treated her as David had love God? Michal must have felt that everything David did was calculated, and that he treated others as he had treated her.

BIBLE BACKGROUND: THE ARK OF THE COVENANT

The ark of the covenant was a box-like object that was to rest in the innermost room of the tabernacle or temple. It was hollow, and contained a sample of the manna God had provided for the Israelites during the wilderness years, the original Ten Commandments, and the staff of Aaron, the high priest. Its most significant feature was the cover, called the "mercy seat," over which two golden figures of angels hovered. Once a year, the high priest of Israel sprinkled the blood of a sacrificial animal there, and God accepted that offering as a covering for all of His people's sins.

The ark of the covenant was the most holy object in Israel, and bringing it to Jerusalem established that city as the religious, as well as political, capital of the nation.

Yet the real tragedy is that Michal's mistreatment by her father and by David made her so bitter that she could not appreciate God. David, for all his flaws, sensed God's presence. As the ark of the covenant was carried into Jerusalem, David's heart was filled with joy. After all the betrayal in her life, Michal was so filled with bitterness she simply could not sense God's presence or feel His love.

Centuries later, the writer of Hebrews, recognizing that the painful events of life can crowd out our awareness of God and His love, urged believers to look carefully, "lest anyone fall short of [miss] the grace of God; lest any root of bitterness springing up cause trouble" (Heb. 12:15).

The true tragedy is not that Michal became a victim of men but that, in her pain, Michal lost sight of God's grace. The root of bitterness that sprang up in her heart grew until it filled her life.

AN EXAMPLE FOR TODAY

◆ While we should be able to trust those we love, we need to remember that they are all too human. The only One we can trust completely is God.

◆ While we can understand Michal's bitterness, she demonstrates the cost of remaining bitter. Even though she was justified in feeling bitter, we need to give our bitterness up to God. Only then will the Holy Spirit work his ministry of healing in us and return our joy.

~ Miriam ~

Scripture References: *Exodus 2:1–10; 15:20, 21;*
Numbers 12:1–15; 20:1;
Deuteronomy 24:9

When They Lived: *About 1520–1420* B.C.

Name: *Miriam [MER-eh-um: "loved by Yahweh"]*

Historical Significance: *Miriam played a vital role as the protective sister of baby Moses, and later as a prophetess partner of the adult Moses in delivering the Israelites from Egypt. Miriam was the leader of the women who led Israel in worship after the deliverance at the Red Sea.*

HER ROLE IN SCRIPTURE

Miriam was the sister of Moses and Aaron, the two men who play the most prominent roles in the grand adventure of the Israelites as God won their freedom from slavery in Egypt. Miriam herself played a significant role in three incidents described in Exodus and Numbers. As a child, she was Moses' sisterly protector. As an adult prophetess, she led the delivered slaves in praising God. And as an unhappy woman, she challenged Moses' special relationship with God.

Miriam, the sisterly protector (Ex. 2:1–10). When Moses' mother hid Moses in a basket-boat floating along the Nile, she set Moses' older sister, Miriam, to watch over him. When Egypt's princess discovered the infant, Miriam quick-wittedly volunteered to find the princess a nurse and called her own mother. Her faithfulness and resourcefulness made her a key figure in shaping Moses' future.

Miriam the prophetess (Ex. 15:20, 21). Miriam was not mentioned in the account of the miracle plagues that forced Pharaoh to his knees. Moses and Aaron were the only two Jewish leaders featured from Exodus 3 through 14. But Miriam reappeared in Exodus 15, after God had opened the Red Sea for His people and wiped out the Egyptian army that pursued them. Exodus 15:20, 21 tells us four important things about Miriam's role in the redeemed community.

Miriam was a prophetess (Ex. 15:20). The Old Testament prophets were God's spokespersons. He gave them words that were not their own but that had the authority of the divine Word. While Moses himself was the prominent prophet of the day, it is significant that he was not the only prophet in the Israelite camp. Miriam, like Moses, had the prophetic gift and calling.

Miriam was the "sister of Aaron" (Ex. 15:20). Miriam was also the sister of Moses, and her connection with Moses, established in Exodus 2, seems much closer to us than her connection with Aaron. Yet Exodus identifies her simply as the sister of Aaron. God called Moses to bring His people out of slavery, give them His Law, and fashion them into an obedient and responsive people. Miriam and Aaron are recognized together, for both held significant leadership positions, but we need to remember that Moses, as a deliverer, stands alone as a type of Christ.

Miriam led "all the women" in worship (Ex. 15:20). The Lord's victory over the Egyptians at the Red Sea lifted the hearts of the Israelites in praise. Miriam led "all the women" to praise God for His victory. Their songs and their dances expressed the joy and wonder of the entire community.

It would be a mistake here to relegate Miriam to the role of the leader of some "women's group." The text portrays women leading the community in worship, and Miriam was the worship leader.

Miriam led in praise (Ex. 15:21). This verse underlines the point made above. In calling for the community to "sing to the LORD," Miriam led in a spontaneous and joyous moment of pure worship.

Miriam, the unhappy challenger of Moses' leadership role (Num. 12:1–16). After leaving Sinai, Miriam and Aaron "spoke against" Moses. This extended passage raises several important issues.

The dispute (Num. 12:1–3). It appears that Miriam instigated the challenge to Moses. Her name is mentioned first in the text and she was the one punished by God. From Aaron's readiness to make a golden calf at Sinai (see Ex. 32), we know he was easily led by others and unlikely to challenge Moses alone.

It began with criticism of Moses for his marriage to an "Ethiopian" (Cushite) woman (12:1). This was not the real problem, but rather an attempt to arouse support by appealing to a people's prejudice. The real motive, and the thing that offended Miriam and probably Aaron, too, was that Moses was recognized as *the* leader. We can sense the jealousy in the words, "Has the LORD indeed spoken only through Moses? Has He not spoken through us also?" (Num. 12:3). Miriam and Aaron truly were leaders whom God was using. Such a rare honor, especially for a woman, had so emboldened Miriam that she wanted to be perceived as being as important as Moses.

The gifts the two had, the privileges they each enjoyed as spiritual leaders, somehow were not enough. Miriam resented being viewed by all as subordinate to Moses.

The resolution (Num. 12:4–8). Miriam and Aaron's attitudes were disruptive and threatened to undermine Moses' authority. God had chosen Moses as the leader. Miriam and Aaron had important ministries of their own, but they were not the ones God had chosen to fulfill the tasks assigned to Moses.

The outcome (Num. 12:9–16). Their challenge to Moses aroused God's anger, and after He rebuked them, Miriam "suddenly became leprous, as white as snow" (Num. 12:10). Leprosy, meaning any infectious skin disease, was a devastating punishment, because the leper had to be put out of the camp, which would make them unable to participate in, much less lead, worship.

We aren't told why Miriam was so harshly punished while Aaron endured only a terrifying rebuke. No double standard should even be considered. It is more reasonable that Aaron was rebuked for his foolishness and Miriam reaped the shameful fruit of her briefly prideful and ungracious heart.

Instead of gaining honor by challenging God's choice of Moses as Israel's leader, Miriam experienced public disgrace and isolation from the camp. Her haughtiness was uncharacteristic of her and her punishment was temporary. In seven days, God fully restored her and we can assume that she continued to serve God and her people as a prophetess and as a worship leader.

A CLOSE-UP

Miriam, as we have noted, was an obedient daughter, a protective big sister, a prophetess, and worship leader. She was not above human frailty, however. Miriam's pride got in her way. She felt jealous that Moses was a more exalted prophet than she was and led her brother, Aaron, into the same negative thinking. She suffered consequences for her disrespect of God and Moses, but God showed her mercy and restored her.

AN EXAMPLE FOR TODAY

- Miriam's role as a prophetess and worship leader suggests that, while some denominations may have trouble with women holding important leadership positions, perhaps God does not.
- That Miriam was a prophetess illustrates that God speaks to the whole community of faith through women as well as through men.
- Miriam's faults teach us as much as her gifts. When she criticized Moses (Num. 12:1, 2), she dishonored God and His prophet. She was a religious leader but she failed in her chief responsibility.

- Above all else, God expects those He puts in leadership positions to humble themselves and to honor Him. "Now the man Moses was very humble, more than all men who were on the face of the earth" (Num. 12:3).
- Miriam reminds us that jealousy and pride stand in the way of our fellowship with God. They also keep God from using us to minister to others.
- We are to rejoice in the gifts God gives us, and use them enthusiastically. Comparing ourselves to others is dangerous and wrong. We can feel fulfillment in serving where we are; we need not feel devalued if we do not have gifts or positions others have been given.

Naaman's Wife's Slave Girl

Scripture References: *2 Kings 5:2, 3*

HER ROLE IN SCRIPTURE

This young girl is another of the unnamed but special women of the Bible. She was captured as a child when the Syrians raided Israel, and as a young girl she waited on the wife of Naaman, an important Syrian military officer who had leprosy.

One day the girl remarked, "If only my master were with the prophet who is in Samaria! For he would heal him of his leprosy" (2 Kin. 5:3). The wife told Naaman what the girl had said, and Naaman set out for Israel.

Naaman's miraculous healing led to his becoming a worshiper of the Lord. It all began with the testimony of a young girl who had faith in God and confidence in the power of God's prophet.

AN EXAMPLE FOR TODAY

◆ Adults often fail to pay attention to children. We need to remember Christ's admonition: "Assuredly, I say to you, unless you are converted and become as little children, you will by no means enter the kingdom of heaven" (Matt. 18:3).

◆ Often in Scripture the lowly are exalted above the high and mighty. Let's watch out that we do not think of ourselves as better than others.

◆ Jesus tells us that the first will be last and the last first. If we fail to humble ourselves in this life, we will surely be humbled in the next.

Noah's Wife & Daughters-in-Law

Scripture References: *Genesis 6—9*

Genesis 6—9 tells the story of the great Flood by which God judged a totally corrupt world. The focus of the story is on Noah, whose godly way of life the Lord praised, and who responded with faith when the Lord told him to build the ark.

THEIR ROLE IN SCRIPTURE

When God determined to cleanse the earth because of sin's corruption, Noah and his family were singled out. Genesis 6 indicates that Noah was a righteous man living in unrighteous times. Nothing is said in the text about the moral character of Noah's sons, wife, or daughters-in-law. Yet we can assume that they were more like Noah than the corrupt society around them.

We know from Scripture that 120 years passed before the giant boat was finished (Gen. 6:3). That massive vessel was 450 feet long, 75 feet wide, and 45 feet high. The size and complexity of the structure make it clear that Noah could not have built it alone. His sons and other family members must have helped.

Interestingly, these women, like Eve, became the mothers of all who lived after them. Yet they are not even named, while each of their husbands is.

EXPLORING THEIR RELATIONSHIPS

We are told nothing specific. Yet for many years the family held together, and focused on a task which must have made them the object of ridicule for a hundred years. We can only assume that any pressures from outside brought them closer together, rather than drove them apart.

AN EXAMPLE FOR TODAY

How important it is for us to stick together and do what is right. Yet studies have shown that many marriages collapse under pressure. The loss of a child is all too often followed by the break-up of the marriage.

Rather than letting pressure drive us away from our spouses and children, we need to draw together and offer each other support. Most of all, we should not give up on relationships in which we have invested our lives.

And, like the other unnamed women of history, we might well be God's agents for changing the future through our relationships and others whom we influence for His glory.

Peter's Mother-in-Law

Scripture References: *Matthew 8:14, 15; Mark 1:30, 31; Luke 4:38, 39*

HER ROLE IN SCRIPTURE

Jesus was at Peter's house in Capernaum. One Sabbath, Peter's wife's mother developed a high fever. When Peter, Jesus, and those with them returned to Peter's house, Jesus discovered the illness. Each of the Gospels includes different details, but they all agree that as soon as she was healed, Peter's mother-in-law got up and served them.

The story, along with 1 Corinthians 9:5, has been used to point out that Peter was indeed married. It has also been used, along with ruins in Capernaum that have been identified as Peter's house, to indicate that Peter was not just a fisherman but was also a businessman who operated a successful fishing business. However, the common features in each account have a different emphasis. These common features are the following: Jesus healed her, and she served them.

The response of Peter's wife's mother to her healing by Jesus acts as an example to each of us. When Jesus comes into our lives, cleansing and healing us from sin, it is fitting to thank and praise Him. The most appropriate response of all is to serve Him.

Pharaoh's Daughter

Scripture References: *Exodus 2:1–10; Acts 7:21, 22; Hebrews 11:24*

When They Lived: *About 1525 B.C.*

Historical Significance: *Her adoption of Moses not only saved his life, but gave him educational and other advantages that equipped Moses for the role he was to play later in life .*

HER ROLE IN SCRIPTURE

Pharaoh's daughter discovered Moses, hidden in a reed boat along the river Nile, and adopted him. While many have speculated, it is impossible to identify this daughter with any certainty. Some believe she was in fact the feminist Queen Hatshepsut, the half-sister to Thutmose III, who ruled Egypt in her own right. Others assume that she was one of Rameses II's fifty-nine daughters. It is interesting that Hebrews 11:24 states that when Moses came of age he refused to be "called the son of Pharaoh's daughter." Some take the phrase, "son of Pharaoh's daughter," as a title. Descent from the mother was significant in establishing title to the throne of Egypt. The title may imply that Moses was actually in line to become the next king of Egypt, but he chose instead to identify himself with the Israelites.

There is no doubt that Pharaoh's daughter played a greater role in God's plan for His people than she could ever have imagined.

A CLOSE-UP

Her father had ordered the destruction of Hebrew male infants, but when she opened the basket containing Moses, he wept. "So she had compassion on him, and said, 'This is one of the Hebrews' children'" (Ex. 2:6). This young woman had everything the ancient world could offer, but her heart, unlike her father's, was not hard. She was so filled with compassion for the beautiful infant that she disregarded her father's edict and drew the baby from the river to save and protect him.

AN EXAMPLE FOR TODAY

◆ A compassionate heart toward children can save them pain and anguish.
◆ This young woman showed compassion, not on one of her own, but on the child of an enslaved race, a child condemned to die. We must be reminded that every child is precious to God and deserves our compassion.
◆ Adoption by a woman with a compassionate heart saved this baby, a child slated by God for greatness. Adoption may do the same today. At a time when abortions are readily available, this should provide an additional reason to consider adoption. We do not know the plans God may have for a life.

The Philippian Slave Girl

Scripture References: Acts 16:16–19

HER ROLE IN SCRIPTURE

We know only four things about the Philippian girl. First, she was a slave. Second, she was possessed by a "spirit of divination," a demon. Third, her owners exploited her plight. And fourth, she was delivered of the spirit by Paul's command.

Like other slaves in the Roman Empire, this girl had no right to choose what was best for her. She was bound by her legal position to do whatever her owners determined was best for *them*. But unlike most slaves, this girl was also subject to a demon who, like her human masters, used her for its own purposes. However miserable the girl's situation might have been, her owners profited by her affliction. They collected money from those who paid to gain some insight into the future or help in making a difficult decision.

When Paul and his missionary team entered Philippi, the demon took possession of the girl's faculties so that she was forced to follow them. As she did, the demon shouted out through her, "These men are the servants of the Most High God, who proclaim to us the way of salvation" (Acts 16:17). After a number of days Paul, "greatly annoyed," commanded the spirit in the name of Christ to leave the girl. "And he came out that very hour" (Acts 16:18).

The incident raises two questions. Why would a demon apparently support Christian missionaries? And why would Paul be "greatly annoyed" at the additional testimony? The answer must be that the cries of the demon *did not support* the missionaries' efforts but harmed them.

The gospel message promises salvation, including deliverance from demons. By publicly supporting the missionaries, the demon undercut their message by associating itself with them.

There may also be other reasons for the demon's "support." By shouting loudly and continuously the demon made it difficult for Paul to speak to people. And by making such a public show, the demon drew the attention of onlookers away from Paul and his message. What Philippi was talking about was the strange phenomenon of the well-known slave girl's behavior rather than the content of the gospel Paul preached.

What may be more puzzling is why Paul waited "many days" before he cast the demon out. Perhaps Paul suspected that casting out the demon without being asked to do so would lead to the trouble that it did. When the demon had been cast out, the girl no longer had any value to her owners. The angry owners, "their hope of profit...gone" (Acts 16:19), seized Paul and Silas and dragged them off to the authorities.

For a study of demon possession, see the book, *Every Good and Evil Angel*. For an extended treatment of Acts 16 and Paul's miraculous release from prison, see *Every Miracle and Wonder*. Both are available from Thomas Nelson at your Christian bookstore.

We do not know what happened to the slave girl. Her masters apparently ignored her to seize Paul and Silas. Whatever they might have done to the girl later, she had been freed from an oppression greater than slavery to any human master. Jesus Christ had torn her from the grip of the dark powers.

AN EXAMPLE FOR TODAY

◆ We don't know how the demon gained control of the slave girl's life. Many people today make themselves vulnerable to demonic influences by dabbling in the occult, and seeking help from psychics, card readers, and other "spiritual counselors."

◆ The slave girl's situation, callously used by her masters, reminds us that all too many of us live in less than ideal situations. Unlike her, we have Christ to comfort us and the Holy Spirit to empower and guide us. When life is difficult, what a blessing it is to focus our thoughts on the promises and freedom that are ours!

Philip's Daughters

Scripture Reference: *Acts 21:9*

THEIR ROLE IN SCRIPTURE

The text simply says that Philip had "four virgin daughters who prophe-sied." We know nothing more about them, nor do we know whether remaining unmarried was important to the exercise of their prophetic gift. What we do know is that the age of the Spirit truly had come. In Peter's first sermon he quoted the prophet Joel's prediction that "Your sons and your daughters shall prophesy" (Acts 2:17).

Perhaps more significant is that these young women are second-gener-ation Christians. Their father was a believer who had a significant ministry (Acts 6:1–6; 8:4–40). Now, some years later, we discover that his four daughters are following in their father's footsteps.

Not everyone's children will welcome and adopt their parents' faith. Yet many do, if not in childhood and youth, as they mature. The promise that "your sons and your daughters shall prophesy" is a word of hope to those whose children stray today.

~ *Phoebe* ~

Scripture References: *Romans 16:1, 2*
When They Lived: *About* A.D. *55*
Name: *Phoebe [FEE-bih:"radiant"]*
Historical Significance: *As a leader in the church in Cenchrea she was a significant help to the apostle Paul.*

HER ROLE IN SCRIPTURE

While we have only two verses on Phoebe in the New Testament, it's clear that she was a significant person in the early church. Those verses read:

> *I commend to you Phoebe our sister, who is a servant of the church in Cenchrea, that you may receive her in the* LORD *in a manner worthy of the saints, and assist her in whatever business she has need of you; for indeed she has been a helper of many and of myself also.*
>
> —Rom. 16:1, 2

EXPLORING HER RELATIONSHIPS

Phoebe's relationship with Paul. These two verses tell us two things about Phoebe's relationship with Paul.

Phoebe is Paul's sister in the Lord (Rom. 16:1). Writers of the New Testament Epistles typically address other believers as "brother" and "sister." All Christians have a relationship with God in which He is our Father. It is appropriate then, that fellow Christians are brothers and sisters, whatever their age, social status, or gender. As Paul wrote in Galatians 3:28, "There is neither Jew nor Greek, there is neither slave nor free, there is neither male nor female; for you are all one in Christ Jesus."

Phoebe had been Paul's "helper" (Rom. 16:2). The word translated "helper" here is prostatis, a word used in classical Greek of trainers who dedicated themselves to assist an athlete competing for a prize. Here it suggests that Phoebe was a person who committed herself to stand by Paul and do all she could to assist him in his mission. The use of this word indicates that her contribution was significant not peripheral.

Paul does not hesitate to commend Phoebe to the Romans (Rom. 16:1, 2). The text suggests that Phoebe was traveling to Rome on a church mission. Some think it was Phoebe who carried Paul's letter to the Roman Christians. The apostle had complete confidence in Phoebe and in her mission.

Phoebe's relationship with the church at Cenchrea. Cenchrea was a port town about seven miles from Corinth. Paul was in Corinth when he wrote his letter to the Romans. These two verses tell us several things about Phoebe's relationship with her home church.

She held office in the church (Rom. 16:1). The word that describes her as a "servant" of the church could be translated "deaconess." For a discussion of this issue, see page 308.

She was commissioned to go to Rome for her church (Rom. 16:2). It was common in the first century to send letters of commendation with itinerant Christian teachers and leaders. Paul requested that the Roman Christians "assist her in whatever business she has need of you." Phoebe was not traveling to Rome to open a branch business. Neither did Paul urge Christians there to "shop at Phoebe's." The "business [in which] she has need of you" would have been church business, and Paul's commendation was intended to enlist the full cooperation of the Romans.

A CLOSE-UP

We know little about Phoebe. We don't know what she looked like. We have no idea how old she was. We don't know her social class, nor whether she was married, widowed, or single.

What we do know is that Phoebe was a committed Christian, who had earned the trust of Paul and of her fellow believers in Cenchrea. Phoebe was not only an officer in her church, but she had been commissioned by her church to go on a mission to Christians in Rome.

Though it would be nice to know more about Phoebe's personal life, what really counted with Paul and her fellow believers was the depth of her commitment to Christ and her readiness to use her gifts to serve Him and His people.

AN EXAMPLE FOR TODAY

◆ Whether or not Phoebe was a deaconess, she was a trusted member of her local congregation. What is important today is not the office we hold but the trust and respect we earn.

◆ Paul set an example for church leaders by demonstrating his confidence that Phoebe was qualified to undertake an important mission for her church. We can thank God for leaders who have Paul's leadership skills...and pray for those who do not.

Pilate's Wife

Scripture Reference: *Matthew 27:19*

HER ROLE IN SCRIPTURE

Pilate's wife may be considered Jesus' last advocate before He was condemned. She is mentioned only in one verse: "While he [Pilate] was sitting on the judgment seat, his wife went to him saying, 'Have nothing to do with that just Man, for I have suffered many things today in a dream because of Him.'"

Even though the ancients considered dreams a source of revelation from the gods, Pilate ignored his wife's unwitting warning. Under pressure from the Jewish leaders, Pilate condemned Jesus to death.

~ Potiphar's Wife ~

Scripture Reference: *Genesis 39*

HER ROLE IN SCRIPTURE

Potiphar's wife played a small but notorious role in Joseph's life. After Joseph had been sold into slavery and eventually found himself overseer of his master Potiphar's estate, Potiphar's wife tried to seduce Joseph. When Joseph refused her advances, she accused him of trying to rape her, and Joseph was imprisoned.

Even though Joseph suffered through many years of unjust treatment, each experience shaped him for the role God intended him to fulfill. His years managing Potiphar's house, and later managing the prison where he was incarcerated, taught him skills that he used to manage the affairs of the nation Egypt. And the position he gained through imprisonment enabled him to save not only much of the population of Egypt but also his aged father and brothers.

Later Joseph told his brothers that "it was not you who sent me here, but God" (Gen. 45:8). Perhaps the same could be said of Potiphar's wife and of all those who mistreat us. Even the evil persons we come in contact with have a role to play in God's plan.

This is important to remember when we encounter persons like Potiphar's wife who cause us to suffer unjustly. We can still trust God, knowing that He is with us. We can still expect God to use our every experience to shape us for something that lies ahead. And we can pity our persecutors, who mean to do us evil but are unaware that God is shaping us through every experience to do good.

~ Priscilla ~

Scripture References: *Acts 18:1–26; Romans 16:3;*
1 Corinthians 16:19; 2 Timothy 4:19

When They Lived: *About A.D. 50*

Name: *Priscilla [prih-SIL-uh]*

Historical Significance: *With her husband Aquila she supported*
Paul's missionary efforts and led a house-church in Ephesus.
Paul and Priscilla had both the trade of leather working and
Christian ministry in common.

HER ROLE IN SCRIPTURE

Priscilla and her husband were Christian Jews who met Paul in Corinth. The couple had moved to Corinth when the Emperor Claudius expelled all Jews from Rome. Paul stayed with this couple, who apparently became Christians before meeting the apostle. When Paul left Corinth after a ministry of some two to three years, Priscilla and Aquila went with him to Ephesus. There they hosted a house-church in their home (1 Cor. 16:19), as they probably did in both Rome and Corinth.

Acts 18:24–28 gives us some insight into the ministry of this couple in telling the story of Apollos, an Alexandrian Jew. Apollos had heard the teaching of John the Baptist on the imminent appearance of the Messiah, and he had traveled to spread the message to Jewish groups in the cities of the Roman Empire. During Apollos's presentation in the synagogue Priscilla and Aquila remained silent. Then they "took him aside and explained to him the way of God more accurately" (Acts 18:26). This ministry of quiet instruction seems to have been one of the gifts of this couple.

EXPLORING HER RELATIONSHIPS

Priscilla's relationship with her husband. As a Jewish wife, Priscilla would have been expected to be subject to her husband. Aquila would have been the one who studied God's Law and who sat with the other men in the synagogue. Priscilla would have been expected to know the laws governing a kosher kitchen, but in all other matters she would have been expected to defer to her husband. In mentioning the couple, if both were mentioned at all, normal mode of speech would have identified Aquila "and his wife."

But here in the New Testament not only is Priscilla identified by name, she is frequently mentioned first:

- Acts 18:2: "Aquila...with his wife Priscilla"
- Acts 18:18: "Priscilla and Aquila"
- Acts 18:26: "Aquila and Priscilla"
- Rom. 16:3: "Priscilla and Aquila"
- 1 Cor. 16:19: "Aquila and Priscilla"
- 2 Tim. 4:19: "Priscilla and Aquila"

It is interesting to compare this with the way Luke states the names of the missionary team of Paul and Barnabas. When the team set out, Luke referred to Barnabas and Paul (Acts 13:2). But almost immediately Luke began to refer to Paul first and Barnabas second. Paul became the recognized leader of the team. The easy exchange of the names of Priscilla and Aquila makes it clear that Priscilla was a full partner with her husband in ministry. In all places where their names are mentioned, neither of the two seem to be given intentional prominence.

Aquila and Priscilla's marriage exemplifies the elevated social status restored to women by the gospel of Christ. The new faith exalted women, making them partners in ministry as well as in life.

Priscilla's relationship with God. As a Jewish woman, Priscilla would not have expected direct access to the Lord. As a Christian she not only had unrestricted access to God through Christ, but she was also given the privilege of serving Him in her own name. Hosting a house-church, supporting Paul's ministry, teaching and instructing, were all privileges that Priscilla enjoyed as a believer in Jesus. We can measure the closeness of her relationship to God by the commitment she and her husband showed to sharing the gospel message. They even moved their business from city to city to be with Paul and support his ministry.

Priscilla's relationship with Paul. Priscilla and Aquila were close to Paul. They shared a Jewish heritage and Christian faith. They also shared the trade of leatherworking. When Paul first came to Corinth, he plied this trade in the couple's shop. The friendship they developed was deep and lasting. Aquila and Priscilla even accompanied Paul when he left Corinth to go to Ephesus. Paul not only trained the couple in ministry, but they kept in touch while apart. When together Paul added their names to the greetings he sent to Corinth. Later when Paul wrote letters to churches in cities where the couple lived, he was sure to say, "Greet Priscilla and Aquila." Priscilla, with her husband, was surely one of Paul's "fellow workers in Christ Jesus" (Rom. 16:3).

Priscilla's relationship with other believers. In writing to Corinth from Ephesus, Paul sent greetings from the couple, calling them "my fellow workers in Christ" (Rom. 16:3). Priscilla and her husband welcomed fellow believers into their home and made it available for Christian gatherings.

The experience with Apollos, however, gives the most insight into the sensitivity the couple brought to ministry. Rather than correct Apollos publicly, Priscilla and Aquila sensed the faith that was in his heart. They took him aside privately to share the good news that the One of whom John spoke had indeed come. Guided by this caring couple, Apollos responded to the gospel and later "greatly helped those who had believed through grace; for he vigorously refuted the Jews publicly, showing from the Scriptures that Jesus is the Christ" (Acts 18:27, 28).

A Close-Up

Genesis tells us that when God created woman, He determined to make a "help meet" for Adam. That phrase emphasizes mutuality. Like Adam, Eve shared those unique qualities of personhood that God granted to human beings. As a helper corresponding to Adam, Eve had the potential of being a true partner in his life here on earth.

In the case of other women in the New Testament, such as Mary of Bethany, we saw how the gospel transformed women's traditional roles. In Priscilla and Aquila we see the transformation of marriage and the restoration of God's original intent that married couples should be partners in all things in their life.

Priscilla is mentioned first in some passages, and some Bible students have concluded that Priscilla's gifts made her the more significant of the two. They suggest that Paul mentioned Priscilla first because she, rather than Aquila, was the "leader" in the relationship. Yet the text guards against this interpretation. That Priscilla is named first in three passages and Aquila is also named first in three indicates that these two truly were *equal* partners. Neither was the leader; neither was the follower. Priscilla and Aquila were one, in the sense that the original text implies: they shared in common all of their life here on earth. They were partners in life and in ministry.

AN EXAMPLE FOR TODAY

- Priscilla worked closely with Paul and earned his respect. If we want a significant role in our church, we need to serve with present leaders so they can know us and administer our spiritual gifts.
- Husband-and-wife relationships may be difficult, but Priscilla's relationship with Aquila reminds us of an important principle. Partnership in a marriage is not achieved by weakening the husband but by elevating the wife. In living together as one in all things, Priscilla and Aquila stand as an example of what Christian marriages are to be—and can be—through Christ.

Prominent Women

Scripture Reference: Acts 13:50

THEIR ROLE IN SCRIPTURE

A cts 13 is a transitional point. From this chapter on, the focus leaves Jerusalem and Judea and ventures into the wider Greek world. The missionaries traveled in an empire where Roman law and Greek culture had created conditions quite different from those in Judea. In the Roman world it was much more common for women to hold wealth in their own right, and women of the social elite were by definition well-to-do.

Acts 13:50 reports that in Pisidian Antioch "the Jews stirred up the devout and prominent women and the chief men of the city" to persecute Paul and the missionaries. In Thessalonica, however, "many ... believed, and also not a few of the Greeks, prominent women as well as men" (Acts 17:12).

In the end it was not social class that determined a person's response to the gospel. The Gentile church encompassed the elite and the poor, the free and slave, men and women.

Puah & Shiphrah

Scripture References: *Exodus 1:15–21*
When They Lived: *About 1525 B.C.*
Names: *Puah [POO-uh]*
Shiphrah [SHIF-ruh:"beauty"]
Historical Significance: *The two midwives thwarted Pharaoh's intent to kill the male infants of Hebrew women at birth. In Egypt women gave birth sitting on a birthing chair.*

THEIR ROLE IN SCRIPTURE

The Hebrews had been slaves in Egypt for some time when the Book of Exodus opens, and the slave population was exploding. What seems to have worried Pharaoh was that these slaves were Semites, from the same stock that was exerting pressure on Egypt's borders. Pharaoh became concerned that in case of war the Hebrews might stage an uprising at home.

The obvious answer seemed to be to reduce the slave population. So Pharaoh commanded these two to see that any male infants the Hebrew women delivered did not survive.

It would be wrong to assume that Puah and Shiphrah were the only two midwives in Egypt. It is likely that they were responsible for overseeing the work of all Egypt's midwives. (Ex. 1:19). While their names are Egyptian, the women were Hebrew. It was not at all unusual for Hebrews serving in an official capacity to be given Egyptian names, as was Joseph, who was given the name Zaphnath-Paaneah (Gen. 41:45).

These two Hebrew women had more reverence for God than for Pharaoh, and were rewarded by the Lord with large families for their role in protecting God's people. Some eighty years later Moses came out of the Sinai as God's agent to set His people free.

BIBLE BACKGROUND: MIDWIVES IN EGYPT

In biblical times midwives rather than doctors assisted women giving birth. In Egypt the expectant mother sat on a stool. Ezekiel 16:4 describes some of the midwife's duties: cutting the umbilical cord, washing the infant in water, rubbing it with salt, and wrapping it in swaddling cloths.

EXPLORING THEIR RELATIONSHIPS

Puah and Shiphrah's relationship with Pharaoh. Puah and Shiphrah knew exactly how it felt to be slaves and be called to appear before the most powerful man in the ancient world. In a personal audience, they were told by Pharaoh to kill all male Hebrews at birth. Refusing to comply would mean their lives. Yet they feared God more than Pharaoh and chose to obey Him.

Puah and Shiphrah were accountable not only for themselves but for all Hebrew midwives. Their handling of this terrible dilemma was crucial. They couldn't kill or order other midwives to kill the babies; yet, they were supposed to obey Pharaoh. Their solution was so wise, surely it came to them as an answer to prayer.

When Pharaoh realized that the Hebrew newborns were being allowed to live, he again called the two midwives in and asked them, "Why have you done this thing, and saved the male children alive?" (Ex. 1:18). The midwives told Pharaoh that the Hebrew women gave birth so easily that they delivered before the midwives could get there. Puah and Shiphrah probably told the other midwives what Pharaoh had ordered. All the midwives must have decided to time their arrival at births so as to be unable to kill the children at birth. Their cleverness notwithstanding, the midwives "feared God, and did not do as the king of Egypt commanded them, but saved the male children alive" (Ex. 1:17).

Pharaoh seemed to believe the women and did not have them put to death for disobeying him. Instead, he gave orders that, "Every son who is born you shall cast into the river, and every daughter you shall save alive" (Ex. 1:22).

Puah and Shiphrah's relationship with God. These midwives feared God and disobeyed the king of Egypt. They understood that ultimately they were responsible to God, and that His is a higher authority. Therefore God dealt well with the midwives, and the people multiplied and grew mighty.

A faith crisis can result when we are confronted with the moral dilemma of being told by a superior to do something that we know is wrong. Who are we to please? We know that the fear of God is the beginning of all wisdom. It gives us a respect for and awareness of God as the present and true King. And it frees us to obey God above human authority.

EXAMPLES FOR TODAY

- The two women remind us that, while leaders and the laws of the land may call certain things safe, legal and good, ultimately, it is God's Law, written on our hearts, to which we are responsible.
- The experience of these midwives illustrates that God does reward our obedience to Him.

The Queen of Sheba

Scripture References: *1 Kings 10:1–10;*
2 Chronicles 9:1–9

HER ROLE IN SCRIPTURE

The kingdom of Sheba lay at the end of the Arabian Peninsula, about 1,500 miles south of Jerusalem, in lands occupied by modern Yemen. In the time of Solomon, the tenth century B.C., Sheba and Israel were both actively involved in trade. Most commentators believe that the queen of Sheba's visit to Solomon was as much intended to establish trade agreements as to satisfy the queen's curiosity about Solomon.

We know little or nothing of this queen beyond the brief reference to her in the passage. The information reported tells us more about Solomon than about the queen.

The Jewish rabbis understood the phrase, "Now King Solomon gave the queen of Sheba all she desired, whatever she asked" (1 Kin. 10:13), to indicate that she had a son fathered by Solomon. It is much more likely that the phrase simply reflects that the visit was successful, and the desired treaties were executed.

~ *Rachel & Leah* ~

Scripture References: *Genesis 29—33; 35:16–19; 46:15–18; Ruth 4:11; Jeremiah 31:15; Matthew 2:18*

When They Lived: *About 1875 B.C.*

Names: *Rachel [RAY-chuhl:"ewe"].*
Leah [LEE-uh:"wild cow"].

Historical Significance: *These two wives of Jacob and their maidservants gave birth to the men who founded the twelve Israelite tribes. The beautiful Rachel was loved, but her plain sister was the mother of six of Jacob's twelve sons.*

THEIR ROLE IN SCRIPTURE

Rachel and Leah were sisters whose lives were closely intertwined. They were the daughters of Laban, and both were married to Jacob, the son of their Uncle Isaac. One sister was loved, the other ignored. Ironically, it was not Jacob's beloved bride, Rachel, who was laid to rest with him in the tomb of his father and mother, but Leah.

Their life stories (Gen. 29:1–30). The two sisters grew up in the family of a sheepherder. As is sometimes the case, one daughter was beautiful, the other unattractive. The biblical text says Leah's eyes were "delicate" [*rakkot*] (Gen. 29:17), better translated "weak." This may imply nearsightedness, light sensitivity that made her squint, or some other defect. The Jewish rabbis resisted this conclusion, and the Talmud argues that there could be no physical blemish in the righteous Leah.

It remains clear, however, that Rachel was far more attractive than her sister. When Jacob first met Rachel in the fields taking care of her father Laban's sheep, he fell deeply in love with her. When Laban offered to employ Jacob and asked him to name his wages, Jacob unhesitatingly offered to serve Laban for seven years for the privilege of marrying Rachel. Jacob had no money to offer Laban for his bride, as custom required, so Jacob offered himself and his services.

The price Jacob offered was actually a handsome one. Old Babylonian contracts from the 19th to 16th century B.C., and contracts from Nuzi dating from the 16th to 14th centuries, spell out the responsibilities of sheepherders to sheep owners, and vice versa. The wages that Jacob would have earned over seven years were far greater than the bride price any suitor might be expected to offer a father!

But when the seven years were complete, Laban substituted Leah for her sister Rachel. And Jacob awoke to discover that the woman he had lain with the night before was not the woman he loved. So Laban offered to make a second deal for Jacob to earn Rachel by serving another seven years (Gen. 29:26–30).

BIBLE BACKGROUND: POLYGAMY

Old Babylonian law prohibited men from having more than one wife except when that wife was childless. Yet 400 or 500 years earlier (second millennium B.C.) at Nuzi, some 25 percent of the men in a census of households had two or more wives. So Jacob's experience was not without parallel. Yet Rachel's and Leah's life as sisters married to a single man was further complicated by a competition to give their husband sons. In this competition each also gave Jacob her slave ["maid"] as a surrogate. As we will see, the complex relationships this created caused extreme pain for each of the women, and undoubtedly for Jacob as well.

So what was the legal relationship between Jacob and his four "wives"? In Old Babylonian law, when a man married two women one was the primary wife, and the other had a lower status. Typically this status was spelled out in a marriage contract, a number of which have been recovered by archaeologists. Despite the fact that no contract is mentioned in Scripture, it is clear from Genesis that Jacob loved Rachel, and considered Rachel his primary wife, while he "hated Leah" [that is, rejected Leah's claim to a primary position even though he had wed her first].

While the two sisters' use of Bilhah and Zilpah as surrogates would make them Jacob's concubines, they continued to be the slaves of Rachel and Leah. Jacob's recognition of Bilhah's and Zilpah's offspring as his sons gave the sons legitimacy, but it did not change the status of their mothers.

Jacob's experience in no way suggests that the Bible teaches or encourages polygamy. Certainly Scripture's description of the relationship between these two sisters married to the same man serves to warn us away from this course.

Sisterly cooperation (Gen. 31:1–35). While within the family fierce competition existed, when threats came from outside the two sisters presented a united front. Jacob served Laban fourteen years for his two wives, and God increased Laban's flocks. For the next six years Jacob oversaw Laban's flocks for payment. God saw to it that Jacob's flocks increased while Laban's decreased. Laban's sons became jealous, complaining to their father that Jacob was getting what was really theirs.

When Jacob's contract with Laban came up for renewal [in Mesopotamia contracts ran from sheepshearing time to sheepshearing time. See Gen. 31:19], God told Jacob it was time to return to Canaan. Jacob held a family counsel and talked it over with his two wives. As slaves, neither Bilhah nor Zilpah were consulted, although by custom their sons would inherit equally with the sons of Rachel and Leah. Jacob explained that God had shown him how to increase his share of the herds he supervised for Laban, and Jacob reviewed the growing hostility of Laban and his sons. Jacob also told them of the visit of the Angel of the Lord instructing him to return to Canaan. Now Rachel and Leah agreed.

> *"Is there still any portion or inheritance for us in our father's house?*
> *... For all these riches which God has taken from our father are really*
> *ours and our children's; now then, whatever God has said to you, do it."*
> —Gen. 31:14, 16

The two might compete within the family, but they were united in their commitment to their own welfare and to that of their children after them.

That Jacob took such pains to consult with and gain the cooperation of his wives is significant. The stereotypical husband of that age is often portrayed as so much the master of his household, and women so subservient, that talking matters over would be unnecessary and demeaning to the man. Incidents such as this recorded in Scripture remind us that one's legal position seldom is an accurate reflection of the true state of interpersonal relationships.

Rachel's theft (Gen. 31:25–35). When Laban discovered that Jacob had left, he and his sons pursued them. On the way, God warned Laban against taking any action against Jacob. However, Laban did have one valid complaint: his household gods were gone.

The mention of household gods reminds us that all the peoples in the ancient world were idolaters. They believed in many deities, and they fashioned wooden or stone images as objects of worship. Abraham alone had had his vision of one God, and what we now take for granted about God was then a belief held only within Abraham's family.

But it would be a mistake to assume that Rachel, who had stolen her father's household deities, did so for religious reasons. In that time possession of the household gods was significant in establishing a claim to the family estate! Rachel was ready to commit herself and her sons to an uncertain future in Canaan. But just in case, she wanted to hedge the bet she had placed on Jacob and his God.

Rachel and Leah in the rest of Scripture. The names of the two are united in the Book of Ruth and in the proverbial blessing still uttered at many Jewish weddings: "The LORD make the woman who is coming into your house like Rachel and Leah, the two who built the house of Israel" (Ruth 4:11).

But Jeremiah recorded a prediction in chapter 31 that harkens back to Rachel's death. When her second son was born the family was traveling near what became Bethlehem. Rachel was dying, and she called her son Ben-oni, "Son of my Sorrow." Jeremiah looks ahead to a time when others near Bethlehem would also weep inconsolably. The prediction was fulfilled in the first century when King Herod ordered the execution of all male children two years old and under in a feverish and futile attempt to kill the infant Jesus (see Matt. 2:18). The ultimate hope for Rachel and for all humankind is not to be found in the future of our children but in the salvation won for us by a descendant of Jacob, Jesus Christ. That descendant of Jacob came to us through the tribe of Judah, Leah's son.

EXPLORING HER RELATIONSHIPS

Rachel's relationship with Jacob. As Rachel headed toward the watering hole with her sheep, the men Jacob was questioning about Laban directed his gaze toward her. Jacob went to Rachel immediately, identified himself as her cousin, kissed her, and wept. After his long journey and the circumstances that necessitated it, and his vision from God, Jacob must have been physically, emotionally, and spiritually drained. When he discovered that God had directed him straight to this lovely shepherdess, his cousin, he was overcome with emotion.

Rachel and Jacob's great love. Laban welcomed his nephew and before long Jacob, who had been sent away without means of procuring a wife, had struck a deal with his uncle. Jacob loved Rachel, who "was beautiful of form and appearance" (Gen. 29:17). He offered to work for Laban for seven years if he could marry Rachel. Jacob's love can be measured in that the seven years' service far exceeded a normal bride price, and that they "seemed only a few days to him" (Gen. 29:20).

It would seem that Rachel must have felt the same toward Jacob. But then Laban committed a dastardly deed. When the seven years were up, Laban gave a veiled Leah to Jacob under cover of darkness. Rachel and Jacob had been double-crossed by Laban and Rachel's older sister, Leah.

After waiting seven years to marry Jacob, Rachel must have been heartbroken to find that her father had given her sister to her beloved. Yet there are many unanswered questions about this incident. Did Rachel know of her father's plan? If so, why didn't she warn Jacob? If she didn't know, where was she when Leah was given to Jacob instead of herself? And why would Leah go along with this scheme when she knew that Rachel and Jacob loved each other and had waited to wed for seven years?

Jacob was more than unhappy when the light of day revealed the sister switch. But it was too late then. The best he could do was to give his unwanted bride the week of individual attention she was due, and then wed her sister Rachel, committing himself to serve yet another seven years.

Rachel's rivalry with Leah poisoned her relationship with Jacob. Jacob and Rachel loved each other dearly. Yet as their years together passed it was heartbreaking to Rachel to see her sister bear children for her husband while she remained barren. Perhaps more than once Rachel complained to Jacob, "Give me children, or else I die!" (Gen. 30:1). Jacob responded angrily as he reminded her, "Am I in the place of God, who has withheld from you the fruit of the womb?" (Gen. 30:2).

While Rachel in desperation blamed her husband, we know he was not withholding himself from her. And while God had opened Leah's womb as a consolation for being unloved by her husband, Rachel remained barren. We are not told that Rachel prayed for a child. Rather she pleaded with Jacob. This may well indicate that Rachel in her love looked to Jacob to provide a satisfaction that only God could provide.

Finally, the desperate Rachel gave her servant Bilhah to Jacob as a surrogate, and Bilhah bore Jacob two sons. In contrast to her great-aunt Sarah, Rachel named these sons herself and considered them her own. Rachel named the first son Dan because, she said, "God has judged my case; and He has also heard my voice and *given me a son*" (Gen. 30:6). For a time at least, Rachel focused on God. But by the time her servant delivered a second son, Rachel's focus is back on her rivalry with her sister. Rachel called this son Naphtali because "with great wrestlings I have wrestled with my sister, and indeed I have prevailed" (Gen. 30:8).

Rachel's relationship with God. We do not know a great deal about Rachel's relationship with the Lord. Jacob had already been chosen by God as the one through whom the Abrahamic Covenant would pass. It is perhaps a significant comment on Rachel's spiritual insensitivity that the line of Christ runs through Leah, not Rachel.

Yet after Leah had borne six sons and a daughter, and felt at last that she had received justice, God opened Rachel's womb. She bore a son named Joseph, and said, "The LORD shall add to me another son" (see Gen. 30:22–24). Now again Rachel's focus shifts toward God, evidence of a real relationship with Him.

Rachel's relationship with her children. The phrase "another son" tells us much about how Rachel felt about the children borne to Bilhah. She did not say that at last God had given her a child, but that God was adding another son. It would appear that Dan and Naphtali were loved as if they were her own flesh and blood.

When Jacob consulted with his wives about returning to Canaan, Rachel and Leah agreed that it was the right thing to do. But shortly after the little company entered the Promised Land, Rachel gave birth again. In one of Scripture's more poignant passages, Rachel, the beloved wife who had yearned for children and resented her sister's fertility, succumbed in childbirth (Gen. 35:18, 19). Ironically, Rachel had thought she would die if she couldn't give birth, but it was in giving birth that Rachel died.

Rachel's relationship with Leah. Little is known about the sisters or their relationship before their marriage to Jacob. We know that Leah was older than Rachel, and that Rachel was prettier than Leah. Perhaps this explains why Leah was willing to marry Jacob through deception, when she knew that Jacob and Rachel loved each other. Leah may have been jealous of her younger sister or even afraid that if she did not participate in tricking Jacob she would have to die unmarried. Tragically, the relationship between the two women that we observe when they were both wives of Jacob is one marked by jealousy, rivalry, and hurt.

A CLOSE-UP

Rachel, like her great-aunt Sarah and her aunt Rebekah before her, was a woman of great beauty. As a shepherdess, she was probably physically fit from walking many miles each day and doing the many other physical tasks that went with that occupation.

Because she was lovely and a hard worker, she was undoubtedly well liked by those around her. She grew up feeling accepted and loved. When Jacob came on the scene, he loved her, too.

It must have been difficult for Rachel when she realized that the man she loved and had waited seven years to marry had been given to another woman. She would never have him to herself. She was the beloved wife, but she always had to share Jacob with her sister.

And how painful it must have been when her sister bore child after child until she had borne seven, and yet Rachel's body was barren. She had given her husband her servant Bilhah, who had borne her two sons and she loved them deeply. Then, at last, she was blessed with Joseph. How her heart must have rejoiced as she held him in her arms.

And then she conceived again! But both her hopes and she herself died giving birth to her second son, leaving Leah to be the sole wife of the man she loved. No wonder she named that infant, Son of My Sorrows. (We know him as Benjamin.)

AN EXAMPLE FOR TODAY

◆ Rachel reminds us again that being beautiful does not bring contentment. Nor does a loving husband guarantee happiness. In the end, only an intimate relationship with our Father can provide true contentment. All other things may fail us, and to the extent we pin our hopes on them, we will remain unfulfilled and hurting.

◆ Rachel also reminds us that despite disappointment we can be a blessing to others. How fortunate Dan and Naphtali were to have her as their "mother," rather than to know rejection like that Ishmael experienced from Sarah.

EXPLORING HER RELATIONSHIPS

Leah's relationship with Jacob. Some surmise that Leah was a victim of her father, who wanted to get another seven years of hard work from Jacob. Had Laban told her to keep quiet on her sister's wedding night because she was so homely no other man would want her? It's hard to imagine Leah obeying her father unless she thought she could make Jacob love her, and she wanted to try.

Leah had to be an accomplice of Laban's on the wedding night. She could have made herself known to Jacob and had him speak to Laban before the marriage was consummated. I can't see any way around Leah's personal responsibility for what happened. Leah knew that Jacob loved Rachel. Was she so jealous of her pretty little sister that she didn't think through the possible consequences of her choice?

Leah could have acted, but she did not. There is no evidence that Jacob ever loved her. But there is one fascinating bit of evidence that perhaps Jacob recognized her qualities in the end. We know that Leah was buried with Abraham, Sarah, Isaac, Rebekah—and Jacob. Jacob seems to have had no interest in transporting Rachel's body or bones to the family tomb. Yet at the end of his life Jacob did ask that his own bones be returned to Canaan, where he lay not beside his beloved Rachel, but the long unloved Leah.

Leah's relationship with God. Leah's life, like that of many women since Eve, reflects an unhappiness symptomatic of the Fall. God told Eve that one of the consequences of her choice would be the twisting of husband/wife relationships. "Your desire shall be for your husband, and he shall rule over you" (Gen. 3:16). Leah kept looking for love, approval, and acceptance from Jacob, and she was continually disappointed until she reoriented her life toward God.

We see this in the names she gave her sons. When the first son was born, Leah named him Reuben ("See, a son!"), for Leah said to herself, "The

LORD has surely looked on my affliction. Now therefore, my husband will love me" (Gen. 29:32). But Jacob did not.

When a second son was born, she called him Simeon ("Heard"). Still hopeful, Leah named him this "because the LORD has heard that I am unloved" (Gen. 29:33). The Hebrew text uses a stronger word for unloved: "hated." Despite Leah's gift of children to her husband, she continued to experience rejection.

When a third son was born, Leah called him Levi ["attached"], believing that "now this time my husband will become attached to me, because I have borne him three sons" (Gen. 29:34). But again she was disappointed.

With the birth of her fourth son, Leah began to look away from her husband for love, and to look to the Lord. She named her fourth son Judah ["Praise"]. When this son was born Leah said, "Now I will praise the LORD" (Gen. 29:35).

There is clear evidence that this change in attitude persisted. After Jacob had had two sons for Rachel by her maid, Bilhah, Leah, still in competition with Rachel, insisted he have sons for her by her maid, Zilpah. The two sons Zilpah bore were named Issachar and Zebulun, and Leah commented, "God has given me my wages" (Gen. 30:18) and "God has endowed me with a good endowment" (Gen. 30:20).

Finally Leah bore a daughter, Dinah ("Justice"), perhaps feeling that, after all, the children she called her own had balanced the lack of a husband's love.

A CLOSE-UP

Leah's name means "wild cow." This is not exactly an attractive appellation with which to brand a young lady, especially in Old Testament times when names were chosen to capture something of the essence of the one named. The only physical description we have of Leah is that her eyes were "delicate." Did this mean extremely light sensitive? That remains uncertain. However, what is sure is that while Sarah and Rebekah and her sister Rachel are all described as beautiful, Leah's weak eyes are highlighted, and she is given the unfortunate name, Wild Cow.

Personal attractiveness is something Leah learned to live without. But her character and her relationship with God did develop. Leah learned to pour out her grief to God. Leah wanted her husband to love her, and she wanted children. While God didn't change Jacob's heart, God did love Leah. He gave her seven children, and in the process God taught her to seek comfort in Him.

In the end, Leah felt God's love, and also felt vindicated. Her seven biological children and her two surrogate children surrounded her, and she at last experienced the love of a family who did not care that she was the sister with weak eyes.

An Example for Today

- Leah's life reminds us that people are overly impressed by appearance. Sometimes it seems that God alone seems to care about what He sees in the heart.
- Yet from Leah we learn to keep our focus on God. He, not the spouse we love, is the one stable force in our existence.
- We can also see in Leah's experience that God blesses each of us in different ways. We need to praise Him for the gifts He gives us and not mourn for what we do not have.

~ Rahab ~

Scripture References: *Joshua 2:1–24; 6:17–25;*
Matthew 1:5; Hebrews 11:31;
James 2:25

When They Lived: *About 1406 B.C.*

Name: *Rahab [RAY-hab:"broad"]*

Historical Significance: *Rahab trusted Israel's God and not only found personal deliverance when Jericho fell, but married an Israelite and produced a son who was in the line of David and Jesus Christ.*

HER ROLE IN SCRIPTURE

When the Israelites under Joshua crossed the Jordan River into Canaan, their access to the heart of the country was blocked by the fortified city of Jericho. The massive fortifications made the city invulnerable to storming. Israel was unprepared for a long siege, which would have given the Canaanites time to unite and send an overpowering force against them. Joshua sent two spies to look the city over. They were discovered, the city gates were closed, and the city guard set out on a house-to-house search to arrest them.

The two spies found refuge in the house of Rahab, whom the text calls a "harlot," or a prostitute. Two kinds of prostitution are mentioned in the Old Testament. One type is ritual prostitution, in which sex acts are engaged in as an element in the worship of pagan fertility gods. The other type of prostitution had commercial but no religious significance: it was simply the usual trade of sexual favors for payment. Archaeological discoveries have made it clear that commercial prostitution was common in drinking establishments and inns. Some have even argued that in identifying Rahab as a harlot, the author of the biblical text is simply saying that she was an innkeeper. The professions were often associated that to call one an innkeeper usually suggested that sex was one of the services ordinarily available.

Whether or not Rahab was a prostitute when the spies entered Jericho is irrelevant to the story. The frequent reference to her as a harlot reminds us that God offers His salvation to sinners, not simply to those whom society accepts as worthy.

Rahab's choice (Josh. 2). When the spies appeared at Rahab's door she was faced with a choice. She could turn them in or hide them. Rahab chose to hide them, but only after making a bargain with them. Rahab's dialog with the spies reveals clearly that the people of Canaan knew what God had done for His people, and were terrified at the appearance of the Israelites on their borders.

> *"I know that the LORD has given you the land, that the terror of you has fallen on us, and that all the inhabitants of the land are fainthearted because of you. For we have heard how the LORD dried up the water of the Red Sea for you when you came out of Egypt, and what you did to the two kings of the Amorites who were on the other side of the Jordan, Sihon and Og, whom you utterly destroyed. And as soon as we heard these things, our hearts melted; neither did there remain any more courage in anyone because of you, for the LORD your God, He is God in heaven above and on earth beneath."*

> —Josh. 2:9–11

What is striking is that while all the Canaanites apparently had this information about God, Rahab was unique in her response. Rather than resist Him, Rahab was determined to commit herself into His care. And so she bargained. Rahab would protect the spies, but the spies had to promise that, when Israel took Jericho, they would spare Rahab and her immediate family.

At Jericho's fall (Josh. 6). God did display the power that the Canaanites feared. Jericho's walls fell. When they did, Rahab and her family survived. The text states, "And Joshua spared Rahab the harlot, her father's household, and all that she had. So she dwells in Israel to this day, because she hid the messengers whom Joshua sent to spy out Jericho" (Josh. 6:26).

In the New Testament. While the text of Joshua tells us no more about Rahab, her name shows up three times in the New Testament.

In the genealogy of Jesus Christ (Matt. 1:5). Four women are mentioned in Matthew's list of Christ's ancestors. One was Tamar, who tricked Judah and became pregnant by her father-in-law. The second is Rahab, who in her life before becoming a member of the Old Testament community of faith was a pagan who probably engaged in commercial prostitution. The third is Ruth, a Moabitess and not an Israelite at all. And the fourth is Bathsheba, whom David took advantage of but later married. Put bluntly, few would be proud to have these four women emphasized in his or her own family line. Of the four, least impressive to our friends might be a pagan woman of Canaan who openly engaged in the world's oldest profession.

It is well for us to remember that God does not measure a person by the sins of their past...Rather God remembers what the life of a person testifies from their heart about who God is. It was Rahab's choice rather than her past that honored her for all time to come.

In faith's hall of fame (Heb. 11:31). Hebrews 11 reviews the wonders faith has worked in human lives. Of Rahab that passage simply says, "by faith Rahab did not perish with those who did not believe, when she had received the spies with peace."

In James's definition of a living faith (James 2:25). James 2 has troubled some people because at first glance the writer's references to Abraham and to Rahab seem to teach a salvation by works rather than by faith alone. This verse asks, "Was not Rahab...also justified by works when she received the messengers and sent them out another way?"

In chapter two, James contrasted "faith" with "faith." Often we use the word "faith" to mean no more than an agreement that certain things are true. In the context, James points out that even demons have this kind of faith in God. They know that He exists and they tremble in fear!

But Christian faith is far more than intellectual agreement or even intellectual certainty. At its root, saving faith involves an act of trust in what is known. What James argued is that not a person, but a person's claim to have saving faith is justified—that is, shown to be true—by the response [works] that a true faith produces. Can we say with certainty that Rahab truly possessed the faith ascribed to her in Hebrews? Yes, without doubt. For Rahab "received the messengers and sent them out another way." Her works did not save her. Her works demonstrated and thus justified the claim that Rahab truly was a woman of faith.

EXPLORING HER RELATIONSHIPS

Rahab's relationship with God. Rahab had heard about God. Unlike others in Jericho, she chose to acknowledge and trust Him.

Rahab's relationship with the Israelite spies. Through Rahab's conversation with these two spies, we discover how familiar the pagan nations of the Promised Land were with the story of the Israelites and the miracles performed by God on their behalf. Further, it's clear that the stories were believed to be entirely true, and that the citizens of the powerful city of Jericho were terrified when they learned that the Israelites were camped outside their city. It seems curious that this woman of ill repute was the only resident of Jericho whose heart was not hardened. Instead, she opened not only her home to the spies, but she opened her heart to the God they served and whom she in turn learned to serve.

A CLOSE-UP

From outward appearance, Rahab the harlot would seem the least likely person to be assimilated by God's chosen people. Yet we can infer much about her character as we examine this story closely. Rahab was a woman of strong courage as evidenced by her willingness to commit treason and help the enemy. When her king called her to bring out the spies who had been seen entering her inn, she said, "Yes, the men came to me, but I did not know where they were from. And it happened as the gate was being shut, when it was dark, that the men went out. Where the men went I do not know; pursue them quickly, for you may overtake them" (Josh. 2:4, 5).

She was also a woman devoted to her family. When she struck the deal to protect the spies, she asked for protection not just for herself but for her family as well. She apparently had some influence in her family; when she told them to come to her place, they showed up there. They trusted her judgment and put their lives in her hands. It seems obvious that Rahab was intelligent and quick-thinking. She used her savvy to protect herself and her family. Her leadership is evidenced by the way her family responded to her.

AN EXAMPLE FOR TODAY

◆ Rahab demonstrates that we don't have to be perfect for God to use us in significant ways. We do need to respond to Him in faith and with integrity. When we do, He will, as He did for Rahab, melt away the impurities of our character and mold us into the kind of women and men He would have us be.

◆ God is free to use whom He will. We pass judgment on what we see, but we can only see the outward appearance. God also passes judgment on what He sees. But He sees inside and out—yesterday, today, and tomorrow.

◆ Rahab reminds believers not to be judgmental. All have sinned, and but for God's grace, all would be doomed. God extends us His grace. We must extend His grace to others regarding not what people may seem to us, but what God may intend them to become.

~ *Rebekah* ~

Scripture References: *Genesis 22:23; 24:15–67;*
26:6–11, 34; 27:1–17, 46;
28:5; 49:31

When They Lived: *About 1925* B.C.

Name: *Rebekah [ruh-BEK-uh]*

Historical Significance: *Rebekah was the mother of two great*
peoples, the Edomites through Esau, and the Israelites through Jacob.

HER ROLE IN SCRIPTURE

It is fascinating how mothers sometimes shape the lives of their children. The story of Rebekah's long-distance courtship may be one of the most romantic in Scripture. Yet as a mother Rebekah made choices that ended in separation from her favorite son.

Rebekah's life story. Rebekah was a granddaughter of Abraham's brother, Nahor. Nahor had accompanied Abraham and their father Terah when the family left the fabled city of Ur and settled in Haran. Haran was located in northern Mesopotamia, along a well-traveled trade route. After the death of his father, Abraham had left his brother in Haran and continued southward to Canaan where God had directed him. Rebekah was of marriageable age, probably in her early teens, when one of Abraham's servants came to Haran in search of a bride for Abraham's son, Isaac. Rebekah's life story is briefly told in that she accompanied the servant back to Canaan, married Isaac, and later bore him two sons, both of whom became famous. But we know much more of Rebekah's life story than this.

Rebekah's courtship (Gen. 24). After Sarah's death Abraham determined to find a bride for their son, Isaac. In ancient times the finding of a suitable bride was the responsibility of the parents, even as it was the responsibility of a young woman's parents to negotiate for a fitting husband. Abraham had lived for decades as an alien among the Canaanites in what we know as Palestine. Abraham was unwilling to link his family with any of them. So Abraham sent a servant back to Haran to find a bride for Isaac from within his own family.

Rebekah is identified as God's choice (Gen. 24:11–27). When the servant finally reached Haran, a journey of some 400 miles, he prayed to the God of Abraham:

> *"Now let it be that the young woman to whom I say, 'Please let down your pitcher that I may drink,' and she says, 'Drink, and I will also give your camels a drink'—let her be the one You have appointed for Your servant Isaac. And by this I will know that You have shown kindness to my master."*
>
> —Gen. 24:14

Before the servant finished his prayer, Rebekah approach the well to draw water.

This is the first recorded prayer for divine guidance in selecting a wife. It is also the first expression of the belief still held by many that there is one person whom God Himself has chosen to be an individual's mate. Later the rabbis asked, What has God been doing since he completed Creation in six days? Their answer? He has been selecting this husband for that woman, and that wife for this man!

Whatever we might draw from the incident, we do know that Rebekah was unusual for more than her beauty. Camels which had completed a journey might drink twenty or thirty *gallons* of water. The servant had proposed a truly difficult test for any future bride to pass. Rebekah's cheerful "I will draw water for your camels also, until they have finished drinking" (Gen. 24:19) convinced the servant that God had answered his prayer.

When the servant learned that Rebekah was indeed the granddaughter of Abraham's brother, he "bowed down his head and worshiped" (Gen. 24:24).

The negotiations (Gen. 24:38–53). As part of the marriage negotiations, the servant told the family the whole story. Rebekah's father, Bethuel, and her brother, Laban, were convinced: God's hand in this marriage was unmistakably clear. When the family had agreed, the servant gave Rebekah and her family the gifts Abraham had supplied.

Rebekah's journey (Gen. 24:54–67). The servant was anxious to start home, but the family urged delay. Rebekah herself was ready to leave. When asked if she was willing to accompany the servant and wed Isaac, she quickly answered, "I will go."

Rebekah's faith and courage are impressive, for this young girl must have known that she would never again see her family or the home in which she had grown up. At the same time we can perhaps imagine the appeal of such a journey to a young girl, and how she must have pressed the servant for tales of Isaac as they took the month-long journey to Canaan.

At journey's end Rebekah found something for which all men and women yearn. The Bible says, "She became his wife, and he loved her."

Rebekah's three disappointments. However romantic courtship may be, the future for any person is sure to hold some disappointments. The Bible describes three experiences of Rebekah's that we may rightly consider disappointments.

Years of childlessness (Gen. 25:19–28). Isaac was forty when he married the teenage Rebekah. As the years passed and Rebekah remained childless, she became more and more concerned. Most women in the ancient world saw childbearing as the most fulfilling role in their lives, and Rebekah was no different. The biblical text tells us that finally "Isaac pleaded with the LORD for his wife" (Gen. 25:21). The phrasing seems significant. Isaac did not plead for a son for himself. He pleaded with God "for his wife." Rebekah desperately wanted children.

Finally God answered Isaac's prayer, and Rebekah conceived twins.

A husband's betrayal (Gen. 26:1–11). When Isaac's father Abraham had met strangers, he had told Sarah to say that she was his sister. This had been a half-truth, for Sarah was also his wife.

Genesis 26 tells us that when Isaac's wanderings took him to the Philistine city of Gerar, he adopted the same strategy. When the men there asked him about his wife, Isaac was afraid and claimed that she was his sister. As God had just previously spoken to Isaac and promised to be with him and bless him, this can hardly be less than a lapse of faith on his part. In time the deception was discovered, and the king of Gerar decreed that neither Isaac nor Rebekah should be touched by any of his people.

Favoritism (Gen. 25:28; 27). Rebekah had been thrilled to become pregnant. Yet her children were also the cause of disappointment and pain. She and Isaac played favorites; Isaac favored Esau, and Rebekah favored Jacob. When Isaac neared death, he sought to bless his successor. Rebekah knew Isaac intended to choose Esau rather than Jacob. The ease with which Rebekah hatched a scheme to divert the blessing to Jacob suggests that she had long been manipulating events to give her favorite an edge.

Rebekah was so determined that Jacob should receive the blessing that she dressed him in his brother's clothing, tied goatskins on his hands to make them feel hairy, and urged Jacob to lie and say that he was Esau. Jacob deceived Isaac and received the blessing Isaac had intended to pass to Esau. But this deceit had tragic consequences.

When the plot was uncovered, Esau became so angry with his brother that he determined to kill Jacob as soon as their father died. Becoming aware of that plot, the desperate Rebekah convinced Isaac to send Jacob to Haran to find a bride among her relations. Jacob fled north...and Rebekah never saw her favorite son again. How much she must have missed him during the last years of her life. Her deceit had deprived her of her favorite son's company, and left her to live out her days with Esau and his wives who Scripture says were "a grief of mind" to her (Gen. 26:35).

Yet Jacob's flight proved to be the making of her son. On the long journey north, God spoke to him. During the twenty long years he spent with his mother's relatives, Jacob grew from a pampered mother's boy into a strong and faith-filled man.

EXPLORING HER RELATIONSHIPS

Rebekah's relationship with her family. Rebekah must have had a good relationship with her family, for when Abraham's servant was negotiating a bride for Isaac, her mother and brother wanted to wait ten days before letting Rebekah depart. When the servant wanted to leave right away, they said they would ask Rebekah's opinion. Such deference to a young woman's feelings was not required by that culture. Laban and Bethuel cared for and respected Rebekah's feelings. The blessing they gave on her departure also reveals the special place she held in their hearts:

> "Our sister, may you become
> The mother of thousands of ten thousands;
> And may your descendants possess
> The gates of those who hate them."
> —Gen. 24:60

Rebekah's relationship with Isaac. Rebekah, on realizing she was about to meet the man who would become her husband, modestly "took a veil and covered herself" (Gen. 24:65). "Then Isaac brought her into his mother Sarah's tent; and he took Rebekah and she became his wife, and he loved her" (Gen. 24:67).

Evidence of Isaac's love. Interestingly, Rebekah had in common with her great-aunt Sarah not only her beauty, but also her infertility problem. Rebekah and Isaac had to wait for twenty years before they were able to have a child. Isaac must have known her broken-heartedness, because when he prayed for a son his plea was "for his wife" (Gen. 25:21). How good it is to see this kind of loving concern twenty years into a marriage.

The changed relationship after childbirth. Most people realize that each time a child is added to the family, the dynamics of family relationships are affected. This was certainly true in the case of Isaac and Rebekah. She gave birth to twin sons. The arrival of the twins, each with a distinct personality, drives, and desires, seems to have impacted the marriage almost from the day of their birth.

Esau, the first-born, was red and hairy. He was an outdoorsman who loved to hunt (Gen. 25:27). Jacob, on the contrary, is described as smooth-skinned and "a mild man, dwelling in tents" (Gen. 25:27). Evidently, each parent chose a favorite. "Isaac loved Esau because he ate of his game, but Rebekah loved Jacob" (Gen. 25:28).

Invisible battle lines were now drawn in the family. Before the twins' birth, God told Rebekah the older would serve the younger (Gen. 25:23). We can assume Rebekah shared this word with her husband. However, when Isaac felt death approaching, he planned to bless Esau. Rebekah, not about to let her favorite lose out, planned a clever ruse to deceive Isaac and steal the blessing for Jacob. Rebekah's premeditated trickery and lying suggest the once intimate relationship between this husband and wife no longer existed.

Rebekah's relationship with Esau (Gen. 25:28). Genesis 25:28 sums up the relationship in a nutshell: "Isaac loved Esau ... but Rebekah loved Jacob." Rebekah had no love for Esau.

Ironically, while Abraham had a servant search for a bride for Isaac, Isaac made no similar effort for Esau. With no arrangements made by his father, Esau chose two Hittite wives. "And they were a grief of mind to Isaac and Rebekah" (Gen. 26:35).

With no love for Esau or either of his wives, Rebekah set out to get Isaac's blessing for her favorite, Jacob. She failed to consider how Esau or Isaac would react to this devious plan. The story does not portray Rebekah as an unconditionally loving mother. She reserved her love for Jacob alone, even excluding her husband from her intentions as time passed.

Rebekah's relationship with Jacob. Rebekah's plot succeeded in deceiving Isaac into giving his blessing to her favorite rather than to Esau. When she realized that Esau was so angry with Jacob that he planned to kill his brother when their father died, Rebekah was forced to act. We're told in Genesis 27 that she spoke to Isaac, complaining,

> *"I am weary of my life because of the daughters of Heth; if Jacob takes a wife of the daughters of Heth, like these who are the daughters of the land, what good will my life be to me?"*
>
> *Then Isaac called Jacob and blessed him, and charged him, and said to him: "You shall not take a wife from the daughters of Canaan. Arise, go to*

*... the house of ... your mother's father; and take yourself a wife from
there of the daughters of Laban your mother's brother."*

—Gen. 27:46—28:2

This guidance, which should have been provided for Esau too, was a
guise for getting Jacob out of his brother's sight. Rebekah told Jacob to go
to her brother's "And stay with him a few days, until your brother's fury
turns away, until your brother's anger turns away from you, and he forgets
what you have done to him" (Gen. 27:44, 45). Ironically, in doing this,
Rebekah sacrificed ever seeing the one she loved most again. Jacob was gone
for twenty years, and his mother died before he returned.

A CLOSE-UP

The story of Rebekah at the well is often featured in children's books.
A pretty young teenage girl went to the well to get water, and as God's perfect timing would have it, she appeared just as Abraham's servant finished
praying about a wife for Isaac.

Rebekah is described as "very beautiful." She also seems to have been
brave, because she was ready to go without delay when she was asked if she
would go with this man on a 400 mile journey to marry her cousin.

As a wife she knew first-hand the sorrow of being barren, but she likewise knew the joy of answered prayer when at last she conceived. We also have
evidence of earlier communion with the Lord. Genesis 25:22, 23 tells us,

*But the children struggled together within her; and she said, "If all is well,
why am I like this?" So she went to inquire of the LORD; And the LORD said
to her: "Two nations are in your womb, two people shall be separated from
your body; one people shall be stronger than the other; and the older shall
serve the younger."*

Rebekah was more than one woman. In her early years she was a virgin, veiling herself modestly before meeting the man she would marry. In
her middle years she was a beloved wife, for whom Isaac labored in prayer.

But as a mother, Rebekah played favorites. The early intimacy with Isaac was lost, and the family unity was shattered with many tragic consequences.

AN EXAMPLE FOR TODAY

◆ From Rebekah we can learn the importance of loving our children for themselves. To play favorites with our children divides a family.

◆ In Rebekah's actions we can see how crucial it is for parents to communicate with each other and have united intentions for their children.

◆ We can also see how deceit creates barriers, even between persons who have had a loving and intimate relationship with each other. The consequences of dishonesty can tear loved ones apart and have an impact on the rest of their lives.

Rhoda

Scripture References: *Acts 12:13–16*

HER ROLE IN SCRIPTURE

All we know of Rhoda is told in these few verses in Acts:

> *And as Peter knocked at the door of the gate, a girl named Rhoda came to answer. When she recognized Peter's voice, because of her gladness she did not open the gate, but ran in and announced that Peter stood before the gate. But they said to her, "You are beside yourself!" Yet she kept insisting that it was so. So they said, "It is his angel." Now Peter continued knocking; and when they opened the door and saw him, they were astonished.*
>
> —Acts 12:13–16

BIBLE BACKGROUND: DOOR KEEPING
ACTS 12:13–16

In Jerusalem, houses were set side by side with their outside walls facing the street. The doors in these walls were kept closed, ensuring the family's privacy and safety. The door had no windows or peepholes. Instead the doorkeeper was expected to recognize the voice of family friends and open the door only for friends.

These verses in Acts accurately depict this situation. Rhoda, the servant girl, answered a knock on the door and was stunned to recognize Peter's voice.

One other element of this event is interesting. The company inside suggested that what Rhoda really heard was Peter's "angel." First-century Jews commonly believed that each person's guardian angel closely resembled him or her. Peter's friends thought it may have been his angel speaking rather than Peter himself!

Even though Rhoda is mentioned only briefly, we know several important things about her. Rhoda was a "girl." The Greek word used suggests that she was probably around twelve years old, but she participated in the prayer gathering. While Rhoda may have been a servant girl, her enthusiasm shows that she was deeply involved in the life of the Jerusalem congregation. When she heard Peter's voice, it was "because of her gladness" (v. 14) that she ran back without opening the door. She was excited and thrilled and eager to share the news with those inside.

Rhoda was also a persistent girl. She didn't let the doubts of those inside sway her. She "kept on insisting" (v. 15) that it was really Peter. While those inside argued, Peter kept on knocking and they were astonished when they saw him.

Rhoda had been right!

AN EXAMPLE FOR TODAY

◆ To see Rhoda, a young servant girl, at prayer with leaders of the Jerusalem church provides us a healthy reminder. In Christ there is no social class. God values the prayers of every believer. As God's children we are to love, accept, and value one another.

◆ Rhoda's life involved menial tasks, as ours often does. No calling or task, when performed in the Lord's name, is so menial that it fails to honor Him.

~ *Rizpah* ~

Scripture References: *2 Samuel 3:7; 21:1–14*
When They Lived: *About 1025 B.C.*
Name: *Rizpah [RIZ-puh: "glowing coal"]*
Historical Significance: *The rumor that Abner had sex with Rizpah, Saul's concubine, led to the unification of Israel under David.*

HER ROLE IN SCRIPTURE

Rizpah was a concubine or secondary wife of King Saul, who bore Saul two sons. As a concubine Rizpah had little status or influence. Yet she proved to be the focus of two defining events.

The fall and rise of kingdoms (2 Sam. 3:7). After Saul's death his commanding general, Abner, had placed Saul's son, Ishbosheth on the throne. While the tribe of Judah anointed David as king, Abner was able to keep the ten northern tribes loyal to Ishbosheth. But then Ishbosheth heard a rumor that Abner had had sex with Rizpah, his father Saul's concubine. Upset because, if true, the act might suggest Abner intended to take the throne of Israel for himself, Ishbosheth confronted and accused Abner.

Abner was deeply offended. It had been his influence and his influence alone that kept the northern tribes loyal to Ishbosheth. Abner's honor impugned, the angry general initiated negotiations with David to transfer the kingdom to him. Thus a mere rumor about Rizpah led to the end of

Saul's dynasty, and the establishment of the Davidic dynasty that is so significant in Israel's history.

A catalyst of reconciliation (2 Sam. 21:1–14). When a three-year
famine devastated Israel during David's reign, David asked God to reveal the
reason. The answer was that the famine was a punishment for Saul's attempt
to exterminate the Gibeonites.

The Gibeonites had tricked Joshua into making a treaty with them some
400 years earlier (see Josh. 9). They had remained in the land ever since,
protected by the ancient treaty, but they were essentially slaves of the
Israelites. Saul apparently decided to wipe them out, possibly in a misguid-
ed attempt to regain God's favor by purging the land of foreign elements.
Saul's campaign against the Gibeonites was a violation of an ancient treaty
sworn to in the name of the Lord, and God was displeased.

David then approached the Gibeonites and asked how he could make
atonement for Saul's sin against them. The Gibeonites refused financial
reparations, and instead asked permission to execute seven of Saul's descendants. David agreed and turned over five sons of Merab (Saul's daughter)
and the two sons of Rizpah, Saul's concubine. It may well be that these men
were asked for specifically because they were involved in Saul's war against
the Gibeonites. At any rate, the seven were executed during harvest time,
and the Gibeonites were appeased.

The story does not end here. Rizpah determined to guard the bodies of
her sons. She spread sackcloth, symbolic of overwhelming grief, and settled
down to keep the bodies safe from birds and animals. Day and night, for five
long months, from harvest to the region's late rains, Rizpah kept vigil over
the remains of her loved ones.

When David was told of what Rizpah was doing, he was so deeply
moved that he went to Jabesh Gilead to collect the bones of Saul and
Jonathan which had been taken there after being recovered from the
Philistines (1 Sam. 31:11–13). He also collected the bones of the seven and
buried them all in the tomb of Kish, Saul's father. The saga of Saul thus
ended with an honorable burial with his ancestors. For David, this may have
been a gesture of reconciliation with the man who had persecuted him in a

vain attempt to keep him from Israel's throne. Following this, the famine ended.

A CLOSE-UP

We know so little about Rizpah's life. The text tells us only that she lived with Saul and bore him two sons. We know that later she was the subject of gossip. We may suspect from Abner's reaction when accused that Rizpah was innocent of any liaison with him.

The only impressions of Rizpah as a person that we can glean are to be found in the story of her sons' execution. That execution left her a childless widow, a terribly vulnerable position for a woman in ancient Israel. Yet rather than mourn for herself, Rizpah set out to guard the remains of her two sons. She spread sackcloth on the rocky outcropping where the bodies had been left exposed and settled down to watch over her children. "She did not allow the birds of the air to rest on them by day nor the beasts of the field by night" (2 Sam. 21:10). Day after day she bore the heat of the sun; night after night she struggled to stay awake and alert. With utter dedication that provoked the sympathy of King David, Rizpah memorialized her sons with a mother's love and loyalty.

Rizpah could have done nothing to save them. But she was determined save them from the ultimate disgrace.

In a real sense Rizpah represents every mother who has grieved over the loss of a child; every mother who has longed for a child's memory to be honored. Her display of courage won for her sons an honorable burial. By her actions Rizpah won the respect and pity of David and all who understand the grief she felt for her sons, and the will she had to sacrifice for their honor.

AN EXAMPLE FOR TODAY

◆ Rizpah grieved in a positive, non-destructive way. Nothing can assuage the pain of losing loved ones, whether they die unfairly or as a consequence of their actions. But there is always a positive way we can answer the loss. Parents who have lost a child to a drunk driver often lobby for enforcement of drunk driving laws. We should do whatever we can to help others redeem the loss and thus find healing.

◆ Rizpah's experience somewhat foreshadows the truth expressed in Romans 8:28. However great the tragedy, God can redeem it. In this case Rizpah's pitiable heroism was the catalyst for closure. After David moved Saul's and Jonathan's bones, along with the remains of the seven who were executed, and buried them in the tomb of Saul's father, the three-year famine in Israel came to an end.

◆ The innocent blood David sacrificed to God's justice for the peace of Israel also foreshadows God's sacrifice of His Son to His justice for the peace of the world.

⌁ Ruth & Naomi ⌁

Scripture References: *The Book of Ruth; Matthew 1:5*
When They Lived: *About 1100 B.C.*
Names: *Ruth [rooth:"friendship"]*
Naomi [nay-OH-mee:"pleasantness"]
Historical Significances: *Ruth the Moabitess, influenced by her mother-in-law Naomi, married an Israelite and their son became the grandfather of David, in the line of Christ.*

THEIR ROLE IN SCRIPTURE

Ruth was a Moabitess who married an Israelite. Her husband's family had left Judah during a famine and migrated to Moab. There all the men of the family died, leaving alone and helpless Naomi and her daughters-in-law, Ruth and Orpah. The women were helpless because property was owned by men. With no men or male heirs left in the family, the women had no property rights or means of support.

Only one course of action seemed open to Naomi. She would return to Judah and seek aid from her relatives. Naomi urged her daughters-in-law to return to their fathers' households, where they would be supported until they could remarry. Orpah reluctantly followed Naomi's advice, but Ruth insisted on staying with her mother-in-law in spite of the risks ahead. The loyalty and support she offered Naomi proved to be the turning point in her own life.

EXPLORING THEIR RELATIONSHIPS

The Book of Ruth is a rich source of insights into healthy interpersonal relationships. It reminds us that even during the dark days of the judges, godly men and women could and did live blessed and happy lives.

Naomi and Ruth's relationship with God (Ruth 1:9–17). Ruth's relationship with God began the way that most relationships with Him do. Ruth came to know and value someone who knew Him well. For Ruth, that person was Naomi.

Naomi spoke easily about God because He was real to her. We see this in the blessing she gave her two daughters-in-law after deciding to return to Judah: "The LORD grant that you may find rest, each in the house of her husband" (Ruth 1:9). Naomi clearly loved her daughters-in-law and loved God. In loving she became the bridge over which Ruth passed to faith.

The biblical text clearly shows that Ruth realized that her decision to go with Naomi called for a faith-commitment to Naomi's God. When Naomi continued to urge Ruth to return home, Ruth answered firmly with her famous words of devotion.

"For wherever you go, I will go;
And wherever you lodge, I will lodge;
Your people shall be my people,
And your God, my God.
Where you die, I will die,
And there will I be buried.
The LORD do so to me, and more also,
If anything but death parts you and me."
                                    —Ruth 1:16, 17

The order in which Ruth expressed her commitment is significant. In Old Testament times Israel alone had a covenant relationship with God. Ruth pledged that "your people shall be my people," fully aware that in committing herself to God's covenant community she was also committing herself to Israel's God.

Ruth's decision to stay with Naomi was also her commitment to God. Ruth had chosen "the LORD God of Israel, under whose wings you have come for refuge" (Ruth 2:12).

Ruth's relationship with Naomi. The first chapter of Ruth makes it clear that Ruth deeply loved and appreciated her mother-in-law. That love was expressed in a loyalty that surpassed all other ties. Rather than return to her father's home, and stay in her own country, Ruth chose to accompany Namoi into an uncertain future in a strange land.

To see how Ruth's commitment to her mother-in-law continued to work itself out is fascinating. For Ruth, Judah was a strange land, with unfamiliar customs. But in Naomi Ruth had a mentor, and she wisely followed her advice. The two women had returned at harvest time. Old Testament Law provided that the poor and landless could gather food in fields owned by others. That law said, "When you reap the harvest in your field, and forget a sheaf in the field, you shall not go back to get it; it shall be for the stranger, the fatherless, and the widow, that the LORD your God may bless you in all the work of your hands" (Deut. 24:19). Naomi sent Ruth out to gather grain that the harvesters missed, a process called gleaning.

Gleaning was hard work, but for the poor each kernel of grain was precious. And Ruth "continued from morning" until late in the day gathering food for Naomi and herself.

Later, after Ruth's modesty and virtue had won the admiration of one of Naomi's relatives, Naomi explained to Ruth the law of the redeeming relative or kinsman redeemer. When a man died childless a near relative could marry his widow. The first son produced by the couple would be given the name of the dead husband and inherit his estate. Hearing of the admiration of such a relative for Ruth, Naomi urged Ruth to approach the man and ask him to take on the redeeming relative's responsibility.

Ruth allowed herself to be guided by her mother-in-law in the selection of a potential husband. Although Naomi's choice was neither young nor especially handsome, Ruth realized that he was a man of quality, and she followed her mother-in-law's advice.

In every way Ruth showed herself to be loyal, hard-working, sensible, and responsive to Naomi's advice. Clearly Ruth had a deep respect for Naomi, as well as a real love for her mother-in-law.

Ruth's relationship with Boaz. It is difficult to overemphasize the importance of a woman's reputation. Long before Boaz met Ruth or knew her by sight, he had heard good things about her.

In the small farming community it was impossible to keep secrets. Everyone knew that Naomi had come back from Moab and that she was accompanied by her daugher-in-law, Ruth. They knew of Ruth's choice to commit herself to Naomi's people and their God, and they had formed definite opinions about her character. When Boaz first met her he was able to say,

"It has been fully reported to me, all that you have done for your mother-in-law since the death of your husband, and how you have left your father and your mother and the land of your birth, and have come to a people whom you did not know before."

—Ruth 2:11

Well aware of her good qualities, Boaz treated her favorably. He invited her to eat with his harvesters, told her to glean with his own servants, and instructed the young men not to molest her. That this instruction was necessary reminds us of how dangerous life could be for a woman alone in the era of the judges. Boaz even instructed his harvesters to be sure to leave handfuls of grain for Ruth to collect.

When Naomi learned of what had happened and realized that Boaz was a near relative of hers, she rejoiced that God was opening a door for Ruth. She instructed Ruth to continue to work in Boaz's fields through the barley and wheat harvests. When the several weeks of the harvests had passed, Naomi took Ruth aside and explained her concern for Ruth's future security.

As a near relative, Boaz was qualified not only to marry Ruth but also to reclaim for her the lands of Naomi's husband. So Naomi told Ruth how to approach Boaz.

During the harvest season workers often slept with the harvested grain. Naomi told Ruth to go at night to the place where Boaz was sleeping and lie down at his feet. Some have taken this as an attempted seduction. However, it is clear that Ruth took a service posture at his feet, not his side. She requested that Boaz take her under his protection as a wife. Boaz clearly understood the symbolism and promised to do as she requested, "for all the people of my town know that you are a virtuous woman" (Ruth 3:11).

Before Boaz could marry Ruth he had to obtain the permission of a man who was an even nearer relative of Naomi. When Boaz explained that to redeem the fields of Naomi's dead husband the man would also have to marry Ruth, the man declined. He already had grown sons. If he should father more than one son with Ruth, he would have to provide for them from the estate he intended to reserve for his first family. With this claim disposed of, Boaz married Ruth.

The marriage was blessed with a son, and that son became the grandfather of King David and an ancestor of Jesus Christ.

A CLOSE-UP

Ruth is one of Scripture's most noble and attractive women. She had a marvelous capacity for love and loyalty. While Ruth was decisive and ready to risk an uncertain future out of loyalty to Naomi, she was far from headstrong. She was wise enough to follow Naomi's advice, ready and willing to work to support the two of them. Ruth quickly established a good reputation in her adopted homeland and won the approval of all who knew her. Her reputation rather than her physical attributes first won the admiration of Boaz, who responded by treating her graciously. The relationship that grew between them was founded solidly on the mutual appreciation of each for the good and gracious qualities of the other.

While Ruth's life truly is a love story, it is far richer than romantic novels that emphasize only passion and physical attraction. The love shared by Ruth and Boaz grew out of a commitment to things valued far more than mere good looks.

A CLOSE-UP

Naomi's name, which means "pleasantness," abbreviates the tender way she cared for her daughters-in-law and earned their love and loyalty. Even Orpah, who chose to remain in Moab, wept when she left Naomi to return home. We can sense in Naomi an especially generous spirit. Although she would be alone, she urged her daughters-in-law to think of their own future rather than Naomi's welfare. Later in Judah, Naomi felt a deep responsibility to Ruth and determined to "seek security" for her, "that it may be well with you" (Ruth 3:1).

With such character, it is not surprising that Naomi was such a powerful influence in Ruth's life. People who love sacrificially tend to draw others to them and through them to the Lord.

EXAMPLES FOR TODAY

- Naomi is a wonderful example of lifestyle evangelism. She didn't try to talk Ruth into the faith. Instead she loved Ruth and lived a life that inspired Ruth to love and trust her. Ruth wanted the peace, character, and loving-kindness she saw displayed in her mother-in-law's life.
- Naomi shows us how to be a gracious in-law. We don't know whether Naomi had counseled her sons against marrying out of their faith. We do know that she loved both her daughters-in-law enough to put their welfare above her own and eventually she did love Ruth to faith in God.
- Many parents hesitate to offer advice to adult children. While we cannot force our will on them, we can share our thoughts and our wisdom with those willing to listen. When advice is given lovingly and with respect for our children's independence, it will often be welcomed.

◆ Naomi is a glorious reminder of how God can transform a life from obscurity to glory. When we feel insignificant we can remember how a starving widow was used to win an ancestor of Jesus Christ to faith in God.

◆ Ruth reminds us that Godly character does count.

Salome

Scripture References: *Matthew 20:20–23; 27:56;*
Mark 15:40; 16:1; John 19:25

When They Lived: *About A.D. 30*

Name: *Salome [suh-LOE-mee:"peaceable"]*

Historical Significance: *She was the mother of Jesus' disciples James and John.*

HER ROLE IN SCRIPTURE

Salome was married to Zebedee and was the mother of the disciples James and John. She herself was a follower of Jesus, and on one occasion tried to influence Christ to favor her two sons.

EXPLORING HER RELATIONSHIPS

Salome's relationship with Jesus. While she is not mentioned frequently, Salome had known Jesus from the beginning of His public ministry.

Salome's early relationship with Jesus (Matt. 4:21; Mark 1:19–20; Luke 5:10). After Jesus was baptised, He spent time in Capernaum, the hometown of Peter, James, and John. Jesus became a familiar figure in the home of Peter and Zebedee. Salome would have known the young Teacher from nearby Nazareth through her two sons. Undoubtedly Jesus had visited Zebedee's home and eaten there with His disciples.

Mark 15:41 lists Salome as one of the women who followed Jesus in Galilee and "ministered to him" there.

Salome's attempt to influence Jesus (Matt. 20:20–24). While we can assume that Salome continued to follow Jesus and help support His ministry, the next time she is mentioned is in Matthew 20:20–23. It was late in Jesus' ministry near the Passover at which Jesus would be crucified.

> *Then the mother of Zebedee's sons came to Him with her sons, kneeling down and asking something from Him. And He said to her, "What do you wish?" She said to Him, "Grant that these two sons of mine may sit, one on Your right hand and the other on the left, in Your kingdom."*
>
> —Matt. 20:20, 21

It's significant that Salome felt comfortable making this request for her sons. She had followed Jesus faithfully, and she knew that He would listen to her. But when Jesus responded, He spoke to the two disciples, not their mother. She had asked, but they had apparently encouraged her.

Jesus was not able to grant Salome's request, but when the other disciples heard about it, they were angry with the two brothers, not with her. Most likely they knew Salome well and realized she would not be so bold if her sons had not urged her.

Salome's presence with Jesus to the end (Matt. 27:56; Mark 15:40; 16:1). The text places Salome at the Cross with the other women who were Jesus' most faithful follows. Salome was also among those who carried spices to the garden tomb that first Easter morning to discover the empty tomb.

And so Salome was one of those disciples who had followed Jesus from the beginning and who continued with Him to the end.

Salome's relationship with her sons (Matt. 20:20–23). Aside from the occasion on which Salome interceded with Jesus on behalf of her sons, we do not see them together. At first we might read her request as the typical attempt of a doting mother to gain an advantage for her sons, but then the reactions of Jesus and His other disciples are evidence that Salome loved her sons and only did as they asked. She surely would have been delighted had Jesus agreed, but we shouldn't assume that the advancement of her sons was any motivation for following Jesus. Her presence at the Cross clarifies this. Any such motivation would have died with Jesus and yet it was Him that Salome was mourning with the other women.

A CLOSE-UP

We are told little of Salome. She was a wife and mother. She was a faithful follower and supporter of Jesus. She knew Jesus from at least the beginning of His mission, and she stayed close by Him to the end.

Salome was not a leader; the leader of the little band of women was Mary Magdalene. Salome was possibly a little older than the others and she was trusted by the women and by the Twelve as well. That she was trusted by the men can be seen in that when "the ten heard" of Salome's request, "they were greatly displeased *with the two brothers*" (Matt. 20:24). Salome's request on behalf of her sons was so out of character that all immediately recognized the hand of James and John, and they may have been offended at their using Salome in that way. Guileless and faithful, Salome was appreciated by all.

AN EXAMPLE FOR TODAY

◆ Salome and her sons learned an important lesson that we would do well to remember. The desire for prominence arises out of our humanity. Putting others before ourselves is a sign of spiritual growth for we are called to be like Jesus.

The Samaritan Mother

Scripture References: 2 Kings 6:25–33

HER ROLE IN SCRIPTURE

The story of this unnamed woman tears at our hearts. Yet it contains a vital warning we need to heed. A Syrian army surrounded Samaria, the capital of Israel. All food was gone, and starvation stalked the narrow streets. Desperate, two women agreed to kill and eat their young sons. After the first woman's child had been eaten, the second hid her child and refused to fulfill her promise.

The first woman appealed to the king. Horrified, the king directed his anger against God and against God's prophet, Elisha, despite the fact that it was the evils done by the king and his people that caused God's judgment to fall on Israel. When the king reached Elisha, the prophet stunned him by announcing that the very next day food would be so plentiful that it would sell at half-price!

That night the Syrian army was overcome by mindless terror and fled, leaving all supplies behind. Elisha's impossible promise was fulfilled.

AN EXAMPLE FOR TODAY

- The woman serves as a warning. Under stress we may be tempted to do something we would never consider under normal circumstances, but it is never right to do wrong.
- The story also encourages us. We cannot know what God might do tomorrow to relieve the situation and the fears that drive us. We need to trust in Him and do right, expecting Him to act.

The Samaritan Woman

Scripture References: *John 4:6–42*

See also pages 297–298.

When They Lived: *About A.D. 30*

Historical Significance: *She believed in Jesus as the Messiah and introduced Him to her fellow villagers.*

HER ROLE IN SCRIPTURE

The woman Jesus met by Jacob's well was a Samaritan. This alone made her unclean in Jewish eyes and meant that no religious Jew would have any contact with her. It is no wonder then that the woman was amazed when Jesus spoke to her as she came to the well (see John 4:9).

In the conversation, Jesus' intimate knowledge of her life convinced the woman Jesus was a prophet. When Christ identified Himself as the promised Messiah the woman believed. She hurried back to her village and told everyone about Jesus, and the people came out to see Him for themselves. The Bible tells us that "many of the Samaritans of that city believed in Him because of the word of the woman who testified, 'He told me all that I ever did'" (John 4:39). After listening to Jesus many more believed, telling the woman, "'Now we believe, not because of what you said, for we ourselves have heard Him and we know that this is indeed the Christ, the Savior of the world'" (John 4:42).

EXPLORING HER RELATIONSHIPS

Her relationship with her "husbands" (John 4:16–18). As the two talked, it became clear the woman was living an immoral life. As Jesus told her, "'You have had five husbands, and the one whom you now have is not your husband'" (John 4:18). Like many today this woman was so hungry for love and a relationship that she welcomed anyone who would have her—even though there was no commitment involved.

Her relationship with the villagers (John 4:5–7). The text tells us that the woman came to the well "about the sixth hour," or 9:00 A.M. She also came alone. This tells us much about the relationship this woman had with other villagers. Normally, early in the morning the women of a village went to the local well together, their water jars balanced on their heads. The early morning walk to and from the well to get the day's water was a valued social time for women. The Samaritan woman's appearance alone at this late hour suggests that she was an outcast.

Her relationship with Jesus (John 4:6–26). John carefully records the conversation and traces the process by which Jesus brought her to faith.

Jesus asked for a drink (John 4:6, 7). Jesus was thirsty, so the request was natural. At the same time it was a wise way to strike up a conversation. In asking for help, Jesus diffused any impression that He had a superior attitude and looked down on the woman.

The woman asked a question (John 4:9, 10). Given the antagonism that existed between Jews and Samaritans the question could have been predicted. The woman was surprised that Jesus would speak to her, much less display a willingness to drink from a cup handed to him by a Samaritan.

Jesus redirected her attention to the "gift of God" (John 4:10). The real answer to the woman's question lay in the identity of the One who spoke to her. Jesus was the One who came bringing "living water." "Living water" meant running water, such as that which comes from a flowing stream. Only "living water" could be used in the baths taken in Judaism to purify a person who was unclean. Christ had come with that gift of God that would purify believers from all sin.

Jesus explained His offer (John 4:13, 14). When the woman expressed confusion (4:11, 12) Jesus continued to speak symbolically. The person to whom Jesus gave His living water would never thirst, but have everlasting life. The water was a symbol of the Holy Spirit who would vitalize and give life to those whom Jesus had come to save.

The woman asked for "this water" (4:15). The woman still did not grasp what Jesus was saying. She continued to take His metaphor literally.

Jesus asked her to "call your husband" (John 4:16). Jesus had initially asked for water because He was thirsty and needed a drink. He then led the woman back to her own true thirst. When she said she had no husband, Jesus revealed that He was fully aware of her life and her brokenness. The woman was lost, empty, and in desperate need of the rebirth Jesus had to offer.

The woman changed the subject (John 4:19–24). When the woman realized that Jesus was fully aware of her life, she acknowledged Him as a prophet and changed the subject by asking a theological question that was a bone of contention between Jews and Samaritans…When feeling convicted, many people tend to follow the path chosen by the woman. If Jesus had been an ordinary rabbi, He might have been distracted by this question. Many scholars are delighted to display their knowledge!

Jesus dismissed her question as irrelevant. The time has come to worship God in spirit and in truth, and God is seeking such people to worship Him in that manner. The issue isn't theology; it's a personal loving relationship with God and His people.

The woman still hesitated (John 4:25). We can read the woman's next remark as another attempt to put off a decision. "'I know that Messiah is coming' (who is called Christ). 'When He comes, He will tell us all things.'" That is, "I think I'd just as soon wait for the Messiah to come for explanations!"

Jesus identified Himself as the Messiah (John 4:26). Jesus now announced:

"'I who speak to you am He,'" and the woman believed. Christ had led her to see both herself and Him more clearly. She had been exposed, and was revealed to Jesus. She had been gently, wisely, led to that point where she truly did believe.

Her new relationship with the villagers (John 4:39–42). Something happened in this woman who had discovered and believed in Jesus. She had been ashamed, hopeless, and isolated. Now she hurried back to tell everyone about Jesus who had "'told me all that I ever did.'" They listened to her, saw the change in her, and some believed because of her testimony. Her thirst had been quenched. Most of the villagers went out to see and hear Jesus for themselves. When Christ enters a life, the change He makes opens doors that once were closed.

A CLOSE-UP

The Samaritan woman was living a hopeless, immoral life, and her choices had cost her. The Samaritans, like the Jews, were a moral people who sought to honor God and keep the Old Testament Law. In such a community she found herself isolated from normal friendships; she was a lonely woman who finally despaired of ever drinking life and lasting love. When she met Jesus and He engaged her in conversation, she was less than open with Him. She perhaps purposely misunderstood what He was saying. When Jesus revealed that He knew her deepest secrets, she quickly tried to distract Him with a theological question. Later she intimated that she'd wait for the Messiah to appear before making any decisions. When Jesus identified Himself as the Savior of the world, all her defenses crumbled. She again knew her sin, her thirst, and her need of salvation. That God was actively pursuing her moved her deeply.

When the change wrought by faith came, it was complete. The woman whose guilt caused her to avoid people now sought them out. The woman who had tried to hide her sins was open about them: "'He told me all things that I ever did!'" (v. 29). Cleansed, filled, and reborn to life, she focused on Christ rather than on herself. The Samaritan woman became a vibrant and successful witness for Jesus Christ.

AN EXAMPLE FOR TODAY

- Sometimes we would rather argue the fine points of theology or doctrine than surrender ourselves to Christ and love others well. Our inner thirsts will only be quenched when we openly allow Christ to take us to our true thirst and fill us with His living water.
- Today's world generally derides biblical morality as Victorian. People are bombarded with the message that anything goes between consenting adults, and increasingly "adult" is being defined as "past puberty!" Yet sin

still evokes a natural awareness of guilt, however we struggle to ignore it. There is no joy to be found.

♦ The woman at the well discovered something in accepting Christ that she had long yearned for. Jesus gave her the unconditional acceptance and love that we all ache for. What the woman may have sought in many failed relationships, she found through faith in Jesus. And so can we today.

~ Samson's Mother ~

Scripture References: *Judges 13*
When They Lived: *About 1200 B.C.*
Historical Significance: *She carefully followed God's instructions concerning Samson's birth and nurturing.*

HER ROLE IN SCRIPTURE

Samson was one of the last judges to appear in Israel. While gifted with extraordinary physical strength, Samson was morally and spiritually weak. His feud with the Philistines who dominated the Israelites in the 11th century B.C. was rooted in personal animosity rather than a passion to free his people. While Samson killed many Philistines during his lifetime, he never won freedom from oppression for his people.

It is clear from the story in Judges that Samson's flaws were his own and cannot be traced to his mother or to his father, Manoah. Both parents are portrayed as godly and good persons who did their best to respond to God and to give their son guidance.

EXPLORING HER RELATIONSHIPS

While the biblical text gives us little insight into Samson's mother's relationship with her son, we do gain insight into her relationship with God and with her husband.

Her relationship with God (Judg. 13:3, 9). Manoah's wife is described as a woman who was sterile and remained childless (13:2). It is impressive that many of the most significant women of the Bible remained childless for long periods of time before giving birth. In almost every case, the children produced had significant roles to play in God's plan for His people. It may be that the delay in bearing children had a significant impact on the spiritual life of the woman. Certainly in Rebekah and Hannah's case, the delay in child-bearing drove the women to seek God's face in prayer.

While we are not told that Manoah's wife went to pray, we are told that the Angel of the Lord appeared not to Manoah but to the wife. He informed her that she would have a child and instructed her to follow the rules imposed on those who made a Nazirite vow. This vow, which was voluntary, is described in Numbers 6:1–21. The person taking this vow was to avoid anything from the vine, anything that would make him unclean, and was not to cut his hair until resolution of the vow. The Lord told Manaoah's wife to follow the same rules until Samson was delivered. Samson then was to keep the vow his entire life. It is believed that Samuel and John the Baptist were also Nazarites from birth.

When Manoah's wife reported the encounter to him, Manoah prayed and asked for additional guidance. The Angel of the Lord appeared again—to Manoah's wife. She then hurried to call her husband, and the Angel instructed them both.

It is significant that the Angel of the Lord chose to appear to the wife rather than the husband. She was the one who would have to follow the Nazarite rules: the Angel informed her directly rather than going through her husband. The Nazaarite vow was an act of special consecration to God's headship often appealed to in times of crisis or injustice. Hence, the Lord's calling to observe such a vow veiled Manoah's headship over his wife during that time.

Her relationship with Manoah (Judg. 13:8, 12, 17–23). While Manoah did not doubt his wife's report of the angel encounter, Manoah was uncertain. He prayed that the "Man of God" might visit them again to tell them how to bring up the boy who was to be born. When the Angel of the Lord came again, he added nothing to the previous instructions.

Manoah pressed for more information and urged the Angel to let them prepare food. When the food was brought, "flame went up toward heaven from the altar" (v. 20) and the Angel of the Lord ascended in the flame. Both husband and wife fell with their faces to the ground, aware that their visitor had been God Himself in human or angelic guise. The couple's reaction is significant. While Manoah wailed, "We are doomed to die," his wife sensibly responded, "If the LORD had meant to kill us, he would not have accepted a burnt offering...nor shown us all these things or now told us this" (Judg. 13:23 NIV).

This reaction suggests there was also wisdom in the Angel's first visiting Manoah's wife, and it shows why Manoah prayed for another visit. Both Manoah and his wife were good people who later tried to guide their unruly son in godly ways. But their roles were somewhat reversed out of necessity. Manoah's wife was the sensible and stable partner in the marriage, while Manoah was the more uncertain and emotional. While she took the Angel's instructions to heart, he worried that they might not know enough to bring up the child who was to be born. While he was overcome with fear at the revelation that their visitor was divine, she accepted that reality and realized immediately that they were in no danger.

It's helpful to remember that stereotypes seldom provide an accurate picture of reality. Each person is different; each couple must work out their relationship in a way that reflects the personality of each individual.

Her relationship with Samson (Judg. 14:3). The text tells us that Samson's father and mother tried to counsel him against seeking a wife among the Philistines when Samson saw a woman he desired. It's clear that the parents were in harmony in urging Samson to marry an Israelite. But Samson was not to be deterred by his parents. As an adult Samson was guided by his passions, rather than by wisdom or by respect for his parents.

Samson insisted that his father "get her for me" (Judg. 14:4). As Samson's father, it was Manoah's responsibility to negotiate for his son's bride. In this case Manoah submitted to his son's demands, rather than the son submitting to his father's guidance. We can only assume that both parents, while they loved their son and had followed the Lord's instructions in raising him, were disappointed in his decision.

A CLOSE-UP

It is appropriate that we know this woman of the Bible only as Manoah's wife, for her unique character was displayed by implicit contrast with her husband. She recognized the "Man of God" as an angelic visitor, but rather than being overwhelmed she carefully noted and remembered His instructions exactly. Her husband is the one who was upset and uncertain, worried that his wife might have overlooked something important. But when the Angel of the Lord returned He had nothing to add to what the wife had remembered. When Manoah and his wife realized that the visitor had been God Himself Manoah was frightened and fell apart. But his wife remained calm and sensible, and reasoned that if God had intended them harm He would not have accepted their offering or spoken of their future. In every way Manoah's wife showed herself to be stable and astute, a truly rational person. In this marriage it was the wife who provided emotional steadiness and strength.

AN EXAMPLE FOR TODAY

- Samson's mother was an obedient and godly woman. When the Lord spoke, she listened and obeyed. We too are responsible to listen and obey.
- Samson's mother did her best to follow the instructions God gave her. Yet Samson made choices she advised against. Parents nurture their children, but children are responsible for their own decisions. They must decide whether they will heed their parents' guidance.
- Samson's choices in women caused his downfall and his death. His parents urged him to find an Israelite wife, but Samson would not listen. It's hard for parents to watch their children make disastrous choices in selecting a spouse. We can offer advice and pray, but we cannot choose for them. Often we will need the grace to live with

things we cannot change and to have faith in the God who works in all things for our good.

~ Sapphira ~

Scripture References: *Acts 5:1–11*
When They Lived: A.D. *35*
Name: *Sapphira [suh-FIGH-ruh:"beautiful"]*
Historical Significance: *Her death for lying to the Holy Spirit inspired awe of God in believers and unbelievers alike.*

HER ROLE IN SCRIPTURE

Sapphira and her husband Ananias were among the first in Jerusalem to become Christians. They were part of those first exciting days after Pentecost that Luke described in Acts 2:44–47.

> *Now all who believed were together, and had all things in common, and sold their possessions and goods, and divided them among all, as anyone had need. So continuing daily with one accord in the temple, and breaking bread from house to house, they ate their food with gladness and simplicity of heart, praising God and having favor with all the people.*

Like others in the little community of faith, Ananias and Sapphira sold property and brought money to the apostle Peter. The two had talked it over and decided to keep part of the proceeds while pretending to give all.

When Ananias brought the money to Peter he lied about the price for which the property was sold. He was immediately struck dead, and his body was carried out. Later, Peter asked Sapphira for the truth. She too lied, dropped dead and was carried out. The text tells us, "So great fear came upon all the church and upon all who heard these things" (Acts 5:11).

EXPLORING HER RELATIONSHIPS

Sapphira's relationship with God. We have no reason to doubt Sapphira's salvation. She and her husband were believers; they were active members of a vital and exciting Jerusalem church that emphasized teaching, prayer, worship, and a deep caring for others. Outwardly everything was going well in the couple's spiritual life.

But inwardly there were nagging doubts and divided loyalties. While the couple seems to have wanted a reputation for selfless generosity, they did not trust God enough to surrender all. They wanted somehow to love both God and money.

Sapphira's relationship with Ananias. It's ironic, but in some ways this pair had an "ideal" marriage. Ananias and Sapphira "agreed together" on the course of action they would take (Acts 5:9). Ananias didn't demand or command. They talked over what they intended to do, and agreed. In modern terms we'd say their relationship was marked by open and honest communication. We would also say that theirs was a mutual relationship: they were partners in life and shared in the decision making. They were in fact "one" in the course they chose, which is why they were one in its consequences!

Sapphira's relationship with other believers. Sapphira, like her husband, wanted to be well thought of by others. When Barnabas sold a piece of property and gave the money to the apostles to use for the needy, Sapphira and her husband may have felt some jealousy. They wanted for themselves the reputation for generosity that Barnabas merited. They wanted to be thought of as generous and selfless—even though they were *not* entirely selfless at all. The admiration of others was so important to them that they did not even consider what God might think of their actions.

Sapphira's relationship with Satan. When Peter confronted Ananias over his deceit, he asked, "Why has Satan filled your heart to lie to the Holy Spirit?" (Acts 5:3). The question does not imply that Satan had a foothold *within* the couple's personalities. Instead it recognizes that the "whole world lies under the sway of the wicked one" (1 John 5:19). Passions, motives, and desires that drove Satan to rebel against God, also drive human culture [the *kosmos*, "world"]. This couple yielded to the world's motives, and they permitted Satan to fill their hearts and direct their way.

Ananias and Sapphira could have resisted the temptation to deceive, and refused to let Satan fill their hearts. Sapphira was even given a second chance to turn from the road she'd chosen. Peter specifically asked her the amount received from the sale, but Sapphira was unfaithful to the end. And so she died.

Sapphira's relationship with Peter. Peter was, at the time, the presumptive leader of the Jerusalem church. He was the one who had preached the first gospel message and he participated in every important event recorded in early Acts. He was the one to whom large contributions were brought for distribution to the poor. It's possible that Sapphira and her husband were as eager to be well thought of by Peter as by others in the Christian community.

But Peter's leadership was rooted in his relationship with God. Both Sapphira and Ananias had overlooked this. When they brought their gift to Peter, God's Spirit revealed the fraud they intended.

A CLOSE-UP

Sapphira was a woman who had so many blessings. She had become a believer in Christ and was secure for eternity. She and her husband seem to have had a good, healthy marriage. She was part of a unique community of faith, marked by warm and caring relationships. Yet Sapphira was unsatisfied.

It wasn't enough for Sapphira and her husband to be ordinary members of that caring fellowship. They yearned to be recognized as special. They wanted others to think of them as "outstanding" believers, not as just two of the many. This concern for appearances, and hunger for the admiration of others proved to be a fatal flaw.

One other thing that we can note about Sapphira: her heart was not focused on the Lord. Despite the wonderful church of which she was a part, she apparently had not truly grasped who God is, nor had she committed herself completely to Him. If she had, she would have been less double-minded and definitely wiser before God who can neither be deceived nor mocked.

AN EXAMPLE FOR TODAY

- ◆ Sapphira reminds us that deceit is never acceptable to the Holy Spirit. We reveal Christ to others by living with them transparently, letting them see the changes that the Spirit works in us over time (see 2 Cor. 3:18). Pretense is still hypocrisy, and we lie not just to others but to the Holy Spirit.

- ◆ Most of us have wished at some time that we could be members of an "ideal" church. Sapphira had the apostles to disciple her and may have even seen Jesus, but rather than count her blessings she wanted more. How important it is to be thankful for what we have instead of lusting for more.

- ◆ Some have felt that the sentence passed on this pair was too severe. But their fate is a reminder that our loving Father usually allows His children to experience the consequences of wrong actions. Thankfully, this doesn't diminish His love for us or the grace and forgiveness He has promised. Nevertheless, it is clear that Sapphira and Ananias were held to a higher standard of single-mindedness, because they witnessed with their eyes many wondrous works of God through the apostles themselves.

- ◆ Jesus commended Thomas for believing so readily once he had seen. But He called them blessed who believe beyond what they have seen. Sapphira's life was forfeited for serving the deceiver after having such revealed assurance of God's work in her.

~ *Sarah* ~

Scripture References: *Genesis 11:29–31; 12:5–17;*
16:1–8; 17:15–21; 18:5–15;
20:2–18; 21:1–12; 24:36, 67;
25:10–12; 49:31; Isaiah 51:2;
Romans 4:19; 9:9; Galatians 4:21–31;
Hebrews 11:11; 1 Peter 3:6

When They Lived: *About 2100 B.C.*

Name: *Sarai [SAR-eye:"Yahweh is prince"],*
changed by God to Sarah
[SAR-uh: "Princess"].

Historical Significance: *She became a mother of nations and kings, and Jesus Christ was her descendant.*

HER ROLE IN SCRIPTURE

S arah was the wife and companion of the patriarch Abraham. In her 90s she became the mother of the miracle-child Isaac. God's covenant promises to Abraham were transmitted through Isaac and his descendants. Sarah thus became honored as the mother of the Jewish people, through whom God gave us not only the Scriptures but also the Savior, Jesus Christ. Sarah also was instrumental in Abraham's fathering of the Arab people.

Sarah's life story (Gen. 11:26–12:14). Sarah's life story rivals the best of modern romance literature.

A privileged beginning (Gen. 11:29). Sarah was married to Abraham in the magnificent city of Ur in Sumer in what is now southern Iraq. Although in 2100 B.C. Ur's glory days were fading, the city remained the center of a flourishing and prosperous society. Archaeologists have excavated Ur and uncovered objects of gold, silver, and precious stones, as well as the remains of chariots, musical instruments, weapons, and even game boards. Trade was carried out over a wide region, with ships going as far as India and Africa via the Persian Gulf. We know that Abraham, first known as Abram, was a wealthy man. So he and Sarai lived a privileged life in one of the ancient world's great cities.

A sudden jolting change (Gen. 12:1). Then God spoke to Abram telling him to leave the city and travel to an unknown land. Abram responded to God's command and assembled his tents, herds, flocks, herdsmen, and serving women suitable for a nomadic life. He and Sarai then left their past lives behind.

Sarai turned her back on all the luxuries and comforts an ancient city could afford a wealthy couple to follow God's call with her husband. She left her friends, her family, and all that was familiar, to share whatever Abram's future might bring. Strikingly, Sarai was probably about sixty years old at the time they started their travels!

Travel they did, going north along an ancient trade route that paralleled the Euphrates River to Haran. After a stay there, Abram, with Sarai and his nephew Lot, turned south until they reached Canaan. For most of their remaining lives, they would wander that sparsely populated land.

The unfulfilled dream (Gen. 16:1–3). Abram and Sarai had been in Canaan for ten years when Sarai gave up hope. She knew that God had promised Abram a son to whom the covenant promises would pass (Gen. 12:1–3). But Sarai became convinced that she was not destined to bear her husband's son.

Sarai's plight was not unusual. While women of nearly all ancient societies saw bearing children as both a duty and a privilege, some women remained childless. But in the Middle East a solution of sorts had been worked out. It was a wife's duty to give her husband sons. If she could not bear sons herself, she could at least provide a surrogate.

An Assyrian marriage contract dating from the 19th century B.C., translated in *The Ancient Near East*, Vol. II (1975), illustrates:

> *Laqipum has married Hatala, daughter of Enishru. ... If within two*
> *years she does not provide him with offspring, she herself will purchase a*
> *slavewoman, and later on, after she will have produced a child by him, he*
> *may then dispose of her by sale wheresoever he pleases. Should Laqipum*

choose to divorce her, he must pay five minas of silver; and should Hatala
choose to divorce him, she must pay five minas of silver. Witnesses: Masa,
Ashurishtikal, Talia, Shupianika.

—p. 72

According to the custom of the times, Abram had been patient with Sarai. But now, after decades of marriage and ten years of wandering in Canaan, Sarai felt compelled to fulfill her obligation to her husband. The Bible describes the turning point.

Now Sarai, Abram's wife, had borne him no children. And she had an
Egyptian maidservant whose name was Hagar. So Sarai said to Abram,
"See now, the LORD has restrained me from bearing children. Please, go in
to my maid; perhaps I shall obtain children by her." And Abram heeded the
voice of Sarai.

—Gen. 16:1, 2

The unexpected consequences (Gen. 16:4–10). This event was to have both immediate and far-reaching consequences. When Hagar conceived, it became immediately clear that even at age eighty-five Abram was not impotent. He had fathered a child! Whatever respect Hagar had for Sarai turned to contempt, and "her mistress became despised in her eyes" (Gen. 16:4). How this birth affected the relationship between the two women will be explored shortly.

The long-term consequences were far more serious. Hagar did bear Abram a child. That child, Ishmael, is the forefather of the Arab peoples, who throughout the centuries have been hostile to the descendants of Isaac who, in God's time, Sarai did give to her husband. We see that hostility today. The headlines continue to be filled with reports of conflict between Palestinian descendants of Ishmael and the Jews in modern Israel—descendants of Ishmael's half-brother, Isaac.

Birth of the miracle child (Gen. 17:1–22; 21:1–7). Ishmael grew up as a member of Abram's family, and Abram loved his son. With the passage of years an uneasy peace existed between Sarai and Hagar. Then, thirteen years after Ishmael's birth, when Abram was ninety-nine years old and Sarai ninety, God spoke to Abram and delivered a stunning message. Sarai was to bear Abram a son, and her son—rather than the son of her bondwoman—would inherit the covenant promises God had given to Abram. God's word to Abram about Sarai was "I will bless her and also give you a son by her; then I will bless her, and she shall be a mother of nations; kings of peoples shall be from her" (Gen. 17:16).

With the giving of that promise, God changed Abram's name to Abraham and Sarai's name to Sarah. And, despite the deadness of Sarah's womb, Sarah did become pregnant. A miracle child, the offspring of Abraham and his wife Sarah, grew in her womb and, when she was ninety and her husband one hundred, Isaac was born.

We can sense Sarah's relief and her delight when Isaac was born. "God has made me laugh," Sarah declared, "and all who hear will laugh with me. ...Who would have said to Abraham that Sarah would nurse children? For I have borne him a son in his old age" (Gen. 21:6, 7).

Conflict and resolution (Gen. 21:8–13). The next critical moment for Sarah came at a celebration marking the weaning of Isaac. In biblical times children were typically weaned at age three or four, so Ishmael would have been sixteen or seventeen years old. At the party Sarah saw Ishmael teasing Isaac (the NKJV says "scoffing"). Sarah exploded and demanded that Abraham "cast out this bondwoman and her son!" The tone of her demand shows both that the relationship of the two women was still marked by hostility, and that Sarah had little or no affection for Ishmael. Yet upon God's instruction, Abraham reluctantly met her demand. Abraham loved his son. To disinherit Ishmael, as Sarah demanded, would go counter to the established custom of accounting all recognized children of one father as equal. (*The Ancient Near East*, II p. 157)

Abraham resisted Sarah's urgings. But then God intervened and explicitly told Abraham to do as Sarah said. For good and compelling reasons, the line of inheritance through which the covenant promises were to pass, must remain clear and certain. Even so, God was more sensitive to Abraham's love for his son Ishmael than Sarah had been. God told Abraham that He Himself would care for Ishmael, and he, like Isaac, would father a great people.

Sarah revisited in the New Testament. If we limit ourselves to the Old Testament, it is clear that Sarai/Sarah played a significant role in the unfolding of God's plan. She was the faithful wife of Abraham, whose faith led him to leave Ur to follow a vision given him by God. She became the mother of Isaac, Abraham's son through whom the covenant promises of God were passed to succeeding generations.

While the Old Testament texts establish these facts and also give us insights into Sarah's personality, the New Testament highlights the significance of several critical points in her life.

Hebrews 11:11 focuses our attention on Sarah's faith, affirming that "by faith Sarah herself also received strength to conceive seed, and she bore a child when she was past the age, because she judged Him faithful who had promised." Sarah is one of only two women mentioned in Faith's Hall of Fame, as Hebrews 11 is often called.

First Peter 3:5, 6 portrays Sarah as a noble wife, who trusted in God and submitted to her husband.

But the most significant passage, Galatians 4:22–31, looks back and highlights the symbolic significance of Sarah and Hagar as symbols of the old and new covenants.

It is written that Abraham had two sons: the one by a bondwoman, the other by a freewoman. But he who was of the bondwoman was born according to the flesh, and he of the freewoman through promise, which things are symbolic. For these are the two covenants: the one from Mount Sinai which gives birth to bondage, which is Hagar—for this Hagar is Mount Sinai in Arabia, and corresponds to Jerusalem which now is, and is in bondage with her children—but the Jerusalem above is free, which is the mother of us all. For it is written: "Rejoice, O barren, you who do not bear! Break forth and shout, you who are not in labor! For the desolate has many more children than she who has a husband." Now we, brethren, as Isaac was, are children of promise. But, as he who was born according to the flesh then persecuted him who was born according to the Spirit, even so it is now. Nevertheless what does the Scripture say? "Cast out the bondwoman and her son, for the son of the bondwoman shall not be heir with the son of the freewoman." So then, brethren, we are not children of the bondwoman but of the free.

We can better see Paul's point that these two women represent two conflicting and irreconcilable systems by looking at the following chart:

The Symbolic Significance of

SARAH	HAGAR
Grace	Law
Reliance on God's promise	Reliance on self-effort
The heavenly Jerusalem	Jerusalem which is now
Christianity	Judaism
Freedom	Bondage

By any criteria, Sarah's role in Scripture is a significant one, both historically and symbolically. Yet Sarah was also a flesh and blood person, a woman of pride and passion, of character and convictions. Let us now examine Sarah the woman, with all her strengths and all her flaws.

EXPLORING HER RELATIONSHIPS

Sarah's relationship with God. A major indication of the nature of the relationship between Sarah and God is that God not only changed Abram's name to Abraham, but also changed Sarai's name to Sarah. Both changes took place in the context of blessing, for God told Abraham, "I will bless her and also give you a son by her; then I will bless her, and she shall be a mother of nations; kings of peoples shall be from her" (Gen. 17:16).

Not only was Sarah a recipient of God's grace, she was a woman with a faith comparable to Abraham's. Hebrews 11:11 says, "By faith Sarah herself also received strength to conceive seed, and she bore a child when she was past the age, because she judged Him faithful who had promised."

The Lord had watched Sarah's faithfulness for sixty years as she waited expectantly to become the mother of Abraham's heir. It is true that she faltered, but only after she could no longer see herself able to conceive. She still did not doubt that God would make Abraham the father of a great nation.

Sarah's relationship with Abraham. Sarah and Abraham had the same father, Terah, but had different mothers. Abraham married his half-sister while living in Ur. Abraham was seventy-five and Sarah sixty-five when they left Haran. They had left family and friends behind once before, but when Abraham told her they were going to move, she went willingly (Gen. 12:4).

Shared worship (Gen. 12:7, 8). While there is no record of direct interaction between Sarah and the Lord, the Genesis account clearly illustrates intimacy between Sarah and Abraham. It is safe to assume that Abraham shared his growing knowledge of and faith in the Lord with his wife. When Abraham and Sarah reached Canaan, the Lord again spoke to Abraham and told him that He would give the land of Canaan to Abraham's descendants. There Abraham built an altar to Him (Gen. 12:7, 8). In this we see Abraham's relationship with the Lord growing, not only as God spoke to him, but also as he responded to God. We assume that Sarah, too, worshiped the Lord with her husband.

Committed love (Gen. 12:11–13). When a famine prevailed in Canaan, Abraham and Sarah went to Egypt. Something strange intruded into Abraham and Sarah's relationship there. Abraham was afraid that the Egyptians would kill him so they could have his wife, because she had such a "beautiful countenance" (Gen. 12:11). Now remember, Sarah was already sixty-five years old!

Abraham asked her, "Say you are my sister, that it may be well with me for your sake, and that I may live because of you" (Gen. 12:13). Some commentaries speculate that Sarah must have had great animosity toward her husband for putting her in the position of becoming an Egyptian concubine. Perhaps she did. But Sarah was a woman with a mind of her own. This is the same woman who insisted Abraham take Hagar so he could have the son God promised. She is the same woman who reacted so strongly when the pregnant Hagar was disrespectful and insisted Abraham send Hagar and Ishmael away. It is hard to see the feisty Sarah as a victim. It is better to assume that Sarah simply loved Abraham dearly and now did as he requested out of love.

Sarah must have assumed there was good reason for her husband's fear. He asked her to say she was his sister to save his life. And, since they shared the same father, there was some basis for what she was asked to say. And so Sarah did as Abraham asked, as an act of devotion to her husband.

Sarah's compliance with Abraham's request may also be seen as an act of faith, much like Abraham's later compliance with God's command to bring Isaac to Mount Moriah to be offered as a sacrifice. God approved Abraham's faith and on the mountain provided a ram for the sacrifice. God may well have approved Sarah's faith too, and it was certainly well placed. For God protected her virtue when she was taken into the Egyptian harem (Gen. 12:17–20), and again later in a similar situation (Gen. 20:2–12).

Selfless giving (Gen. 16:1, 2). Sarah has often been criticized for giving Hagar to her husband as a surrogate. But consider. We don't know how many years Sarah was married to Abraham before they left Ur, but we do know that it was common in those days to marry by age thirteen or fifteen. It is likely that Sarah and Abraham had been married thirty-five years even before leaving Ur. Abraham was eighty-six when he became Ishmael's father and Sarah was ten years younger. If they married at age fifteen, Sarah had waited some sixty years, not the commonly accepted two years, before giving her slave to Abraham to produce his heir!

Why after waiting so long did she act when she did? We know that when women stop producing estrogen their skin begins to age more quickly. We also know that kings wanted Sarah in their harems when she was sixty-five (Gen. 20:2–8). The fact that she was still a ravishing beauty at this age would tend to indicate that Sarah remained fertile late in life. We can conjecture that as long as Sarah felt able to become pregnant she waited in faith, and only after she ceased menstruating did she consider the culturally approved alternative.

Commentators say that Sarah gave up too soon. In reality, Sarah waited faithfully, trusting far longer than any of us could imagine. When at last she believed she had passed her years of childbearing, she unselfishly offered her husband Hagar to provide the gift she thought she was now unable to give.

A shared burial (Gen. 23). Sarah's death is a poignant moment in the biblical record. The love this couple shared for each other during their life-long marriage is legendary. Abraham mourned his loss and he purchased a cave for his beloved's resting place. Forty-eight years later his sons laid Abraham to rest in that same cave.

Sarah's relationship with Hagar (Gen. 21:16). We have no record of the relationship between Sarah and Hagar before Sarah offered her slave to Abraham. But we have a clear record of what happened afterward.

After Hagar conceived (Gen. 16:1–11). When Hagar found herself pregnant, "her mistress became despised in her eyes" (Gen. 16:4). Hagar did not disguise her attitude, and Sarah then dealt harshly with her (Gen. 16:6). Hagar responded by running away, returning only after the Angel of the Lord sent her back and promised that her son Ishmael would father an innumerable people (Gen. 16:15). Hagar obeyed and submitted to Sarah.

Following this, there appears to have been at least a cool, civility between Hagar and Sarah. While Sarah may have eased up on the pregnant woman, there is no reason to believe that they were ever mutually warm or benevolent. Sarah's reference to Hagar as "this bondwoman" (Gen. 21:10) would indicate the opposite.

The final break (Gen. 21:8–18). The final break took place years later when Sarah demanded Abraham cast out this bondwoman and her son.

The text gives Sarah's motive and records God's support:

"For the son of this bondwoman shall not be heir with my son, namely with Isaac." And the matter was very displeasing in Abraham's sight because of his son. But God said to Abraham, "Do not let it be displeasing

in your sight because of the lad or because of your bondwoman. Whatever Sarah has said to you, listen to her voice; for in Isaac your seed shall be called."

—Gen. 21:10–12

Clearly God wanted no mistake about the line through which His covenant with Abraham would pass. God honored Abraham's son Ishmael by making him the father of the Arab nations. But God purposed that the covenant promises were passed on through Sarah's lineage, the freewoman, and not through Hagar, the bondwoman.

Sarah's relationship with Ishmael (Gen. 21:10). It is clear from at least two verses (Gen. 17:18; 21:11) that Abraham loved his son Ishmael. But there is no evidence that Sarah ever felt any affection for the child. Legally, Ishmael was Sarah's son. But Hagar was not Abraham's wife. She was Sarah's property, used to produce an heir for Abraham and Sarah. Sarah had followed the culturally approved course in providing Abraham with a surrogate, but Sarah apparently wanted no part of the boy who was legally her son.

Some sixteen or seventeen years later Sarah angrily demanded that Abraham cast out Ishmael and his mother. And it was done.

While Sarah never acknowledged Ishmael and was the cause of his removal from the family, Ishmael was present forty-eight years later at the burial of his father, Abraham (Gen. 25:9). It would appear that Abraham and Ishmael were reconciled, probably after Sarah's death.

Sarah's relationship with Isaac (Gen. 24:67). Even though advanced in years, Sarah was able to raise her son and spend thirty-seven years with him before her death. How could one even imagine finally having a child after more than seven decades of marriage? He was a promised child, long awaited, and certainly loved and cherished. Evidence of the closeness and love of this mother and son can perhaps best be seen three years after Sarah's death, when Isaac married Rebekah. The Bible says Isaac took her to his mother's tent to consummate the marriage, and "so Isaac was comforted after his mother's death." The fact that he took his bride to his mother's tent suggests a special bond of love and tenderness had existed between them, and that Isaac felt her loss even three years after Sarah's death.

A CLOSE-UP

Sarah was a woman of astonishing beauty even well into her sixties. We have looked at passages in which Abraham was actually in fear of his life just traveling with her. She must have been physically stunning to not only evoke this fear, but then to be taken into the harems of Egypt's pharaoh and of King Abimelech.

But Sarah's beauty did not bring her a life without grief. She left the city of her birth and its comforts to spend the last half of her long life as a nomad. While God blessed Abraham and Sarah with great wealth, the thing she desired most eluded her.

Sarah longed to feel the life of a child quickening in her womb. She longed to give her beloved husband the heir he had been promised by the God of the universe. And so she waited decade after decade, until more than half a century had elapsed. And then she waited another quarter of a century.

How much it must have hurt Sarah to realize that, after maintaining hope all those barren years, her aged body had passed the time of child-bearing. She had loved Abraham most of her life, but at age seventy-five Sarah assumed that while God had promised Abraham that he would father a great nation, she would not be the mother of that people. How it must have pained her to give her young slave to Abraham as she tried to help God make good on His promise.

Sarah had given up the life she had known in Ur for an uncertain life of wandering, and finally even gave the man she loved into the arms of another woman so she could provide Abraham what Sarah had not been able to give him—a son. It must have been a shocking blow when Hagar conceived so quickly. But the grief and anger was worsened by Hagar's attitude toward Sarah.

Understanding Sarah's emotional state helps us understand her harshness with Hagar. Any other response under these circumstances would have been miraculous. It also gives insight into why Sarah could not accept Ishmael as her own. Every time Sarah looked at Ishmael, she was reminded of her failure to provide an heir and of her slave woman's disdain.

Isaac means "laughter." Abraham and Sarah were full of joy to the point of laughter when finally at ages one hundred and ninety respectively they became parents. God is so good. He then granted Sarah thirty-seven more years, to watch her son grow into manhood, to revel in the miracle of new life as mothers do. In Sarah we see both the trial of faith and faith's reward.

AN EXAMPLE FOR TODAY

- Abraham and Sarah's hearts were focused on being faithful to God. And God is responsive to such faith.
- Abraham and Sarah were married over a century. While each made some unfortunate choices over the years, they remain a great example of the mutual submission Christ calls for in marriage.
- God asked Sarah if anything could be too difficult for Him (Gen. 18:14). She came to understand that even those things that appear impossible to us are not impossible for Him.
- From Sarah we learn that God does not set His timetable according to our schedule. In His time, what He elects will come to pass. He does not need us to jump in and make things possible for Him. Sometimes, this may mean we are to wait for a lifetime.
- From Sarah we also learn that God makes no promises that He does not keep.
- Sarah's life story reminds us that God does not normally interfere when we make a bad choice, as in the case of Sarah's gift of Hagar to Abraham. Instead God may well let us live with consequences, and learn from them. But as the expulsion of Hagar and Ishmael illustrates, if our mistake infringes on His overall plan, He may step in.
- Sarah's life story also illustrates the importance of commitment. This, plus valuing our partner, can build a relationship that will withstand the pressures and the ravages of time.

Shelomith

Scripture Reference: *Leviticus 24:11*
When They Lived: *About 1445 B.C.*
Name: *Shelomith [Shih-LOE-mith:"peaceful"]*

HER ROLE IN SCRIPTURE

Shortly after God gave the Israelites His Law, a fight broke out in the Hebrew camp. In the heat of the struggle, the son of an Israelite woman named Shelomith and her Egyptian husband "blasphemed the name of the LORD and cursed" (Lev. 24:11). In so doing he broke the third commandment, "You shall not take the name of the LORD your God in vain" (Ex. 20:7).

The meaning of the commandment and the incident itself is often misunderstood. The phrase "in vain" renders a Hebrew word that indicates something that is empty or meaningless; it is frequently linked with idolatry. The "curse" mentioned here is not profanity, but rather an occult curse: an attempt to invoke supernatural powers to harm an enemy. What Shelomith's son did was to invoke God's name in a curse hurled against his adversary in the same way pagans used the names of their demons and deities.

This serious violation of the third commandment led to the execution of Shelomith's son and became an unforgettable reminder to Israel that God is to be honored always as real and present.

AN EXAMPLE FOR TODAY

◆ For those who are unmarried, Shelomith serves as a reminder that God does not want us to be unequally yoked to nonbelievers. She was an Israelite married to an Egyptian who worshiped pagan deities. This undoubtedly gave her son knowledge of these pagan gods and occult worship that led him down a path toward a capital sin. Our choice of a life-partner affects not just us but our children as well.

◆ Shelomith had not modeled the behavior that her son acted out. If she had, she too would have died. Even if she were a wonderful mother who taught her son God's commands, he still had the power to make his own choices. Society likes to blame parents, especially mothers, for all the faults of children. Parents truly have an awesome responsibility in raising children, but we must remember that our children have been given the choice to respond to authority or to rebel. Adam and Eve had the perfect Father, yet they chose to rebel. Surely, we do not hold God responsible for their sinful choices.

The Shunammite Woman

Scripture References: *2 Kings 4:8–37; 8:1–6*

HER ROLE IN SCRIPTURE

The third unnamed woman in Kings is not a widow but a childless wife. She was "notable"—that is, a respected member of her community. As Elisha the prophet often passed by her home, this woman had her husband prepare a special room where Elisha could stay for the night.

Later, when Elisha asked the woman what he could do for her, she had no request. But Elisha's servant Gehazi observed that the woman was childless, and that her husband was old. So Elisha promised the woman a son. The child was born as Elisha had promised, but some time later the boy suffered sunstroke and died. The woman immediately set out to get Elisha. Elisha came and prayed for the child, who was restored to life.

Later Elisha warned the woman and her son of a coming seven-year famine, and told her to leave. She moved to the land of Philistines during the famine. When the famine was over, the woman returned to Israel and sought the return of her property. It happened that when the woman reached the palace, the king was listening to stories about Elisha's miracles, told by Elisha's former servant. When the Shunammite woman arrived,

Elisha's servant recognized her and identified her and her son! Impressed, the king ordered that her lands be restored.

A CLOSE-UP

While much of the story in 2 Kings is narrative, three revealing quotes provide insight into this "notable woman."

The first quote (2 Kin. 4:13). When asked by Elisha what he could do for her, the woman responded simply, "I dwell among my own people." She was saying that she was content: she had found her place, and was reconciled to her situation.

The second quote (2 Kin. 4:16). When Elisha announced that she would have a son, the woman responded, "No, my lord. Man of God, do not lie to your maidservant!"

The reaction seems strange at first until we link it to her first statement. It wasn't that she didn't want a son, but she had determined to be satisfied with what life had provided. She feared she would make herself miserable if she hoped for what she thought she could not have. For those who have tried to insulate themselves from hurt by determining not to dream, the sudden introduction of hope can be frightening.

The third quote (2 Kin. 4:28). After her son died the woman hurried to Elisha. When she found him her words reflect the deep distress she felt: "Did I ask a son of my lord? Did I not say, 'Do not deceive me'?"

The Shunammite had resolved to live a life marked by the rejection of hope until Elisha appeared and gave her hope despite herself. Her hope had borne fruit: she had a son. But now the son was dead, and in her dark despair it seemed preferable to have lived the empty, hopeless life she had known before the boy was conceived than to experience the pain that now tore at her innermost being.

But the woman's story doesn't end there. Elisha's God restored the child to life and to his mother's arms. And the woman learned an important lesson about life.

What was the lesson? Simply that the logic of abandonment is wrong. We may, like the Shunammite, reason, "If I want nothing, I cannot suffer from its lack. If I have nothing, I cannot be hurt by its loss." Such a life is stark and empty. God invites us to live in hope and expectation rather than in resignation. While it is true that living in hope may bring us unexpected pain and that every gain brings with it the possibility of loss, the God who guards and guides us is gracious indeed. In opening our lives to whatever the future may bring, whatever pain we know will be more than balanced by His joy.

AN EXAMPLE FOR TODAY

◆ Non-believers may dismiss the woman's appearance at the exact moment Elisha's former servant was telling the king about her as a coincidence. But we are not to lose sight of the fact that we have a wonderful God who exercises sovereign control. Even now He is weaving many "coincidences" into the fabric of our lives.

◆ We seem to have forgotten that hospitality is a spiritual gift. The woman of Shunem practiced this gift, and she was greatly blessed because she did.

The Syro-Phoenician Woman

Scripture References: *Matthew 15:21–28; Mark 7:24–30*

HER ROLE IN SCRIPTURE

On first reading, the story is troubling. Here was a woman in need, and Jesus seemed unwilling to help. It's true that she was a Canaanite, a pagan woman who had no personal relationship with God. Matthew 15:21–28 states:

Then Jesus went out from there and departed to the region of Tyre and Sidon. And behold, a woman of Canaan came from that region and cried out to Him, saying, "Have mercy on me, O Lord, Son of David! My daughter is severely demon-possessed." But He answered her not a word. And His disciples came and urged Him, saying, "Send her away, for she cries out after us." But He answered and said, "I was not sent except to the lost sheep of the house of Israel." Then she came and worshiped Him, saying, "Lord, help me!" But He answered and said, "It is not good to take the children's bread and throw it to the little dogs." And she said, "Yes, Lord, yet even the little dogs eat the crumbs which fall from their masters' table." Then Jesus answered and said to her, "O woman, great is your faith! Let it be to you as you desire." And her daughter was healed from that very hour.

Understanding the story. We need to clarify several things before we can understand this event or draw applications from it. When the Canaanite woman first approached Jesus, she appealed to Him as "Lord, Son of David." In so saying the woman was appealing to Christ as the Jewish Messiah, for Son of David is a messianic title. Jesus did not respond to this appeal, for as a Canaanite the woman had no rights under the Davidic Covenant. When His disciples urged Jesus to "send her away" they were asking Him to grant her request and so stop her from bothering them. Christ's response, "I was not sent except to the lost sheep of the house of Israel," was made to them, not to the woman.

But the woman, who had been listening, sensed Jesus' dilemma and shifted the basis of her appeal. She addressed Him simply as "Lord," and begged, "help me." Jesus responded with an analogy: food prepared for children isn't fed to household pets. But the woman had an answer. Household pets do eat the crumbs that fall from the children's table. In healing her daughter Jesus would not be defrauding the children of Israel to whom He had come as their Messiah. Since Jesus was Lord, the very Son of God, there was plenty for all.

Jesus' reply caps the story: "O woman, great is your faith! Let it be to you as you desire."

EXPLORING HER RELATIONSHIPS

Her relationship with Jesus. This woman had no claim on Jesus. He was not *her* Messiah, and she was not one of the covenant people. As soon as she sensed the reason why Jesus could not respond to her request, she shifted the grounds of her appeal. As Lord, Jesus was Sovereign over all God's Creation. She might have no *right* to appeal to Him on the basis of a covenant relationship, but she could and did appeal to Him as a needy creature, who recognized that as God there was no limit to Jesus' ability to meet every human need.

AN EXAMPLE FOR TODAY

◆ There's an important reminder here for us. Jesus once said that God "makes His sun to rise on the evil and on the good, and sends rain on the just and on the unjust" (Matt. 5:45). God in grace is good to all.

◆ Surely God may choose to hear and answer the prayers even of those who do not yet have a covenant relationship with Him. Jesus honored this pagan woman's faith when it was placed in Him, and undoubtedly she later learned to follow the Christian Way.

~ *Tamar* ~

Scripture References: *Genesis 38*
When They Lived: *About 1850 B.C.*
Name: *Tamar [TAY-mur: "palm tree"]*
Historical Significance: *She became the mother of Perez, through whose line David and Jesus Christ came.*

HER ROLE IN SCRIPTURE

Tamar was the young woman selected by Judah, one of Jacob's twelve sons, as a bride for his oldest son, Er. When Er died childless, Judah instructed his second son, Onan, to marry Tamar and produce an heir for Er.

This practice, called leverite marriage, is authorized in Old Testament law but clearly was a custom long-practiced in the ancient Middle East. To protect the line of a married man who died childless, his closest relative would impregnate his wife. Any son born of this union would be considered the son of the childless husband and would inherit not only any property but also his name and identity.

But Onan was unwilling to fulfill his duty to his brother and Tamar. It would mean Onan would have to raise a child that would inherit his brother's estate instead of him. Yet he did marry Tamar but refused to impregnate her. Onan deceived Tamar and took advantage of her by interrupting sex with her in time to spill his seed on the ground. This vile abuse angered God, and before long Onan died, too.

After Onan's death Judah told Tamar to return home but to live there as a widow until Judah's youngest son, Shelah, was grown. But when Shelah reached maturity, and no arrangement had been made for him to wed Tamar as Judah had promised, Tamar took action. She pretended to be a prostitute, and was impregnated by her father-in-law, Judah. The twin sons she bore him were named Perez and Zerah.

Why is this story included? It seems strange that the inspired Scriptures drop the story of Tamar and Judah into the middle of chapters dealing with Joseph's adventures. Why include the story here? Why include the story at all?

One reason is clear. In a chapter following this story, a list of those who went to Egypt with Jacob will be recorded. It was important to the Jewish people to maintain accurate genealogies, for they were God's chosen people. The purity of their line was important, and the births of Perez and Zerah, included in Judah's line, needed to be accounted for.

There may be another reason as well. In later Judaism the notion developed that salvation depended to a large extent not on the individual, but on the merits of the forefathers. Abraham and the men of the patriarchal age were deemed so good that the merit they accrued could be applied to cancel out the sins of thousands of individuals multiplied generations later.

We can see how a person might imagine that the Joseph portrayed in Genesis might possess such merits. Placed beside the account of Joseph's life, the story of Tamar and Judah seems tawdry and out of place. Yet if we look more closely, we make an important discovery. Jesus the Messiah did not come from Joseph's line, but from Judah's. And specifically from Perez, Tamar's son! And Tamar herself is one of four women named by Matthew in his genealogy of Jesus (Matt. 1:3)!

It is not in the merits of the ancients that we find hope. It is in the sinless descendant of sinners, who came to bring forgiveness and to break the hold sin has on us.

EXPLORING HER RELATIONSHIPS

Tamar's relationship with Judah. Legally Tamar was a member of Judah's household and under his authority. Yet Judah ignored his obligations to Tamar. So Tamar took matters into her own hand and by cunning became pregnant with Judah's child.

Judah's reaction when the parentage was finally revealed is significant. He "did the right thing," and not only acknowledged that she had been more righteous than he (Gen. 38:26), but also acknowledged her twins as his own sons.

In this situation each of the two central figures, Tamar and Judah, displayed strengths and weaknesses. Each acted on what seemed to be "right" in the situation—as wrong as each may have been. Yet the years Judah had disregarded Tamar's needs, and her understandably hostile feelings for him, made it impossible for a personal relationship to develop between them.

We need not approve of what Tamar did to acknowledge that she was one of the exceptional women of patriarchal times.

AN EXAMPLE FOR TODAY

Ultimately, we are all responsible for our own life and accountable to God. We are called to pursue God and His purposes diligently. If we count on others to do what they should, we may be accomplices in our own victimization. Yet in making choices, we must be sure that we avoid acting as if the end justifies the means.

~ *Tamar* ~

David's Daughter

Scripture References: *2 Samuel 13*
When They Lived: *About 975 B.C.*
Name: *Tamar [TAY-mahr:"palm tree"]*
Historical Significance: *Tamar's rape by a half-brother led to murder and ultimately rebellion against David.*

HER ROLE IN SCRIPTURE

Tamar was one of David's daughters, the full sister of Absalom and half-sister of Amnon. She is described in Scripture as "lovely" (2 Sam. 13:1). She was in fact so lovely that her half-brother Amnon fell in love with her. A friend of Amnon's suggested that he pretend to be sick, ask Tamar to bring him food, and then take her. Amnon followed this advice, and when Tamar rejected his advances, Amnon raped her.

Tamar left, crying bitterly. When her brother Absalom discovered what had happened, he advised Tamar, "hold your peace" and "do not take this thing to heart" (2 Sam. 13:20). The text says simply, "So Tamar remained desolate in her brother Absalom's house" (2 Sam. 13:20).

While nothing more is said of Tamar, the rape had consequences beyond the young woman's desolation. Absalom hated Amnon for what he had done, and he deeply resented David's failure to deal with the matter. Two years later Absalom conspired to murder his half-brother. Then Absalom fled into exile for a time, but later he returned and led a rebellion against David that resulted in a devastating civil war.

EXPLORING HER RELATIONSHIPS

Tamar's relationship with Amnon. Tamar seems to have been a total innocent, unaware of Amnon's passion for her. When asked to bring him food, she prepared it herself and brought it to him. Even when Amnon sent everyone from the room, Tamar seems to have suspected nothing. She was shocked when Amnon propositioned her.

The rape. Tamar tried to reason with Amnon. First she argued: "No, my brother, do not force me, for no such thing should be done in Israel. Do not do this disgraceful thing!" (2 Sam. 13:12).

Tamar then appealed to Amnon: "And I, where could I take my shame?" (v. 13)

Finally Tamar offered Amnon hope: "Now therefore, please speak to the king; for he will not withhold me from you" (v. 13).

But Amnon was unmoved and unwilling to settle for any delayed gratification. His passion demanded that he take her immediately. "Being stronger than she, he forced her and lay with her" (v. 14).

The reaction of Amnon. Here the story takes a strange but understandable twist. The text tells us, "Then Amnon hated her exceedingly, so that the hatred with which he hated her was greater than the love with which he had loved her. And Amnon said to her, "Arise, be gone!" (v. 15).

What happened to so change Amnon's feelings for Tamar? Amnon had acted against what he himself knew was right. No person can violate deeply held personal convictions without drastically affecting himself as well as others. The passion Amnon had had for Tamar was transformed into hatred, for now he saw her as the cause of his own moral failure. Rather than take responsibility for his actions, as David had in the case of Bathsheba, Amnon acted as though Tamar had been the responsible party. He transformed the guilt he felt into hatred of Tamar.

Again Tamar protested, for Old Testament Law required that a man who raped a virgin who was not betrothed had to marry her (Deut. 22:28, 29). "'No, indeed! This evil of sending me away is worse than the other that you did to me!' But he would not listen to her" (2 Sam. 13:16).

Tamar's relationship with Absalom. Tamar was Absalom's full sister, and his concern when she put ashes on her head and tore her robe—cultural symbols of extreme grief and distress—was obvious. That Absalom immediately asked whether Amnon was the cause of her distress indicates that Absalom was aware of Amnon's infatuation with his sister.

But Absalom's advice—"hold your peace" and "do not take this thing to heart"—shows how little Absalom understood how devastating the rape was to Tamar. Rape is not something any woman can or should simply shrug off. Rape is a violation that must be reported and dealt with if the victim is to find any sense of closure or recover her self-respect. However innocent a woman may be of responsibility for her rape, the emotional damage is severe and must be dealt with.

Clearly Absalom was not thinking of his sister's welfare but of how he might take revenge on Amnon. It served Absalom's purposes to have Tamar remain silent; it did not serve Tamar's needs.

Two full years later Absalom had Amnon murdered, and Absalom fled the country. Absalom had his revenge, but had done nothing to help Tamar. The text simply tells us, "Tamar remained desolate in her brother Absalom's house" (2 Sam. 13:20).

Tamar's relationship with David. Another telling comment in the biblical text reports that "When King David heard of all these things, he was very angry" (v. 21). What the text does not report is any action on David's part to right the wrong.

He did not punish Amnon. He did not rebuke him. He did not follow the law and force Amnon to marry Tamar. David did nothing.

We can perhaps understand David's reticence. David himself had done what Amnon did in taking Bathsheba. It is likely that David felt he had lost the moral authority required to condemn another for what he himself had done. While we can understand David's reticence, we cannot excuse it. As king and as a father, David was responsible to deal with his son's actions. David's failure to act left Tamar to suffer in silence and ultimately led not only to Amnon's murder but also to the rebellion that Absalom led against him.

A Close-Up

From all we can tell in the text, Tamar was a lovely and innocent young woman whose life was destroyed by Amnon's brutal rape. Her hope of recovery was thwarted by Absalom and David's failures to deal honestly with the crime. Yet, what a future we might have projected for Tamar. Her recorded words to Amnon suggest a high moral quality and sensitivity like that displayed by Abigail when she first met David. But unlike David, Amnon refused to be persuaded to take the right course.

All we know of Tamar after this is that she remained desolate in her brother's house. In all likelihood, she stayed there until she died.

Later Absalom named his own daughter after his sister. The gesture was, tragically, too little—and much, much too late.

An Example for Today

- Tamar is a tragic reminder that sometimes dreadful things happen to godly people. And at times those we look to for help harm us instead. Only God's healing mercy and grace can restore our sense of self-worth and provide a fresh beginning.
- Tamar's experience serves as a warning not to keep quiet should we be violated as she was. For our own sake we need to do all we can to see that justice is done and closure achieved.
- Tamar, although innocent, found herself alone with her brother. We need to be on guard against letting ourselves be put in vulnerable situations even if we trust our companions.

Two Harlots

Scripture References: *1 Kings 3:16–27*

THEIR ROLE IN SCRIPTURE

Not long after Solomon became king a dispute between two prostitutes was brought to him for settlement. Each had had a child, but one of the infants died during the night. Each prostitute claimed that the live child was hers, and the dead child belonged to the other.

Solomon announced that he would split the live child in two, with half given to each. One of the women agreed; the other begged the king to give the living child to the other rather than kill him. Solomon's subterfuge had been intended to find out which woman truly cared for the child. The harlots' reactions showed this clearly, and Solomon decreed that the child be given to his real mother—the one who wanted him to live. The incident helped to establish Solomon's reputation for wisdom.

Vashti

Scripture References: *Esther 1:10–22*

HER ROLE IN SCRIPTURE

Vashti was the principal wife of King Ahasuerus (Xerxes), around 475 B.C. Her name means "beautiful woman," and she was included in Scripture because her sense of personal dignity or perhaps her natural obstinacy led her to refuse the king's command to display herself at a banquet he was hosting. Vashti's subsequent divorce by Xerxes led to the search for a new queen of Persia that resulted in the crowning of Esther. This enabled Esther to save the Jewish people from extermination.

Aside from this significance, the account in the first chapter of Esther reveals part of the injustice of a social system that includes men dominating their wives instead of partnering with them.

> *Then the king said to the wise men who understood the times (for this was the king's manner toward all who knew law and justice ...) "What shall we do to Queen Vashti, according to law, because she did not obey the command of King Ahasuerus brought to her by the eunuchs?"*
>
> *And Memucan answered before the king and the princes: "Queen Vashti has not only wronged the king, but also all the princes, and all the people who are in all the provinces of King Ahasuerus. For the queen's behavior will become known to all women, so that they will despise their husbands in their eyes, when they report, 'King Ahasuerus commanded Queen Vashti to be brought in before him, but she did not come.' This very day the noble ladies of Persia and Media will say to all the king's officials that they have heard of the behavior of the queen. Thus there will be excessive contempt and wrath. If it please the king, let a royal decree go out from him, and let it be recorded in the laws of the Persians and the Medes, so that it will not be altered, that Vashti shall come no more before King Ahasuerus; and let the king give her royal position to another who is better than she. When the king's decree which he will make is proclaimed throughout all his empire (for it is great), all wives will honor their husbands, both great and small."*
>
> —Est. 1:13, 15–20

As we might expect, this recommendation pleased the king, and he acted immediately to prevent a possible women's movement.

What makes this account even more humorous is that the husband's position as ruler of the household was thoroughly established in both law and custom in the ancient world. How amazing that the king and princes of such a mighty kingdom felt so insecure in their home life!

AN EXAMPLE FOR TODAY

- The characters and good will of a husband and wife will contribute more to a marriage than will the laws and expectations of society.
- What is important in a marriage is that the husband and wife love one another completely and seek each other's best interest first.

The Widow with the Mite

Scripture References: *Mark 12:42, 43; Luke 21:2, 3*

HER ROLE IN SCRIPTURE

This is another woman whose name we do not know. We know that she was a widow, and thus one of the poorest of the poor. We know that she loved God, for although she had almost nothing, she contributed everything she had to the temple treasury.

What is fascinating about her is that she alone attracted Jesus' attention as He and His disciples sat by the treasury. A stream of people, many of whom were wealthy, made contributions. The rich put in large amounts—some no doubt doing so ostentatiously so their generosity could be applauded. Jesus put the scene in perspective when He praised the widow's tiny gift as more significant than all the others "'for they all put in out of their abundance, but she out of her poverty put in all that she had, her whole livelihood'" (Mark 12:44).

AN EXAMPLE FOR TODAY

- This generous widow is an interesting contrast with the young man who asked Jesus what he had to do to inherit the kingdom (Mark 10:17–22). When the young man insisted that he had kept the commandments, Jesus told him to sell his possessions, give them to the poor, and follow Him. The young man walked away. For him, money had priority over following Jesus. What we do with our money reveals our priorities.

- No one would have thought less of the widow if she had kept those copper coins—worth less than a single cent. But she wanted to give, and Jesus saw her gift as more significant than the wealth others contributed. Never think that the little we have, in time or money, won't make a difference. God measures the significance of our giving by what we have, not by the size of the gift.

- The Lord loves a cheerful giver. He has given us the money, the time, and the personal gifts that we possess. What could make us more cheerful than graciously returning a portion of what He has given us?

The Widow of Nain

Scripture References: *Luke 7:11–15*

Luke is the only Gospel writer to record this event.

HER ROLE IN SCRIPTURE

Now it happened, the day after, that He went into a city called Nain; and many of His disciples went with Him, and a large crowd. And when He came near the gate of the city, behold, a dead man was being carried out, the only son of his mother; and she was a widow. And a large crowd from the city was with her. When the Lord saw her, He had compassion on her and said to her, "Do not weep." Then He came and touched the open coffin, and those who carried him stood still. And He said, "Young man, I say to you, arise." So he who was dead sat up and began to speak. And He presented him to his mother. Then fear came upon all, and they glorified God, saying, "A great prophet has risen up among us"; and, "God has visited His people."

—Luke 7:11–16

The text does not name the woman featured in this story, but it does tell us much about her. The dead man was her "only son," and she was a "widow." What this tells us is that the woman was in desperate straits. Without a husband or son she had no one to provide for her. When Jesus saw the funeral procession, He had compassion on *her*—not on her dead son. Jesus responded to her needs; the son had gone to a far better world.

Two additional things are significant about the story. The first is that Jesus was not asked to help as He had been asked to help Peter's wife's mother. At the time no one imagined that Jesus' power extended to the raising of the dead.

The second is that Jesus was motivated by *compassion*. The Greek word here is *splanchnizomai*. *The Expository Dictionary of Bible Words* notes:

> *The word originally indicated the inner parts of the body and came to suggest the seat of the emotions—particularly emotions of pity, compassion, and love...When Jesus' response is such that he is described as being moved by compassion, the occasion is often the turning point in someone's life.*
>
> —p. 180

Surely the compassion Jesus felt for the woman was the turning point in her life. Before Jesus acted, she faced a bleak and frightening future, but at Jesus' act of raising her son, her future was transformed. Not only was the one she loved and had lost restored, but she herself was now secure. Her son would inherit her husband's estate and care for her until it was her own time to die.

Jesus' compassion has proven to be the turning point in the life of all who trust Him. Without a personal relationship with Jesus, how bleak our future would be! Jesus, moved by love, chose to take the path that led to the Cross and thus flung open the door to eternal life to all who will trust in Him.

The Widowed Wife of a Prophet

Scripture References: *2 Kings 4:1–7*

HER ROLE IN SCRIPTURE

When the destitute wife of a prophet appealed to Elisha for help, the prophet questioned her about her resources. All she had was a jar containing some olive oil.

Elisha told her to send her two sons to borrow containers. Then Elisha told her to pour oil from her jar into the containers. She poured and poured, but the oil did not run out. Soon all the jars were filled. Only then did the oil cease to flow. Elisha then told the woman to sell the oil, pay off the family debt, and live on the leftover money.

While we know little of the woman as an individual, we do respect the faith she displayed in doing as Elisha commanded. We also note that had she displayed even greater faith, and assembled more vessels, she and her family would have had even more.

Faith still opens the door to God's blessing. The greater the faith, the more blessings God will pour out on us.

The Widow of Zarephath

Scripture References: *1 Kings 17; Luke 4:26, 27*

HER ROLE IN SCRIPTURE

The unnamed widow lived in Zarephath, a town in Sidonian territory. The Lord sent Elijah there during the drought that Elijah had announced to King Ahab. While Ahab scoured Israel to find Elijah, the prophet was in Zarephath, the homeland of Jezebel, the evil queen who was intent on wiping out worship of the Lord.

The widow, who recognized Elijah as a worshiper of the Lord (1 Kin. 17:12), displayed an unusual and growing faith.

Her first test of faith (1 Kin. 17:10–16). When Elijah first saw the woman, she was gathering sticks to make a fire. Elijah called to her and asked for water and food. The text describes this meeting.

> So she said, "As the Lord your God lives, I do not have bread, only a hand-ful of flour in a bin, and a little oil in a jar; and see, I am gathering a couple of sticks that I may go in and prepare it for myself and my son, that we may eat it, and die."
>
> And Elijah said to her, "Do not fear; go and do as you have said, but make me a small cake from it first, and bring it to me; and afterward make some for yourself and your son. For thus says the LORD God of Israel: 'The bin of flour shall not be used up, nor shall the jar of oil run dry, until the day the LORD sends rain on the earth.' "
>
> So she went away and did according to the word of Elijah; and she and he and her household ate for many days.
>
> —1 Kin. 17:12–15

It took considerable faith for the woman to trust Elijah's word, and to feed him *first*, hoping there would be enough for her and her son later.

Her second test of faith (1 Kin. 17:17–24). Some time after, the woman's son became sick and died. The distraught woman came to Elijah and cried, "Have you come to me to bring my sin to remembrance, and to kill my son?" (1 Kin. 17:18). The woman feared that by coming to her home Elijah had brought her to God's attention and that God had remembered her sins and punished her by killing her son.

Elijah took the boy to his room and prayed fervently. God restored the child's life "and he revived" (v. 22). When Elijah brought the child to his mother, the woman cried, "Now by this I know that you are a man of God, and that the word of the LORD in your mouth is the truth" (1 Kin. 17:24).

The widow in the New Testament (Luke 4:26, 27). Jesus referred to the widow of Zarephath when speaking in the synagogue in his hometown. Jesus confronted His neighbors concerning their lack of faith in Him and reminded them that although there were many widows in Israel in Elijah's time, God sent Elijah to a woman of Sidon, a pagan. This reminder that God had shown special compassion for the pagan widow aroused the anger of Christ's neighbors. Yet it clearly reflects the wonderful truth that God has always cared for the lost of every nation and has compassion for all.

A Close-Up

Although a widow and in poverty, this woman showed both courage and a growing faith. She was aware of Israel's God, and immediately she recognized Elijah as one who worshiped Him. Her readiness to feed Elijah when He made a promise in God's name showed that the widow had some confidence in Him. At the same time, she showed a limited understanding of God's justice. When her son sickened and died, the widow concluded that God was punishing her for past sins. The miracle of restoring her son to life did two things for the widow. It strengthened her faith in God as Elijah gave his word to her. It also taught her that God is a God rich in grace and forgiveness for those who trust Him.

An Example for Today

◆ The story of the widow reminds us that God can use those outside the faith to help believers. Some Christians wonder if it is all right to see non-Christian physicians. This Scripture reminds us that God used a non-believer to minister to His prophet.

◆ The widow's encounter with Elijah ultimately led to her belief in the God of Israel. This is another important reason to have contact with non-Christians. As they help us, God may well speak to them (Matt. 10:41).

◆ It is fascinating that although the widow was a pagan rather than one of God's covenant people, she listened when God's prophet asked her to make him a loaf of bread first, and then prepare food for herself and her starving son. What an example this was of obedience to God when obedience was hard. And this from a pagan! Probably without realizing it, the widow was tithing the last of her food to God by giving the first part to Elijah.

The Wise Woman of the City

Scripture References: *2 Samuel 20:16–22*

HER ROLE IN SCRIPTURE

After David's forces killed Absalom, a man named Sheba continued the rebellion. David's forces under Joab pursued Sheba, who took refuge in a walled city.

When Joab seemed about to batter the wall down, a "wise woman" called out to him. When Joab offered to spare the city if Sheba were executed, the wise woman said, "Watch, his head will be thrown to you over the wall" (2 Sam. 20:21). The wise woman persuaded the people, Sheba was killed, and the city was spared.

The Wise Woman of Tekoa

Scripture References: *2 Samuel 14:2–22*

HER ROLE IN SCRIPTURE

After Absalom had murdered Amnon, Absalom fled the country. Joab, the commanding general of David's army, sensed that David loved

Absalom and wanted to bring him back home. So Joab enlisted the aid of a "wise woman" from Tekoa, who told a story that could by analogy be applied to Absalom's case.

The descriptive term "wise woman" is found three times in the Old Testament (2 Sam 14:2; 20:16; Prov. 14:1). In 2 Samuel the phrase suggests an older woman who is notable for giving good counsel and thus has gained influence with others.

AN EXAMPLE FOR TODAY

- The wise woman let herself be used by Joab for his own purposes. Let's be careful not to let others use our reputation or us for their own purposes unless we fully understand and agree with those purposes.
- We have a responsibility to those who see us as wise and understanding to pray for discernment that we may help others and not harm them.

The Witch of En Dor

Scripture References: 1 Samuel 28:5–25

HER ROLE IN SCRIPTURE

We know little of the "witch of En Dor," who was not a witch but a medium, a woman who had contact with a familiar spirit. It is not at all certain that this woman was a Hebrew. During the conquest, En Dor was a Canaanite stronghold that the Israelites had not been able to possess (Josh. 17:11). The city did lie in Israelite-controlled territory, however, and Saul, in obedience to Deuteronomy 18's condemnation of occult practices of every kind, had set out to exterminate all mediums and spiritists (1 Sam. 28:9).

However, when the Philistines invaded Israel, and Saul's prayers met with silence, the desperate king demanded that his servants find him a medium. When one was located at En Dor, Saul went there in disguise to consult with the demon that was her spirit contact.

BIBLE BACKGROUND: *MEDIUMS & SPIRITISTS*

The Old Testament teaches the reality of demonic beings that seek to influence and harm human beings. These demons are actually fallen angels who followed Satan in his great prehistoric rebellion against God. While some so-called occult practices are mere trickery, true occult practices do tap into the supernatural and serve as avenues through which demons can contact and influence human beings. For this reason the Bible condemns every occult practice, from the reading of horoscopes to the seeking contact with demons. According to Old Testament Law, these things were to be condemned as capital crimes. Deuteronomy 18:9–12 states:

"When you come into the land which the LORD your God is giving you, you shall not learn to follow the abominations of those nations. There shall not be found among you anyone who makes his son or his daughter pass through the fire, or one who practices witchcraft, or a soothsayer, or one who interprets omens, or a sorcerer, or one who conjures spells, or a medium, or a spiritist, or one who calls up the dead, For all who do these things are an abomination to the LORD, and because of these abominations the Lord your God drives them out from before you."

For a thorough examination of demonism and the occult, see the book *Every Good and Evil Angel in the Bible*.

The woman was reluctant to conduct a seance for the disguised Saul. When promised immunity, however, she did as asked. But then, when a spirit actually appeared, the woman "cried out with a loud voice" (v. 12). Her reaction showed that the spirit that appeared was not the familiar spirit she had called upon, but Samuel himself, who then informed Saul that he was destined to die in the coming battle with the Philistines.

Saul, weak from hunger and shock, then fainted. The woman encouraged him to eat. Then Saul and his servants left her.

A CLOSE-UP

Like others dedicated to the occult, this woman had linked her future to evil forces. Despite the campaign Saul had launched to exterminate such persons, the medium of En Dor had been unable to break the spiritual bonds that held her. She lived in fear of exposure, yet was addicted to the relationship that had been established.

At the same time, her shock at the sudden appearance of Samuel makes it clear that she knew the difference between holy and evil spirits.

What a tragic life this medium must have lived, knowing that her spiritual bondage was wrong. She was no doubt fearful that her secret might be discovered, and yet unwilling or unable to rid herself of the demonic.

AN EXAMPLE FOR TODAY

◆ We must not be lured by television ads for psychic hot lines, or respond to magazine ads or articles with phone numbers promising help from a "friend" with supposed spiritual powers. It's not surprising that so many lonely people, depressed teens, or desperate single parents respond to these appealing but deceptive promotions. But let no Christian be among them.

◆ When we do feel the need for guidance, we should turn to God and Christian friends and then wait for the Holy Spirit to confirm His way for us. Trusting God's perfect timing and faithfulness sometimes means we must wait a while for such confirmation, so we need to wait.

The Woman Who Blessed Jesus' Mother

***Scripture References:** Luke 11:27, 28*

HER ROLE IN SCRIPTURE

The woman, mentioned only here, intended to compliment Jesus in saying, "Blessed is the womb that bore You, and the breasts which nursed You." It was common in the first century to praise an individual by praising his or her parent. In responding as He did, Jesus did not discount His mother, but reminded all those who heard of the true source of blessing: "Blessed are those who hear the word of God and keep it!" (Luke 11:28).

That is, "Don't praise Me. Listen to what I say and do it!"

The Women Disciples

***Scripture Reference:** Acts 1:14*

THEIR ROLE IN SCRIPTURE

The new freedom is symbolized in this brief verse, which mentions only one woman by name. The text says,

These [the eleven disciples] all continued with one accord in prayer and supplication, with the women and Mary the mother of Jesus, and with His brothers (Acts 1:14).

What is significant for us here is the simple phrase, "the women."

When the Jews gathered for study or prayer, it was a meeting of men. It took ten men, a *minyan*, to convene for worship in Judaism, and in this case women literally did not "count." Yet here we see the followers of Christ assembled to pray and not only are women among them, but verse 15 counts them among the 120 "disciples" who were present.

While modern readers would likely pass over these two words, they reflect a radical change in first-century attitude. Believers had gathered for prayer and worship, and the text specifically says that "the women" were among them.

Other subtle indications in Acts point to this change of attitude. The Gospel account of the feeding of the 4,000 and 5,000 specifically says that the count is of "men...in number about five thousand" (John 6:10). But in Acts 1:15 the figure 120 is not based on the number of men, but "the *number of names* was about a hundred and twenty" [italics mine]. Similarly when Luke reported on the response to Peter's first presentation of the gospel, he noted that "that day about *three thousand souls* were added to them" (Acts 2:41).

It might seem that Acts 4:4, which relates the response to Peter's second sermon, says, "the number of men came to be about five thousand." Why "the number of men" here? The answer is that Peter was in a court of the temple to which women were not admitted. So Peter's audience there was made up *only* of men, while Peter's first sermon was preached in the city where both men and women could hear.

Without laboring the point, the first mention in Acts of women pictures them gathered with men, for prayer and worship. This scene alone indicates that the new freedom Christ offered to women had begun to be experienced by those who trusted in Him.

The Women of Israel

Scripture References: *1 Samuel 18:6–8*

THEIR ROLE IN SCRIPTURE

It's strange. Saul seems to have cared nothing for the feelings of his daughters or for their opinion of him. But he cared deeply about the opinion of strangers. After David had killed Goliath, David became a folk hero. As David led his troops to victory after victory, his fame surpassed that of the king. The "women of Israel" came out of all the cities of Israel to celebrate, singing:

> *"Saul has slain his thousands,*
> *And David his ten thousands."*
> —1 Sam. 18:7

How fascinating that it was the song of women celebrating David's triumphs that aroused Saul's anger and jealousy, and turned the king against his loyal supporter.

AN EXAMPLE FOR TODAY

- How like Saul we are at times, playing to the crowd while not taking our family's feelings into account. The image of Saul burning against David should help us remember that "the crowd" should not influence our thinking.
- As a member of our own crowd we also have a personal responsibility. A crowd may call for someone to jump from a ledge. Perhaps that's the time we should start another chant: "Don't jump!"
- Saul would fit right in with some politicians, not only playing to the crowd but also being swayed by what the crowd thinks—a waffle king.

The Daughters of Zelophehad

Scripture References: *Numbers 27:1–11; 36:1–13;*
Joshua 17:3–5

When They Lived: *About 1400 B.C.*

Names: *Mahlah [MAH-luh:"weak, sickly"]*
Noah [NOE-uh:"rest," or "comfort"]
Hoglah [HOG-luh:"partridge"]
Milcah [MILL-kuh:"counselor"]
Tirzah [TUR-zuh: meaning unknown]

Historical Significance: *These daughters of a sonless father*
brought about a significant clarification of inheritance law.

THEIR ROLE IN SCRIPTURE

On the last stages of the journey to Canaan, Moses set down a process for dividing the Promised Land after the Israelites were victorious. Land would be given to each family and was to be held by that family in perpetuity as a gift from God.

Like other societies of the era, Israel society was patriarchal in structure. This meant that land would pass from father to son with the provision that sons would support their widowed mothers and unmarried sisters. But a man named Zelophehad, who had been among those rescued from Egypt and later died on the journey to Canaan, had five daughters but no sons. The process for dividing the land that Moses outlined made no provision for passing the inheritance of a man who died with daughters but no sons.

Rather than sit back quietly, the daughters of Zelophehad brought their complaint to Moses and the leaders of the congregation.

"Our father died in the wilderness; but he was not in the company of those who gathered together against the LORD, in company with Korah, but he died in his own sin; and he had no sons. Why should the name of our

*father be removed from among his family because he had no son? Give us
a possession among our father's brothers."*

—Num. 27:3, 4

Moses listened to their complaint and took it to the Lord. God responded, "The daughters of Zelophehad speak what is right" (Num. 27:6), and laid down a series of principles covering cases in which a man died without having a son eligible to inherit his property.

This incident is significant, for the story told first here in Numbers 27 is repeated in Numbers 36. And Joshua 17 makes it clear that these five daughters did inherit their own lands.

The incident is significant not only as an account of a clarification of biblical inheritance law, but also for the insight it provides into the relationship of women to those in authority. Apparently women as well as men were free to bring their concerns to Moses in this era. Apparently, too, women's concerns were evaluated on the merits of the case rather than summarily dismissed. While Moses was convinced by the daughters' argument, it was not Moses' place to modify the divine Law. Moses transmitted the Law; God originated it. Moses' decision to inquire of God was appropriate.

EXPLORING THEIR RELATIONSHIPS

Their relationship with Moses. These five sisters went before Moses with a legitimate concern. They asked why their father's name should be removed from among his family because he had no sons. They asked to receive their father's portion of land after he had died, since he left no sons to inherit it.

A few things are noteworthy in this history. First, God used these five young women to emphasize the inheritance rights of women and establish justice for them in the Law. Secondly, they responded to the problem appropriately. They took their case before Moses and presented it to him in a logical and respectful manner.

Noteworthy, also, is that they were allowed access to Moses. They were not told they couldn't see this important leader because they were young women who didn't want to obey the Law. Furthermore, Moses listened to them with an open mind and heard the merit of their complaint. He in turn went respectfully to his Superior and the Judge of all revealed more of His Law for all Israel.

A CLOSE-UP

These daughters of Zelophehad were intelligent, assertive young women. They were not militants; neither were they doormats. They did not say, "It's a man's world," hang their heads and go through life dejectedly, because they had been treated unfairly. Neither did they instigate a negative campaign of complaints, which had become the custom of many of these Israelites who had been set free from captivity. Many of the people murmured when they grew tired of manna and wanted meat and other things they missed about Egypt. In today's terms, these young women were "pretty awesome," and a credit to themselves and their father.

EXAMPLES FOR TODAY

These sisters are a splendid example of how powerfully and wisely women can handle prejudicial or unjust treatment even if it is spelled out in laws or bylaws. They went to the proper authority and laid out the facts of their case respectfully. The greatest difficulty today is finding an authority with an open heart and mind who will seek the spirit and wisdom of God and then advocate for what is just in His sight regardless of the political consequences.

Zipporah

Scripture References: *Exodus 2:21, 22; 4:25; 18:1–6;*
Numbers 12:1

When They Lived: *About 1450 B.C.*

Name: *Zipporah [zip-POE-rah: "bird"]*

Historical Significance: *She circumcised her sons as Moses*
began his mission for the Lord.

HER ROLE IN SCRIPTURE

When Moses was forced to flee from Egypt he settled in a desolate part of the Sinai Peninsula. The area supported a few sheepherders, and long before Moses' time it had been mined for semi-precious stones. Moses attached himself to the family of Jethro, a Midianite who lived in the Sinai. In time Moses married Zipporah, one of Jethro's daughters.

We know little of Zipporah or of her life with Moses. We know that the couple had two sons, and that Moses brought her along when he set out for Egypt after God's call (Ex. 4:20). Apparently Zipporah and her sons turned back after an incident reported in 4:24–26, for after the Israelites had been freed from Egypt Jethro brought Zipporah and the two sons to rejoin Moses at Mount Sinai (Ex. 18:1–6).

Some have assumed that Zipporah died and that Moses remarried, because Numbers 12:1 speaks of Moses' marriage to an "Ethiopian," or "Cushite." It is more likely that the reference is to Zipporah. Cush was an imprecise term during most of the biblical era, but at all times it referred to lands south of Egypt where the Sinai lay.

The one passage in which we catch a glimpse of Zipporah in action is a puzzling one. The passage describes an incident that occurred as Moses set out with his family for Egypt to carry out the mission he had been given by God.

And it came to pass on the way, at the encampment, that the LORD met
him and sought to kill him. Then Zipporah took a sharp stone and cut off
the foreskin of her son and cast it at Moses' feet, and said, "Surely you are
a husband of blood to me!" So He let him go. Then she said, "You are a
husband of blood!"—because of the circumcision.

—Ex. 4:24–26

These verses have puzzled ancient Jewish commentators as well as Christian scholars. A few elements seem clear, however. Moses had failed to have his sons circumcised, a rite given to Abraham that functioned as a sign and seal of membership in the covenant community. When God "attacked" Moses [perhaps through a sudden illness?], Zipporah was apparently aware of the importance of circumcision to Moses' heritage but was nevertheless hostile enough to her son being so used that Moses capitulated. This was a family trait considering Aaron's like behavior. Zipporah must have realized why judgement was upon Moses and quickly acted to avert disaster by circumcising their son.

One of the puzzles here is the meaning of Zipporah's repeated reference to Moses as a "husband of blood." This may have been an invective for her having to cut her son to save Moses. But she may have also realized that her son's innocent blood was necessary to appease God for Moses' sin of disobedience concerning his son. But Zipporah, and not even Moses, could have understood how deep was the gospel significance of this incident. What is significant in the context of the passage, however, is that Zipporah's quick analysis of the situation and her willingness to act removed the threat to Moses, and he was able to continue on his mission.

EXPLORING HER RELATIONSHIPS

Zipporah's relationship with God. Zipporah was not raised in the Covenant yet she responded to God when it became clear what He required. God was angry that Moses had neglected to circumcise his son to honor the covenant God had made with Abraham. That Zipporah knew enough to do this points to Moses having told her about this covenant and custom.

Zipporah's relationship with Moses' siblings. When Miriam and Aaron attacked Moses on account of his "Ethiopian woman" and complained that Moses was not the only one through whom God spoke, "Miriam became leprous, as white as snow" (Num. 12:10). After God intervened, there is no more unfair criticism about Zipporah.

AN EXAMPLE FOR TODAY

Just as Miriam and Aaron criticized Zipporah, many times wives or families of religious leaders will be unfairly criticized. It is better to focus on Christ's example of love and acceptance of others than Miriam and Aaron's negative example. Zipporah's instant willingness to repent on Moses' behalf, whether graciously or not, shows that she had the certain knowledge of God we call faith. She may not have liked injuring her son, but she chose to acknowledge God and her son's place in His will.

Quick Reference

of Every Named Woman in the Bible

A

ABIGAIL *[AB ih gale:"father rejoices"]*. Two women named Abigail are mentioned in the Bible.

1. Abigail was the name of the wise wife of a foolish rancher named Nabal, who lived around 1000 B.C. When Nabal insulted David, Abigail hurried to head off David's planned attack on the rancher's homestead. Her courage and wisdom so impressed David that when Nabal died of a stroke a short time later, David married her. Abigail's story is featured in 1 Samuel 25. We're told in 2 Samuel 3:3 that she bore David a son named Chileab. See page 1.

2. The "other Abigail" lived about the same time, and was David's sister. Perhaps the two women were friends. The "other Abigail" is mentioned in 2 Samuel 17:25 and 1 Chronicles 2:16,17. David's general, Joab, killed her son, Amasa, an officer in David's army.

ABIHAIL *[AB ih hail:"father is strength"]*

1. Closely related to King David, this Abihail was the daughter of one of David's brothers, Eliab. She married David's obscure son, Jerimoth. She is perhaps most notable as the mother of Mahalath, who married Rehoboam, the son and successor of Solomon. Although quite possibly an influential woman around 950 B.C., she is mentioned only in 2 Chronicles 11:18.

2. The only other woman with this name is found in a genealogy of Judah's descendants. According to 1 Chronicles 2:29 she was married to Abishur, of the line of Jerahmeel. Her date is uncertain.

ABIJAH *[a BUY jah:"my father is Yahweh"]*. Two Bible women shared this name with six men, one of whom was the second king of Judah.

1. One feminine Abijah was the wife of Hezron, a descendant of Judah. Her name is found only in a genealogy found in 1 Chronicles 2:24.

2. The other female Abijah was the mother of King Hezekiah, one of Judah's godly kings. She lived about 750 B.C. She is mentioned in 2 Chronicles 29:1, and also in 2 Kings 18:2, where she is called Abi.

ABISHAG *[AB ih shag:"my father was a wanderer"]*. This attractive young Shunammite woman cared for David during his last days, around 970 B.C. Later she became a pawn in a power struggle between Solomon and his brother Adonijah. Adonijah's request for permission to marry Abishag was viewed as an effort to strengthen his claim to Israel's throne and led directly to his execution for treason. Abishag is mentioned in 1 Kings 1:3, 15 and 2:17–22. See pages 25, 26.

ABITAL *[ah BY tuhl:"father is the dew"]*. She was one of David's wives around 1000 B.C. Nothing is known of her or her son by David, Shephatiah. See 2 Samuel 3:4 and 1 Chronicles 3:3.

ADAH *[A duh:"adorned"]*. The two women of this name had very different roles in Scripture.

1. In prehistory, Adah was one of Lamech's two wives whose story is told in Genesis 4:19–23. Adah is identified as the mother of Jabal and Jubal, whose birth marked the transition of human civilization from a subsistent level economy to an economy that supported the arts, music, and metallurgy. See pages 7, 8.

2. The second Adah lived about 1950 B.C. She was a Canaanite woman who married Esau, the oldest son of Isaac. Isaac was offended by Esau's choice of brides, which reflected Esau's insensitivity to spiritual issues. Adah is mentioned briefly in Genesis 36.

AHINOAM *[ah HIN oh am:"brother is delight."]*. The two women who bore this name lived around 1000 B.C.

1. According to 1 Samuel 14:50 Ahinoam was the name of Saul's wife. As no other wife is mentioned, Ahinoam would have been the mother of Jonathan, who became David's closest friend.

2. Another woman named Ahinoam was married to David and was the mother of his firstborn son, Amnon. She is mentioned in every list of David's family although we know nothing else about her. See 1 Samuel 25:43; 27:3; 30:5 and 2 Samuel 3:2.

AHLAI *[A lih: meaning unknown]*. The only woman with this name is listed in the genealogy of Jerahmeel, a descendant of Judah, in 1 Chronicles

2:31. As Hebrew genealogies characteristically skipped generations to mention the most significant individuals, we can't assign her a date. Yet the inclusion of Ahlai and several other women in this genealogy is significant.

AHOLIAMAH (See Oholibamah.)

ANNA *[AN ah: "grace"]*. Anna is identified in the New Testament as a prophetess, who had dedicated herself to serve God in the temple. When Mary brought the baby Jesus to the temple to offer the sacrifices required after childbirth, Anna recognized Jesus as the promised Messiah. Due to the fact that the calculations establishing our calendar were faulty, the event involving Anna, reported in Luke 2:36–38, likely took place in 4 B.C. See page 130, 299, 306.

APPHIA *[AF ih uh: meaning unknown]*. Paul greeted this unknown woman by name in his letter to Philemon (v. 2), written about A.D. 60. Paul's frequent mention of women in his letters reminds us that the apostle valued Christian women and respected their contribution to the spread of the gospel.

ASENATH *[AS ih nath: "belonging to Neit," an Egyptian deity]*. Asenath's name reflects the common practice in the ancient world of incorporating the names of deities in personal names. This Egyptian wife of Joseph (Gen. 41:45, 50; 46:20) who lived around 1875 B.C., was the mother of his two sons, Manasseh and Ephraim. We do not know whether Joseph influenced her to trust the living God. Yet each of her sons is counted with Jacob's sons as the founder of an Israelite tribe.

ATARAH *[AT ah rah: "crown"]*. She is one of several unknown women listed in the genealogy of Jerameel, a descendant of Judah, in 1 Chronicles 2:26. We know nothing of her life, or the dates during which she lived.

BASEMATH *[BASE math: "fragrant"]*. Also written as Bashemath, and Basmath.

1. Genesis 26:34 identifies Basemath as a daughter of Elon the Hittite and a wife of Esau. She is probably the same woman called Adah in Genesis 36:2.

2. Another wife of Esau who is identified as a daughter of Ishmael is called Basemath in Genesis 36:3, 4, 10, and 13. She is called Mahalath in Genesis 28:6–9. Each of these

women would have lived around 1950–1925 B.C.

3. A thousand years later (around 925 B.C.), Solomon named one of his daughters Basemath. She was married to the governor of one of the new administrative districts Solomon set up in an attempt to break down tribal loyalties in favor of a national identity. She is mentioned only in 1 Kings 4:15.

BATHSHUA *[bath SHOO uh: "daughter of abundance"]*. This Canaanite woman (called Shua in NKJV) was married to Judah, one of the sons of Jacob about 1875 B.C. She is mentioned in 1 Chronicles 2:3, and called "Shua" in Genesis 38:2, 12.

BITHIAH *[bih THIH uh: "daughter of Yahweh"]*. First Chronicles 4:18 identifies Bithiah as a daughter of a Pharaoh, who was married to Mered, of the family of Judah. The date is uncertain.

CANDACE *[KAN duh see: probably a title rather than a proper name]*. She was the queen of Ethiopia in A.D. 35 served by the government official whom Philip baptized after explaining the meaning of Isaiah 53. The government official's story is told in Acts 8.

CHLOE *[KLOH ee: "tender shoot"]*. A Christian woman in Corinth about A.D. 55. According to 1 Corinthians 1:11 members of her household informed the apostle Paul of the problems he discussed in that Epistle.

CLAUDIA *[CLAW dih uh: meaning unknown]*. A Christian woman of Rome, whose greetings are forwarded in 2 Timothy 4:21.

D

DAMARIS *[DAM uh riss: "heifer"]*. A woman of Athens who converted to Christianity about A.D. 50. The fact that Damaris was among those listening to Paul preach indicates that she was a hetaera, an educated woman valued as a companion of men, rather than someone's wife. She is mentioned in Acts 17:34. See page 305.

DEBORAH *[DEB uh rah: "honey bee"]*

1. The first Bible woman to bear the name was the nurse of Rebekah, who later became Isaac's wife (Gen. 35:8). She lived around 2025 B.C.

2. The most famous Deborah served as a "judge." This title was given to individuals who served as political, military, and spiritual leaders in Israel after Joshua's death up to the crowning of Israel's first king, hundreds of years later. We cannot accurately date Deborah's judgeship, although it was early in the period. It is clear from the biblical text that Deborah's leadership was accepted by the people of her time, and that her many gifts won her a position generally reserved for men. This exceptional woman's career, described in Judges 4 and 5, is evidence that gender did not in itself disqualify individuals from significant leadership in the Old Testament faith community. See page 42–48, 288, 289.

EGLAH *[EGG la:"calf"]*. A wife of David around 1000 B.C. Neither she nor Ithream, her son by David, played a significant role in Scripture. She is mentioned only in genealogies in 2 Samuel 3:5 and 1 Chronicles 3:3.

ELISHEBA *[ee LISH ih buh:"God is an oath"]*. She was the wife of Aaron, Moses' brother. She was the mother of the priests Nadab, Abihu, Eleazar, and Ithamar in the exciting era of the Exodus around 1400 B.C. She is mentioned only in Exodus 6:23.

EPHAH *[E fah: meaning unknown]*. Caleb's concubine whose name is listed in the genealogy of Judah in 1 Chronicles 2:46. Her date is unknown. Her sons' names are recorded.

EPHRATH *[EF rath: meaning unknown]*. The second wife of another Caleb in Judah's line, who is named in 1 Chronicles 2:19. Her name is rendered Ephrathah in 1 Chronicles 2:50 and 4:4.

GOMER *[GOAM ur: meaning unknown]*. The wife of the prophet Hosea around 750 B.C. Gomer left her husband and children and became a prostitute. The prophet's commitment to his straying wife became a metaphor for God's faithfulness to His covenant people who had abandoned Him to worship idols. See Hosea 1–3.

HADASSAH *[hah DAH shuh:"myrtle," or "bride"]*. Another name of Esther.

HAGGITH *[HAG ith:"born on a feast day"]*. One of David's wives around 1000 B.C. According to 2 Samuel 3:4 and 1 Kings 1:5 she was the mother of Adonijah, who competed with Solomon to succeed David.

HAMUTAL *[huh MOO tuhl: meaning unknown]*. Hamutal was the wife of godly king Josiah, around 650 B.C. She was the mother of Jehoahaz and Zedekiah, each of whom became kings of Judah. Her name is given in 2 Kings 23:31; 24:18; and Jeremiah 52:1.

HAZELELPONI *[haz ih lehl POE nigh: meaning unknown]*. An otherwise unknown woman whose name is listed in the genealogical record of the tribe of Judah in 1 Chronicles 4:3.

HODESH *[HOE desh:"new moon"]*. All we know of Hodesh is that she is listed in Benjamin's genealogy in 1 Chronicles 8:8.

HOGLAH *[HOG luh:"partridge"]*. One of the five daughters of Zelophehad, a descendant of Manasseh. After the conquest of Canaan, around 1390 B.C., she and her sisters petitioned Moses for the right to inherit their father's property since he had no sons. When their request was brought to the Lord, God confirmed their right to inherit, and the Law was modified appropriately. Their story is told in Numbers 27:1–11, and repeated in Numbers 36 and Joshua 17:3–6. See page 256-258.

ISCAH *[IZ kuh: meaning unknown]*. A daughter of Haran and sister of Nahor, Abraham's brother. She lived about 2075 B.C. and is mentioned only in Genesis 11:29.

ISHTAR *[ISH tahr: possibly "bride"]*. Ishtar was the Assyrian goddess of sexuality and fertility. While not named in the Bible, Jeremiah 7:18 and 44:17, 18, 19, and 25 refer to her by her title, the "queen of heaven."

JECHOLIAH *[JEK uh LIGH uh: meaning unknown]*. She lived around 825 B.C. and was the mother of Uzziah (also known as Azariah), the tenth king of Judah. See 2 Kings 15:2 and 2 Chronicles 26:3.

JEDIDAH *[juh DIGH duh:"beloved"]*. She was the mother of godly King Josiah, the sixteenth descendant of David to rule Judah. She lived around 650 B.C. She is named in 2 Kings 22:1.

JEMIMAH *[juh MIGH muh: "little dove"]*. The daughter of Job, born after his time of trouble, probably lived sometime in the age of the patriarchs. See Job 42:14.

JERIOTH *[JER ih ahth: "tents"]*. A wife of Caleb, Jerioth is listed in the genealogy of Judah in 1 Chronicles 2:18. Her date is unknown.

JERUSHA *[juh ROO shuh: "possession"]*. Also spelled Jerushah. She was the wife of Uzziah and mother of Jotham, both of whom were kings of Judah. She is mentioned in 2 Kings 15:33 and 2 Chronicles 27:1 where she is referred to as Jerushah.

JUDITH *[JOO dith: meaning unknown]*. A Hittite wife of Isaac's son Esau, around 1950 B.C., named in Genesis 26:34. Probably the same as Aholibamah, named in Genesis 36:14, 18, 25.

JULIA *[JOOL yuh, feminine form of Julius]*. Paul greeted this woman living in Rome around A.D. 55 as he concluded his letter to the Romans. See Romans 16:15.

JUNIA *[JOO ni uh: meaning unknown]*. A woman whom Paul identified in Romans 16:7 as a fellow countryman and "of note among the apostles." While "apostles" here is used in its weaker sense as "missionaries," the fact that a woman bore this title around A.D. 55 is significant.

KEREN-HAPPUCH *[KER uhn HAP uhk: "horn of antimony" (eye shadow)]*. The youngest daughter of Job, she was born after his time of trouble, probably sometime in the age of the patriarchs. See Job 42:14.

KETURAH *[keh TUR uh: "incense"]*. Abraham's second wife, taken after Sarah's death, around 2025 B.C. She is called a concubine in 1 Chronicles. See Genesis 25:1, 4 and 1 Chronicles 1:32, 33.

KEZIAH *[kih ZIE uh: "cassia" or cinnamon]*. Job's second daughter. Keziah, born after Job's time of trouble, probably lived sometime in the age of the patriarchs. See Job 42:14.

LO-RUHAMAH *[LOH roo HAH muh: "not loved"]*. The prophet Hosea gave this symbolic name to one of his daughters around 725 B.C. The name was intended to communicate God's unwillingness to forgive the sins of a stiff-necked and unrepentant Israel. See Hosea 1:6–8; 2:23.

MAACAH *[MAY ah kah: "oppressed"]*. The Hebrew name is also spelled Maachah, Michaiah, and Michaiah in our English versions. Five women by this name are identified in the Old Testament.

1. The concubine of a man named Caleb, the son of Hazron, mentioned in the genealogy of Judah in 1 Chronicles 2:48.

2. The wife of Makir, listed in the genealogy of Manasseh in 1 Chronicles 7:15, 16.

3. The wife of Jeiel, an ancestor of King Saul, who lived about 1125 B.C. She is named in 1 Chronicles 8:29 and 9:35.

4. This wife of King David gave birth to Absalom, who led a rebellion against his father and temporarily drove David from Jerusalem. She is mentioned in 2 Samuel 3:3 and 1 Chronicles 3:2.

5. This favorite wife of King Rehoboam was the mother of Abijah, who succeeded his father on Judah's throne. Later Maacah was deposed as queen mother by her grandson Asa because she made an Asherah pole, used in the worship of a pagan goddess. She was likely the granddaughter of Absalom. She is mentioned in 1 Kings 15:2–13 and 2 Chronicles 11:20–22 and 13:2.

MAHALATH *[MAY huh lath: meaning unknown]*. Two women by this name are mentioned in the Old Testament.

1. Around 1925 B.C., a daughter of Ishmael who later married Esau, bore this name. See Genesis 28:9.

2. Another Mahalath in 925 B.C., who was a daughter of David's son Jerimoth, married King Rehoboam. See 2 Chronicles 11:18.

MAHLAH *[MAH luh: "weak, sickly"]*. A daughter of Zelophehad who, with her sisters, around 1400 B.C., brought about a significant development in Israel's inheritance laws. See Numbers 26:33; 27:1–7 and pages 256–258.

MARA *[MAY ruh: "bitter"]*. This name was assumed by Naomi, Ruth's mother-in-law, after her husband and two sons died in Moab, some time during the era of the judges. See Ruth 1:20, and pages 194–200.

MARY *[MAIR ee: the Greek form of Miriam, "loved by Yahweh"].* Mary was a common name in first-century Palestine.

1. Mary, Jesus' mother. Mary was a teenager when the angel Gabriel appeared to her to announce she had been chosen by God to be the mother of the Savior. Mary's immediate and trusting response makes her an appealing example of faith for all. See Matthew 1:16–25, Luke 1:26–56 and pages 126–135, 299, 303.

2. Mary, the sister of Martha and Lazarus. She violated custom by sitting at Jesus' feet as a learner rather than retreating to the kitchen. Jesus supported her action, saying she had "chosen the better part." See Luke 10:39–42, John 11, and pages 114, 296, 299.

3. Mary called Magdalene after the city from which she came. She became a dedicated follower of Jesus after he expelled a demon from her. She was also the first witness of the resurrected Christ. See Luke 8:2, John 20:1–18, and page 120.

4. Mary, the mother of James the younger and Joseph (Joses). Most believe she was also the Mary identified in John 19:25 as the wife of Clopas, and the "other Mary" of in Matthew 27:61; 28:1. See also Mark 15:40, 47.

5. Mary, the mother of John Mark. After the resurrection Jesus' followers often gathered in the Jerusalem home of this well-to-do woman. When Peter was miraculously released from prison, he hurried to her home, where a prayer meeting was in progress. See Acts 12, and pages 136–138, 304.

6. A sixth Mary is mentioned in the last chapter of Paul's letter to the Romans dated about A.D. 55. See Romans 16:6.

MEHETABEL *[meh HET uh bel: "God is doing good"].* She is named in Genesis 36:39 as the wife of a ruler of Edom, whose date is unknown.

MERAB *[MEE rab: "increase"].* This older daughter of Saul was promised to David, but instead Saul married her to Adriel of Meholah. After Saul's death her five sons were executed by the Gibeonites, whose ancient covenant with Israel Saul had violated. See 1 Samuel 18:17–19 and 2 Samuel 21:8 (where the NKJV has "Michal.").

MESHULLEMETH *[meh SHUL uh meth: "reconciliation"].* The wife of evil King Manasseh of Judah, and mother of King Amon who was no better. She lived around 675 B.C. See 2 Kings 21:19.

MILCAH *[MILL kuh: "counsel"]*

1. This grandmother of Rebekah lived around 2075 B.C. She was married to Abraham's brother, Nahor. See Genesis 11:29; 22:20–23.

2. One of the daughters of Zelophehad who around 1390 B.C. won the right for women to inherit their father's land. See Numbers 26:33; 27:1, and pages 256–258.

NAAMAH *[NAY uh muh: "pleasant"].* Two Old Testament women bore this name.

1. Long before the Genesis Flood one of the daughters of Lamech was named Naamah. See Genesis 4:22.

2. About 950 B.C., another Naamah was the mother of Rehoboam, who succeeded his father Solomon on the throne of the then-united Hebrew Kingdom. See 1 Kings 14:21–31.

NAARAH *[NAY a rah: "girl"].* Mentioned only in 1 Chronicles 4:5, 6 as the wife of Ashur.

NEHUSHTA *[neh HUSH tuh: meaning unknown].* Identified in 2 Kings 24:8 as the mother of Jehoiachin, who ruled Judah in 587–586 B.C.

NOADIAH *[NO uh DIE uh: "Yahweh assembles"].* A prophetess who opposed Nehemiah around 450 B.C. See Nehemiah 6:14.

NOAH *[NOH uh: "rest," "comfort"].* One of the daughters of Zelophehad who together brought about a change in Israel's inheritance laws around 1390 B.C. See Numbers 27:1–11, and pages 256–258.

O

OHOLIBAMAH *[o HOLE ih bah mah: "tent of the high place"].* Also spelled Aholiamah. The name of a Hittite wife taken by Esau, the son of Isaac, around 1850 B.C. See Genesis 26:34 where she is referred to as "Judith the daughter of Beeri the Hittite."

ORPAH *[AWR pah: meaning unknown].* The sister-in-law of Ruth. After her husband died, she returned to her father's home in Moab rather than accompany Naomi and Ruth to Judah. See Ruth 1.

P

PENINNAH *[pih NIN uh:"coral"]*. A wife of Elkanah, she made her co-wife Hannah miserable by ridiculing her for her inability to have children. She lived around 1125 B.C. and is mentioned briefly in 1 Samuel 1:2–7.

PERSIS *[PUR sis:"Persian woman"]*. A member of the church in Rome in A.D. 55, she was identified as a dear friend who "labored much in the Lord." See Romans 16:12.

R

REUMAH *[ROO muh: meaning unknown]*. The concubine of Nahor, Abraham's brother, about 2075 B.C. See Genesis 22:24.

S

SALOME *[suh LOE mee:"peaceable," feminine of Solomon]*. The two New Testament women who bore this name could hardly have been more different.

1. Salome, the follower of Jesus, was probably the wife of Zebedee and mother of James and John (see Matt. 27:56). She was a true believer and a witness to Christ's resurrection. See Mark 15:40, 41; 16:1, and page 200.

2. Salome (although not mentioned by name in the Bible), the daughter of Herodias and Herod Philip. About A.D. 30 and at the urging of her mother, Salome asked for the head of John the Baptist as a reward for a dance that had pleased King Herod Antipas and his guests. See Matthew 14:3–11.

SARAI *[SAY ri:"Yahweh is prince"]*. Sarah's original name. See Genesis 11:29; 16:1–9.

SERAH *[SEE ruh:"extension"]*. Mistranslated Sarah in some versions, this daughter of Ashur is mentioned in Genesis 46:17 and Numbers 26:46.

SHEERAH *[SHEE uh ruh:"blood relationship"]*. Spelled Sherah in some versions. This descendant of Ephraim is credited with founding three towns. See 1 Chronicles 7:24.

SHELOMITH *[shih LOE mith:"peaceful"]*

1. The mother of a blasphemer who was stoned to death around 1475 B.C. See Leviticus 24:11.

2. A daughter of Zerubbabel listed in the genealogy of the royal family after the return of the Jewish exiles to their homeland, about 500 B.C. See Ezra 8:10.

SHIMEATH *[SHIM ee ath:"fame"]*. The Ammonite mother of one of the conspirators who murdered King Joash of Judah, around 825 B.C. See 2 Kings 12:21.

SHIMRITH *[SHIM rith:"watch"]*. The Moabite mother of an official who helped murder King Joash of Judah, around 825 B.C. See 2 Chronicles 24:26 and SHOMER below.

SHOMER *[SHOW muhr:"keeper" or "watcher"]*. The mother of one of the men who conspired to murder King Joash of Judah, about 825 B.C. See 2 Kings 12:21. She is mistakenly called Shimrith in 2 Chronicles 24:26.

SHUA *[SHOO uh:"prosperity"]*. A daughter of Heber, mentioned in the genealogy of Ashur in 2 Chronicles 7:32.

SUSANNA *[SUE zan nah:"lily"]*. A follower of Jesus who helped support Him and His disciples financially. See Luke 8:3.

T

TAHPENES *[TAH puh neez: meaning unknown]*. An Ethiopian queen about 925 B.C. She was a contemporary of David and Solomon. See 1 Kings 11:18–20.

TAMAR *[TAY mur:"palm tree"]*. Three Old Testament women shared this name.

1. The first Tamar was the widow of a son of Judah, founder of one of Israel's twelve tribes. She lived about 1850 B.C. When her father-in-law failed to marry her to another of his sons, as custom required, she pretended to be a prostitute, seduced Judah, and became pregnant. See Genesis 38 and page 233.

2. The second Tamar was a daughter of David, who lived around 975 B.C. Her half-brother, Amnon, raped her. Subsequently Tamar's full brother, Absalom, murdered Amnon and led a rebellion against David. See 2 Samuel 13 and page 236.

3. Around 950 B.C. Absalom named one of his own daughters after his sister, Tamar. See 2 Samuel 14:27.

TAPHATH *[TAY fath: meaning unknown]*. A daughter of Solomon who was married to one of his high officials around 950 B.C. See 1 Kings 4:11.

TIMNA *[TIM nuh:"restraining"]*

1. In 1950 B.C. a concubine of Eliphaz, a son of Esau. See Genesis 36:12.

2. In 1975 B.C., a sister of Lotan, a Horite chief in Esau's family line. See Genesis 36:22.

TIRZAH *[TUR zuh: meaning unknown]*. The youngest of the five daughters of Zelophehad, around 1400 B.C. She and her sisters petitioned Moses to inherit their father's land and brought about a change in Israel's inheritance laws. See Numbers 27:1–8 and pages 256-258.

TRYPHENA *[trigh FEE nuh:"dainty"]*. A Christian woman whom Paul greeted in his letter to the Romans, about A.D. 55. See Romans 16:12.

Z

ZERESH *[ZEE resh:"gold"]*. The wife of Hamaan, the enemy of the Jewish people in 425 B.C. Zeresh suggested that her husband build a gallows on which to execute the Jew Mordecai. In the end, Hamaan himself died on those gallows. See the Esther 5:10, 14; 6:13.

ZERUIAH *[zeh roo EYE ah: meaning unknown]*. This sister of David was the mother of several commanders in David's army. See 1 Samuel 26:6; 1 Chronicles 2:16.

ZILPAH *[ZILL pah: meaning unknown]*. Leah's slave in 1925 B.C. Leah used Zilpah as a surrogate in a competition with her sister Rachel to give their husband Jacob the most sons. See Genesis 30 and pages 28–30, 168, 174, 280.

Appendix A

Historical Panorama of Women in the Bible

In the Bible, we meet many different women, some with vital roles to play in salvation history. We also find teachings about women's essential nature as human beings, and teachings about their relationships with men in society, in marriage and the family, and in the community of faith.

The Bible also contains a wide variety of literary devices that feature women. There are similes and there are metaphors. Some women serve as symbols, while Sarah and Hagar are even referred to as "types." Women often appear in illustrations, and parables featuring women are used frequently to make a point. In this appendix, we survey and explain passages in Scripture where Bible imagery features women.

Imagery Involving Women in the Old Testament

Imagery in the Pentateuch

The books of Genesis through Deuteronomy contain narrative history and Law. They contain little imagery involving women. However, they contain two passages in which Israel is warned of the consequences of abandoning the Lord and His Law.

Leviticus 26:26: "When I have cut off your supply of bread, ten women shall bake your bread in one oven." In Bible times, each family baked bread in its own hive-shaped oven. The image of ten women baking in one oven powerfully conveys the idea of starvation, when ten families must survive on bread needed to feed a single family.

Deuteronomy 28:56: "The tender and delicate woman among you, who would not venture to set the sole of her foot on the ground because of her delicateness and sensitivity, will refuse to the husband of her bosom, and to her son and daughter..." The passage goes on to describe a horrible famine. The famine would be so great that even this pampered, upper-class woman would hide her placenta after giving birth so she might gnaw on it in private and thus assuage her hunger.

Imagery in the Books of History

While the bulk of the content of these books is also narrative, a few passages contain imagery involving women.

2 Samuel 1:26. This image is found in David's lament at the death of Saul and Jonathan:

> I am distressed for you, my
> brother Jonathan;
> You have been very pleasant to me;
> Your love to me was wonderful,
> Surpassing the love of women."

—2 Sam. 1:26

Some have misused this verse to argue that David and Jonathan had a homosexual relationship. Just the opposite is implied. David recalls a friendship so deep that each person was unselfishly loyal to the other. David emphasized that no element of passion or self-gratification was present in the friendship these two men enjoyed. The relationship was both pure and unique.

Ruth 4:11, 12. "And all the people who were at the gate, and the elders, said, 'We are witnesses. The LORD make the woman who is coming to your house like Rachel and Leah, the two who built the house of Israel; and may you prosper in Ephrathah and be famous in Bethlehem. May your house be like the house of Perez, whom Tamar bore to Judah, because of the offspring which the LORD will give you from this young woman.'"

In this expression of best wishes to Boaz on his forthcoming marriage to Ruth, the women are representative of both fertility and significance. Rachel and Leah were considered "mothers" of the race, and Tamar was the "mother" of Boaz's family line, from whom King David sprang (see Ruth 4:18–22).

2 Kings 14:9; 2 Chronicles 25:18. "And Jehoash [Joash] king of Israel sent to Amaziah king of Judah, saying, 'The thistle that was in Lebanon sent to the cedar that was in Lebanon, saying, "Give your daughter to my son as wife"; and a wild beast that was in Lebanon passed by and trampled the thistle.'"

Amaziah of Judah wanted war with Israel. Jehoash replied with a parable, emphasizing the superiority of the "cedar of Lebanon" [Israel] to the "thistle" [Judah]. Just as the thistle was above itself in seeking an alliance by marriage with the cedar, so Judah had overreached itself in challenging Israel. Jehoash proved to be correct. Amaziah insisted on war anyway, and Israel thrashed Judah.

Imagery in the Poetic Books

Hebrew poetry relies heavily on imagery to convey meaning. Yet relatively few images that involve women appear in the poetic books.

Psalm 87:4; 89:10. "I will make mention of Rahab and Babylon" (Ps. 87:4). In these two verses, "Rahab" is a poetic name for Egypt. This is not a reference to the biblical woman of this name.

Proverbs 30:15. "The leech has two daughters; Give and Give!" Here, "daughters" is a metaphor for characteristics or qualities. Like the leech, those who demand "give" and "give" drain others without ever giving back to them.

Proverbs 31:14. "She is like the merchant ships, / She brings her food from afar." In this poem praising the virtuous woman, the poet uses a simile that he then limits.

The land of Israel is blessed with a variety of climatic zones that support many different kinds of food plants. Grain, figs, olives, melons, and oranges—all of which require different soils and amounts of rainfall—can all be grown in Israel. Many Israelite farm families relied on what their own land produced to feed the family. Therefore, they had a limited diet. The woman of Proverbs 31 provided a more varied diet for her family, by purchasing food "from afar," that is, food grown in other climatic zones in Israel.

Ecclesiastes 7:26. "'And I find more bitter than death / The woman whose heart is snares and nets, / Whose hands are fetters.'" Here again, Solomon relied on metaphor to picture a particular type of woman. As similar images are found in Solomon's description of the immoral woman in Proverbs 7, we can conclude that here, too, he has in mind women who use their sexuality to draw men into sin.

Ecclesiastes 12:4. "And all the daughters of music are brought low." Frequently Hebrew idiom uses "sons of" or "daughters of" to designate a class. In this passage, Solomon is describing the debilitating effects of old age. This image describes the loss of hearing, so that the "daughters of music," that is, the sound of music or music itself, can hardly be heard.

Imagery in the Prophets

As we might expect, it is the prophets who most often use imagery involving women. There are a number of such uses throughout the prophetic writings.

Isaiah 3:12. "As for My people, children are their oppressors, / And women rule over them." The image is a lament. The metaphor depicts the rulers of the kingdom as being unqualified.

Isaiah 4:1. "In that day seven women shall take hold of one man, saying, / 'We will eat our own food and wear our own apparel; / Only let us be called by your name, / To take away our reproach.'"

This verse goes with Isaiah 3:16–26 rather than with 4:2 and following. Isaiah is describing the disastrous effects on the haughty women of Jerusalem of the coming enemy invasion made certain by their sins. In that day, men will be so scarce that women will be desperate for marriage and children. Rather than asking the man to provide the customary bride price, the women will offer to provide the money needed to feed and clothe themselves if only the man will accept them into his household.

Isaiah 13:8. "And they will be afraid./Pangs and sorrows will take hold of them;/They will be in pain as a woman in childbirth."

The pangs of childbirth are symbolic of anguish and agony. This powerful image is found in each of the following passages in the Old Testament:

◆ "in childbirth": Isaiah 13:8; Jeremiah 50:43; Hosea 13:13
◆ birth pangs": Psalm 48:6; Jeremiah 48:41; 49:22; Micah 4:10
◆ "in labor": Isaiah 21:3; 42:14; 66:7; 66:8; Jeremiah 4:31; 6:24; 13:21; 22:23; 30:6; 49:24; Micah 4:9; 5:3

The simile is used frequently by the prophets to depict the extreme suffering associated with divine judgment and especially of the judgment to come on Israel and the world at history's end.

Isaiah 19:16. "In that day Egypt will be like women, and will be afraid and fear because of the waving of the hand of the LORD of hosts, which He waves over it."

The simile depicts the helplessness of biblical women in wartime. They had no way to defend themselves and waited in fear and uncertainty on the outcome of the battles in which their men took part.

Isaiah 21:3. See the note on Isaiah 13:8.

Isaiah 42:14. See the note on Isaiah 13:8.

Isaiah 49:15. "Can a woman forget her nursing child.../Surely they may forget,/Yet I will not forget you."

In Israel, as in our culture, mother-love was symbolic of selfless commitment. The prophet pointed out that even mothers "may forget" their nursing children, but God will not forget His people. His loyalty and love far exceeds that of the mother who is the ultimate symbol of human commitment.

Isaiah 54:6. "'For the Lord has called you/Like a woman forsaken and grieved in spirit,/Like a youthful wife when you were refused,'/Says your God."

Isaiah used a simile to depict the reconciliation of God's people to the Lord at history's end. Israel is likened to a divorced woman, and to a young wife who had been "refused" [that is, cast off] because of her own faults. Yet Israel's faithful God will call His people back into the intimate relationship they

enjoyed before their spiritual unfaithfulness led to a "divorce."

Isaiah 66:7, 8. See the note on Isaiah 13:8.

Jeremiah 3:1. "They say, 'If a man divorces his wife,/And she goes from him/And becomes another man's,/May he return to her again?'/Would not that land be greatly polluted?/But you have played the harlot with many lovers;/Yet return to Me,' says the LORD."

Jeremiah draws an analogy between a man and wife and God and Israel. According to Moses' Law a woman who, after a divorce, married a second husband could not return to the first (Deut. 24:4). Yet God loves Israel so much, even after the nation has been unfaithful to Him, He is willing to take it back.

Jeremiah 3:20. "'Surely, as a wife treacherously departs from her husband,/so have you dealt treacherously with Me,/O house of Israel,' says the LORD." This verse reflects the thought of Jeremiah 3:1, above.

Jeremiah 4:31. See the note on Isaiah 13:8.

Jeremiah 6:2. "I have likened the daughter of Zion/To a lovely and delicate woman." This simile is intended to convey Jerusalem's helplessness when at history's end "disaster appears out of the north" (6:1).

Jeremiah 6:24. See the note on Isaiah 13:8.

Jeremiah 9:17. "Consider and call for the mourning women,/That they may come;/And send for skillful wailing women,/That they may come."

Jewish funerals featured loud wailing and mourning as a sign of respect for the deceased. To make sure that a person who died was so honored, many families hired professional mourners. But Jewish funerals were conducted the day a person died. The call to "send for" mourning and wailing women was the prophet's way of saying that the disaster he had predicted was almost upon his homeland.

Jeremiah 9:20. "Teach your daughters wailing,/And everyone her neighbor a lamentation." See the comment on Jeremiah 9:17. Jeremiah urged mothers to equip their daughters with a skill they would be able to use to support themselves. The only thing mothers could do to prepare their daughters for the future God had in store was to teach them to become professional mourners, for there would be funerals aplenty!

Jeremiah 13:21. See the note on Isaiah 13:8.

Jeremiah 22:23. See the note on Isaiah 13:8.

Jeremiah 30:6. See the note on Isaiah 13:8.

Jeremiah 31:22. "How long will you gad about,/O you backsliding daughter?/For the LORD has created a new thing in the earth—/A woman shall encompass a man."

The phrase "encompass a man" is obscure in English, and might better be translated as in the Tanakh [a Jewish translation of the Old Testament], "a woman courts a man." Normally men initiated the courtship. Here, Jeremiah is looking forward to a day when God's people will again yearn for Him, and court His presence rather than "gadding about" as backsliders.

Jeremiah 48:41. See the note on Isaiah 13:8.

Jeremiah 49:22, 24. See the note on Isaiah 13:8.

Jeremiah 50:43. See the note on Isaiah 13:8.

Jeremiah 51:30. See the note on Isaiah 13:8.

Lamentations 1:1. "How like a widow is she,/Who was great among the nations!/The princess among the provinces/Has become a slave!"

In this poetic simile, the author of the poem portrays the transformed condition of Jerusalem. The once-great city has become a ruin. Its changed condition is like the changed condition of a wife who is widowed, or a princess who has become a slave.

Ezekiel 16:32. "'You are an adulterous wife, who takes strangers instead of her husband.'"

The prophet likened the city of Jerusalem to an unfaithful wife. Idolatry was often pictured as spiritual adultery for each involved the breaking of a covenant commitment.

Ezekiel 16:46. "Your elder sister is Samaria, who dwells with her daughters to the north of you; and your younger sister, who dwells to the south of you, is Sodom and her daughters."

In an extended passage, Ezekiel portrays Judah and its people as sisters of Samaria–the capital of the fallen northern Hebrew kingdom Israel—and of Sodom. The imagery conveys a clear and simple message. The people of Jerusalem and Judah have adopted the ways of the two sinful cities. Through the prophet the Lord says, "'Neither your sister Sodom nor her daughters [that is, the inhabitants of the city] have done as you and your daughters have done'" (16:48). God destroyed the two sinful sister cities, and Jerusalem will surely suffer the same fate.

Ezekiel 23:1–49. Ezekiel returns to the "sisters" imagery, this time focusing on "two women, the daughters of one mother" (v. 2). In this passage, the sisters are the kingdoms of Israel and Judah. Ezekiel gave each a symbolic name. Israel is called Oholah ["her own tabernacle"], a reference to the counterfeit religious system set up by Jeroboam I (1 Kin. 13) and maintained by all the succeeding kings of Israel. Judah is called Oholibah ["My tabernacle is in her"], a reference to the fact that God's temple lay in Jerusalem in Judah. Each of the two "sisters" turned to harlotry and was unfaithful to the Lord. Each would experience divine judgment.

Ezekiel 24:18. "So I spoke to the people in the morning, and at evening my wife died; and the next morning I did as I was commanded."

One of the distinctives of Ezekiel's ministry is that he was often called on to act out his prophecies. For instance, when predicting the siege of Jerusalem, he constructed a model city and set up siege works around it. He subsisted on a starvation diet for the same number of days as the city would be under siege.

Then the Lord warned Ezekiel that his wife, the "desire of your eyes" (24:16) would die suddenly. But Ezekiel was not to show any of the traditional signs of mourning, even though he loved her dearly. His demeanor was a sign that when God destroyed Jerusalem as He had promised, the survivors would be so concerned with their own escape that no one would mourn the loss of loved ones.

Ezekiel 36:17. "'Son of man, when the house of Israel dwelt in their own land, they defiled it by their own ways and deeds; to Me their way was like the uncleanness of a woman in her customary impurity.'"

Here, the Lord Himself introduced a simile, comparing the ways of the people of Israel before the Assyrians took the people away to "'the uncleanness of a woman in her customary impurity.'" As a woman with her menstrual flow was ritually unclean and could not be touched by a man, so Israel's sins made the people untouchable by God. As Isaiah 59:2 says, "Your iniquities have separated you from your God;/And your sins have hidden His face from you,/So that He will not hear."

Daniel 11:37. "'He shall regard neither the God of his fathers nor the desire of women, nor regard any god; for he shall exalt himself above them all.'"

The phrase "the desire of women" is not a reference to sex, but to the Messiah. It was the desire of every Jewish woman to become the mother of the Messiah. Daniel's point is that the Antichrist, to whom this verse refers, has no respect for Israel's God, for the coming Messiah, or for any people's deity. Instead, he wants to be treated as a god himself!

Hosea 1:2. "When the LORD began to speak by Hosea, the LORD said to Hosea: 'Go, take yourself a wife of harlotry/And children of harlotry,/For the land has committed great harlotry/By departing from the LORD.'" See the comment on Hosea 3:1, below.

Hosea 3:1. "Then the Lord said to me, 'Go again, love a woman who is loved by a lover and is committing adultery, just like the love of the LORD for the children of Israel, who look to other gods and love the raisin cakes of the pagans.'"

God called the prophet Hosea to marry a woman named Gomer. Either before or after the marriage, Gomer's true character was revealed, and she deserted her husband and children to take many lovers. The heartbroken Hosea was called to act out in this relationship God's own relationship with Israel. Hosea continued to love his wife and to provide for her despite her unfaithfulness. Ultimately, Hosea took his straying wife back.

Here, both Hosea and Gomer are symbols. Their experiences reflected Israel's own unfaithfulness to the Lord, but also foreshadowed the ultimate restoration of Israel's relationship with God at history's end.

Hosea 13:13. See the note on Isaiah 13:8.

Micah 4:9. See the note on Isaiah 13:8.

Micah 4:10. See the note on Isaiah 13:8.

Micah 5:3. See the note on Isaiah 13:8.

Nahum 3:13. "Surely, your people in your midst are women!" Here "women" symbolizes weakness. The prophet emphasized Nineveh's helplessness to resist the invaders God sent against it.

Zechariah 5:7, 9. "'Here is a lead disc lifted up, and this is a woman sitting inside the basket'; ...Then I raised my eyes and looked, and there were two women, coming with wind in their wings; for they had wings like the wings of a stork, and they lifted up the basket between earth and heaven."

The women in this vision are symbolic. Both the woman in the basket and the two winged women stand for something other than themselves. Also, the basket is an *ephah*, holding approximately half a bushel of grain, so the woman in it is not of normal size. The text explains the woman in the basket; she symbolized wickedness (Zech. 5:8). In the vision, the two women carried the basket containing "wickedness" to Shinar [Babylon].

The question is, why should a woman represent wickedness? Several reasons have been suggested.

- ◆ "Wickedness" is a feminine noun.
- ◆ The prophets viewed idolatry as "wickedness" and used the figure of prostitution to represent it. Thus, a woman is an appropriate symbol (see Hos. 2:2; Jer. 3:1).
- ◆ The woman in the basket is not a living woman, but an idol; a figure of the "queen of heaven" (Jer. 44:17–19) whose worship originated in Babylon.

Whichever is correct, it is clear that women, in themselves, do not represent wickedness. It is perhaps to avoid this interpretation that the two beings who symbolize the removal of wickedness from the land are also described as women.

Imagery Involving Women in the New Testament

Matthew 13:33. "'The kingdom of heaven is like leaven, which a woman took and hid in three measures of meal till it was all leavened.'"

This verse is found in a series of kingdom parables, each of which contrasts the form of the kingdom Christ will institute with the form of the kingdom expected by the Jewish people. This parable points toward the gradual growth of the church in contrast to the full-blown expression of God's rule in the messianic kingdom the Jews expected.

Matthew 18:25. "'As he was not able to pay, his master commanded that he be sold, with his wife and children and all that he had, and that payment be made.'" This line from Jesus' story of the unforgiving servant is a reference to debtor law that allowed a creditor to sell a man and his assets—including his family—to pay a debt. However, Old Testament law limited servitude for Hebrews to seven years, after which they must be freed.

Matthew 22:23–33. "'Teacher, Moses said that if a man dies, having no children, his brother shall marry his wife and raise up offspring for his brother.'"

This is the first line of a hypothetical case the Sadducees—who denied the resurrection—used to confound the Pharisees. The Pharisees insisted that the Scriptures taught the resurrection of the body. The hypothetical case postulated a woman who contracted Leverite marriages with seven brothers, remaining childless through all the unions. The climax came when the Sadducees challenged, "'In the resurrection, whose wife of the seven will she be?'" (Matt. 22:28).

The Pharisees had no answer for this challenge, which was intended to reduce the idea of resurrection to absurdity. But Christ did have an answer. The institution of marriage is for our life on earth; it will not exist in heaven. So the question is irrelevant. And, Christ added, the Sadducees were wrong about resurrection because they knew neither the Scriptures nor God's power.

Matthew 24:41. "'Two women will be grinding at the mill: one will be taken and the other left.'" In this passage, Jesus is taught about the end of the age and His own Second Coming. Grinding grain was a task first-century women performed daily. Christ will come unexpectedly while people are going about their ordinary work. When He returns, God will then distinguish between the saved and unsaved.

Matthew 25:1–7. "'Then the kingdom of heaven shall be likened to ten virgins who took their lamps and went out to meet the bridegroom.'"

In this extended simile, Jesus again drew on contemporary customs to make His point. When a Jewish man married, he led a contingent of friends to his bride's house at night, carrying torches and lamps. He then led her back to his own home. The bridegroom's male friends accompanied him; female friends who were also equipped with lights escorted the bride. Jesus pictured the institution of His coming kingdom as a wedding in which He [the bridegroom] comes to take His people [the bride] to His home.

In the story Jesus told, ten young women were waiting for the bridegroom. Only five of them had prepared for a long wait and brought along extra olive oil for their lamps. When the bridegroom finally arrived, only those five who were prepared and ready were allowed inside to join the celebration.

Jesus will come again, but no one knows when. We must take care to be ready when He comes.

Mark 12:18–27. See the discussion of Matthew 22:23–33.

Luke 4:25, 26. "'I tell you truly, many widows were in Israel in the days of Elijah, when the heaven was shut up three years and six months, and there was a great famine throughout all the land; but to none of them was Elijah sent except to Zarephath, in the region of Sidon, to a woman who was a widow.'"

Jesus had been speaking in the synagogue of His hometown, Nazareth. He quoted Isaiah 61 and announced that He Himself was the Messiah spoken of there. The people could not imagine that Jesus, known to them as the son of Joseph the carpenter, could actually be the Messiah.

Christ responded by pointing out that their own people had never honored God's prophets in their own time. He then referred to the widow of Zarephath, a pagan woman whose life Elijah preserved and to Naaman the Syrian leper whom Elisha healed. God will bless pagans should His own people reject Him.

This meaning was clear to all those in the synagogue. They "were filled with wrath, and rose up and thrust Him out of the city" and attempted to throw Him off a cliff (Luke 4:28,29).

Luke 13:21. See the discussion of Matthew 13:33.

Luke 14:20. Still another said, "'I have married a wife, and therefore I cannot come.'"

Christ came offering Himself to the Jewish people as their Messiah, but they refused His invitation. Luke 14 records Jesus' analogy of a man who invited friends to a feast but whose invitation was refused. This verse relates one of several excuses: one guest had just married and had to spend time with his new wife.

What then would the host do since the invited guests refused to respond to his invitation? Jesus said the host sent His servant to invite all those whom society dismissed as insignificant. Since room was still available, the servant was sent to hedges and highways to locate even more guests.

What a picture of what did happen. Israel rejected Jesus, the Messiah died on the cross to become the Savior, and through His death, the door of salvation was thrown open wide to all who will respond.

BIBLE BACKGROUND: INVITATION OF GUESTS

Some have questioned the host's sensitivity in sending his servant "at supper time" (Luke 14:17) to invite his guests to the meal. But first-century etiquette called for guests to be sent a first invitation well ahead of time, and then to be informed when the feast was ready. Luke 14:17 says that the servant was sent "'at supper time to say to *those who were invited*, "Come, for all things are now ready"'" [italics mine]. These guests knew of the feast well ahead of time and should have been ready rather than making excuses.

The message of the Old Testament prophets was God's first invitation to His people to enter the Messiah's kingdom. Jesus' coming was the announcement that "'all things are now ready'" (14:17). But rather than responding to Jesus, who was God's servant, the Jewish people made excuse after excuse for rejecting Him.

Luke 15:8. "'Or what woman, having ten silver coins, if she loses one coin, does not light a lamp, sweep the house, and search carefully until she finds it?'"

This parable is one of three stories Jesus told to illustrate God's attitude toward sinners. In each story, the object that was lost was precious, and finding it caused great rejoicing.

Why was a simple silver coin so precious? The ten coins may have been the woman's dowry. Often dowry coins were strung on a string and worn by the wife. They represented that she brought assets into the marriage. They were also a symbol of security. Should she be divorced, the dowry would be hers. As such, the coin would have significant symbolic and monetary value. Jesus' listeners would have understood this.

Luke 17:26, 27. "'As it was in the days of Noah, so it will be also in the days of the Son of Man: they ate, they drank, they married wives, they were given in marriage, until the day that Noah entered the ark, and the flood came and destroyed them all.'"

Jesus drew an analogy between conditions existing in the days of Noah and conditions that will exist just before He returns. All will seem normal—until God intervenes!

Luke 17:32. "'Remember Lot's wife.'" Jesus further illustrated that people will be surprised when He returns to intervene. When God acted in the days of Noah, people were surprised, and another generation was equally surprised in the days of Lot.

Jesus warned His listeners that when the day He is revealed finally comes, not to hesitate, but flee immediately. It is then, Jesus said, "Remember Lot's wife." The analogy seems clear. Lot's wife hesitated when fleeing Sodom, looked back, and was turned into a pillar of salt. When the day of which Jesus is speaking comes, those who hesitate to flee are doomed.

Luke 17:35. See the discussion of Matthew 24:41.

Luke 18:1–8. "'Now there was a widow in that city; and she came to him, saying, "Get justice for me from my adversary."'"

This parable features a judge who cared nothing for God's opinion and who had no compassion for a widow who had been defrauded. The judge ignored her pleas, but she persisted until the judge finally avenged her, just so she would no longer bother him.

The parable is intended to *contrast* the unjust judge with the Lord, who does have compassion on people and cares deeply for the plight of widows and orphans. While God cares and will avenge His own, we need to be as persistent in prayer as the widow was in pursing her case.

Luke 20:27–38. See the discussion of Matthew 22:23–33.

1 Thessalonians 2:7. "But we were gentle among you, just as a nursing *mother* cherishes her own children." Paul likened his relationship with the young Christians he led to Christ in Thessalonica to that of a nursing mother with young children. The image is striking, particularly since the earliest description we have of the apostle is that of a bent, little man with piercing eyes peering out from under a heavy brow, and whose nose almost touched his chin! Yet it's unlikely that anyone in Thessalonica laughed, for they knew the love Paul had for them and the tenderness with which he nurtured them.

Revelation 2:20. "'Nevertheless I have a few things against you, because you allow that woman Jezebel, who calls herself a prophetess, to teach and seduce My servants to commit sexual immorality and eat things sacrificed to idols.'"

This verse is found in a letter from Christ to one of seven churches in Asia Minor. The name "Jezebel" is applied to an actual but otherwise unnamed woman who, like the Old Testament Jezebel, had gotten believers to commit sexual immorality and idolatry.

Revelation 12. This chapter features two symbolic figures: a "woman clothed with the sun" (v. 1) who gave birth to a male child, and "a great, fiery red dragon" (v.3) who was the dedicated enemy of the woman and the child. The child is the Messiah, the woman represents Israel, and the dragon stands for Satan. The chapter uses symbolic language to describe future events that involve Satan and Israel.

Revelation 17. This chapter of Revelation features another symbolic female figure. Here, the figure is a woman "arrayed in purple and scarlet, and adorned with gold and precious stones and pearls, having in her hand a golden cup full of abominations and the filthiness of her fornication. And on her forehead a name was written: MYSTERY, BABYLON THE GREAT, THE MOTHER OF HARLOTS AND OF THE ABOMINATIONS OF THE EARTH" (17:4, 5).

Commentators generally agree that this woman is symbolic of religion and especially of a great world religion that, at history's end, will at first support the government of the Antichrist and subsequently be destroyed by him.

Revelation 21:9. "Then one of the seven angels who had the seven bowls filled with the seven last plagues came to me and talked with me, saying, 'Come, I will show you the bride, the Lamb's wife.'"

John portrayed the descent of the heavenly Jerusalem to the new earth God created, saying the city was "prepared as a bride adorned for her husband" (Rev. 21:2). The city itself however is not described as a bride, and it is not in view here in verse 9.

The Lamb's wife (v. 9), is the body of believers who, because of faith in Him, have not been consigned to the lake of fire (v. 8). These believers will join Christ in the new and perfect universe God will create at history's end.

What a wonderful prospect to look forward to! No wonder, as John nears the end of this great book, he writes, "and the Spirit and the bride say, 'Come!'" (Rev. 22:17).

Come indeed! Even so, come quickly, Lord Jesus!

Appendix B
Women of the Old Testament

Woman in Creation and the Fall
(Genesis 1–11)

The answers to all our most basic questions are found in Genesis. What is the origin of the world? What is special about human beings? What lies at the heart of our male and female identities?

These questions and many others are answered decisively in the first chapters of Genesis. Here, we find affirmation that the universe is the creation of God who has revealed Himself as a Person. God infused the material world and all living things with structure and order. Genesis 1 immediately defines what is so special about human beings. And Genesis 1 and 2 strongly affirm the common identity of men and women.

Men and Women Are Created in God's Image
(Genesis 1:26, 27)

Then God said, "Let Us make man in Our image, according to Our likeness; let them have dominion over the fish of the sea, over the birds of the air, and over the cattle, over all the earth and over every creeping thing that creeps on the earth." So God created man in His own image; in the image of God He created him; male and female He created them."

There are several things we notice in Scripture's first statement about human beings.

"Man" is a term for the whole human race (Gen. 1:26). The Hebrew word translated man is `adam. This familiar word is also the name of the first man, Adam. In most cases we should understand `adam as "mankind," "human beings," or "humankind." Both male and female are included in *man*. When the biblical text wishes to make a gender distinction, the word `ish is usually used of male human beings, and the word `issah is used of female human beings.

Other Hebrew words are used to make a strong sexual distinction. *Zakar* is used to assert maleness eighty-three times in the Old Testament, and nᵉqebah is used twenty-two times to designate the female.

When God said, "Let Us make *man*," He was not speaking of male human beings, but of both men and women. Male and female are equally, and alike, *man*.

All human beings are created in God's image (Gen. 1:27). The biblical text takes great pains to maintain the essential equality of the genders. Notice the phrases in Genesis 1:27:

- ◆ God created man (`adam) in His own image
- ◆ Male and female
- ◆ He created them

Not only does the text use a word that encompasses all human beings (`adam), but to avoid any possible misunderstanding it adds "male and female," and uses the plural "them."

God wants us to understand that men and women *share the same essential identity*. While there are differences between men and women, these are not differences of essence. The essence of humanity, the thing that sets humankind apart from all other living creatures, is that only human beings have been created in God's image and likeness!

The image of God (Gen. 1:26). Genesis 1:26 uses two Hebrew words to communicate the uniqueness of human beings. In the original text, the two terms, *selem* [image] and *demut* [likeness], are linked. Together, they make a grand theological statement: Human beings bear the image-likeness of God.

Only *human beings* possess this amazing gift. While theologians have debated implications of the phrase, we can best understand image-likeness in a simple way. God has revealed Himself as a Person, with all the attributes of personhood. He thinks, plans, remembers, appreciates beauty, establishes priorities, distinguishes right from wrong, makes decisions and carries them out, and so forth. When God made human beings in His image, He gifted us with this same wonderful range of capacities. These capacities of His, reflected in human nature, make us *persons* too, and constitute the image-likeness of God.

What Genesis 1:27, 28 teach us is that all human beings, *men and women*, share these gifts equally. Some of us will be more intelligent than others, some more sensitive to beauty. The existence of these and other human capacities, not the amount of any one capacity a person may possess, makes each of us human and reflects something of the glory of a God who possesses every quality to perfection.

What we should always remember as we look into Scripture's teaching on women is that women, equally with men, have been gifted by God with His own image-likeness. The women we meet in Scripture display these gifts just as clearly as do the male heroes of our faith.

In *essence,* men and women are the same.

The Creation of Eve
(Genesis 2:18–23)

One of the truly fascinating passages in Scripture is the report in Genesis 2 of Eve's creation. God created the first man, Adam, and placed him in Eden. There, Adam explored the wonders of God's creation. But wherever Adam looked, he was reminded that something was missing. He could not find another creature like himself.

And the Lord God said, "It is not good that man should be alone; I will make him a helper comparable to him."

Out of the ground, the Lord God formed every beast of the field and every bird of the air, and brought them to Adam to see what he would call them. And whatever Adam called each living creature, that was its name. So Adam gave names to all cattle, to the birds of the air, and to every beast of the field. But for Adam, there was not found a helper comparable to him. And the Lord God caused a deep sleep to fall on Adam, and he slept; and He took one of his ribs, and closed up the flesh in its place. Then the rib that the Lord God had taken from man He made into a woman, and He brought her to the man.

And Adam said: "This is now bone of my bones And flesh of my flesh; She shall be called Woman, Because she was taken out of Man."

"A helper comparable" (Gen. 2:18). One of the fictions on which the view of women held by some Christians rests is that women were created subordinate beings. The NIV translates this phrase as a "helper suitable for him," offering further support to those who argue that as "helpers," women were created to be subservient to men and to meet men's needs. The implication is that it is men who count, and women's concerns are to be subordinate to men's.

But the Hebrew phrase here is `ezer kᵉnegᵉdu`, which is best understood as a "helper corresponding to him." Commenting on this phrase, the *Expository Dictionary of Bible Words* (1985) notes:

> In Eve, God provided a "suitable helper" (Gen. 2:20). Eve was suitable because she shared with Adam the image and likeness of God—the image that permits human beings to relate on every dimension of personality (emotional, intellectual, spiritual, physical, etc.). Only another being who, like Adam, was shaped in the image of God would be suitable.

The word for "helper" here is `ezer`. It means "a help," "a support," "an assistant." Before we understand this concept to imply inferiority or subordination, we should note that the root is used in the Old Testament to speak of God as helper of His nation and of individuals. God is man's helper in all kinds of distress (Ex. 18:4; Deut. 33:7, 26, 29; Ps. 20:2; 33:20; 70:5; 89:19; 115:9–11; 121:1, 2; 124:8; 146:5; Hos. 13:9). We do not conclude from this that God is inferior to the person He helps (p. 433).

"That was its name" (Gen. 2:19). A fascinating feature in the story of woman's creation is the way God prepared Adam for his mate. The text tells us that God brought Adam every beast and bird to name. In the Old Testament, names were more than labels. Names were understood to capture and express something of the essence of the things named. The implication is that Adam carefully observed each creature over a significant period of time so he might understand something of its peculiar nature. Then Adam assigned that creature a name that accurately reflected that nature.

In the process of carefully studying birds and animals, Adam made a significant discovery. As wonderful as living creatures were, none among them corresponded to him. There was no creature suited by its nature for him to relate to it.

It was only after Adam had made this discovery, and had begun to feel the emptiness of his isolated life, that God caused him to fall into a deep sleep and set about preparing Eve.

"Flesh of my flesh" (Gen. 2:23). Genesis 2:23 records Adam's words when God brought Eve to him. We can sense his wonder and excitement. "This, at last, is flesh of my flesh!"

What Adam is saying, of course, is, "Now, at last, here is one who shares my identity—one to whom I can relate because she is everything I am, and I am everything she is. Here, at last, is another *person!*"

Again, we have the strongest kind of biblical affirmation of the essential identity of men and women. In terms of essential identity, men and women alike bear the image-likeness of God, and because of it, men and women can relate to each other on every level of the human personality.

The creation story in all its details strongly affirms woman as the full equal of man. Woman's "otherness" or her inferiority and subordination to man simply is not supported by the story of creation.

The Fall

While "otherness" and female inferiority cannot be found in the story of creation, some claim to see it in Scripture's account of the Fall. The theory is that while men and women were created equal, when Adam and Eve sinned God assigned womankind an inferior place as punishment for Eve's behavior.

So we need to examine closely the consequences of the choice of Adam and Eve to eat the forbidden fruit.

Consequences of the Fall

The two fled silently, desperately. They averted their gaze from each other until they had covered themselves with broad leaves torn from low-lying plants. Then they crept into the bushes to hide.

But they could not hide from Him. They heard His voice calling them, and they cowered deeper into the concealing branches. Once they had loved that voice; now it terrified them. What would He do to them? Truly, as the serpent had promised, their eyes had been opened to good and evil—and they had discovered that now *they* were evil!

The voice drew nearer. "Where are you?" The branches they crouched behind parted, and the first pair felt His eyes on them. Still crouching, Adam answered. "I heard Your voice in the garden, and I was afraid because I was naked; and I hid myself."

With infinite sadness, the Lord questioned them, heard their excuses, and explained the consequences of their choice to eat the forbidden fruit. God addressed the three central parties separately. To the serpent and the fallen angel who had spoken through him, God said:

"Because you have done this, you are cursed more than all cattle, and more than every beast of the field. On your belly you shall go, and you shall eat dust all the days of your life. And I will put enmity between you and the woman, and between your seed and her seed. He shall bruise your head, and you shall bruise His heel."

To the woman He said:

"I will greatly multiply your sorrow and your conception; In pain you shall bring forth children. Your desire shall be for your husband, and he shall rule over you."

Then to Adam He said,

"Because you have heeded the voice of your wife, and have eaten from the tree of which I commanded you, saying, 'You shall not eat of it.' Cursed is the ground for your sake. In toil you shall eat of it all the days of your life. Both thorns and thistles it shall bring forth for you, and you shall eat the herb of the field. In the sweat of your face you shall eat bread till you return to the ground. For out of it you were taken; For dust you are, and to dust you shall return."

—Gen. 3:14–19

When we look closely at these pronouncements, we note a striking parallelism. Each explanation of the consequence of the Fall has physical, psychological, societal, and spiritual aspects.

God curses Satan (Gen. 3:14,15). Only God's words to the serpent that hosted Satan are identified as a curse. In biblical language, a curse (*'arar*) is a binding act and a punishment. In this case, the physical consequences of the curse were visited on the serpent. It must forever crawl on the earth's surface on its belly.

Psychological and societal consequences were visited on Satan, and are expressed in 3:15a. God speaks to the devil of "enmity between you and the woman, and between your offspring and hers." The psychological consequence for Satan as explained here is a settled animosity toward the human race, rooted deep in his essential being. The second phrase, "and between your offspring and hers," directs our attention to a unique relationship between fallen human beings ["your offspring"] and God's Son [her Seed].

The Hebrew word for "offspring" is a collective noun, always found in the singular and never in the plural. Thus we are to understand Satan's "offspring" as humanity itself, alienated from God by the Fall and attuned by the Fall to Satan's ways. The "offspring" imagery is used throughout Scripture, and is clearly seen in New Testament passages describing unredeemed human beings as related to Satan morally and spiritually (cf. John 8:44–47; Eph. 2:2; Col. 1:21; 1 John 3:10). And evidence of this antagonism is seen in history, for humankind has displayed a marked antipathy to the God of revelation, and a strange attraction to gods of its own invention.

It is important to realize that this enmity has an impact on society. Every culture significantly institutionalizes values and behaviors. These values and behaviors are not only actively hostile to that which is godly and good, but they are also harmful to human beings. The enmity between God and a world that adopts Satan's values is real indeed, and it is important to discern which values and behaviors reflect Satan's standard rather than God's.

The spiritual consequences to Satan are defined in the last two phrases of this verse, "He will crush your head, and you will strike his heel." It is clear from the use of "he" and "his" that "offspring" refers to an individual. What is normally a collective noun is used in a singular sense. One day a Deliverer will come. He will crush Satan and strip him of his power, despite being terribly bruised in the process. Satan will suffer defeat, as through Eve's promised offspring, God acts to set all things right.

God explains the consequences of the Fall for women (Gen. 3:16). When we look at God's words to Eve, we note first of all that she is not cursed. Rather, God spells out for Eve the implications of her choice, for herself, and also for all her daughters.

> *"I will greatly multiply your sorrow and your conception; In pain you shall bring forth children; Your desire shall be for your husband, and he shall rule over you."*

> —Gen. 3:16

This verse has long puzzled commentators. The rabbis tended to interpret Genesis 3:16 in a sexual way. Childbirth will be painful. A woman's desires [Heb. *T*^e*shuga*: cravings, hungers, focused intent] have generally been understood as a reference to the conjugal act (as by Rashi, and see Midrash; v. Niddah 31b). However N`Tziv comes closest to the text's meaning when he observes that "in the most literal sense, the woman always strives to find favor in her husband's eyes."

When we look at this verse (Gen. 3:16) carefully, we see that the consequences spelled out to Eve and Satan are parallel. The Fall had a physical, psychological, societal, and spiritual impact on Eve. These consequences extended beyond Eve and apply to all her daughters, for in Genesis, Eve represents not just herself but all womankind.

Physical consequences of Eve's fall. Physically, the pains associated with childbirth are increased. Commentators remain puzzled by these images. However, it is best to understand the increased pains as an acceleration of the menstrual cycle to a monthly rather than perhaps an annual rhythm, and to view the pain of childbirth, like many contemporary diseases, as the result of the gradual mutation of an originally perfect genetic code.

Psychological consequences of Eve's fall. Psychologically, the desires of Eve's daughters now focus on men. The translation "your desire will be *for your husband*" is unfortunate but understandable. The Hebrew term translated "husband" is *ish*, which sim-

ply means "man." As Adam stands in this passage not only for himself but also for male humanity, the text is better understood as "your urge will be directed toward men." This is not necessarily a reference to sexual desires, but rather a description of the psychological reorientation of women toward seeking to please not just husbands, but men in general. The psychological orientation of Eve's daughters shifted with the Fall so that their *urges* or *cravings*, as *teshuqa* is best understood, are to please men.

The social consequences of Eve's fall. Societally, this reorientation is expressed in the ways human cultures define men's dominion over women in social institutions, in the family, and even in the Christian church.

The spiritual consequences of Eve's fall. Spiritual consequences of the Fall for women are clearly implied in God's words to Eve. Women, in shifting their urges from a desire to please God to a desire to please males, lose sight of who they have been created to be. Similarly, in exercising a distorted dominion over women, men not only usurp the role of God, but also hold women down and defraud society of the gifts that individual women might bring to enrich all.

God explains the consequences of the Fall for men (Gen. 3:17–19). The passage continues with an explanation to Adam of the consequences of the Fall for the human male.

> *"Cursed is the ground for your sake. In toil you shall eat of it all the days of your life. Both thorns and thistles it shall bring forth for you, and you shall eat the herb of the field. In the sweat of your face you shall eat bread till you return to the ground. For out of it you were taken; For dust you are, and to dust you shall return."*

> —Gen. 3:17b–19

Here again, Adam is not cursed. Rather, God explains the consequence of Adam's disobedience.

Physical consequences of Adam's fall. The first physical consequence is death, reflected in mankind's return to dust. Death, as a process of decay and degradation, is also reflected in nature. The beauty we see in nature reflects the goodness of God's original creation. But the pain, struggle, and decay we see corrupting all of God's creation are a consequence of Adam's sin.

Psychological consequences of Adam's fall. Why the repeated emphasis on labor and toil? Because, just as the Fall stripped Eve of her longing for God and replaced this healthy desire with an urge to please men, so Adam was stripped of his longing for God. What has replaced this healthy desire for God in males has been a desire to achieve by their own efforts. The psychological consequence of the Fall in men has been the emergence of a competitive desire to surpass other men—to bend every effort to excel.

Genesis 3 depicts this struggle in agricultural terms and also describes its futility. Strive as a man will to build, whether kingdoms or companies or fortunes or power, dust awaits the individual. "Dust you are," the text reminds us, "and to dust you will return," leaving every meaningless accomplishment behind.

Societal consequences of Adam's fall. Societally, the urge to excel is expressed as a drive to dominate and control others. Women, whose desire is toward men, are terribly vulnerable to male domination. How ironic it is! Eve used her influence to lead Adam to disobey. As a consequence, the tide of influence has been reversed, and Eve's daughters are carried away on the flood of that urge which makes them desire men's approval.

Spiritual consequences of Adam's fall. Spiritually, men have been corrupted just as women have by the relational reversals of the Fall. Men's desires, which refocused from pleasing God toward personal achievement and the urge to dominate, have also trapped them psychologically and societally. Rather than having a clear image of what they were created to be, men have replaced God's best with pitiful human substitutes. Even as women have lost their intended identity, men have lost theirs also.

And so, in warping and distorting humanity, the Fall has had a disastrous impact on individual women and men and on the institutions and values of society.

We can sum up the impact of the Fall in the following chart:

IMPACT OF THE FALL

Impact of the Fall	On Satan	On Women	On Men
PHYSICALLY	Satan's host (the serpent) is doomed to crawl.	Frequency of menstruation is increased; childbirth becomes painful.	Earth cursed; achievement now involves struggle.
PSYCHOLOGICALLY	Satan to be intensely hostile toward mankind. The lost become antagonistic to the God of revelation.	The urge to please men replaces the desire to please God.	The urge to achieve and to dominate replaces the desire to please God.
SOCIETALLY	Satan corrupts institutions, values.	Women's roles are distorted, opportunities limited.	Male dominance institutionalized, women subjugated.
SPIRITUALLY	Satan and his followers are doomed.	Women replace orientation to true self and God with orientation to men.	Men replace orientation to true self and God with orientation to achievement, domination.

God's words to Satan and to the first pair help us understand the underlying nature of the pressures that increasingly corrupt our society and cause terrible damage to girls and women, as well as distort relationships between them and men. Once we understand these pressures, much that we find in Scripture takes on fresh and new meaning. We realize that notions we have uncritically accepted about the "proper" roles of men and women, and in some cases have even justified as biblical, are far from God's will for a people who have been redeemed and restored in Christ.

The distortions of God's ideal for women and for men that were introduced at the Fall are not to be accepted as normative by Christians. They are to be rejected, and we are to find our way back to God's original ideal.

We can do this by looking to Scripture and discovering in its teachings, and in the women whose lives are portrayed there, a clearer vision of what all of us—men and women alike—are to affirm in womankind. All men and women were created in God's image, and in Christ we are to recover the equality and partnership which Adam and Eve lost.

Women in the Days of the Patriarchs
(Genesis 12—50)

The first meaning of "patriarch" found in most dictionaries is "the paternal leader of a family or tribe." Biblically, the patriarchs are Abraham, Isaac, and Jacob—male heads of that family from which the Hebrew people sprang. Their stories are told in Genesis 12—50.

While the Bible takes note of the wives of the patriarchs—Sarah, Rebekah, Rachel, and Leah—the focus of sacred history never shifts from their husbands. We cannot say that the women of Genesis are unimportant. But it is clear from the biblical text that they are of secondary importance.

One might argue from the perspective of our own time that, in the world of the patriarchs, women were "oppressed." Some feminists have condemned the Old Testament as a sexist document and criticized its failure to demand reform of the patriarchal structure of ancient societies. But to a great extent, this criticism is unreasonable.

All people are born into an existing culture. That culture, to a large extent, will define and limit our views, experiences, and roles in life. A son born in the first century into the family of a Roman senator had vastly different expectations than a son born into the family of a slave in one of Rome's provinces. Whatever these children's native intelligence or gifts, the cultural setting into which they were born defined both opportunities and limitations. One may argue that this was not fair. But "fair" is irrelevant to the reality of a culture's influence on an individual's station or role in life.

In meeting the women of the Bible, our task is not to speculate on what might or should have been. Rather, we should try to understand what we can of the reality of a woman's experience in a given period of history. There is much to learn about a woman's life in the ancient Middle East some 2,100 to 1,800 years before Christ. To do so, we must strive to grasp the existing culture's view of women and to explore the interpersonal relationships of the women found in the patriarchal narratives.

Women in the Ancient Middle East

Women in the ancient Middle East were born into a man's world. During childhood and early adolescence, a woman "belonged" to her father and was under his authority. When a woman married, she then "belonged" to her husband. In either case, the woman's situation had to be described as "dependent." The father or husband was legally and economically responsible for the women in his family.

Assumptions about women as daughters. The dependence of women as daughters is illustrated in a number of laws whose codification ranges from before Abraham to some 500 years afterward. All of these laws reflect cultural views commonly held during the age of the patriarchs.

The laws of Eshnunna, a city-state in what is now Iraq, illustrate a woman's dependence on her father and the father's rights over his daughter.

> 26: If a man gives bride-money for a man's daughter, but another man seizes her forcibly without asking the permission of her father and her mother and deprives her of her virginity, it is a capital offense and he shall die.

> 27: If a man takes a man's daughter without asking the permission of her father and her mother and concludes no formal marriage contract with her father and her mother, even though she may live in his house for a year, she is not a housewife.

> 28: On the other hand, if he concludes a formal contract with her father and her mother and cohabits with her, she is a housewife.

Rape was an offense against the father, for it deprived him of the bride price. And marriage involved the legal transfer of the woman from her father to the husband. Without a formal contract, "even though she may live in his house for a year," the woman was not considered a housewife.

The Code of Hammurabi envisions a situation where a father dies without stating in writing that an unmarried daughter can control her dowry (her share of his estate, which was to be transferred to her husband when she married). In this case, provision 178 of the Code states:

> After the father has gone to [his] fate, her brothers shall take her field and orchard and they shall give her food, oil, and clothing proportionate to the value of her share and thus make her comfortable; if her brothers have not given her food, oil, and clothing proportionate to the value of her share and so have not made her comfortable, she may give her field and orchard to any tenant that she pleases and her tenant shall support her, since she shall have the usufruct of the field, orchard, or whatever her

father gave her as long as she lives, without selling [it, or] willing [it] to another, since her patrimony belongs to her brothers.

This provision was intended to protect the legally helpless, single woman from exploitation by her brothers. Yet the law never envisions truly independent ownership of such property by a woman. Women were dependent, and ownership of a father's property passed to the sons. The daughter in this case had a lifetime benefit from the property, but she did not own it.

Assumptions about women as wives. A similar provision concerns the case of a wife whose husband leaves a document giving his wife discretion in the distribution of his property.

> 151: If a seignior, upon presenting a field, orchard, house, or goods to his wife, left a sealed document with her, her children may not enter a claim against her after [the death of] her husband, since the mother may give her inheritance to that son of hers whom she likes, [but] she may not give [it] to an outsider.

Again we see that a woman did not own outright even what her husband left her. She could pass it on to the son of her choice, but she could not dispose of it to an outsider.

The Code of Hammurabi clearly gives priority to the rights and interests of men while attempting to guard women against exploitation. Take for example the case of a husband whose wife develops an interest in activities outside the house, thus depriving her husband of expected household labors.

> 141: If a seignior's wife, who was living in the house of the seignior, has made up her mind to leave in order that she may engage in business, thus neglecting her house [and] humiliating her husband, they shall prove it against her; and if her husband has then decided on her divorce, he may divorce her, with nothing to be given her as her divorce-settlement upon her departure. If her husband has not decided on her divorce, her husband may marry another woman, with the former woman living in the house of her husband like a maidservant.

Clearly, in this law the husband's interests are paramount, and while a wife has some ability to set the course of her own life, neglecting the housewife role had serious consequences. Normally, in a divorce, a woman's dowry from her father was to be returned, so she might have assets that would help attract another husband. But a woman who tried to build a life for herself separate from her husband forfeited this right, and thus was severely punished.

Perhaps even more significant, each of these laws is addressed to men, and treats women as objects who are virtually possessions of their fathers or husbands. While not intentionally demeaning, they reflect the common view that women are dependent, and in essence they are designed to keep women dependent on their fathers or husbands.

This was the world in which women lived in the time of Abraham, Isaac, and Jacob—a world shaped by assumptions which, as peculiar or shocking as they may seem to us today, appeared natural and "right" to the men and women of the patriarchal age. When we read stories of the women who are portrayed in Genesis, we need to remember that the women in each story did not see themselves as oppressed, but rather assumed that they lived the way women were intended to live.

The report of Dinah's rape (Gen. 34). Whatever the assumptions of the men and women of the patriarchal age about a woman's role, cultural practices often spelled serious violence for women. Some of the practical implications for women are revealed in two stories imbedded in Genesis. The first is the story of Dinah's rape.

The Old Testament records the names of Jacob's twelve sons, born to his wives Rachel and Leah and their maids Bilhah and Zilpah. We know of only one daughter of Jacob: Dinah, who was born to Leah.

The event that features Dinah took place after Jacob led his large family back to Canaan following twenty years in Haran. As the family traveled in the sparsely settled land, Dinah went in search of other young women to talk with. A young man from the leading family of the nearby town raped her and took her back to his home. The young man, Shechem, fell in love with Dinah and asked his father to "Get me this young woman as a wife" (Gen. 34:4). The father approached Jacob with the intent of negotiating a marriage contract.

The rape angered Dinah's brothers, "because he had done a disgraceful thing in Israel by lying with Jacob's daughter, a thing which ought not to be done" (Gen. 34:7). When Shechem and his father requested marriage, Dinah's brothers conducted the negotiations. They hid their anger, and falsely promised to permit the marriage if the men of the city would accept circumcision. The men of the city agreed. But while they were incapacitated by the operation, Dinah's two full brothers entered the city, killed all the men, and brought their sister home.

The report is significant for the insights it provides into the true situation of women of the era. We are not told anything about Dinah's feelings. Was she glad to be rescued, or had she fallen in love with Shechem? What happened to Dinah after her rescue? How did her father, her brothers, and other family members relate to Dinah after her disgrace? We are told nothing in the text, nor is there any intimation that her brothers tried to speak with her and ask what she wanted. Instead, we are shown the reaction of the brothers, who feel disgraced and who are intent on restoring the family honor by taking revenge. When rebuked by Jacob for potentially arousing the hostility of the peoples inhabiting Canaan, the brothers' only reply was, "Should he treat our sister like a harlot?" (Gen. 34:31).

Women were dependent on the family, and certainly the men of the family felt a responsibility toward them. But the report of Dinah's rape conveys the clear impression that the brothers' strongest motive in plotting revenge was the belief that, in raping Dinah, Shechem had affronted *them*. Because Dinah was in some sense "owned" by her father and brothers, the rape was an insult to the family that called for repayment. What Dinah herself had experienced and what she felt was of little importance to them.

Tamar's deceit (Gen. 38). A second story in Genesis that brings home the true situation of women is found in Genesis 38. Judah, one of the sons of Jacob, "took a wife for Er—his firstborn" (Gen. 38:6). Er died, leaving the wife, Tamar, a childless widow.

According to the custom of that time, Judah gave Tamar to another son, Onan. The first son born of this union would be considered Er's heir, and would receive Er's share of his father's estate. Onan was unwilling to dilute his own share of the estate, and whenever he had sex with Tamar, he "emitted on the ground, lest he should give an heir to his brother" (Gen. 38:9). This displeased the Lord, and Onan too died. Judah then told Tamar to remain with the family, promising that when his third son, Shelah, reached maturity, she would become his wife. But when Shelah matured, Judah did not keep his promise.

Finally Tamar "took off her widow's garments" and posed as a prostitute by the side of a road Judah frequented. Judah, assuming she was a harlot, had sex with her, and left his signet and staff with her as a pledge until he could send a lamb to pay the price she demanded. When he left her, Tamar returned to Judah's camp with Judah's signet and staff.

Later, when Tamar was discovered to be pregnant, Judah condemned her to death. Before the sentence could be carried out, Tamar produced Judah's signet and staff. Judah was forced to admit that "she has been more righteous than I, because I did not give her to Shelah my son" (Gen. 38:26).

The story further illustrates the situation of women in the patriarchal age. Tamar, married to a son of Judah, was totally dependent on Judah, the head of the family. She was misused by Onan, and then defrauded of her right to marriage by Judah. The story reminds us that while Judah retained rights to his own sexuality, and could traffic with a prostitute, Judah also claimed rights to Tamar's sexuality. When her pregnancy showed that she had had sex outside of marriage, Judah was fully prepared to execute her!

Yet clearly, Judah was an honorable man, and when Tamar revealed that Judah himself had made her pregnant, he admitted that he had wronged Tamar by not giving her to his third son. Although Judah never again had sex with Tamar, her two sons, Perez and Jerah, were accepted by Judah as his sons, and are so listed in biblical genealogies (see Num. 26:19–22).

The situation of women in patriarchal times: A Summary. While we can appreciate the concern for women's welfare imbedded in ancient Near Eastern laws and customs, at the same time we must recognize that a double standard existed. In the days of the patriarchs, women simply were not viewed as equals, nor did women enjoy the same rights and freedoms enjoyed by men. Women were acted upon rather than actors; they were possessions that, though perhaps treasured by their men, were not fully persons in their own right.

It is important when we look at the situation of women of this period to remember that the Genesis account is descriptive rather than prescriptive. Descriptive passages portray without making value judgments. Prescriptive passages do make value judgments and reflect what ought to be rather than what is. As we read the stories of Sarah, Rebekah, Rachel and Leah, Dinah, and the others in Genesis and indeed in much of the Old Testament, we need to remember these passages are descriptive. As told, the stories reveal much about the lives of women in this era, but they do not imply that the patriarchal society in which the women lived reflects God's will for humankind.

The situation of women reflected in these stories is a powerful witness to the truth of God's revelation to Eve of certain consequences of the Fall. It is sin, not God's will, that is displayed in the way women were viewed and treated at that time. When God told Eve "and he shall rule over you" (Gen. 3:16), the Lord was not revealing the shape man/woman relationships *should* take, but rather the shape sinful human societies would impose on womankind.

The status of women as dependent on men and subservient to them, so clearly reflected in Genesis 12—50, simply reminds us that God knows all too well the sinfulness of the human heart and understands how sin warps not only individuals but also the cultures in which we live.

Interpersonal Relationships of Bible Women

While the narrative accounts in Genesis reflect a view of women current in the ancient Middle East in patriarchal times, these same accounts provide fresh evidence that law and custom cannot fully depict the reality of any individual's life. What do the portraits of Genesis women tell us about the real lives of women in patriarchal times? Let's delve into a few of the most noted women of the Old Testament.

Sarah

Sarah and Abraham. Three incidents provide insight into Sarah's relationship with Abraham.

Sarah's request (Gen. 16:1–3). After ten years in Canaan, Sarah urged Abraham to have a child with her Egyptian slave, Hagar. According to the custom of the time, Hagar was a surrogate, and the child would be considered Sarah's own. Abraham "heeded the voice of" (listened to) Sarah. It's clear from the text that Sarah took the initiative and influenced Abraham to do what she wished.

Sarah's changed relationship with Hagar (Gen. 16:4–6). When Hagar became pregnant she felt contempt for the childless Sarah. Clearly, Abraham was able to father children; Sarah was not fertile. The change in her slave's attitude infuriated Sarah, and she blamed Abraham (Gen. 16:5). Abraham's response was to remind Sarah that, according to the law and custom of that era, she had the right to discipline Hagar. And so Sarah "dealt harshly" with Hagar—so harshly that Hagar fled. Only after the intervention of the Angel of the Lord did Hagar return to Abraham's camp, where she bore his son, Ishmael.

Sarah demands Ishmael's expulsion (Gen. 21:9–14). When Ishmael was a teenager, God supernaturally enabled Sarah to give Abraham a son, Isaac. Sarah had never bonded with Ishmael, even though, technically, he was "her" son. When Isaac was three, Sarah saw Ishmael teasing his younger half-brother. Infuriated, she went to Abraham and demanded that he send Ishmael away.

Abraham was unwilling to do this for two reasons. He cared for his son, and the law and custom of the time required that a father who had acknowledged a child born to a slave as his own should divide his estate equally between such a child and any born to his wife. Only when God instructed Abraham to listen to Sarah, and promised to be with Ishmael, did Abraham send Hagar and Ishmael away.

These three incidents remind us that, whatever culture may decree, the interactions between a husband and wife remain functions of their relationship and their personalities. A strong bond of love existed between Abraham and Sarah, and Sarah was free within that relationship to urge, to complain, to initiate, and even to insist that her husband take a specific course of action. The fact that a woman was legally dependent was less important in determining her status than her own personality and the character of the relationship that she developed with her husband.

Rebekah

Rebekah and her family. Rebekah was the daughter of Abraham's relative. When it came time for Isaac to marry, Abraham sent a servant on the long journey to Haran, where the family still lived, to negotiate for a bride for Isaac.

The servant's prayer for divine leading was answered, and Rebekah was identified as God's choice of a bride for Isaac. Genesis 24 describes the servant's negotiation on Abraham's behalf and records the response of Rebekah's brothers who, since her father was dead, were responsible for her well-being:

> Then Laban and Bethuel answered and said, "The thing comes from the LORD; we cannot speak to you either bad or good. Here is Rebekah before you, take her and go, and let her be your master's son's wife, as the LORD has spoken."
>
> —Gen. 24:50, 51

If we were to stop here, we would see only a reflection of the law and custom that made women objects to be bartered by their men. But the story does not stop here. The Genesis account goes on:

> So they said, "We will call the young woman and ask her personally." Then they called Rebekah and said to her, "Will you go with this man?" And she said, "I will go." So they sent away Rebekah their sister and her nurse, and Abraham's servant and his men.
>
> —Gen 25:57–59

The fascinating point in this narrative account is the fact that, while the brothers conducted the marriage negotiations, they still consulted their sister. The text seems to imply that Rebekah could have refused to go with the servant, even though the brothers were willing to contract her marriage to Abraham's son.

Once again, we're reminded that the nature of relationships existing within the family had a great impact on a woman's experiences. While law and custom gave a father or brothers the right to marry off their daughter or sister, in reality, a young woman's wishes might be taken into account.

Rachel and Leah

Jacob consults with Rachel and Leah (Gen. 31). Later, Jacob, the son of Isaac and Rebekah, also traveled to Haran. There he fell in love with his uncle Laban's daughter, Rachel. Tricked by his uncle into a loveless marriage with Leah, Jacob later was given Rachel as a wife also.

Jacob remained in Haran for some twenty years, working for his uncle and building his own estate. Toward the end, Laban and his sons became more and more hostile toward Jacob. As the situation became tense, the Lord told Jacob it was time to return to Canaan, the land God had promised to Abraham's descendants.

According to law and custom, Jacob was head of the family and responsible for its future. We might suppose then that Jacob would simply tell his wives and sons to pack and lead them back to his homeland. But again, the narrative in Genesis surprises us. What actually happened was that Jacob sent for Rachel and Leah, reviewed the growing tension with Laban, and shared the vision in which God had told him to return to Canaan. Then Jacob waited for his two wives' response. Genesis tells us:

> Then Rachel and Leah answered and said to him, "Is there still any portion or inheritance for us in our father's house? Are we not considered strangers by him? For he has sold us, and also completely consumed our money. For all these riches which God has taken from our father are really ours and our children's; now then, whatever God has said to you, do it."

—Gen. 31:14–16

How striking that Jacob conferred with his wives, explained the situation, and then waited for them to respond. The wives carefully considered the situation, realized that they and their children had no future in their father's household, and encouraged their husband to take the path God had laid out for them.

The process Jacob initiated seems more in harmony with an egalitarian than a patriarchal family structure. Yet, as we have seen, Jacob and his wives lived in an era where law and custom defined the family structure in strict hierarchical terms and made wives dependent and subservient. What we conclude is

that, in reality, the relationship between husband and wife (or wives) was more important in shaping the experience of women than was the cultural definition of their roles.

The Real Lives of Women in the Patriarchal Era

If we were to assume that law and custom provide a totally accurate picture of women's experience in any culture, we would be driven to the conclusion that women in patriarchal times truly were oppressed. There is no doubt that, in many cases, the needs of women were disregarded, and that they were treated unfairly. This is powerfully illustrated in the stories of Dinah's rape and Tamar's deception of Judah.

Yet we would be wrong to conclude that law and custom, or "worst case scenarios," convey a totally accurate picture of women's place. As we've looked at incidents from the lives of each of the wives of the three patriarch's—Sarah, Rebekah, and Rachel and Leah—we've discovered evidence that softens the stark portrayal of women's lives seen in the era's law and custom. We've seen that a woman like Sarah had a powerful influence on choices made by her husband; that sisters like Rebekah had more choice in the selection of a mate than the laws would indicate; and that husbands like Jacob felt it was important to consult wives when making decisions that affected the future of the family.

Each of these discoveries reminds us that the quality of the relationships that develop in a woman's life is probably more determinative of the quality of her life than anything else. Where there is mutual love and concern, lives will be enriched, and the well-being of women, as well as men, will be strengthened.

Women of the patriarchal age must be understood in the context of their time and place. Yet the women of this era still were individuals. While beliefs and attitudes were shaped by immersion in culture, each individual displayed traits of character and personality that remind us that, although environment may be significant, it does not alter human nature. Both the wonderful gifts God gave human beings and the Fall's twisting of those gifts is revealed as powerfully in biblical women of this period as in the women of our own time.

Women's Rights in the Ancient World: Moses' Law

(Exodus—Joshua)

There is no question that in the cultures out of which ancient Israel emerged, law and custom favored men over women. Society was organized along patriarchal lines, and the legal status, as well as the social and economic position of women, reflected the words of Genesis 3:16, "and he shall rule over you."

Only in the past few decades have feminist and non-feminist scholars begun to argue that Old Testament Law is different, and that an egalitarian theme can be discerned in the rulings contained in Exodus, Leviticus, and Deuteronomy. These scholars have emphasized provisions made in biblical laws for the offspring of unloved as well as loved wives and also provisions that protect dependent family members. They have argued that such laws promote relationships that are distinctively non-hierarchical.

The debate raises two important questions. First, is the position of women reflected in Old Testament Law really radically different from their position in other law codes of the era? And second, what assumptions underlie Old Testament laws concerning women, and what is their real purpose?

Women in Law Codes of the Era

There are no less than ten ancient law codes from the biblical world that we can compare in a study of women's rights. The ten are:

The Code of Ur-Nammu	About 2200 B.C.
Sumerian Laws	About 2200–1900 B.C.
Laws of Eshnunna	About 1900 B.C.
Code of Lipit-Ishtar	About 1800 B.C.
Code of Hammurabi	About 1700 B.C.
The Edict of Ammisaduqa	About 1600 B.C.
Middle Assyrian Laws	About 1400 B.C.
Mosaic Laws	About 1400 B.C.
Hittite Laws	About 1300 B.C.
Nuzi Laws	About 1300 B.C.

In comparing these codes we find both similarities with and differences from biblical law. In some cases,

legal provisions are parallel. For instance, most ancient codes protect the inheritance rights of sons born to a concubine when the father has acknowledged those sons.

In some cases, the Mosaic code seems less lenient than others. For example, a Hebrew woman sold into slavery to a fellow Hebrew was to be freed after six years. But the Code of Hammurabi freed a woman after only three years. The Laws of Eshnunna seem even to take the side of the woman against her husband in the following:

If a man divorces his wife after having made her bear children and takes another wife, he shall be driven from his house and from whatever he owns.

—Law #59

There is nothing like this in the biblical code.

In other provisions, Mosaic Law seems more sensitive to a woman's rights and concerns than the contemporary codes. Mosaic Law holds guiltless a woman who is raped in the field, in that there was no one to help her should she have cried out. In contrast, Middle Assyrian law A55 punishes a rapist by ordering that the rapist's own virgin daughter be raped by the father of the victim. But A56 adds: unless the rapist simply swears that the woman consented.

It is not surprising that the law codes of the era should have a number of similarities. After all, each of the peoples the codes governed lived essentially the same kind of life and were faced with resolving the same kinds of legal issues—issues of inheritance, of marriage and divorce, of personal injury, of contract violations, and so forth. We should not be surprised that many of the legal rulings are similar.

It is difficult to sustain the argument that the biblical code introduces egalitarian principles that cannot be discerned in the others. The problem is, if we compare the position taken in the codes on one issue (to argue that the Mosaic code is more sensitive to women), someone else can make just as strong an argument that Mosaic Law is less sensitive by comparing the position taken in the codes on another issue.

Even more significantly, when we adopt a case-by-case comparison approach, we in essence concede the point. If the Mosaic code truly were *radically* different from the other codes, such comparisons would not be possible. That provisions in the Law of Moses can be set side by side with similar provisions in other law codes makes it clear that underlying assumptions about the role of women are the same in biblical and contemporary law codes.

Assumptions Underlying Old Testament Law– Family Law

How then can we determine whether Old Testament Law moves toward an egalitarian rather than patriarchal view of society and the role of women? The best way is to identify the assumptions underlying the Law's provisions rather than by trying to compare codes case by case. When we do this, we find clear evidence that the Mosaic code is not designed to promote egalitarian gender relationships.

The language of Old Testament Law assumes a patriarchal society. When we examine the language of Old Testament Law, we are led to the conclusion that Mosaic law is not egalitarian at all, but assumes a patriarchal and male-dominated society. This is revealed in the following features of the Mosaic code:

◆ The law is generally addressed to males. It assumes that the man is the actor.
◆ Laws that protect the rights of dependents acknowledge the father's authority, even as they limit it (Deut. 21:14).
◆ A woman's legal status is determined by her relationship to men—either to her father or to her husband.
◆ A woman's economic well-being is dependent on membership in the household of her father, her husband, or her sons. A widow, like a fatherless child, is depicted in the Old Testament as both poor and powerless, and thus worthy of special consideration (Ex. 22:22).
◆ Even when a law protects a woman's interests, it does so by limiting a man's freedom of action (Deut. 22:19,29).
◆ In the case of first marriages, the woman is object rather than agent. It is the man who "takes" his wife and who brings her into his household (Deut. 21:12).
◆ There is a significant difference in the status of sons and daughters, especially in the area of inheritance (Deut. 25:5–10).
◆ Property, children, and family name are all owned by and transmitted from the father to sons, not daughters (Deut. 21:15–17).
◆ The law of divorce assumes that the husband initiates a divorce (Deut. 24:1–3). There is no provision stated by which the wife could initiate divorce.

◆ When a man slandered or violated a young woman, damages were to be paid to the father, not the young woman (Deut. 22:19, 29).
◆ The family is the father's household (Deut. 22:21). When divorced, a woman leaves her husband's household (Deut. 21:14; 24:2, 3). The woman does not own the household, but belongs to it.

The fact that this kind of language is used throughout the Mosaic code makes it abundantly clear that Old Testament Law is not egalitarian. It is instead distinctly patriarchal in orientation and in its underlying assumptions.

Some provisions of Old Testament Law do affirm equal rights of husbands and wives. While the structure of Old Testament Law is clearly patriarchal, and assumes that males retain the dominant position in society, the Law does not *depersonalize* women. This is seen most clearly in two features of the Law.

First, women, like men, are held responsible for violations of criminal law. The idolater or the person involved in occult practices, whether man or woman, was dealt with the same way (Deut. 18:9–11).

Second, children are to honor their mothers as well as their fathers (Ex. 20:12). When a rebellious son refused to respond to the authority of his parents, mother and father together were to bring him to court, where the charge was lodged against "our" son (Deut. 21:18–21). The rebellious son's refusal to heed the voice of his mother is equally damning as his refusal to listen to his father's voice.

While there are few such indications of equality of the spouses, it is important to avoid assuming that patriarchy in itself depersonalized women. Or that bonds of real affection did not exist between many husbands and wives, and fathers and daughters. The patriarchal structure of the Old Testament did make men *responsible* for the well-being of their families. But it did not make women mere chattels.

One function of Old Testament Law required the patriarchal orientation. In all probability, those who examine Old Testament Law to support either chauvinist or feminist agendas will miss a vital point. The central concern of the Mosaic Law was not *gender* but *family*.

God did not shape His law to make a statement about male/female relationships. The Law was shaped to accomplish a different purpose entirely.

God had chosen Abraham and his descendants for a great and wonderful mission. Through the seed of Abraham, Isaac, and Jacob, God would give the world His Word and, ultimately, the Savior. The Israelites truly were the chosen people—chosen not simply for their own sake, but chosen as an instrument through which God in Christ would bring salvation and renewal to all who believe.

This overarching purpose of God required the preservation of the Jewish race across not just centuries but millenniums. For God's purpose to be achieved, Israel would have to retain its identity and racial integrity despite living among similar peoples whose languages might be comparable but whose religions and immorality were virulently corrupting. Israel would have to retain its identity and racial integrity even when the Jewish people were torn from their homeland and scattered through a pagan empire, subject to many attractive and insidious influences. (*If Israel were to remain distinct, a powerful sense of family and national identity had to be established and maintained.*)

Old Testament laws relating to men and women invariably function to strengthen and preserve family identity. This concern—not the gender agenda of our day—drives biblical family law. Simply put, the Law embodies priorities other than the priority of those who argue for or against gender equality.

When we understand biblical family law as a mechanism for preserving and strengthening family identity, we can better understand its patrilinial orientation. Laws relating to inheritance, marriage, divorce, and other family matters are all structured to support a sense of unity with past and future generations as each generation becomes a strand in a single, unbroken line of descent from fathers to sons. It is not because of their gender that women are minimized in the Law, nor because of their gender that men are emphasized. Rather, family laws are woven together to create a cord strong enough to bear the weight of an entire people's sense of personal and corporate identity. From the beginning, that identity was transmitted from father to son—from Abraham to Isaac to Jacob to the sons of Israel to their sons and their sons' sons.

Yes, God's Old Testament Law is patriarchal and male-dominated, but this is not because God favors one sex over the other. The patriarchal structure was required if the Law was to accomplish one of its essential purposes and strengthen every Israelite's sense of national and personal identity.

What implications does this have for those today who are concerned about women and their roles in the home and the church? First, it makes arguing from Old Testament Law irrelevant to the contemporary concerns. The economic, legal, and social relationships defined in the Law were designed to strengthen the sense of identity of God's people. Given this priority, the roles of men and women in the Law were *subordinate to that purpose. Based on the Law,* we cannot draw any conclusions about gender,

for the Law's specific provisions were not shaped by any assumptions about gender.

Back to Genesis 3:16. But can't we argue that God might just as easily have chosen to give the Law with a matriarchal rather than patriarchal structure? Isn't the fact that He chose the patriarchal significant? It is significant—but significant because of consequences of the Fall that God explained to Eve in Genesis 3:16. To Eve He said, "Your desire shall be for your husband, and he shall rule over you" (Gen. 3:16). As we noted, this was neither a curse nor an announcement of punishment, but rather the statement of a consequence.

The Fall twisted Adam and Eve's very nature out of the shape that God had created, warping every dimension of the human personality. For Eve, this meant that she and her daughters would find themselves wanting and needing male approval. In this vulnerable state her husband would rule her, not because she was inferior, but because sin had corrupted the relationship between men and women, as it had all things. The relationship of complete equality that Adam and Eve had known was altered, and since the Fall, human societies have reflected the dominant, and all too often oppressive, rule of men over women.

The Old Testament Law's patriarchal structure is in harmony with that reality—a reality other societies of the time reflect as well.

Thus the women we meet in the days of the Exodus and the Conquest are women who lived in a patriarchal society. While the women may be gifted, as Miriam surely was, or assertive, as Caleb's daughter was, they lived in a day when, insofar as the law that governed their lives and society's expectations were concerned, women truly were less significant than men.

Daily Life
in Ancient Israel
(Judges; Ruth)

For most of the Old Testament era, the majority of people lived a rural life. This was certainly the case in the time of the judges, which extended roughly from the 1370s, after the death of Joshua and the elders who ruled with him, to David's organization of a united monarchy around 1000 B.C. Even after Israel became a united nation, daily life changed little for most men and women. The majority lived in small village settlements, not in cities. Most people grew their own food and met other needs within the household. A few developed household industries, such as making pottery or catching and drying fish.

Now, we will look briefly at the daily life of women in this kind of society.

Political and Social Conditions in the Age of the Judges

Life in the age of the judges was difficult in Israel. Hebrew armies under Joshua had put down organized resistance in Canaan and divided the land among the twelve Hebrew tribes, but pagan strongholds still existed. God ordered the tribes to drive out the remaining Canaanite peoples as their own population grew and they needed additional land. However, Judges 1:19 sums up in a single verse the reality of the situation:

So the LORD was with Judah. And they drove out the mountaineers, but they could not drive out the inhabitants of the lowland, because they had chariots of iron.

Archaeology has confirmed the significance of this verse. During the age of the judges, the Israelites were largely confined to the rocky highlands while the Canaanites occupied the fertile valleys. During the age of the judges, Israel's primary enemy, the Philistines, held prime land along the Mediterranean and knew the secret of working iron. This knowledge provided both an economic and military advantage. Not until David's day did the Israelites gain access to iron-working technology.

The restriction of the Israelites to the highlands and their lack of access to iron largely defined economic conditions during the time of the judges. These two factors kept God's people in relative poverty.

However, the presence of Canaanites in the land was even more significant. Again and again, God's people abandoned the Lord to adopt the idolatry and the immoral practices of the nations God had commanded them to drive out. Time and again, God's response to Israel's unfaithfulness was to permit foreign enemies to oppress His people. When life became unbearable, God's people turned back to Him and prayed for relief. God responded by raising up a judge—a military, political, and spiritual leader—who repelled the enemy and led the tribe or group into a period of peace. However, after a short time, the people once again turned from God to idolatry.

These repeated cycles of crushing defeats and temporary recoveries kept the people divided and impoverished. Not until the time of David and Solomon, when Israel became the dominant power in the Middle East, did the Israelites enjoy general prosperity.

Life during the time of the judges was hard for men and for women. Yet daily life was hard for most men and women throughout the world in Old Testament times. In most families, men and women simply had to work as a team if the family was to survive.

Mr. Outside, Mrs. Inside

In general, this describes the way tasks were divided in the typical Israelite household. The husband was responsible for tasks outside the house, the wife for tasks inside. This meant that the woman prepared the food, made the family clothing, cared for young children, and trained their daughters in the skills needed to run a household. The husband worked the fields, planted and cared for crops, maintained stone fences and grape or olive presses, and trained the boys for their future role as husbands and providers.

The house itself. The typical Israelite house was built of stone or mud brick on a four-room plan. A room ran across the back, with three open rooms running perpendicular to it. Inside walls were coated with plaster, while the floors were clay. The roof was typically about six feet from the floor. It was made with wooden beams layered with branches and packed mud. The rooftop was flat and could be reached by an outside staircase. The roof provided extra space where the family could work or sleep in the summer, and where flax could be laid out to dry. Doorways in the four-room house were low; a few windows were placed high in the wall.

Household furnishings. The Israelite home had few furnishings—a few cooking utensils, a raised platform for sleeping, food storage jars or sunken storage pits, and perhaps a brazier for heating. Most cooking was done outside the home, in a small beehive-shaped oven. Each day, the women ground grain to make bread, which was formed into flat cakes and slapped against the outside of the oven to cook, or was formed into loaves the size of our dinner rolls to be cooked inside the oven after the fire's ashes had been swept out.

Family meals. Meals were simple—a bit of bread and some fruit was eaten in the middle of the morning, and a larger meal in the evening. The evening meal was generally eaten with the family seated on the floor, with one or more common dishes placed on a circular leather or skin mat. Family members ate with their hands, soaking up any juices with bits of bread. Meat was a rarity in the Israelite daily diet; protein came from milk or cheese, and occasionally from dried fish.

Indoor cisterns. About the time the Israelites invaded Canaan, a means of storing water in porous soil was invented. Bell-shaped hollows were dug in loose rock and sealed with a waterproof plaster. Rainfall was sparse in the hills where the Israelites settled, so this invention was essential to the people's survival. A complicated system of channels collected rainwater and fed it into an indoor reservoir. The channels were filled with traps designed to filter out impurities.

Most household cisterns of this period held twenty to thirty cubic yards of water, enough to provide a year's drinking water for six to twelve people. Because children were so highly valued, large families were the norm, and the four-room house was normally crowded.

Making clothing. A major task of women in Old Testament times was clothing the family. Most wore woolen garments. The women and girls carded the wool to strip fibers from it. They then spun the fibers together to create threads. Then they wove the threads together on a loom to create cloth. Women frequently wove cloth on a ground loom. Parallel rows of pegs were driven into the ground. Threads were tied between the pegs to form the warp of the cloth, and other threads were then interwoven. Upright looms also were used. To create an upright loom poles, were driven into the ground and a crossbeam was set between them. Threads weighted with stones were hung from the crossbeam to create the warp of the cloth. Other threads were interwoven and tied to the vertical poles.

Linen clothing was made from flax. The plant was dried, beaten to extract fibers, and the same process used in weaving woolens was then followed.

It is no wonder, given the work involved in making cloth, that most Israelites used the heavier outer robe they wore on colder days as a blanket at night.

Helping outdoors at harvest time. While these in-house tasks kept women and girls busy, when harvest time came they worked beside their men in the fields. While the men cut grain with hand sickles, the women followed closely behind to tie the stalks into bundles that were then tented upright for drying. When grapes or olives were harvested, the women also worked beside the men. Harvest time involved hard outdoor work, but it provided a break from normal routine and a time for feasting and celebration.

Today, we would hardly call the lifestyle just described as fulfilling. It was a hard life, with none of the stimulating advantages we appreciate so much today. Yet there was no question about the significance of women in this society. Women and men were truly interdependent. The contribution of each to the family was understood and appreciated. Men and women faced life's challenges together as partners.

While there were undoubtedly both happy and unhappy marriages, few marriages existed in which people were uncertain about their roles or in doubt about the importance of their contribution to spouse and family.

The Women Mentioned in Judges

The judges era extended from around 1350 B.C. to the anointing of Saul as king of the Israelites, in 1050 B.C. It was a time of spiritual and political stagnation. The pagan peoples they had permitted to stay in Canaan after the conquest pressured the children of Israel. Events during this period are reported in the books of Judges, Ruth, and the first seven chapters of 1 Samuel.

Successful women in Old Testament times needed similar gifts and abilities to carry out their responsibilities that successful men of the same period used. That a woman's tasks were focused inside the household and a man's tasks were focused in the fields does not change the fact that there was no essential difference in the personal qualities needed to fulfill their social roles. We can hardly support modern stereotypes of supposed men's and women's roles from data in the Old Testament. Women were no less equipped for success by nature than were men.

At the same time, we must remember that ancient Israel was a patriarchal society. The priesthood passed from father to son, and no woman served the Lord as a priest. The Levites who served the tabernacle and later in the temple were also men, although later there were women singers in choirs that led the people in worship. Throughout this period, male elders led local communities. Ultimate responsibility for the well-being of the family did rest on the men, who retained veto power over certain choices that might be made by their wives or daughters. It is not surprising that we do not find women filling such roles. In a strongly patriarchal society, we would not expect women, however gifted, to be accepted in social roles that violated the social expectations.

Deborah

This, of course, makes the emergence of Deborah as a judge even more remarkable. Israel's judges were the recognized leaders of the tribes they served. A judge in those days combined in one person all branches of government: executive, legislative, and judicial. The fact that the Bible describes Deborah as a prophetess in no way explains the nation's acceptance of her as a judge. While later rulers assembled prophets to advise them, possession of the gift of prophecy was never viewed as a qualification for any governmental office or for any position in Israel's cult. Religious positions were inherited: only a male descendant of Levi could serve at the worship center; only a male descendant of Aaron was qualified to serve as a priest.

Yet in this unmistakably patriarchal society, where men held every significant leadership role, Deborah emerged as a judge. All of the people in the tribes she served submitted to her leadership.

Without the example of Deborah, we might perhaps conclude that gender somehow was disqualifying in itself, and that women may have been viewed as inferior in Old Testament times. But Deborah's judgeship prevents us from jumping to this kind of conclusion. In a strongly patriarchal society, we *expect* men to function as leaders. But Deborah reminds us that what restrained more women from serving as leaders was not inherent in a woman's nature, but rather was inherent in those expectations that were deeply imbedded in society.

Far more significant for our understanding of women as persons is the description of the virtuous woman of Proverbs 31 (see Appendix E). That passage clearly testifies to the fact that to successfully fulfill a woman's role in Old Testament times required an exercise of the very same abilities required to become a successful man in that day. In this respect, women were understood to be the equals of men, and their contributions to the family were as necessary and as important as that of their husbands.

The Condition of Women in the Age of Kings
(1 Samuel–Malachi)

The introduction of the monarchy around 1050 B.C. caused hardly a ripple in the lives of most women in ancient Israel. The same household chores needed to be done each day. They could look forward to the same seasons: harvest, with its gleaning in the fields; the joyous religious festivals that punctuated the year and brought relief from toil. Young girls outside the nation's capital still helped their mothers, and then sat in the shade playing "house" as they dreamed of having their own husbands and children.

But the introduction of the monarchy did have a dramatic impact on women who would become members of the royal family. To be married to a king, or to be born into the royal family, brought a few privileges but many duties, and many, many disappointments. Essentially and with few exceptions,

women in the royal families of the ancient world were pawns, moved on the chessboard of geopolitics by men who were far more concerned with policy than with the well-being and happiness of wives or daughters.

This new political role for women of the royal family is clearly illustrated in the Old Testament: in the multiple wives taken by Israel's kings, in stories of familiar figures like David and Michal, and in the few unusual women who broke the mold and, rather than be used by their husbands, became political themselves and eagerly grasped for personal power.

Royal Wives

The Book of Deuteronomy (17:14–20) includes a section of laws that applied only to Israel's kings.

"When you come to the land which the LORD your God is giving you, and possess it and dwell in it, and say, 'I will set a king over me like all the nations that are around me,' you shall surely set a king over you whom the LORD your God chooses; one from among your brethren you shall set as king over you; you may not set a foreigner over you, who is not your brother. But he shall not multiply horses for himself, nor cause the people to return to Egypt to multiply horses, for the LORD has said to you, 'You shall not return that way again.' Neither shall he multiply wives for himself, lest his heart turn away; nor shall he greatly multiply silver and gold for himself.

"Also it shall be, when he sits on the throne of his kingdom, that he shall write for himself a copy of this law in a book, from the one before the priests, the Levites. And it shall be with him, and he shall read it all the days of his life, that he may learn to fear the LORD his God and be careful to observe all the words of this law and these statutes, that his heart may not be lifted above his brethren, that he may not turn aside from the commandment to the right hand or to the left, and that he may prolong his days in his kingdom, he and his children in the midst of Israel."

While other monarchs of the ancient world were absolute rulers, Hebrew kings were to be ruled by God and to remain conscious of His sovereignty. They were to govern as one among many fellow Hebrews, rather than as one above them. The commandments governing the king were designed to strip him of significant symbols of royalty and keep him humbly subservient to the Lord. There was to be no ostentatious wealth, no great chariot armies, and no multiple wives to produce multiple sons and daughters.

Yet from the beginning, the limits placed on kings were ignored. Though Saul had only one wife, he did have a concubine named Rizpah. And Saul was hardly a typical Hebrew king. It was David who truly established the monarchy in Israel. It was David who welded the Hebrew tribes together as one, designed a central government and bureaucracy, and who established Jerusalem as both a political and religious capital of the emergent Hebrew nation. It was David who defeated surrounding nations and expanded Israelite territory tenfold. And it was David who first asserted the privilege of kings and, when his throne was firmly established "took more concubines and wives from Jerusalem" (2 Sam. 5:13).

The pattern of multiple marriages was followed to excess by David's son, Solomon, who according to 1 Kings 11:3 had "seven hundred wives, princesses, and three hundred concubines." While the text tells us that "King Solomon loved many foreign women" (11:1), it would be wrong to assume that Solomon simply illustrates the adage that power is the ultimate aphrodisiac. What is significant is that his 700 wives were "princesses."

In the ancient world, it was customary to make treaties between nations and peoples more binding by intermarriage between the royal families. Most of Solomon's foreign wives, like the "daughter of Pharaoh" mentioned in 11:1, came into Solomon's harem as a clause in an international agreement worked out between governments.

Despite the fact that the multiplying of wives was forbidden in God's Law, and despite the example of Solomon's fall from grace, the practice of solidifying international agreements by intermarriage was too deeply imbedded in ancient cultures to be ignored by Israel's and Judah's kings. Rehoboam, the son of Solomon, who "loved Maachah the granddaughter of Absalom more than all his wives and his concubines," still had "eighteen wives and sixty concubines, and begot twenty-eight sons and sixty daughters" (2 Chr. 11:21). Ahab, thoroughly dominated by his wife Jezebel, also had multiple wives and children (1 Kin. 20:5).

We can hardly imagine what it must have been like to be just one of some ancient king's sixty daughters. Certainly, there would have been no close relationship with a loving father. Instead there would have been the certain knowledge that you were a coin in your father's political treasury, likely to be paid out to some foreign ruler as part of the price of some political advantage your royal father desired. As a member of the royal family, a young girl would have had material advantages. But from her earliest years, she would have been made aware of her duty and that she was more a commodity than a person with dreams and desires of her own.

The young woman brought up in poverty on some rural farm with a loving mother and father, looking forward to a husband and family of her own, was in many respects more blessed than the princess brought up in the empty luxury of the royal court.

The Story of David and Michal

The story of David and Michal, a younger daughter of King Saul, illustrates the plight of women in the royal family. Although Saul, Israel's first king, hardly ruled an established monarchy, his relationship with Michal shows that he fully understood the political use of women. Sadly, the story makes it clear that David fully understood this, too.

A young girl's dream of love (1 Sam. 18:20–28). When Goliath, the giant Philistine warrior, was terrifying the Israelites, Saul promised that whoever defeated him would receive riches, tax exemptions, and would be given the king's daughter as a wife. After David killed Goliath, Saul reneged. He offered David a commission in his army instead, vaguely promising his older daughter Merab to David if only he would "be valiant for me, and fight the LORD's battles" (1 Sam. 18:17). At the time, Saul was already jealous of David, and hoped that the prospect of marrying into the royal family would lead David to take foolish risks in battle.

Of course, a daughter of the king was too valuable to spend on a nobody like David, and when the time came that Merab should have been given to David, Saul married her to a man named Adriel for reasons unspecified in the biblical text.

But then Saul's younger daughter, Michal, fell in love with David. She dreamed day and night of the handsome young officer, and like girls in love everywhere, spoke of him to her friends. When word reached Saul of his daughter's infatuation "the thing pleased" the king (1 Sam. 18:20). How thrilled Michal must have been, and how delighted, when she was told that her father would actually permit her to marry the man of her dreams.

But Saul was not moved by a desire to please his little girl. In fact, Saul saw her love as a weapon to use in his secret campaign against David. Saul imagined that "she may be a snare to him" (1 Sam. 18:21), tripping David up and ridding Saul of a potential rival. If Michal's heart was broken in the process, well, that was of little consequence to Saul.

Saul had his servants speak to David of the king's admiration and of Saul's desire to have David in his family. David, both humble and poor, objected. He had nothing to bring into the marriage that could equal the value of a king's daughter.

Saul had counted on just this reaction. Saul told David that all he wanted as a dowry were tokens proving that David had killed a hundred Philistines—hoping that the Philistines would kill David instead.

When David quickly procured the required tokens, the frustrated king permitted the marriage to take place, the happiness of his daughter dampened not at all by his dark looks.

Michal sides with David (1 Sam. 19:11–17). David's marriage into the royal family did nothing to resolve Saul's jealousy or his fear of the gifted, young soldier. The king's hostility became more and more evident, and at last, Saul attempted to "pin David to the wall with the spear" (19:10). David hurried home, and after conferring with Michal, agreed that he would have to flee to survive. Michal let David down through a window, and he slipped safely away.

Michal, who had been left behind, did all she could to give David a head start. When messengers came from Saul demanding that David come to the palace, Michal told them David was sick. She placed a dummy in David's bed and covered it so cleverly that, when the messengers later carried the "ill" David before the king, the masquerade went undetected until the blankets were thrown off in Saul's presence.

When Saul angrily accused Michal, she told him David had threatened to kill her. What could she, a mere woman, do? And all the while her heart sang, for the man she loved had escaped, and she had saved him.

But Michal paid a price. With her husband David an outlaw, Saul later exercised his prerogative as king and gave "Michal his daughter, David's wife, to Palti the son of Laish, who was from Gallim" (1 Sam. 25:44).

David demands Michal's return (2 Sam. 3:13–16). At least ten years passed before David and Michal met again. David remained a fugitive until after Saul's death. He was then recognized as king by the tribe of Judah. But Abner, Saul's military commander, set up Saul's son, Ishbosheth, as puppet ruler of the northern tribes. For seven and a half years, David ruled the one Hebrew tribe. Then Abner had a falling out with Ishbosheth and offered to influence the northern tribes to make David king of a united Hebrew nation.

As negotiations for reunification were taking place, David announced his one demand. He told Abner, "I will make a covenant with you. But one thing I require of you: you shall not see my face unless you first bring Michal, Saul's daughter, when you come to see my face" (2 Sam. 3:13). At the same time David sent messengers with the same demand to Ishbosheth, who immediately did as David asked.

> *And Ishbosheth sent and took her from her husband, from Paltiel the son of Laish. Then her husband went along with her to Bahurim, weeping behind her. So Abner said to him, "Go, return!" And he returned.*

—2 Sam. 3:15, 16

It would be encouraging to suppose that David was moved by love for Michal, and that she was filled with delight at the prospect of reunion. However, by then, David had several other wives and children as well. And certainly there is no hint in the text that any of the principals—David, Abner, or Ishbosheth—consulted Michal. David demanded. Ishbosheth commanded. And Abner, for his own reasons, sent Michal's weeping second husband home.

Why would David have sent for Michal? Not for love, but for politics. David was soon to be proclaimed king of a united Israel, the northern tribes as well as southern Judah. It was important that there be some visible connection with Saul to legitimize David's ascension to what had been Saul's throne. What better connection could there be than David's marriage into the royal family? But for that connection to exist, David must be reunited with Michal. David simply had to require her return, so that she could be by his side when the crown of a united Israel was placed on his head.

Saul had used Michal for his own ends, utterly disregarding her feelings. He had persecuted the husband whom she had loved in her youth, and then married her to another man. And now her first husband tore her from the arms of her second husband, not because he hoped to revive their love, but for reasons as selfish and political as those that had moved her father to use and then discard her.

A final confrontation (2 Sam. 6:20–23). Years later, we catch a glimpse of Michal. David had triumphed over all his foreign enemies, and had established Jerusalem as the political capital of the nation. He had just succeeded in bringing the ark of the covenant to the city, making it the nation's religious capital as well.

David was flushed with the joy of this victory, still filled with the gratitude to God and with the delight that moved him to lead the procession of priests carrying the holy ark through the city streets. For this, David had taken off his royal robes, and clad in a simple linen garment had danced before the Lord, a simple worshiper. Michal had watched him from one of the palace windows, and as she watched was overcome by feelings of bitterness and contempt. The Scriptures describe the scene in the palace:

> *Then David returned to bless his household. And Michal the daughter of Saul came out to meet David, and said, "How glorious was the king of Israel today, uncovering himself today in the eyes of the maids of his servants, as one of the base fellows shamelessly uncovers himself." So David said to Michal, "It was before the LORD, who chose me instead of your father*

and all his house, to appoint me ruler over the people of the LORD, over Israel. Therefore I will play music before the LORD. And I will be even more undignified than this, and will be humble in my own sight. But as for the maidservants of whom you have spoken, by them I will be held in honor." Therefore Michal the daughter of Saul had no children to the day of her death.

What a change had occurred in Michal. The young girl, so in love with her hero-husband, had become a bitter and disillusioned woman. Her love for David had turned into contempt, and she couldn't wait to strike out at him. David, perhaps aware of his own responsibility for the woman she had become, struck back. She was no longer a princess, far above the humble officer she married. Her father was dead, rejected by God, and now David ruled. It was David who determined what was dignified and what was not, and even the servant girls Michal despised could sense the love for God that motivated David's unseemly praise and honor him for it. With this reply, David turned away from Michal forever. She remained in his house, a symbol, but he never touched her again. She died childless and alone.

What a tragic figure Michal was, and what a price she paid for being born into a royal family. As a woman in the ruling house, Michal had lost her primary identity as a person and had become instead a pawn for men to use.

Jezebel

Not all women in the royal houses of Israel and Judah were as helpless as Michal seems to have been. Some women then as now were gifted with unusually strong personalities and were able to grasp and to hold power.

One of these women was Jezebel, the wife of King Ahab of Israel. Jezebel was the daughter of Ethbaal, the king of Sidon. The marriage was undoubtedly arranged between the two royal houses, but Jezebel proved to be no minor clause in an international treaty. She brought into the marriage a passion for the religion of her homeland and a strength of will that enabled her to dominate her often-indecisive husband.

The royal couple quickly set out to replace the worship of the Lord in Israel with the worship of Baal. They imported prophets from Jezebel's homeland and sought to exterminate the prophets of the Lord. Only the intervention of Elijah and miracles that God enabled him to perform turned the general population back to the Lord and thwarted Jezebel's plans.

One incident reported in Scripture reveals the relationship between the two rulers and the power Jezebel held in her own hands.

Ahab coveted a vineyard, owned by a man named Naboth, that lay just beyond the palace. The king asked Naboth to sell the plot of land to him, offering either a better field or money in exchange. But Naboth refused. When the land of Canaan had been distributed to the members of the twelve tribes centuries before, the plot Naboth now owned had been given to Naboth's ancestors. It was as if God Himself had chosen that particular plot for Naboth's line, and he refused to give the king "the inheritance of my fathers" (1 Kin. 21:4).

Disappointed and sullen, Ahab returned home to sulk. When Jezebel asked what was wrong, Ahab told her of Naboth's refusal. First Kings 21 continues:

Then Jezebel his wife said to him, "You now exercise authority over Israel! Arise, eat food, and let your heart be cheerful; I will give you the vineyard of Naboth the Jezreelite." And she wrote letters in Ahab's name, sealed them with his seal, and sent the letters to the elders and the nobles who were dwelling in the city with Naboth. She wrote in the letters, saying,

Proclaim a fast, and seat Naboth with high honor among the people; and seat two men, scoundrels, before him to bear witness against him, saying, "You have blasphemed God and the king." Then take him out, and stone him, that he may die.

So the men of his city, the elders and nobles who were inhabitants of his city, did as Jezebel had sent to them, as it was written in the letters which she had sent to them. ...Then they sent to Jezebel, saying, "Naboth has been stoned and is dead." And it came to pass, when Jezebel heard that Naboth had been stoned and was dead, that Jezebel said to Ahab, "Arise, take possession of the vineyard of Naboth the Jezreelite, which he refused to give you for money; for Naboth is not alive, but dead." So it was, when Ahab had heard that Naboth was dead, that Ahab got up and went down to take possession of the vineyard of Naboth the Jezreelite.

—1 Kin. 21:7–11, 14–16

This account makes clear that Jezebel wielded royal power. She wrote letters in Ahab's name. She sealed them with the royal seal. Yet everyone knew that she had penned the letters, for when the elders and nobles of Naboth's city carried out the thinly disguised judicial murder, they reported not to Ahab but to Jezebel. All the people feared Jezebel. She was feared so much that her evil command was obeyed without protest.

It was not easy to be a woman of the royal family in the age of kings. Yet strong women like Jezebel succeeded by the force of their personalities to gain a power which enabled them to treat men as men treated women: as objects to be used for the ruler's ends, without consideration and without concern.

When Eve chose to disobey God's command in Eden, she could not have imagined the consequences, for her, and for all her daughters. God's announcement "your desire shall be for your husband, and he shall rule over you" (Gen. 3:16), spelled out consequences that history has confirmed in tragedy after tragedy. Seldom has the calamitous effect of the Fall on women been more clearly seen than in the experience of women like Michal, whom we meet in the age of kings. And seldom has the nature of men and women alike been more viciously twisted than in women like Jezebel who, rebelling against her subservient state, adopted as her own the traits of woman's oppressors.

~ *Appendix C* ~
Women of the New Testament

Jesus' Relationships with Women
(The Gospels)

The rabbis of Jesus' day had little use for women. Their attitude, reflected in the sayings and rulings of the sages recorded during the two centuries after Christ, seem especially strange today. Take, for example, the dictum of Yose b. Yohanan of Jerusalem, "Talk not much with womankind" (*mAbot* 1.5). Rabbinic writings contain many comments on this pronouncement. The *Mishna* (IV, 493) notes, "They said this of a man's own wife; how much more of his fellow's wife," while the Talmud says, "It was taught: Do not speak excessively with a woman lest this ultimately lead you to adultery" (*bNed.* 201).

While the dictum was originally intended for rabbis, the *Abot de Rabbi Nathan* extends the advice to include all males, noting "a man should not speak with a woman in the market, even if she is his wife, much less another woman, because the public may misinterpret it" (ARNA 2, p.9). Indeed, R. Eliezer b. R. Shimeon determined that "we have not found that the Almighty spoke to a woman except Sarah" (*ySot.*7.1,21b).

In view of the attitude toward women displayed here and reflected in many rulings governing the lives and relationships of first-century Jews, the Gospels are truly stunning documents. The Gospel writers portray women in a vastly different light. When Jesus interacts with women He often directly violates rules laid down and scrupulously kept by the Pharisees, who were the strongest proponents of what has come to be known as rabbinic Judaism.

It is not an overstatement to affirm that the Gospels portray Jesus as liberating women and lifting them to an equality with men unknown in first-century Palestine. This clearly is a major theme in the Gospel of Luke, which frequently sets up contrasts between a man and a woman that reflect favorably on the woman and unfavorably on the man.

The current debate on the role of women is focused on a few passages in the Epistles of Paul. However, to interpret them correctly we must realize that a startling redemptive and transformational process is initiated in the Gospels.

Jewish Women in First-Century Palestine

The women we meet in the Gospels lived in a strongly patriarchal society. It was also a society structured by a religious faith that shaped every aspect of people's lives. Yet first-century Jewish society was not monolithic.

A heterogeneous population. Some Jewish people in Palestine lived in urban settings; others lived in rural areas. Some were wealthy; most were poor. Some were members of the religious elite; others were despised for supposed religious failings. The Jewish people also were divided into religious and political factions, with Pharisee and Sadducee, Zealot, and Essene, all convinced that their view of the Law's teachings was correct. These divisions had an impact on the role of women, as well as on other aspects of life.

Geographical differences. For instance, the people of Jerusalem and Judea were stricter in their observance of the Law as the rabbis interpreted it than were the people of Galilee. Understandably, most sages and rabbis chose to live in Jerusalem, the holy city, and their influence was strongest there.

Wealth and religious party. The Sadducees, who controlled the temple and the high priesthood, were among the wealthiest in Jerusalem. They were also the most open to Greek culture and ideals and the most supportive of the Roman government. In contrast, ordinary priests lived rural lives, sharing the poverty of the majority. The lives of Sadducean women were undoubtedly different from the lives of most women in the Holy Land, and it is not possible to identify any of the women we meet in the Gospels with this social and religious class.

Scholarship and religious party. In most societies, status is ascribed on the basis of wealth and power, but in the Jerusalem of Jesus' time, a transition was already taking place. The piety of the Pharisees made a great impression on the general population, and the rabbis and sages associated with the Pharisee party were viewed as "the" religious authorities. The Sadducees, much to their dismay, were even forced to adopt the rulings of the Pharisees concerning temple functions. Increasingly in Judaism, status was a matter of scholarship in the Law, rather than a matter of wealth.

While the Pharisees' rulings concerning women's matters were extremely strict, it would be wrong to assume that they describe the lifestyle of every Jewish family. For instance, the rabbis held that women should have their own rooms and, as much as possible, stay in them. For the average Jewish family of six living in poverty, this was simply impossible. So there is no doubt that the wives of the sages and Pharisees, to whom the strictest of rabbinical rulings were actually applied, had different lives than most women.

The "typical" first-century Jew. The great majority of the population of Judea and Galilee, whether they lived in urban or rural settings, were relatively poor. The men were farmers who often worked as day laborers to supplement their incomes. Or they were fishermen, artisans, or shopkeepers. By necessity, many wives worked alongside their husbands and sold produce in the market or sold their husband's products in a shop. We meet these ordinary women most frequently in the Gospels. Luke provides clear clues to the social position of most of the persons mentioned in his Gospel and in Acts. We can identify the class of the women mentioned in his Gospel, most of whom are also referred to in the other Gospels.

Social Class of Women in Luke's Gospel

Governing Classes
Ruling families
Herodias (Luke 3:19)

Relative Prominence
Due to income
Joanna (Luke 8:3)
Susanna (Luke 8:3)
Jairus' daughter
(Luke 8:41–42, 49–56)
Due to husband's religious role
Elizabeth (Luke 1:5–7, 24–25)

Rural Poor
Mary, Jesus' mother
(Luke 1:27–36; 2:4–51; 8:19–21)
Mary, mother of James (Luke 24:10)

Urban
Landowner
Mary and Martha (Luke 10:38–42)
Artisan
Peter's mother-in-law (Luke 4:38, 39)

Slaves
Servant accusing Peter (Luke 22:55–62)

Unclean and Degraded
By sickness
Peter's mother-in-law (Luke 4:38, 39)
Hemorrhaging woman (Luke 8:43–48)
Daughter of Jairus (Luke 8:41, 42, 49–56)
Woman bent double (Luke 13:10–17)
By demonization
Mary Magdalene (Luke 8:2; 24:10)
Joanna (Luke 8:3)
Susanna (Luke 8:3)
Woman bent double (Luke 13:10–17)
As prostitutes
"Sinful" woman (Luke 7:36–50)
As pagans
Widow of Zarephath (in story)
(Luke 4:26, 27)

Widows
Anna (Luke 2:36–38)
Widow with dead son (Luke 7:12–15)
Widow of Zarephath (in story)
(Luke 7:36–50)
Persistent widow (in story)
(Luke 18:1–18)
Poor but generous (Luke 21:1–4)

When we identify women by social class, we note, first of all, that most of Jesus' interactions were with women who were distressed. Even the relatively prominent, like Joanna and Susanna who provided Jesus with financial support, were demon-possessed when Jesus first met them. Mary and Martha, although of a relatively well off landowning class, were single women living in their brother's home. This role was minimized in a society that emphasized the importance of marriage and family.

Jesus' contact with the women in Luke's Gospel invariably lifted them. Jesus saw in these women a significance that they were denied in their society!

The Gospels introduce their liberating note at this point. Without contesting the patriarchal structure of first-century society, Jesus interacted with women in ways that challenged contemporary views of women. Jesus' coming initiated a transformation of attitudes toward women that, we will see, continued on into the church age. Jesus' actions, when contrasted with the dictums of the rabbis, makes it clear that *Christ's coming introduces a redemptive process designed to lift and restore women to the position they enjoyed in original creation.*

We will see this as we examine Jesus' interaction with several women, and as we later look at the way Luke structured his Gospel to challenge his readers to reevaluate their attitude toward women.

Jesus' Interactions with Women

Each of the Gospels relates the words and actions of a Man who lived as a first-century Jew in Palestine. Each of the Gospels requires us to know something of Jewish thought and life if we see the full significance of what Jesus Christ did and said. This is particularly true of Jesus' reported interactions with women. In this section of our study we will look at selected women of the Gospels, and see how their treatment by Jesus contrasted with that of the rabbis.

The Bleeding Woman

Jesus and the woman with the issue of blood (Matt. 9:20–22; Mark 5:25–34; Luke 8:41–49). Luke tells the familiar story:

And behold, there came a man named Jairus, and he was a ruler of the synagogue. And he fell down at Jesus' feet and begged Him to come to his house, for he had an only daughter about twelve years of age, and she was dying. But as He went, the multitudes thronged Him.

Now a woman, having a flow of blood for twelve years, who had spent all her livelihood on physicians and could not be healed by any, came from behind and touched the border of His garment. And immediately her flow of blood stopped. And Jesus said, "Who touched Me?" When all denied it, Peter and those with him said, "Master, the multitudes throng and press You, and You say 'Who touched Me?'" But Jesus said, "Somebody touched Me, for I perceived power going out from Me."

Now when the woman saw that she was not hidden, she came trembling; and falling down before Him, she declared to Him in the presence of all the people the reason she had touched Him and how she was healed immediately. And He said to her, "Daughter, be of good cheer; your faith has made you well. Go in peace."

While He was still speaking, someone came from the ruler of the synagogue's house, saying to him, "Your daughter is dead. Do not trouble the Teacher."

—Luke 8:41–49

We know the rest of the story. Jesus went to Jairus' house, and there raised their daughter from the dead. Yet what happened on the way must have stunned the original witnesses.

The relative value of women. In rabbinic thought, men were primary; women were secondary. The religious leaders, being men, looked on women as "other." Indeed, their formulations of religious law treat women more as objects that men experience than as persons in their own right. While women were portrayed as weak-minded and fragile, men in contrast were viewed as courageous, strong, and wise. This attitude is expressed in Genesis Rabba 17:8, which describes male-female differences. One of those differences is that "the man makes demands on the woman whereas the woman does not make demands on the man."

How startling then to see Jesus, making his way through the crowds at the request of an important man, stop to respond to the silent cry of a woman! To Jesus the woman was at least as important as the man was, for both their needs were urgent.

The danger of "contamination" by women. There is little doubt that her contemporaries would consider the woman in the story *niddah.* This term was applied to women suffering a menstrual flow. During this period, women were ritually unclean, and a husband could not have sex with his wife. Of course, any menstrual bloodstains on objects women came in contact with were held to pollute the objects, so Jewish women had to be especially careful in the kitchen and around the house.

The rabbis went beyond the Old Testament teaching on menstrual uncleanness. They urged that a man separate from his wife several days before and after her period to avoid contamination. The Scripture, "You shall separate the children of Israel from their uncleanness" (Lev. 15:31), was used as a proof text for this ruling. Rabbi Yoshayah even warned men that they might die if they failed to keep away from their wives when they approached their periods. A later story recorded in *bShub.13a-b* illustrates:

It once happened that a certain scholar who had studied much Scripture and mishna, and had served scholars much, yet died in the prime of life. ...I said to her: My daughter! How was he to you in your days of menstruation? She said to me: God forbid! He did not touch me even with his little finger. And how was he to you during your days of white garments [from the end of the period to the time of ritual bathing]? He ate with me, drank with me and slept with me in bodily contact, and it did not occur to him to engage in sex. I said to her: Blessed be the Omnipresent for slaying him!

Mere contact, even after the flow of blood ceased, was assumed to explain *and justify* the early death.

While some sages were willing to make distinctions between menstrual flows and discharges of blood from injuries or illness, only lengthy and careful examination of individual cases could lead to a declaration of cleanness. In most cases, it was deemed better to err on the side of safety.

The horror with which menstrual blood was viewed in rabbinic Judaism reflected and intensified the suspicion and distrust with which women themselves were viewed.

Against this background, it is striking to see Jesus' untroubled reaction to the woman's touch. Even more striking, rather than contaminating Jesus, this woman's touch released a flow of spiritual power *from Him* that cleansed *her*.

Christ showed concern for women's unique needs. The New Testament never directly attacked the patriarchal structure of first-century society. Nor does it ever imply that the differences between men and women are irrelevant. But the New Testament does call for a transformation of men's attitudes toward women, and thus seeks to reform rather than replace patriarchy. Certainly Jesus did not pause to talk with the woman simply because He felt power flow from Him. He paused because He knew that the woman, fearful and trembling at her boldness in violating strictures imposed by the men who ruled her world, needed to hear Christ address her as "daughter," tell her to "be of good cheer," and then to receive His commendation for her faith.

Some people reading this story in the Gospels have viewed it as an "anti-Pharisee polemic." The attitude Jesus displayed in this encounter departs strikingly from the attitude toward women expressed in rabbinic writings. Christ's concern for the woman as a person clearly condemns the dismissive and slighting ways women were viewed in that day.

Mary and Martha

Jesus at Mary and Martha's home (Luke 10:38–42). Luke is the only Gospel writer to relate a striking story about Jesus' visit to the home where Mary and Martha lived.

Now it happened as they went that He entered a certain village; and a certain woman named Martha welcomed Him into her house. And she had a sister called Mary, who also sat at Jesus feet and heard His word. But Martha was distracted with much serving, and she approached Him and said, "Lord, do You not care that my sister has left me to serve alone? Therefore tell her to help me."

And Jesus answered and said to her, "Martha, Martha, you are worried and troubled about many things. But one thing is needed, and Mary has chosen that good part, which will not be taken away from her."

—Luke 10:38–42

Unmarried women (John 11). We do not know a lot about Mary and Martha, although we meet them again in John's Gospel. We do know, however, that they were relatively well off and frequently hosted Jesus and His disciples when they came to Jerusalem. We also know that they were unmarried. We know this because, even though Luke depicts Martha welcoming Jesus "into her house," John tells us the two women lived with their brother, Lazarus. This means that the house had been their father's, and first-century Jewish inheritance laws required the home to pass to the son, not the daughters. If Mary or Martha had been married, they would have lived in the homes of their husbands, not with their brother.

In a society that emphasized marriage for both men and women, and where thirteen years and one day was the marriageable age for women, Mary and Martha's unmarried state was a disgrace. Although relatively well off, we would have to consider Mary and Martha disadvantaged persons in that society. Like so many other women we read of in the Gospels, these two women were oppressed by the expectations of others—expectations neither had been able to meet.

Martha's view of her role (Luke 10:40). Luke pictures Martha as a flustered homemaker. She rushed around the kitchen, frantic to prepare and serve food for her visitors. Jewish society made a clear distinction between "women's work" and "men's work," and the kitchen was the woman's responsibility. Martha did not question this view of herself and her role. She may not have been married, but she unquestioningly accepted society's definition of a woman and her duties.

Martha not only accepted society's view of her role; she became upset when her sister Mary did not. When Mary sat down to learn at Jesus' feet, Martha became angry. In first-century Judaism, *men*, not *women*, were supposed to learn from rabbis. It may well be that Martha's agitation is not so much a reflection of her need for kitchen help as it is anxiety at Mary's "inappropriate" behavior.

Finally Martha went to Jesus and asked Him to "tell" Mary to help her. She desperately wanted Jesus to confirm her idea of what was right and wrong for women.

Mary's rejection of the woman's role (Luke 10:39). There is some debate today concerning how much Scripture Jewish women knew. There is evidence that the rabbis deferred to women as far as rulings governing the kitchen were concerned. Evidence also shows that studying was considered inappropriate for women.

Sifre Deuteronomy 46 comments on Deuteronomy 11:19, "'And you shall teach them to your sons,' your sons and not your daughters." R. Eleizer is quoted as saying, "They shall burn the teachings of Torah rather than convey them to women" (*ySot.3.4,19a*). Rabbi Eleizer also stated, "A woman has no wisdom except in handling her spindle, for it is written, 'And all the women that were wise-hearted did spin with their hands.'" While this rabbi is the most hostile to the idea of Torah-study for women, there is no doubt that women were not expected, as men were, to probe deeply into God's Word.

Mary, then, in setting household tasks aside to sit as a disciple at Jesus' feet, was taking a bold step. She was claiming a right that those in first-century Judaism assumed was for men only. In so doing, she was abandoning the role that both men and women in her society had assigned her.

Jesus affirms Mary's choice (Luke 10:42). After hearing Martha's complaint, Jesus did what no rabbi of His time would have considered. He affirmed Mary's action, saying, "Mary has chosen that good part, which will not be taken away from her."

In making this statement, Jesus was not denigrating the tasks women performed for their families. Rather, Jesus was opening the door for women to a privilege that had long been denied them. Women,

like men, are called by God to explore the depths of His Word. Women, like men, are invited to listen to Jesus and to grow in spiritual maturity.

Today in our churches, many debate whether a woman can teach. Despite the intensity of the debate today, that issue is hardly as inflammatory as the issue Mary's bold action raised in the first century. Are women capable of mastering God's Word? Are women called to be students of the Scriptures and disciples of the Lord? Jesus' affirmation of Mary's eager desire to learn from Him opened a door for women that had long been closed.

Jesus' affirmation of Mary should lead those of us who would deny the privilege of teaching to women to question whether our attitude toward women and the Word reflects the view of women held by the Pharisees or the view of women held by our Lord.

The Samaritan Woman

Jesus and the Samaritan woman (John 4:6–42). A third report of Jesus' contact with a woman further illustrates the transformation of attitudes toward women that Jesus initiated. Because the dialog quoted by John is so lengthy, we'll look only at the most significant verses for this study.

Jesus shocked a Samaritan woman by speaking with her (John 4:7–9). These verses underline how unusual Jesus' action was.

> *A woman of Samaria came to draw water. Jesus said to her, "Give Me a drink." For His disciples had gone away into the city to buy food. Then the woman of Samaria said to Him, "How is it that You, being a Jew, ask a drink from me, a Samaritan woman?"*
>
> —John 4:7–9

Samaria. The district of Samaria lay between Judea and Galilee on the west side of the Jordan. The land had once been part of the northern Hebrew kingdom, Israel. When Israel fell in 722 B.C., the Assyrians deported most of the Jewish population and resettled the area with people from other lands. The new settlers adopted the God of the land, Yahweh, while also holding to their old deities. The Samaritans of the first century were descendants of these peoples, who claimed an allegiance to Yahweh, but whose claims were rejected by "pure" Jews. A deep hostility existed between these neighboring peoples. Many Jews, rather than pass through Samaria on their way to or from Jerusalem, would take the much longer route around Samaria to the east, crossing and then re-crossing the Jordan River.

Samaritan women. The woman who came to the well was shocked that Jesus would speak to her. This was not simply because she was a Samaritan, but a Samaritan woman.

First, it was unusual for a Jewish rabbi to speak to any woman directly. Several rabbinical quotes exist that advise men to "talk not much to womankind."

Second, the rabbis were just as concerned about looking at a woman. In the *Testament of Judah* (17:1), Judah laments that he succumbed to a Canaanite woman, and warns his sons against looking at *any* woman. And *BBer.21a* states, "Our rabbis taught: He who pays a woman by counting out coins from his hand to hers in order to gaze at her, even if the level of his *Torah* knowledge and good deeds has reached that of Moses our teacher, he will not escape the punishment of *Gehenna*."

Surely Jesus' conversation in private with the woman at the well would have been viewed as shocking if not depraved.

But there is another reason why Jesus' moments alone with the Samaritan woman would have shocked the Pharisees. Earlier, we saw that during their periods women were considered *niddah*, and were to be avoided by men lest they become contaminated. Rabbinic expositions on *niddah* classify Samaritan women as *niddah* from the day of their birth (*mNidd.*4:1; *mNidd.*5:1). Thus, according to the Pharisees, men of Christ's time should *strictly avoid any kind of contact with Samaritan women*.

Against this background, we can understand the surprise of Jesus' disciples, recorded in John 4:27: "At this point His disciples came, and they marveled that He talked with a woman; yet no one said, 'What do You seek?' or, 'Why are You talking with her?'"

The woman's response to Jesus (John 4:28–30). John records both the lengthy conversation Jesus held with the woman and her response.

> The woman then left her waterpot, went her way into the city, and said to the men, "Come, see a Man who told me all things that I ever did. Could this be the Christ?" They then went out of the city and came to Him.

—John 4:28–30

The woman of Samaria responded to Jesus' offer of eternal life with faith, and she showed her faith by hurrying into her village to tell others about Him.

The implicit comparison with Nicodemus (John 3). It is hardly by chance that John places the story of the Samaritan woman immediately after his account of Nicodemus's interview with Jesus. Nicodemus was not only a Jewish man, he was a "man of the Pharisees, ... a ruler of the Jews" (John 3:1). This description identifies Nicodemus as a member of the Sanhedrin, the Jewish ruling council. As a Pharisee,

he was devoted to keeping every detail of God's Law as interpreted by the rabbis. This description marked him as a person who had studied the Old Testament intensely, and who was supposedly qualified to interpret and to apply God's Law to every situation.

In contrast, the Samaritan woman is a person whose understanding of Scripture is limited by her race and her sex, and whose classification as *niddah* made her an object of revulsion.

Yet it is the Pharisee who does not understand or respond to Jesus' teaching, while the Samaritan woman not only responds, but immediately hurries away to tell others about Him. Ultimately, Nicodemus became a disciple (see John 9:39), but the Samaritan woman's ready response and her joyful witness to Christ is a far better example of discipleship. Strikingly, it is the "ignorant" and "outcast" *woman* rather than the learned and respected *man*, who illustrates a true faith-response to Jesus' words.

Implications of Gospel stories about women. The stories we read in the Gospels are so familiar that we tend to miss their significance. Yet these incidents highlighted above and many others depicting Jesus' interaction with women are truly revolutionary. They directly challenge the view of women held in the first century. And they powerfully affirm women who were restricted or held down on the basis of religious ideas that Jesus, by His example, decisively rejected.

Jesus' interactions with women affirmed the worth and value of women as persons, overturned stereotypes, and opened the door to new and fulfilling roles for women of faith. Before we follow the example of the religionists of Jesus' day, and deny significant roles to women today, we must seriously reconsider the liberation of women that the coming of Jesus clearly introduced.

Women Jesus Knew and Other Women in the Gospels

A quick survey of the Gospels shows that they clearly reflect first-century patriarchal society. Daughters are mentioned 24 times in the Gospels, sons 327 times. Mothers are mentioned 72 times, fathers 293 times. "Woman" or "women" occur 78 times, "man" or "men" occur 295 times. There can be no doubt that the society portrayed in the Gospels was patriarchal.

Yet Jesus rejected the attitude toward women the religious leaders of His day held. Incident after incident depicting Jesus' relationships with women indicates that Christ, by His example, sought to restore to women prerogatives that were forfeited in the Fall. Even in that most patriarchal of societies, the Savior lifted up women and women's role.

Our goal is not to construct a more biblical theology of womankind, but rather to meet individual women. Thus the stories in the Gospels will not be cited as evidence to advance a feminine agenda. Rather, these stories will be explored to learn more about each woman as a person, so that we might gain insights into our own lives and callings.

Who are the women of the Gospels we need to visit? Taken in the likely order of their first contact with Jesus, these are the women we should consider.

Women Jesus Knew or Met

Mary of Nazareth (see page 126)
Elizabeth (see page 57)
Peter's mother-in-law (see page 148)
The Samaritan woman (see page 204)
The adulteress (see page 8)
Widow of Nain (see page 243)
Anointing sinner (see page 13)
Mary Magdalene (see page 120)
Hemorrhaging woman (see page 87)
Jairus' wife and daughter (see page 94)
Syro-phoenician woman (see page 231)
Mary and Martha of Bethany (see page 114)
Widow with the mite (see page 242)
Crippled woman in synagogue (see page 38)
Anointer at Simon the leper's (see page 16)
Salome, mother of James and John (see page 200)

Other Women in the Gospels

Bride at Cana (see page 30)
Herodias and her daughter (see page 89)
Woman who blessed Jesus' mother (see page 253)
Caiaphas' maid-servant (see page 32)
Pilate's wife (see page 156)

Women in Luke's Gospel

It has long been noted that Luke's Gospel, shaped to reveal Jesus as the ideal human being, pays special attention to Christ's concern for the poor and oppressed. For instance, Luke frequently mentions widows, and always in a positive light (see Luke 2:36–38; 4:26; 7:11–17; 18:1–8; 20:47; and 21:1–4). Luke also pays unusual attention to women, often pairing them with men in ways that are less than flattering to the male. In fact, most references to women in Luke's Gospel are not only positive, but

seem to be crafted to break stereotypes and to cast women as equal with men in those qualities which count in Christ's kingdom.

We can see this clearly in a brief survey of Luke's portrayal of women in his Gospel and especially in the way Luke pairs women with men. Each pairing shows that in Jesus' kingdom women are lifted up.

Luke's Portrayal of Women

Mary, the mother of Jesus (Luke 1). Gabriel, an angel of the highest rank, visited Mary, the betrothed teenager. She was the first to hear that God was about to break into history in the person of the Messiah, her Son-to-be, and Mary was the first to hear His name—Jesus. Mary responds to the stunning announcement with a beautiful and simple faith expressed both in her submission to God's will and in the Magnificat, her prophetic song of praise (Luke 1:46–55). In every way Mary is shown not only to be favored by God, but also an example of that simple faith that welcomes divine grace and then rejoices in the privilege of serving God.

Elizabeth (Luke 1:40–45). Elizabeth was pregnant with John the Baptist when Mary, pregnant with Jesus, visited her. When Mary entered her house, Elizabeth "was filled with the Holy Spirit" and spoke prophetically.

Anna, the prophetess (Luke 2:37, 38). Anna, who had dedicated her life to serve God in the temple, is the third woman mentioned by Luke. She is identified as a prophetess. She not only recognized the Babe in Mary's arms, but proclaimed Him to "all those who looked for redemption in Jerusalem."

While Anna is the only one of the three identified as a prophetess, the work of the Holy Spirit experienced by Mary and Elizabeth enabled each of them to prophesy also. What a powerful suggestion that in the coming age of the Spirit ordinary women will have extraordinary gifts!

Mary and Martha (Luke 10:38–42). The portrayal of Mary and Martha, discussed earlier, is very significant. Mary throws off her traditional role to take what was then considered a man's role, to learn as a disciple at Jesus' feet. As Ben Witherington III points out:

Luke 11:27–28, unique to the Lukan account, implies that a person's chief blessedness is in one's response to God's Word. This implies a criticism of any attempt to see a woman's chief blessedness in her traditional gender-specific roles. Luke 10:38–42, also unique, implies a similar criticism of any attempt to suggest a woman's traditional roles were more important than hearing and heeding the words of Jesus. The "one thing needful" for women as well as men is a response to the Word, the "best portion" of which they should not be prevented from partaking. (*Women in the Earliest Churches* [1988], 130).

Again Luke's portrayal of women indicates a restoration to privileges long denied to them in male-dominated society.

Women witnesses to Christ's resurrection (Luke 24). While the New Testament does not challenge the patriarchal structure of society, it does transform the relationships of men and women within that structure. This concept is powerfully illustrated in Luke 24. The apostles whom Jesus chose retain their roles, but in this chapter, women are cast in new and partnering roles.

> Now on the first day of the week, very early in the morning, they, and certain other women with them, came to the tomb bringing the spices which they had prepared. But they found the stone rolled away from the tomb. Then they went in and did not find the body of the Lord Jesus. And it happened, as they were greatly perplexed about this, that behold, two men stood by them in shining garments. Then, as they were afraid and bowed their faces to the earth, they said to them, "Why do you seek the living among the dead? He is not here, but is risen! Remember how He spoke to you when He was still in Galilee, saying, 'The Son of Man must be delivered into the hands of sinful men, and be crucified, and the third day rise again.'" And they remembered His words. Then they returned from the tomb and told all these things to the eleven and to all the rest. It was Mary Magdalene, Joanna, Mary the mother of James, and the other women with them, who told these things to the apostles. And their words seemed to them like idle tales, and they did not believe them.
>
> But Peter arose and ran to the tomb; and stooping down, he saw the linen clothes lying by themselves; and he departed, marveling to himself at what had happened.

—Luke 24:1–12

A number of features of this description are significant for the present study.

"They came to the tomb" (Luke 24:1). The women came to the tomb that morning to bind spices in the linen cloths in which Jesus' body was wrapped. In the first century, this was "women's work." What is significant is that in doing their women's work, God opened the door to a unique and wonderful privilege.

"Remember how He spoke to you when He was still in Galilee" (Luke 24:6). The angels, in remind-

ing the women of Jesus' words, made it clear that these women were disciples who had been taught by Christ—just as the Twelve had been. Jesus had taught the women the same truths He taught the men. Their gender, and even their willingness to do "women's work," in no way limited their status as Christ's disciples.

"And they remembered His words" (Luke 24:8). As the angels spoke, the women remembered what Jesus had taught. The implication was that they suddenly understood both the meaning of the cross and the grand miracle of Jesus' resurrection.

Here, Luke contrasts the insight of the women with the confusion of the male disciples. When the same message was conveyed to them, "their words seemed to them [the Apostles] like idle tales, and they did not believe them" (Luke 24:11). The women who had chosen to follow Jesus were more perceptive spiritually than the male disciples Christ Himself had chosen!

"Then they returned ... and told all these things to the eleven and to all the rest" (Luke 23:9). Today we might miss the significance of this verse. But in first-century Judaism, while there were exceptions, the testimony of women was not considered valid. Sifre Deuteronomy states the general principle in commenting on the requirement for two witnesses to establish a fact in court.

"Is a woman also qualified to give testimony? It is stated: 'two' (*Deut. 19:15*), and further on, 'the two [men]' (*ibid. 17*). As the meaning of 'two' in one instance is men and not women, so the meaning of 'two' in the other instance is men and not women."

Yet that first Easter morning, women served as the first witnesses to Jesus' resurrection. In fact, Matthew's account emphasizes the fact that they were God's *chosen* witnesses, for the angel tells the women, "Go quickly and tell His disciples that He is risen from the dead" (Matt. 28:7).

Implications. In Luke's account of the first Easter as well as throughout his Gospel, we see the status of women undergoing a striking transformation. Women, so quickly dismissed in first-century Judaism, are implicitly initiated into full discipleship, commended for superior spiritual insight, and commissioned as witnesses to the apostles of Christ's return to life. The consequences of the Fall, spelled out so clearly in Genesis 3, are in the process of being reversed. Women are being restored to the role Eve played in Eden, as a full partner with men in the new creation breaking into our world in Jesus Christ.

Luke's Pairing of Women with Men

The transformation of the place of women within the dawning kingdom of God is even more striking in settings where Luke pairs a woman and man. We can sense the revolutionary view of women that Luke clearly supported by looking at just a few of these pairs.

Zacharias versus Mary (Luke 1). These two are the focus of Luke's first chapter. Zacharias, an aged and respected priest, was serving God in the temple when the angel Gabriel appeared to announce that he and his wife would have a son. Stunned and unbelieving, Zacharias's first words were, "How shall I know this?" He is then temporarily struck mute by Gabriel "because you did not believe my words" (Luke 1:20).

Shortly after this, Gabriel appeared to Mary, a young peasant girl in Galilee. Unlike Zacharias, who doubted "whether" the promise would be kept, Mary believed, asking only "how." With a beautiful and simple faith, Mary accepted God's gift and rejoiced in Him. How striking the contrasts are.

	Zacharias	**Mary**
Location	The temple	Galilee
Status	A priest	A commoner
Characteristics	Male	Female
	Mature	Young
Response	Unbelief	Trust
	Challenge	Praise
Consequence	Silenced	Blessed

In comparing these two, Mary models how all are to live in Christ's kingdom. Zacharias, for all his geographical closeness to God and the status ascribed to him by society on account of his priesthood and of his age, is rejected as a model. In the coming kingdom it is Mary's simple faith that brings blessing, while the supposed advantages enjoyed by Zacharias have no value at all.

The Pharisee versus the sinful woman (Luke 7:36–50). Jesus was invited to eat at the home of a Pharisee named Simon. While they were eating, a woman "who was a sinner" slipped into the house. Weeping, she "began to wash His feet with her tears, and wiped them with the hair of her head; and she kissed His feet and anointed them with fragrant oil" (Luke 7:38). Simon, knowing the woman was a prostitute, concluded that Jesus could not be a prophet. A prophet would know the kind of woman she was. And the Pharisee assumed no man of God would permit the polluting touch of such a person.

Jesus challenged Simon's assumptions, telling the story of two borrowers whose debts were freely forgiven. Jesus then asked which would love more, the person forgiven a great debt, or a small debt? When the Pharisee answered correctly, Jesus pointed out that when He came to dinner, Simon had not shown Him even normal courtesies, while the woman's actions showed exceptional love.

Christ concluded that her loving actions showed that she had been forgiven much, and He told her, "Your sins are forgiven" (Luke 7:48). The reaction from Simon and his Pharisee friends was outrage that Jesus claimed the right to forgive sins.

In this incident, too, we see a number of implied contrasts.

	Simon	**The Woman**
Status	A Pharisee	A "sinner"
Characteristics	Male	Female
	Wealthy	Poor
	Respected	Outcast
Response to Jesus	Dismissive	Loving
	Doubting	Believing
Consequences	Unforgiven	Forgiven

Again, we see a striking reversal. The Pharisee was admired and respected and even held in awe for his apparent piety, while the sinful woman was despised and rejected. However, it is one's attitude toward Jesus that opens the door to God's kingdom. Simon's attitude toward Jesus was dismissive and unbelieving. The sinful woman's attitude toward Jesus was shaped by awareness of her need and trust in Christ's willingness to forgive. She had found forgiveness in Christ, and as a result, she loved Him deeply. In turn, Jesus accepted her love, commended her faith, and confirmed her forgiveness.

In this pair, we see the theme of reversal again. Simon, respected in his society, is dismissed by Jesus, and we discover that it is the sinful woman, transformed by Jesus' forgiveness, who is significant in God's eyes.

The synagogue ruler versus the bent woman (Luke 13:10–17). A third incident in Luke shows a similar pattern. Jesus was teaching in a synagogue one Sabbath where there was "a woman who had a spirit of infirmity eighteen years, and was bent over and could in no way raise herself up" (Luke 13:11). Jesus laid hands on the woman, and immediately she was healed and stood up straight.

The ruler of the synagogue was scandalized. He considered the healing "work," and criticized Jesus for working on the Sabbath. Christ responded:

"Hypocrite! Does not each one of you on the Sabbath loose his ox or donkey from the stall, and lead it away to water it? So ought not this woman, being a daughter of Abraham, whom Satan has bound—think of it—for eighteen years, be loosed from this bond on the Sabbath?"

—Luke 13:15, 16

Jesus' response shamed all His adversaries:

"and all the multitude rejoiced for all the glorious things that were done by Him."

—Luke 13:17

Again we note the implicit contrasts.

	The Ruler	The Woman
Status	Spiritual leader	Member of congregation
Characteristics	Male	Female
	An authority	A victim
	Healthy	Victim
Jesus	Rebuked him	Restored her
	Condemned him	Affirmed her
Outcome	Was shamed	Became a cause of rejoicing

Here, we see a high-status man contrasted with a low-status woman. The man was a respected religious leader, who saw himself as an authority on God's Law. Yet his behavior showed that he cared less for a crippled woman in his synagogue than for his farm animals In contrast, Jesus saw the woman as a "daughter of Abraham"—a valued member of God's covenant community. He acted immediately to free her from bondage and restore her to complete health and wholeness. The result of the miraculous healing is that the ruler of the synagogue was shown as a hypocrite, and the restored woman became a cause of rejoicing for "all the multitude" (Luke 13:17).

Without in any way challenging the historicity of the event recorded, we can sense a powerful symbolic message. Christ has come to release women from the bondage caused by the Fall. The restoration of women is a cause of rejoicing for all.

The poor widow versus rich men (Luke 21:1–4). This familiar story contrasts the rich, who publicly deposited large sums in the temple treasury, with a poor widow who gave a tiny offering. Jesus commended the widow and announced that she had "put in more than all."

	Rich Men	The Widow
Location	The temple	The temple
Status	High	Low
Characteristic of Gifts	Large	Small
	Abundance	Poverty
	A part	All she had
Evaluation	Insignificant	Significant

Again, Luke chose to tell the story of a woman to make an important point. Again, the woman chosen was from the lowest strata of society. And again, her actions showed that what she could contribute was extremely significant to the Lord. Christ's commendation marks a striking reversal of status. The great gifts given by wealthy men were dismissed, while the tiny gift given by the widow was commended as "more than all" (v. 3).

The significance of male-female pairings in Luke's Gospel. Mary's words of praise recorded in her Magnificat in Luke 1 expressed a significant truth. In coming to earth as a Babe to be born into a poor family, heaven's King turned our values upside down. The things human beings deemed important were shown to be trivial, and the things the world considered minor were filled with significance. In Mary's words:

He has put down the mighty from their thrones, and exalted the lowly.

—Luke 1:52

How women are exalted. Luke's consistent treatment of women in his Gospel and, as we will see, in Acts, shows that women are among the exalted. Women, who since the Fall had taken a lowly place in human society and even in Israel's faith, are lifted up and given striking prominence by Jesus Christ. Christ consistently displayed a concern for women that contrasts sharply with the way women were viewed and treated in first-century Jewish society.

Our Lord's concern for women is not the only striking feature of their portrait in the Gospels. Jesus is shown exalting women far above the limited positions they were granted in the first-century Jewish world. Women were filled with the Holy Spirit and privileged to prophesy. Women were welcomed as learners and disciples. Stereotypes were shattered as women were commissioned as the first witnesses of

Jesus' resurrection. Women, dismissed by Jewish leaders as light-minded and silly, or cloistered and avoided as threats to male spirituality, are set forth in the Gospels as models of godliness and examples of faith.

When women are paired with men. The transformation of women's position in the community of faith is even more strikingly shown when Luke pairs men and women. In most cases the pairing presents women in a strongly positive light. The men in such pairs share certain characteristics. They have a relatively high status, a reputation as religious leaders—and often are dismissive of the concerns or needs of the women with whom they are paired. In contrast, the women have low status, are lightly regarded, and have deep needs to which the men are insensitive.

Yet in these pairings, the men are shamed and the women praised. Zacharias the priest was exposed for his unbelief while the peasant girl Mary was exalted as a woman who trusted God completely and was richly blessed. Simon the Pharisee stood in judgment on Jesus and concluded that He was no prophet. The sinful woman with whom he is paired found forgiveness and went on to model loving service to our Lord. Christ condemned the ruler of the synagogue as a hypocrite. The full restoration of the crippled woman with whom he is paired became a cause of rejoicing for all.

Those of us who view Scripture as God's inspired and trustworthy Word can hardly dismiss this evidence as irrelevant. The Gospels mark decisive shifts in the way Jesus' followers are called to view women. Our Lord shatters the older sex-biased and role-limited categories, and we clearly are called to rethink our assumptions about womankind.

Women in Acts

The Gospels are striking for their revolutionary depiction of women. Jesus displayed a respect for women that was in stark contrast with the attitude expressed in rabbinic literature. In Luke's treatment of women in his Gospel, we can see a conscious effort to demonstrate that Jesus' coming radically changed women's status in the community of faith.

Luke also wrote the Book of Acts, in which he continued his account of "all that Jesus began both to do and teach" (Acts 1:1). In his Gospel, Luke traced the ministry of Christ "until the day in which He was taken up" (Acts 1:2). In Acts, Luke related Jesus' continuing activity in the early church through the agency of the Holy Spirit and His human followers. Here, we will see if Acts continues to depict women in new roles and relationships. If Acts does continue to portray women in Christ's church in ways that dif-

fer radically from the way they were viewed in Judaism, we have further evidence that one purpose in Christ's coming was to restore to women that equality with men that was lost in the Fall.

Acts mentions a number of women, most of whom are viewed positively. Arlandson (*Women, Class, and Society in Early Christianity*, 1997) suggests we classify these women as persons who are receptive to or favored by the kingdom of God. He suggests a second classification of women who were resistant to or not favored by God's kingdom. While Arlandson identifies twenty-three individual women or groups of women as favored, only Sapphira (5:1–11), Candace (8:27), prominent Antiochenes of Pisidia (13:50), Philippian women (16:13), Drusilla (24:24) and Bernice (25:23) fall into the "not favored" category.

Here, we'll look briefly at women who are mentioned favorably in Acts, and then we'll look closely at some women who display how the new faith has changed their lives.

Women Mentioned Positively in Acts

Several of Luke's references to women in Acts seem to stress a transformation of women's traditional roles. He presents models for new ministries available to women in the Christian community. We need to look especially at Tabitha, Mary the mother of John Mark, Lydia, Priscilla, and Philip's daughters.

Mary (1:14). Mary, the mother of Jesus and "Jesus' brothers," is identified in reference to disciples who met in Jerusalem for prayer between the ascension of Christ and Pentecost. Luke is not exalting Mary, but is making it clear that members of Jesus' earthly family are among those who trusted Him as Savior and Lord.

Praying Disciples (1:14). The text names the eleven men whom Jesus selected to lead the church as apostles. Luke took pains to make clear that 120 of Jesus' earliest followers included "the women."

On Pentecost (2:4). This same group was gathered on the day of Pentecost when the Holy Spirit was given. The text says "They were all filled with the Holy Spirit and began to speak with other tongues." In neither the filling nor the gift was a distinction made between men and women.

Jerusalem disciples (5:14). The text says, "Believers were increasingly added to the Lord, multitudes of both men and women." Again, we see Luke's habit of specifically mentioning women.

Hellenistic widows (6:1–7). Jerusalem was a cosmopolitan city. Many Jews had been born in other cities of the Roman Empire. Many lived in Jerusalem and primarily spoke Greek. The primary language of those born in Judea was Aramaic, a language closely related to Hebrew. The Aramaic-speaking or local widows are called "the Hebrews" in this text. Since few occupations were open to women in Jerusalem, widows with no adult sons were especially vulnerable to poverty. The city provided food for Jewish widows but may have refused to feed those who became Christians. So the early church set up its own distribution system to provide for the needy.

Hebrew widows (6:1–7). Some in the early church felt the Hebrew widows were favored in the distribution. The apostles suggested the church select trustworthy men to make sure all were treated fairly. Significantly, every man selected bore a Greek name.

Persecuted disciples (8:3). When persecution drove most Christians from Jerusalem, many believers were dragged from their houses and imprisoned. Again Luke expressly states both "men and women."

Samaritans (8:12). Luke again takes pains to report that "both men and women" were among the first Samaritan converts to Christianity.

Tabitha (9:36–42). Peter brought this woman, identified as a disciple, back to life. Some take Luke's description of her to indicate she was a deaconess.

This passage relates two miracles performed by Peter. The first is the healing of a Christian man named Aeneas (vv. 32–35). The second is the resurrection of a Christian woman named Tabitha or Dorcas.

As we see in his Gospel, Luke frequently pairs a man and a woman. When he does, he generally presents the woman in the better light. Here, Luke's brief mention of Aeneas stands in contrast to the detail he provides about Tabitha.

Tabitha is specifically called a "disciple"; Aeneas is not.

Tabitha's important ministry to Christians is emphasized. Nothing of any ministry Aeneas might have had is mentioned.

Tabitha's death deeply affected many Christians. Nothing similar is said of Aeneas's paralysis.

In Luke's view, the healing has priority in Aeneas's case. However, Tabitha and her role in the Christian community are emphasized in the second incident, despite the fact that raising a person from the dead is a more spectacular miracle than healing a paralytic.

Some have felt that Luke describes Tabitha so carefully because she was a deaconess in the church, and Luke is providing a description of the ministry of a first-century deaconess. The phrase "full of good works" (9:36) indicates continuing activity. Whether or not Tabitha held office as a deaconess, she is presented as a model disciple, and Aenaes is not.

Widows (9:39–41). Tabitha (or Dorcas) is portrayed as providing clothing for widows in Joppa.

Mary (12:12-17). "Mary" was a common first-century name. This Mary is identified as the mother of John Mark. Luke reports that "many were gathered together praying" in Mary's house. This indicates an unusually large Jerusalem residence and marks Mary as a well-to-do and influential woman.

When Herod Antipas imprisoned Peter, members of the Jerusalem church gathered to pray at Mary's home. This tells us several important things about Mary. We know that she was well-to-do. The typical house in Jerusalem was quite small and would not have provided room for a number of people to gather. Mentioning Mary's household slave, Rhoda, strengthens the impression of membership in the upper class.

For at least the first two centuries of the Christian era, believers met in homes rather than in church buildings. Mary's home served as a place of worship for part of the Christian community in Jerusalem. On his release, Peter went immediately to Mary's home. He knew where the believers would be gathered and where he would be welcomed.

"James, and...the brethren" [the other apostles?] were not at the prayer meeting. Peter commissioned Mary to carry word of his release to them.

Finally, we should not forget that in opening her home, Mary showed great courage. Herod Antipas had recently executed the apostle James and imprisoned Peter. A period of official persecution had already been launched. Yet Mary did not hesitate to continue to offer her home as a place of worship and prayer.

Mary, then, was a vital and trusted member of the early Christian community and the hostess of a church that met at her home. There men, women, and even slaves participated as communing members of an early Christian church.

Rhoda (12:13–15). The servant girl Rhoda was a household slave. In stating that Rhoda "came to answer" the door when Peter knocked indicates she was inside. It is possible she was praying with the others. If so, the incident reflects the fact that in the young church, a person's sex or social role was no barrier to full participation in the shared life of the congregation.

Timothy's mother (16:1). Timothy's mother is simply mentioned here as a believer. In a later letter to Timothy, the apostle Paul credits his mother Lois and grandmother Eunice with leading Timothy to faith when he was a child.

Lydia (16:13–15, 40). Lydia was the first convert in Macedonia. Her occupation as a seller of purple and her later sponsoring of Paul and the Philippian church in her own home indicate that she was both wealthy and influential.

She was the first of Paul's converts in Europe after he crossed from Asia Minor into Macedonia. Women had more freedom in Macedonia than in other parts of the Roman Empire, so it is not surprising that Paul should meet an independent and successful business-woman there. It is not even surprising that Lydia, a Jewish "seller of purple" should have moved there from Thyatira, famous for its purple dye.

What is unusual is that Paul, trained as a Pharisee, should have been willing to launch a local church with a group of women. For when Paul found no syn-agogue in Philippi, on the Sabbath he went to a spot on the riverbank where Jewish women gathered to pray. These women, possibly Lydia and her employ-ees, responded to the gospel, were baptized, and formed the core of the first Christian church in Europe, which long remained one of Paul's favorite churches.

In Judaism, ten *men* were required to constitute a *minyan*, the minimum number for a worship service. The difference in the status of women in Christianity could hardly have been demonstrated more powerful-ly than by Paul's willingness to launch a church with a congregation made up only of women.

Lydia then invited the apostles to stay at her home and make it the base from which to evangelize the city.

After being released from prison, Paul and Silas went to Lydia's home. In stating that "when they had seen the brethren" there, Luke makes it clear that the church met in Lydia's home. Clearly Lydia, a woman, continued as a central figure in the local Christian church.

Demonized slave girl (16:16–24). In Philippi, Paul cast a demon from a slave girl. Her owners had exploited her as a fortune-teller. Their anger at Paul's freeing the girl from demonic domination vividly contrasts the treatment of women in pagan society and the valuing of women as persons in the Christian community.

Cultural Background
Women in Pagan Society

The society into which the church burst in the first century was strongly patriarchal. Women may have governed the household, but men were dominant in the larger society. Most men would have agreed with Aristotle, who held that "the male is by nature superior and the female inferior, the male ruler and the female subject" (*Politics* 3.2.10).

Yet in the Roman Empire wealth brought women a surprising degree of personal free-dom, and some even held public office. But only in Macedonia do we have a situation like the following:

The women were in all respects the men's counterparts. They played a large part in affairs, received envoys, and obtained conces-sions from them for their husbands, built tem-ples, founded cities, engaged mercenaries, commanded armies, held fortresses, and acted on occasion as regents or even co-rulers...(W. W. Tarn and G. T. Griffith, *Hellenistic Civilization*, 1952, page 74).

In Asia Minor, too, women could hold pub-lic and cultic offices, which in other parts of the world could be held only by men.

In the Roman upper-classes, divorce had become an option for women as well as men. But Roman upper-class marriages were still contracted by families for political or econom-ic reasons, and girls could not refuse marriages arranged by their fathers unless they could prove the proposed husband was morally unfit. In general, freedwomen were in a better posi-tion in the Roman Empire than women in Greek or Jewish communities. A number of occupations were open to them, and Rome's liberal property laws permitted women to inherit property.

Despite the differences that existed between one part of the Roman Empire to another, the whole society retained its patriar-chal structure. The differences remind us that a patriarchal society is not *necessarily* oppressive although it surely may be.

Prominent Thessalonians (17:4). Luke mentions the "leading women" of Thessalonica. These were undoubtedly influential women. Some of the women may have gained their status by their husband's posi-tion, but many of them were likely influential because of personal wealth.

Prominent Bereans (17:12). The phrase "promi-nent women" of verse 12 has the same meaning as "leading women" in verse 4.

Damaris (17:34). Luke mentioned this woman among the Athenians who heard Paul speak and who responded to the gospel. Given the roles of women in Greek society, it is likely that she was a hetaera, a woman educated to be a companion of men rather than a wife. In Athens, wives were still secluded with-in the home.

Priscilla (18:2, 3, 18, 26). Priscilla is mentioned six times in the New Testament, always with her husband, Aquila. However, four times Priscilla is named first, a peculiarity that indicates she was likely more influential in the church than her husband.

In Acts 18, Luke introduced Priscilla and Aquila, a couple who had been expelled from Rome with other Jews and had recently settled in Corinth. When Paul arrived, he stayed with this couple. Later, when Paul moved to Ephesus, Priscilla and Aquila moved their leatherworking business to that city. The couple stayed in Ephesus when Paul moved on. Commenting on this, Chrysostom, an early church father, says "He left them at Ephesus with good reasons, namely that they should teach" (in Stevens, *Pre-Nicene Fathers*, Vol. XI, 1975, p. 346).

Luke reports a particular incident concerning this couple that highlights their teaching ministry.

> Now a certain Jew named Apollos, born at
> Alexandria, an eloquent man and mighty in the
> Scriptures, came to Ephesus. This man had been
> instructed in the way of the Lord; and being fervent
> in spirit, he spoke and taught accurately the things
> of the Lord, though he knew only the baptism of
> John. So he began to speak boldly in the synagogue.
> When Aquila and Priscilla heard him, they took
> him aside and explained to him the way of God
> more accurately.

—Acts 18:24–26

The key to understanding Apollos is that he "knew only the baptism of John" (Acts 18:25). Luke tells a parallel story in Acts 19. Many Jews had heard reports of John's preaching only and were looking for the Messiah. They had not yet heard of Jesus or that He had fulfilled John's prophecies.

When this Jewish Christian couple who still attended synagogue heard Apollos speak accurately of the Old Testament prophecies and their meaning, "*they* took him aside" [emphasis ours]. Apollos, to his credit, received *their* instruction.

While Acts 18 depicts team teaching, it is clear that Priscilla as well as Aquila instructed this powerful preacher. That Priscilla is named first in one verse here, as well as whenever the two are mentioned in the Epistles (Romans 16:3; 2 Timothy 4:19), makes it clear that Paul reckoned her among his fellow workers in the gospel. This also suggests that Priscilla's spiritual gifts and contributions at least equaled those of her husband.

Tyrian disciples (21:5). Again Luke mentions that women were among the disciples who said farewell to Paul as he set out on his final journey to Jerusalem.

Philip's daughters (21:9). Philip was one of the original deacons. He is mentioned in Acts 6 and is featured in Acts 8 for initiating a revival in Samaria and

for leading an Ethiopian official to Christ. Luke wrote that Philip "had four virgin daughters who prophesied." First Corinthians 12:28 states, "God has appointed these in the church: first apostles, second prophets."

Luke mentions Philip's daughters only briefly: "Now this man had four virgin daughters who prophesied."

The reference to Philip, with whom Paul's party stayed in Caesarea, fits Luke's careful tracing of Paul's journey to Jerusalem. But the mention of Philip's daughters is clearly unnecessary, and puzzling.

The best solution to the puzzle is found in Luke's tendency to emphasize the transformed role of women in Christianity. Luke saw an opportunity to demonstrate in these four women the fulfillment of an Old Testament prophecy that Peter had quoted on Pentecost:

> And it shall come to pass in the last days, says God,
> That I will pour out of My Spirit on all flesh;
> Your sons and your daughters shall prophesy.

—Acts 2:17

The age of the Spirit had come indeed. Daughters as well as sons were prophesying.

The critical question we need to raise is, What does this imply concerning women's roles in the new community formed by the Spirit around Jesus Christ? Ben Witherington III (*Women in the Earliest Churches*, 1988, p. 151, 152) has done a study of prophets and prophecy in Luke's writings. The following are among his observations:

- Luke makes a point of establishing that his most important, or at least his most exemplary, characters are prophets: John the Baptist (Luke 1:76, 7:26, 20:6); Jesus (Luke 4:18–24; 7:16, 39; 9:19; 13:34; 22:64; 24:19); Peter (Acts 1:20; 2:4–21; 5:3, 9; 11:15–17); Paul (Acts 13:1, 9–11; 17:2, 3); Elizabeth (Luke 1:41–45); Mary or Elizabeth (Luke 1:46–53); Anna (Luke 2:36–38); Agabus (Acts 11:27, 28; 21:10,11); Judas and Silas (Acts 15:32).
- Luke appears to limit the Greek term *prophetes* to a select group; that is, some of the church leaders (see Acts 15:32).
- NT prophets are seen as engaged primarily in discerning the fulfillment of the predictive prophecy of the OT, rather than in giving new predictive prophecy on their own, though the latter is somewhat in evidence (see Acts 11:28; 27:10, 23, 24, 31–34).

◆ Prophets are shown to have a supernatural ability to discern people's character (Luke 7:39–50; Acts 6:3).

Paul's sister (23:16). We know nothing of Paul's sister from Luke's brief reference to his nephew in this verse.

Several things stand out in this brief review. Luke clearly takes pains to include "the women" where other first-century writers and certainly the rabbis would never think of mentioning them. Where "the women" are included, it is clear that they are active participants with men in significant events. In naming Priscilla before her husband in contexts where convention called for the reverse, Luke suggests a leading role for her in the church. Of course, the simple fact that so many women are referred to in Luke's history is significant.

However, when we look closely at selected women in Acts, we see even more clearly the revolutionary change in the status of women that Luke highlighted in his Gospel.

Whatever we might say about prophets and prophetesses, it is clear from Luke-Acts and from the epistles that this is a truly significant gift or office in the early church. Luke makes sure that we understand women are to be counted among the prophets.

Conclusions. From the way Luke treats women in Acts, and particularly from his descriptions of five women, we can validly draw several important conclusions.

◆ Women like Mary (John Mark's mother) and Lydia played a vital role in the spread of the gospel. They offered hospitality to missionaries and opened their homes as meeting places for Christians. Their sponsorship of first-century congregations made such women important members in the believing community.

◆ Women like Tabitha actively served others in local Christian communities. While Luke does not identify Tabitha as a deaconess, the kind of services she provided clearly fit that role. Luke's reference to her as a "disciple" suggests that she is set forward as an example for others in the church to follow.

◆ Paul's reference to Philip's daughters as prophetesses indicates that women shared in the most significant of spiritual gifts—and possibly offices—in the early church. Some have suggested that Luke's identification of Philip's daughters as *virgins* is significant. Clearly they had not adopted the traditional "feminine" role as wives and mothers. Like Paul, they may have chosen to remain unmarried to devote themselves to God's work (see 1 Cor. 7:34, 35).

◆ Luke wants us to see Priscilla as a teacher. What is more, she is portrayed teaching Apollos, a man with a deep understanding of the Old Testament Scriptures. Priscilla was equipped for teaching the deeper issues of the gospel, not simply the basics.

Why does Luke make an effort to show us women in ministry roles that they were denied in Judaism? We can only conclude that, under the inspiration of the Holy Spirit, Luke intended to portray some of the ways in which the gospel transformed the roles and the significance of womankind. In Christ, women were no longer second-class citizens, although they still lived in a patriarchal society. In the Christian gospel, we have the promise of restoration from every impact of the Fall. Surely this must include relief from the diminished status of women, which was clearly a consequence of Adam's and Eve's foolish choices.

Appendix D
Paul's Teaching on Women

Paul on Women
(The Pauline Epistles)

One of Jesus' fascinating sayings is recorded in Matthew 12:36. Christ had just commented on the fact that good things flow from the heart of a good man, for "out of the abundance of the heart the mouth speaks" (Matt. 12:34, 35). He then warned that in the judgment, people would be held accountable "for every idle word" (Matt. 12:36). What did Jesus mean by "idle" words?

When we're aware that people are listening to us, we are careful to say only those things that make a good impression. It's what we say spontaneously, when we're not trying to make a good impression, that reveals our most basic attitudes.

Surprisingly, we can apply the principle of "idle" or incidental words to help us understand the apostle Paul's real attitude toward women. This in turn will help us interpret passages in which he gives explicit teaching on women in the home and church. We apply this principle by looking through Paul's Epistles for references to women in contexts other than those in which he is specifically teaching about them. What Paul says about women in such passages will indicate a basic attitude toward women.

Understanding that attitude will guard us against reading our own prejudices into those explicit passages where there is so much debate.

Paul's Idle Words About Women

A quick survey of several "idle words" passages reveals several insights. His idle words most certainly demonstrate that the apostle is no male chauvinist. His attitude toward women is dramatically different from that of the Pharisees under whom Paul trained.

Romans 16:1–27

The last chapter of his letter to the Romans contains greetings to Roman Christians Paul knew. There is no intent here to teach on any subject, much less on the role of women. So the contents of this chapter qualify as incidental, or "idle," words.

When we first look through the list of those whom Paul greets, we're struck by the fact that six of the twenty-four are women. Remembering the rabbi's injunctions against even speaking with a woman, this would be an anomaly. It becomes even more striking when we note how Paul referred to four of the six women.

Phoebe, a deaconess of the church in Cenchrea (16:1). The Greek word, *diakonia* ("servant" in the NKJV), except for the feminine ending, is the same word all English versions translate "deacon" when referring to men. Similar bias is shown in 1 Timothy 3:11. The Greek *gyne* can be translated either "woman" or "wife." The logic of the passage indicates that Paul referred here to women deacons, not to wives of deacons.

Bible Background: Are the Women in 1 Timothy 3 Deaconesses?

1 Timothy 3 defines qualifications for those holding church office. In 3:2–7 Paul described character qualifications for bishops (equivalent to elders). Verse 8 begins, "Likewise deacons," and lists character qualifications for deacons. Verse 11 also begins "likewise," followed by the Greek word for "women/wives," and a similar list of character qualifications.

There are several reasons to believe Paul's first readers understood these women to be deaconesses rather than the wives of deacons.

The passage structure. The use of "likewise" in verses 8 and 11 suggests that in each case Paul discussed a distinct church office.

The logic of the passage. Why would Paul note qualifications for deacons' wives, and not mention qualifications for the wives of bishops/elders, a more important office?

The subject of the passage. Paul's overall subject in 3:1–13 is church offices. In verses 8–13 he looks at the office of the deacon, using the masculine form of the word. This title (deacon) would control, leading first-century readers to understand that verse 11 refers to women deacons.

"Mary, who labored much for us" (Rom. 16:6). Paul clearly acknowledges that Mary has made an important contribution to Paul's ministry. Tryphosa (Rom. 16:12) is another woman commended for laboring in the Lord.

"Junia ... who [is] of note among the apostles" (Rom. 16:7). This reference is especially significant. The word translated "of note" (*episemos*) in this context means "prominent." Paul is saying that Junia, with (probably her husband) Andronicus are prominent *apostles!*

In the New Testament, the word "apostle" is used in several senses. First, it is used of the Twelve Jesus chose to be His disciples. These are *the* apostles. Second, Paul applies the term to himself with the additional meaning of "emissary," a person commissioned by a particular church to go on mission, to spread the gospel (see 2 Cor. 8:23; Phil. 2:25). It also is used in the general sense of "itinerant missionary" (see Acts 14:4, 14). This may be the sense in which "apostle" is used in 1 Corinthians 12:28 and Ephesians

4:11. Paul refers to God's gift of apostles to the church and ranks apostles as of first importance.

How striking then that Paul identifies Junia, a woman, as a prominent missionary-evangelist, who was "in Christ before me" (Rom. 16:7).

Whatever our view of the specific ministries of Phoebe, Mary, Tryphosa, and Junia, Paul had a high regard for them and for their ministries in the church.

Bible Background: Prominent Women

What made persons prominent in the Greco-Roman world was not only the possession of wealth, but its expenditure for the public good. An inscription in Corinth dating to A.D. 43, memorialized one of Corinth's prominent women in these words:

A woman of highest esteem ... who with full measure and generosity aided many of our citizens from her own means, and welcomed them in her home, and in particular never ceased benefiting our citizens regarding any favor asked, the majority of the citizens have met in assembly to give testimonial on her behalf. In gratitude our people agreed to vote to commend Junia and to give testimonial of her generosity to our native city and her good will, and declares that it urges her to increase her generosity to our city, knowing that our people too will not cease in their good will and gratitude to her, and will do everything for the excellence and glory she deserves. For this reason—may good fortune abound—it was decreed to commend her for all that she has done (David Gill, *The Book of Acts in Its First-Century Setting*, page 116).

1 Corinthians 7. In this chapter, the apostle Paul corrects distortions of his teaching on marriage that had cropped up in Corinth. Some there insisted that Paul was anti-marriage. They abandoned sexual relations with spouses in favor of a more "spiritual" relationship. Some had initiated divorces. Others were confused as to whether they should marry those they were engaged to, or break the engagements.

Paul's response to the issues that confused the Corinthians provides further insights into his basic attitude toward women.

Authority over a spouse's body (1 Cor. 7:4). Paul made it clear that he did not endorse the idea of "spiritual" marriage. Sex in marriage is important (1 Cor. 7:1–5). In this passage Paul made a striking statement. He argued that "the wife does not have author-

ity over her own body, but the husband does. And likewise the husband does not have authority over his own body, but the wife does" (7:4). In contemporary Greek society as well as in Judaism, one of the wife's roles was to be sexually available to her husband. He "owned" rights to her sexuality. But the reverse was not true. The husband also had rights to *his own* sexuality; thus the so-called "double standard." A man could have sex outside of marriage, or in Judaism, have more than one wife. A woman could not have extramarital affairs, and certainly could not have more than one husband.

Paul dramatically broke with this pattern and taught that "the husband does not have authority over his own body, but the wife does." At least insofar as sexual availability is concerned, the partners in a Christian marriage are *truly equal!*

While the Jewish rabbis felt that a man owed a sexual duty to his wife and even regulated the minimum frequency of intercourse, they never imagined that a wife should have "authority over" the body of her husband! That idea never entered the thoughts of men whose whole orientation to family life presupposed a strong patriarchal structure. Paul displayed a view of women's equality in marriage that is truly striking.

Male/female parallelism. As Paul continued his instruction in 1 Corinthians 7 his approach further reflects a radical equality in his treatment of men and women. Even those rabbinic discussions that were about women were addressed to men, with women treated as objects. Paul, however, addressed his instruction on marriage and divorce to both together (see vv. 5, 7, 8, 17, 28, 32, 35). He clearly viewed the rights and responsibilities of men and women as parallel (see vv. 2, 3, 4, 10–16, 28, 33, 34). In expressing the wish that all were unmarried (vv. 7, 8, 37, 38, 40), Paul was at odds with rabbinic thought that assumed the significance of women is rooted in their roles as wives and mothers.

Paul was not anti-marriage. He made it clear that whether a person marries is a matter of that individual's gift and calling. He simply believed that single persons are freer to dedicate themselves completely to God's service. This principle applies equally to men and to women.

In this passage, then, the way Paul handles this subject reveals a strong orientation to women's equality in marriage and a rejection of a number of assumptions deeply rooted in both Hellenistic and Hebrew cultures. Paul even seems to suggest that a woman should consider remaining single so that she might focus solely on serving the Lord.

1 Corinthians 12. In this basic treatment of spiritual gifts, the apostle Paul makes it clear that "the manifestation of the Spirit is given to each one for the profit of all" (1 Cor. 12:7). Spiritual gifts are:

◆ distributed to each believer, male and female
◆ a manifestation of the Holy Spirit
◆ given "for the profit of all"

This critical passage makes no male/female distinctions between either the gifts given or their use. In specifying that the gifts are intended "for the profit of all," Paul did not state that the gifts of *men* are intended for the profit of all, while the gifts of women are intended only for the profit of women and children.

In a study entitled *Women in the Church: Biblical Data Report* (1997), the faculty of Dallas Theological Seminary noted the following concerning women's relationships to the Holy Spirit:

◆ The Holy Spirit fell on men and women on the Day of Pentecost (Acts 2:1–4).
◆ The Holy Spirit used women as His prophetic mouthpiece (Philip's four daughters were prophetesses, Acts 21:8, 9).
◆ Like men, the Holy Spirit indwells women (Rom. 8:9), and women's bodies also serve as a sanctuary of the Holy Spirit (1 Cor. 6:9–20).
◆ In Christ, a woman is given the same spiritual gifts available to men today, including pastoring, teaching, and evangelism (1 Cor. 12:7–11, 27–31; Rom. 12:3–8; 1 Pet. 4:10, 11).
◆ Paul recognized that the Holy Spirit used women as His prophetic mouthpiece (1 Cor. 11:5).

The presence of the Holy Spirit and the gifts the Spirit gives believers are essential to ministry. Paul taught that women share equally with men in these gifts. Therefore, we can conclude that Paul's attitude toward women's ministry is a distinctly positive one.

Philippians 4:2, 3. In Paul's letter to the Philippians, he urged two women, Euodia and Syntyche, to "be of the same mind in the Lord." Then Paul addressed a "true companion" and urged him to "help these women who labored with me in the gospel, with Clement also, and the rest of my fellow workers."

In this passage Paul was not teaching about women *per se*, so once again we can view what he says as "idle words" that reveal his underlying attitude toward women. How then does Paul view these women who have apparently come into conflict?

"Labored with me in the gospel" (Phil. 4:3). The word translated "labored with me" is *synathleo*, a term drawn from athletic contests, which might be better

translated "fought together with me side by side." The choice of this word cannot possibly be taken to suggest a supportive "female" role, but rather casts these two women as persons actively engaged with Paul in his ministry of communicating the gospel in Philippi or perhaps elsewhere.

"With...the rest of my fellow workers" (Phil. 4:3). The Greek word here is *sunergos*. Paul used it twelve times in his letters but never of believers in general (see 1 Corinthians 3:9; 2 Corinthians 1:24; 8:23; 1 Thessalonians 3:2; Romans 16:3, 9, 21; Philippians 2:25; Philemon 24). Rather, *sunergos* implies a leadership role in the Christian community. While Paul did not define the particular leadership function implied here by *sunergos*, he clearly viewed these two women, who struggled side by side with him for the gospel, as significant persons in the Philippian church.

The implications of Paul's "idle words" about women. While we could look at other passages that also contain "idle words" about women, those we've reviewed clearly reveal Paul's basic attitude toward women. Paul is often portrayed as a chauvinist who wants nothing more than for women to shut up and stay home. Yet our look at the biblical data reveals quite a different person indeed.

Paul's words to and about individuals make it clear that Paul had close and warm relationships with a number of women. Paul's descriptions of these women reveal that he saw them as partners in his ministry of spreading the gospel and as significant leaders in their own local congregations. In referring to Phoebe as a deaconess and to Junia as an apostle, we have evidence that Paul saw nothing unusual in women having significant offices in the early church.

As far as women in the family are concerned, Paul (1 Cor. 7) accorded women equal rights and responsibilities with their husbands. This equality was unthinkable in Judaism, the faith from which Christianity sprang.

This biblical data is especially vital if we are to appraise accurately those passages in which Paul dealt specifically with women in the home and the church. Alternative interpretations are hotly argued for or against each of these passages. Yet the data about Paul's basic attitude toward women that we have developed here makes one thing clear: *any interpretation of such passages which imply a negative or repressive view of women simply cannot be correct.* The "idle words" in Paul's letters make it clear that Paul valued and appreciated Christian women as partners in marriage and in ministry as well.

Paul's Teaching on Women in the Christian Family

Paul's Epistles were written to predominantly Gentile Christian churches. Their members lived in cities across the Roman Empire. In contrast, the Gospels presuppose a Jewish rather than Gentile setting. Yet common to both broad cultures, the Jewish and the Gentile, was an assumption of the patriarchal structure of family and society.

The view of wives in the Gentile world. Greek and Roman thinkers saw the family much as did the Jewish rabbis. This can be established from several sources.

Women and wives in Roman legal theory. Roman legal theory viewed women as subject either to their fathers or their husbands. Gaius's *Institutes* summarizes this relationship:

48: Some persons are sui iuris (legally independent); some are alieni iuris (subject to another).

49: Again, of those subject to another, some are in potestas (power), and some are in manus (subordination) to a husband.

104: Women cannot adopt by any method, for they do not have potestas even over their biological children.

108: Now let us consider those persons who are in our manus, that is, subordinate to us as wives. This is also a right peculiar to Roman citizens.

115b: But whereas it is customary for both males and females to be held under potestas (power), only women come into marital subordination.

Here, as in rabbinic Judaism, the laws are addressed to men, and again women are treated as objects.

The implications of "subordination" as the Romans understood it is illustrated in Plutarch's criticism of women who adopted foreign religions.

A wife ought not to make friends on her own, but to enjoy her husband's friends in common with him. The gods are the first and most important friends. Wherefore it is becoming for a wife to worship and to know only the gods that her husband believes in, and to shut the front door tight upon all queer rituals

and outlandish superstitions. For with no god do stealthy and secret rites performed by a woman find any favor.

Wives viewed through their epitaphs. "Ideal" first-century wives were often praised in epitaphs erected by their husbands. Like Roman legal theory, epitaphs give us insight into the view of women held in the Roman Empire when Christianity burst on the scene. Two typical epitaphs illustrate this attitude.

"Here lies Marcus's Amymone, the best and most beautiful. Busy at her wool-working, devoted, modest, thrifty, chaste, happy to stay at home," and "Visitor, what I have to say is not much, stand a moment and read. This tomb is not beautiful, but it is for a beautiful woman. Her parents gave her the name Claudia. She loved her husband with her whole heart. She bore two children, of whom she left one above ground, and buried the other under the earth. Her conversation was agreeable, her bearing pleasing. She stayed at home, she worked at her wool. I have finished speaking. You may go."

These and other inscriptions reflect the deep affection that often existed between spouses, and at the same time, provide a clear reflection of society's view of wives and their subordinate position.

Women in first-century contemporary satire. Of course, neither the legal nor idealized vision of women necessarily reflected reality. Even in a strongly patriarchal society, a wife might be the dominant spouse. The satirist Juvenal frequently mocked such relationships as in this passage from his *Satires*, 6:434–56:

"Crucify that slave!" says the wife. "But what crime worthy of death has he committed?" asks the husband; "where are the witnesses? ...give him a hearing at least; no delay can be too long when a man's life is at stake!" "What, you numbskull? You call a slave a man, do you? He has done no wrong, you say? Be it so; but this is my will and my command; let my will be voucher for the deed." Thus does she lord it over her husband.

Juvenal not only mocked the domineering wife; he also implied that the cruel and capricious nature of women made it necessary for men, who possess judgment and a sense of justice, to rule them.

First-century upper-class Roman women actively challenged the traditional patriarchal structure of the family. However, the writings of men of that era strongly affirm the traditional patriarchal view.

The view of wives in household codes in Paul's Epistles. Paul's specific teaching on husband-wife relationships is embedded in several "household code" passages in his Epistles. When we compare Paul's views as expressed in these codes with the view expressed in contemporary literature, legal theory, and epitaphs, we gain significant insights.

The household code passages are Colossians 3:18–4:1; Ephesians 5:22–6:9; 1 Timothy 2:8–15; 6:1, 2; and Titus 2:1–10. First Peter 2:18–3:7 is also viewed by many as a household code. An examination of just the first two household code passages reveals underlying concepts reflected in the other code passages in Paul's writings.

Patriarchal assumptions of "household management" literature. Ancient writers frequently discussed the topic of household management. They affirmed the authority of the *paterfamilias*, the father as the head of the house, and discussed the duties of wives, children, and slaves. In pagan as well as Jewish families, the patriarchal structure of the family was assumed. Paul also assumed the same patriarchal structure. Yet in these household codes, or *haustafel* [household tables] as they are commonly called, we have a significant innovation. Similarities to pagan and Jewish material are rooted in the fact that a man's household from Aristotle, well past the time of Paul, included wives, children, and slaves. What is unique to the New Testament is that Paul's household codes define *reciprocal* duties.

Paul's patriarchal assumptions. Scripture assumes the patriarchal structure of the family and of society that existed in every ancient and first-century society. Paul did not challenge this assumption. Throughout his writings, Paul operated on a principle expressed in 1 Corinthians 7:20: "Let each one remain in the same calling in which he was called." In this context, Paul pointed out that a slave could remain a slave and serve Christ; a married person can remain married and be a good Christian; a single person doesn't have to marry to have a fulfilling Christian life. Paul went on to show that the principle of remaining in one's calling does not mean that a person *cannot* change his or her situation. A slave can gain freedom or a single person can marry without violating God's will. What Paul intended to communicate was simply that Christianity, far from requiring radical or revolutionary change in the social order, offered every person the opportunity to find spiritual fulfillment—whatever that person's station in life.

What the apostle Paul did in his household codes was teach that knowing Christ *transforms relationships between persons of different stations.* Husbands would still head the *Christian* household, but Christ will transform the relationship between husband and wife. *Christian* masters in the first century may still own slaves, but Christ will transform the relationship between master and slave without necessarily changing the institution. The household codes redefined the relationship between *Christian* husbands and wives, Christian parents and their children, Christian masters and their slaves.

With this background, we can now look at two of the household code passages.

The household code in Colossians 3:18–4:1.

Wives, submit to your own husbands, as is fitting in the Lord. Husbands, love your wives and do not be bitter toward them. Children, obey your parents in all things, for this is well pleasing to the Lord. Fathers, do not provoke your children, lest they become discouraged. Bondservants, obey in all things your masters according to the flesh, not with eyeservice, as men-pleasers, but in sincerity of heart, fearing God. And whatever you do, do it heartily, as to the Lord and not to men, knowing that from the Lord you will receive the reward of the inheritance; for you serve the Lord Christ. But he who does wrong will be repaid for what he has done, and there is no partiality. Masters, give your bondservants what is just and fair, knowing that you also have a Master in heaven.

(1) There is a reciprocal structure to the code. The truly unique element in the New Testament household codes is that they define duties of each pair to one another. Pagan and Jewish literature deal with duties household members owe to the head of the house. Only in the New Testament is duty owed to the head of the house matched with duty owed by him.

We can chart the reciprocal duties as follows.

RELATIONSHIP	DUTY OF THE SECOND	DUTY OF THE FIRST
Husband/wife	Submit	Love, do not be harsh
Father/child	Obey parents	Do not provoke
Master/slave	Obey, work hard	Be just, be fair

While the family's patriarchal structure was retained, Paul's focus is on how positive Christian relationships are to be maintained within it. While this treatment of relationships did not criticize patriarchy, Paul should not be understood as actively supporting it. Paul's concern is simply that Christian members of the household please God in whatever role society has assigned.

(2) The significance of "submit." A glance at the chart above shows that while children and slaves owe a duty of obedience, the wife's duty is to "submit." The Greek word is *hypotasso*, found here in the present tense and middle voice. The present tense indicates a continuous activity, while the middle voice indicates that submission is something the wife chooses and does for herself. There is no indication here that the husband has a right to coerce or demand submission.

But what does the Greek verb itself mean, and how is it used in the New Testament? Perhaps the first thing to note is that it is used in 1 Corinthians 15:28 of Jesus' relationship to God the Father. Clearly "submission" does not imply inferiority, as in essence Christ and the Father are equally and together God. *The Expository Dictionary of Bible Words* (1985) has the following helpful discussion on the concept of submission in Scripture:

> The voluntary submission of believers involves existing social structures. Christians are to "submit…to the governing authorities (Rom. 13:1), to "every authority instituted among men"(1 Pet. 2:13). The NT applies this specifically to slaves. They are to submit and provide good service, even to harsh masters (Tit. 2:9; 1 Pet. 2:18). This calls for voluntary submission in roles defined by one's culture and makes no judgment at all on the justice or validity of particular institutions. It simply calls on the believer to live in the world as it is and in one's own culture to do what is expected of a good citizen or good slave. If we wish, we can call this situational submission—a voluntary choice by the believer to do what is deemed right according to the norms of his or her own culture. (Of course, Scripture is not dealing here with the exceptional case in which the culture calls "right" what God calls "wrong.")
>
> Another area in which believers are called on to submit voluntarily is that of Christian interpersonal relationships. In their various roles in the body of Christ, Christians are to "submit to one another out of reverence for Christ"(Eph. 5:21). This responsiveness and willingness to yield to one another out of love should be extended not only by younger to older (1 Pet. 5:5) but also by everyone to those who devote themselves "to the service of the saints (1 Cor.

> 16:15, 16). This is in perfect harmony with the NT portrait of mutual concern among Christians and the surrender of one's own interests to those of others (Rom. 12:10; Phil. 2:3, 4).
>
> One of the critical questions in our day is that of the submission that the NT calls for from the wife to her husband. In the light of the times in which the NT was written, we may take this as situational submission in some contexts and perhaps as an interpersonal submission in others. What is important for us to realize is that however we understand "submission" in such passages, it does not imply an inferiority of person.
>
> Submission is not a confession of inferiority but a demonstration of the fact that personal significance does not depend on one's role in society. The Christian is responsive to God, fulfilling his or her highest destiny in choosing to obey the Lord in the matter of submission.

—pp. 584–585

(3) Submission is a husband/wife issue, not a male/female issue. The household codes explore relationships in the family. We cannot generalize from them to other gender issues, such as the roles of women in the church or the gender appropriateness of roles in society in general.

The household code in Ephesians 5:21–6:9. This is Paul's lengthiest statement of mutual responsibilities in household relationships. Here, we will look only at what he said to husbands and wives, remembering that Paul also expanded his teaching on father/child and master/slave relationships.

> … submitting to one another in the fear of God. Wives, submit to your own husbands, as to the Lord. For the husband is head of the wife, as also Christ is head of the church; and He is the Savior of the body. Therefore, just as the church is subject to Christ, so let the wives be to their own husbands in everything. Husbands, love your wives, just as Christ also loved the church and gave Himself for her, that He might sanctify and cleanse her with the washing of water by the word, that He might present her to Himself a glorious church, not having spot or wrinkle or any such thing, but that she should be holy and without blemish. So husbands ought to love their own wives as their own bodies; he who loves his wife loves himself. For no one ever hated his own flesh, but nourishes and cherishes it, just as the Lord does the church. For we are members of His body, of His flesh and of His bones. "For this reason a man shall leave his father and mother and be joined to his wife, and the two shall become one flesh." This is a great mystery, but I speak concerning Christ and

the church. Nevertheless let each one of you in particular so love his own wife as himself, and let the wife see that she respects her husband.

—Eph. 5:21–33

This is certainly the most significant New Testament passage on husband/wife relationships. We must be careful in defining what it does and does not teach. The following elements are of special note:

(1) Ephesians 5:21 introduces the topic. The Greek text of the New Testament was not divided into verses or paragraphs. These were added later. Thus paragraph divisions are hardly inspired. This is well illustrated in Ephesians 5, where verse 21 goes with verse 22, rather than verse 20. Paul introduced this statement of the Christian household code by reminding us that Christians are to submit "to one another." He then went on to explore how mutual submission works itself out in the Christian household containing a husband and wife, parents and their children, masters and their slaves.

(2) "Wives submit to your own husbands, as to the Lord" (5:22). We note several things about this instruction.

◆ Wives, not "women" are to submit
◆ Submission is to one's own husband, not men in general
◆ Submission is hupotasso, discussed above
◆ The wife's submission to the husband is like her submission to Christ

(3) The husband is called the "head" [*kephale*] of the wife "as also Christ is head of the church" (5:23). Only in contexts where Christ is affirmed as head of the church is the husband spoken of as the head of the wife.

The headship of the husband is paired with the submission of the wife. The interaction of these two creates a relational climate in which Christian marriage flourishes. The term "head" in itself does not define what the husband does as head to enrich the relationship. So Paul develops an analogy between Christ's headship and the husband's.

We need to remember that here, Paul is teaching by analogy. There is always a danger that a reader will extend the analogy: that is, find more points of comparison than the writer intends. So Paul wisely makes clear just what points of comparison he intends us to make:

◆ Husbands are to love as Christ loves (5:25)
◆ Husbands are to value their wives as Christ values the church (5:29)

◆ Husbands are to view wives as their "own flesh," which is how Christ views Christians as members of His body (5:29, 30)

In this passage, Paul illustrates how the love, the valuing, and the view of Christ are to be expressed in practice. Jesus gave Himself for the church (5:25). Jesus committed Himself to enable the church to reach its full potential (5:26, 27). Jesus continues to nourish and cherish the church (5:29). We conclude that Paul wants us to understand that while headship may imply authority, the Christian husband's headship is exercised by *a loving commitment to see to his wife's good.*

(4) The wife responds to the husband with submission (5:22) and respect (5:33). It is, as many have pointed out, not difficult to respond in this way to a person who takes the lead in showing the kind of loving concern Christ displayed in serving the church.

Paul's View of Women as Wives: a Summary

Paul was not a reformer, but a transformer. He did not challenge institutions; he challenged individuals. Paul was convinced that anyone in any situation could please God, and he encouraged believers to use whatever opportunities they had to do so. This approach to the Christian life is expressed in the general principle: "Let each one remain in the same calling in which he was called" (1 Cor. 7:20).

When Paul wrote about the Christian household, he did not concern himself with its patriarchal structure. It is irrelevant whether this structure is "good" or "evil." Paul called on believers to live Christian lives *within society as it is*, and made no judgment on whether institutions are flawed or whether they should be changed.

But Paul was deeply concerned about how believers related to one another. In assuming patriarchy, Paul rejected the notion that persons' roles can strip them of worth and value as human beings. He also rejected the notion that a person's role conveys the right to depersonalize another. In the household codes in his Epistles, Paul simply instructed husbands and wives, fathers and children, masters and slaves, on how to relate to one another as Christians.

The striking thing about these household codes is that here, relationships are viewed reciprocally. In contemporary pagan and Jewish thought, patriarchy was assumed to imply a strict hierarchy. The husband/father/master was viewed as "above" the wife, child, or slave. The man dominated; the others served his desires and needs. The man was important; the others were relatively unimportant except as they affected his well-being. While the wife, children, and slaves owed a duty of obedience to the husband, he owed no duty to them except whatever his own feelings of love or sense of justice moved him to grant.

Paul's treatment of patriarchy is truly revolutionary in that it introduces an equalizing element that is at odds with the traditional hierarchical view of patriarchy. The husband/father/master is still head of the household, but he is as responsible to serve the members of the household as they are to serve him. The other members of the household become important *in themselves*, and the husband/father/master owes duties to the wife/child/slave, just as they owe duties to him. Without directly challenging the hierarchical view in his culture, Paul applied the gospel in such a way that it transformed relationships between family members and created something non-hierarchical and truly new.

Problem Passages in Paul's Epistles

Several passages in Paul's epistles have been interpreted as severely restricting women's participation in the Christian church. In the last quarter of the 20th century, these passages have become the focus of a debate. On the one hand are those who teach a gender-based hierarchy with church leadership restricted to men, and those who hold an egalitarian view insisting that Scripture calls for equal access by men and women to leadership positions. A number of books by conservative Christians, all of whom carefully exegete the text, argue for each of these views. A survey of studies of these key passages offered by both sides clearly shows that each passage raises not just one, but several interpretive difficulties. Christians equally committed to the inspiration and authority of Scripture can and do reach carefully reasoned conclusions that differ dramatically.

What seems significant to me, however, is that in focusing the argument on a limited number of passages in the Epistles, most have failed to take into account data from the New Testament as a whole. Earlier, we saw that Christ's relationships with women were truly transformational. He broke the rigidly hierarchical patterns long established in rabbinic Judaism. He frequently gave priority to women and honored them as disciples and witnesses to His resurrection.

We explored the way Luke portrayed the transformation of women's traditional roles and the removal of restrictions that existed in Judaism. Luke frequently paired a woman with a man in ways that give women new significance. He developed this same theme in Acts where we meet women cast in leadership roles in the church that were unthinkable in Judaism. Earlier, we looked at Paul's casual references to women in his Epistles. The apostle saw individual women as partners in his ministry of spreading the gospel and as significant leaders in their own local congregations.

When we consider this mass of evidence from the New Testament as a whole, we are reminded of an important hermeneutical principle: Scripture does not disagree with itself. Our interpretation of any given passage must not only be consistent with the immediate context but also with the whole Word of God. *Where two or more possible interpretations of a passage dealing with women exist, we must prefer an interpretation in accord with the transformation of women's roles as* witnessed to in the Gospels, in Acts, and in the incidental or "idle words" about women in Paul's Epistles.

Keeping this hermeneutic principle in mind, and without examining every competing interpretation, we can profitably examine the most hotly debated passages in Paul's writings: specifically 1 Corinthians 11, 1 Corinthians 14, and 1 Timothy 2, each of which deals with women in the gathered church.

A call for a head covering (1 Cor. 11:2–26). Paul instructed women in Corinth to wear head coverings when they participated in church gatherings. This teaching has been taken to imply a general subordination of women to men in the church and to support a gender-based hierarchy of church leadership.

> Now I praise you, brethren, that you remember me in all things and keep the traditions just as I delivered them to you. But I want you to know that the head of every man is Christ, the head of woman is man, and the head of Christ is God. Every man praying or prophesying, having his head covered, dishonors his head. But every woman who prays or prophesies with her head uncovered dishonors her head, for that is one and the same as if her head were shaved. For if a woman is not covered, let her also be shorn. But if it is shameful for a woman to be shorn or shaved, let her be covered. For a man indeed ought not to cover his head, since he is the image and glory of God; but woman is the glory of man. For man is not from woman, but woman from man. Nor was man created for the woman, but woman for the man. For this reason the woman ought to have a symbol of authority on her head, because of the angels. Nevertheless, neither is man independent of woman, nor woman independent of man, in the Lord. For as woman came from man, even so man also comes through woman; but all things are from God. Judge among yourselves. Is it proper for a

woman to pray to God with her head uncovered?
Does not even nature itself teach you that if a man
has long hair, it is a dishonor to him? But if a
woman has long hair, it is a glory to her; for her
hair is given to her for a covering. But if anyone
seems to be contentious, we have no such custom, nor
do the churches of God.

—1 Cor.11:2–16

General observations. Paul expressed concern
here about "proper" (v. 13) behavior in church meetings. He tells the Corinthians that it is "proper" for
women to wear a head covering when praying or
prophesying. It is clear from Paul's discussion that he
is concerned that the church maintains rather than
blurs gender distinctions. It is also clear that in
Corinth, women did pray and prophesy when
Christians gathered for worship.

The debate over this passage has focused on *why*
gender distinctions are important. Is it because men
are to hold superior positions in the church, and
women inferior positions, as many argue? Or is there
some other rationale for Paul's teaching?

"Every woman who prays or prophesies" (1
Cor. 11:5). There is no doubt that women both
prayed and prophesied in Corinth. Paul will shortly
argue that prophesying is the premier spiritual gift (1
Cor. 14:1), and list prophets as second among those
"God has appointed...in the church" (1 Cor. 12:28).
Paul's problem with the praying and prophesying at
Corinth is not that women participate, but that
women participate with their heads uncovered.

Women taking a leading role in the church did not
trouble Paul. What Paul objected to was *the manner in
which* they prayed and prophesied.

"With her head uncovered" (1 Cor. 11:5). Paul
objected to women participating with heads uncovered. What was this head covering? Was it a veil? A
particular way of wearing a tunic? Why were women
enjoined to wear it? What did going about uncovered
imply in first-century society? Was it the mark of a
prostitute as some have suggested?

Many different theories have been offered. We
know from the passage that whatever the rationale in
first-century Corinth, women wore head coverings
and men did not. So the one thing we can say with
certainty is that the head covering was gender dis-
tinctive. We can also say that Paul insisted women
dress as women when they prayed or prophesied in
church.

**"The head of every man is Christ, the head of
woman is man, and the head of Christ is God"** (1
Cor. 11:3). Paul launched this teaching with a strong
affirmation. Those who hold a hierarchical view of the
relationship between the sexes view this as a state-

ment about authority and subordination. They read it
as if Paul had written, "Every man is under Christ's
authority, woman is under man's authority, and
Christ is under God's authority." This, however, is not
what Paul wrote.

While "head" in Greek may mean leader or "boss,"
this meaning is unusual. Even in the Greek translation
of the Old Testament, in nine of ten cases where the
Hebrew Old Testament uses *rosh* (head) in the sense
of "leader," a different Greek word than *kephale* (head)
is chosen to translate it. Thus, the argument that
"head" here must mean "authority over" is hardly
compelling.

Another problem exists with this interpretation.
The second phrase in the Greek text is *de gunikos ho
aner kephale*. Gunaikos may mean either "woman" or
"wife," and *aner* may mean either "man" or "husband."
Here the definite article *ho* suggests Paul meant "the
husband is head of the wife," rather than "man is the
head of woman." If we take this phrase in the first
sense, we see that Paul is making a distinct statement
about three different relationships:

- ◆ Christ is the "head" of "every man"
- ◆ The husband is the "head" of the wife
- ◆ God is the "head" of Christ

"Head" in this passage cannot be used here to
ascribe superiority or subordination; Christ is not
inferior to God the Father. "Head" cannot mean that
men are "the source" of women, for husbands are not
the source of wives. In what metaphorical sense can
"head" be used to fit all three applications?

In the next chapter (1 Cor. 12), Paul again used
"head" to refer to Christ. Paul described the relationship Christ has to the church that is His body. In chapter 12 Paul used "head" and "body" to indicate that a
true, organic relationship exists between Jesus and
Jesus' people. If we take "head" to have a similar
metaphorical meaning in 1 Corinthians 11 that it has
in 1 Corinthians 12, what Paul says fits the rest of his
argument beautifully. Every man has an organic relationship with Jesus—so that each man reflects glory
or dishonor on Jesus (see 1 Cor. 11:7). Wives have an
organic, one-flesh relationship with their husbands,
so what they do reflects glory or dishonor on their
husbands. Jesus had an organic relationship with God
the Father, and what He did reflected glory and honor
on God.

Why then should women cover their heads when
praying or prophesying in church? Because it is proper behavior, and when wives behave properly they
reflect glory on their husbands. By behaving improp-
erly, women would dishonor not only their husbands
but also Christ.

"Man is not from woman, but woman from man" (1 Cor. 11:8, 9). Paul added that man was not created to complete woman, but woman was created to complete man. Here the meanings of *gunikos* and *aner* shift back to "woman" and "man." Paul's argument is that in creating humans, God made gender distinctions. It follows that it is wrong to blur these God-designed distinctions. Men and women remain distinct, with women completing men. Women who pray with heads uncovered deny a distinction between the sexes that God Himself made.

"For this reason the woman ought to have a symbol of authority on her head, because of the angels" (1 Cor. 11:10). The NKJV text rightly adds "a symbol of" to the Greek, for the head covering is symbolic. The question is, "What 'authority' does the head covering symbolize?"

The person who interprets the passage in a hierarchical way argues that the head covering is a symbol of male authority over women in the church. But the text does not say this, even though Paul could have done so easily. The head covering is a symbol of *the woman's* own authority to pray and prophesy *as a woman*!

We can understand why women, excited about their newfound freedom to participate equally with men in Christian assemblies, would want to express that freedom symbolically. It may well have seemed to the Corinthian women that abandoning their head-coverings was an appropriate symbol of what Christ had done for them. But Paul saw this as totally inappropriate. God created humankind male and female, and the Scriptures as well as human societies preserve this distinction. In assuming that to be equal women must behave like men, the Corinthian women denied rather than affirmed the good news of spiritual equality.

To Paul, what is glorious is that now in Christ women can be full participants in the Christian community *as women!* Only by dress and behavior that affirms their femininity will women show the world that their gender truly has been lifted up by Jesus Christ, to reclaim a heritage forfeited by Eve so long ago.

"Because of the angels" (1 Cor. 11:10). Why does Paul add this mysterious phrase? We know that angels, who do not die, were created before humans. They witnessed creation and the Fall. They participated in the exodus; observed the giving of the Law at Sinai; and were present at the birth, death, and resurrection of Jesus. Throughout history angels have been awed witnesses as the grand drama of sin and redemption has been played out on earth's stage.

The apostle Peter wrote of the long-prophesied grace now experienced by Christians through the gospel, and said these were "things which angels desire to look into" (1 Pet. 1:12).

The image Peter evokes is that of wondering angels participating in our meetings, observing our lives, awed at each new indication of the grace that God pours out on us in Jesus Christ. And so women simply must retain the head coverings that mark them as women. For one of the wonders accompanying salvation is that in Christ, humanity recovers all that was lost in Adam's Fall—and more. As witnesses to the angels of God's transforming power, women are to minister as *women*, gifted partners with men in the many ministries of Christ's church.

Let your women keep silent (1 Cor. 14: 34, 35). At first glance these verses seem decisively to support those who hold the hierarchical position. Yet even a moment's thought raises troubling questions.

How can Paul, in chapter 11, speak of women praying and prophesying in a church meeting and three chapters later insist that women are to "keep silent"? Has he forgotten what he wrote? Has he changed his mind? Or does 1 Corinthians 14 invalidate 1 Corinthians 11? Again, if we hold to an inspired Word of God, we are convinced that Scripture cannot contradict itself. Yet 1 Corinthians 14:34, 35 sounds decisively clear.

> *Let your women keep silent in the churches, for they are not permitted to speak; but they are to be submissive, as the law also says. And if they want to learn something, let them ask their own husbands at home; for it is shameful for women to speak in church.*

Interpretive problems with 1 Corinthians 14: 34, 35. When we look more closely, we see a number of difficulties in interpreting these verses. Carroll D. Osburn (*Essays on Women in Earliest Christianity*, I, 1993) describes some of the difficulties.

> *Do vv. 34–35 occur after v. 33, as in most ancient mss and modern editions, or after v. 40, as in only a few mss? Does v. 33b, "as in all the churches," go with v. 34–35, as is the case in most modern editions, or with v. 33a as in all ancient mss? What are vv. 34–35 doing in a context of tongues and prophecy? What is the actual problem behind vv. 34–35? Does gunaikes (v. 34) mean "wives" or "women"? What is meant by "silence"? What is meant by "to speak"? To whom are the women to be in submission? What is meant by "as the law says"? How do vv. 34–35 relate to v. 36, which some see directed only to males? How is one to understand the possible contradiction with 11:2–16, where Paul approves women praying and prophesying? Is the message of vv. 34–35 consistent with Pauline theology?*

—p. 219

Each of these questions, and others, has been debated in lengthy articles and books. Any interpretation we accept must be in full accord with the principle of the harmony of Scripture. We must understand these verses in a way that fits the immediate context, and we must test our understanding to see if it is in harmony with the rest of the New Testament.

General observations. These verses are found in a particular context. In chapters 11 through 14, Paul dealt with what was to happen when the church met. He considered several issues in these chapters. He taught that women are not symbolically to deny their gender when praying or prophesying in church (11:2–16). He taught that believers are not to deny the symbolic significance of the Lord's supper by turning the sacrament into an ordinary meal (11:17–34). Paul taught that the church is not to deny the Spirit's ministry through each believer by overemphasizing the gift of tongues (12:1–13). Paul taught that the true test of spirituality is not what gifts a person exercises, but the experience and expression of Christ's love for others (13:1–13). Finally, Paul taught that church meetings are to be focused on the edification of believers (14:1–40).

These verses fall under the fifth theme of edification in church meetings. Paul first established the priority of edification in meetings where all are free to participate (14:26). He went on to examine disruptive issues: tongues (14:27, 28), prophecy (14:29–33), and talkative women (14:34, 35). Paul concluded with an exhortation to the Corinthians to acknowledge his instructions as from the Lord, and "let all things be done decently and in order" (14:40).

We can chart the disruptions Paul deals with as follows.

DISRUPTIONS IN CORINTHIAN CHURCH MEETINGS DISCUSSED IN 1 CORINTHIANS 14

Verses	The Problem	The Solution	The Result
27-28	Tongues	Keep silent unless an interpreter is present.	The church will be edified.
29-33	Prophets interrupt each other	Take turns and be silent when others are speaking.	The church will be edified.
34-35	Talkative women	The women are to be silent and ask questions at home.	The church will be edified (implied).

In this context of congregational disruptions, Paul told certain women of Corinth to "keep silent." So our interpretation of 1 Corinthians 14:34, 35 must be shaped by this immediate context. Then it must be tested against the larger context of the New Testament's expressed view on the role of women in the church.

What I am pointing out is that Paul's teaching is situation-specific. We can hardly apply a situation-specific injunction as if it had universal application. Because Paul told some women to "keep silent," we are not justified to insist that all women in all meetings of every church throughout history keep silent. Yet this is just what some would have us do. What we must, in fact, do is examine the text carefully to see if we can discern what that specific situation was and how Paul's instruction to "keep silent" was intended to correct it.

"It is shameful for women to speak in church" (14:35). Two clues to the solution are found in this verse. The first is in the present infinitive ("to speak"). While the Greek word *speak* does not indicate any specific kind of speech, the present infinitive portrays *continual speaking up*. These women continually, repeatedly, and disruptively spoke out in church meetings.

The second clue is "let them ask their own husbands at home, for it is shameful for *gunaikin* (women or wives) to speak in church." This tells us that the word rendered "women" in 14:35 should be translated "wives." It is far more natural in this context to understand Paul to be speaking of the wives of the husbands mentioned rather than of all women.

These two clues suggest that the specific problem in Corinth involved certain wives (not all women) creating chaos by repeatedly and inappropriately speaking up in church gatherings.

"Let your women keep silent" (14:34). Paul's solution is for the disruptive wives to "keep silent." Many have noted that this verse need not be understood to require total silence, but rather silence in the specific situation. But what is "the situation"?

One suggestion links this verse with the similar injunction in 14:28, where the person who speaks in tongues is told to keep silent unless a person with the gift of interpretation is present.

Another suggestion is that it refers back to "let them ask their own husbands." The women were apparently raising so many [irrelevant?] questions that no positive teaching could take place.

A third suggestion links the inappropriate speech with 14:29. When a prophet spoke, others in the congregation were to "judge." The Greek word here means to discern, to examine for authenticity, and thus to judge. In the first century, there was no completed New Testament against which to measure a person's teaching. It was important that each congregation have believers who were gifted by the spirit to evaluate and authenticate messages delivered by those who claimed to be prophets. It is possible that the women in Corinth to whom Paul refers were continually intruding in the authentication process.

"To be submissive, as the law also says" (14:34). The middle form of the verb indicates that Paul is addressing the women, calling on them to "submit yourselves." The phrase "as the law says" indicates a principle understood to govern all Christian behavior. Some have thought that Paul was calling on these wives to submit to their husbands, while others have assumed he was calling on them to submit to the authority of the church leaders, whose responsibility it was to evaluate the words of the prophets. However, it is most likely that the universal principle Paul has in mind is the principle of mutual submission. This principle is expressed in Ephesians 5:21 ("submitting to one another in the fear of God") and is also expressed in Philippians 2:2, 3 and 1 Corinthians 16:16. Paul appealed to the Corinthian wives, whose interruptions were so disruptive, to consider others and voluntarily stop their continual speaking up so that church meetings might be edifying rather than chaotic.

Applying Paul's teaching. Paul and the Corinthians were fully aware of the nature of the problem addressed here. They knew which women were disruptive and should be silent as an expression of submission to others. Unfortunately, no one today knows what was actually happening in Corinth.

That we do not know the details, however, does not justify tearing Paul's words in 1 Corinthians 14:34, 35 out of context and reading them as a command to all women to "shut up and listen." Such an application of these verses ignores the immediate context. It also ignores Paul's own words in 1 Corinthians 11 about women praying and prophesying in church. It also ignores a great mass of evidence in the Gospels, Acts, and Paul's other Epistles that in Christ, the consequences of Eve's original sin truly have been reversed.

We can confidently say that, while the details of the situation in which Paul called for wives to be silent are lost to us, Paul's words are *not* addressed to all women. They do not prevent women from participating actively and vocally with men in gatherings of Christ's church.

The prohibition against women teaching (1 Tim. 2:9–15.) This passage is undoubtedly the most difficult to interpret in harmony with the positive and supportive view of women that we have identified throughout the New Testament. Yet given a high view of Scripture as God's inspired Word, we cannot accept an interpretation that rules women out of all teaching roles in the gathered church without totally compelling evidence. So we must examine this passage and its immediate context carefully.

General observations. 1 Timothy is one of three "pastoral" letters written by Paul to instruct the next generation of church leaders. Paul states the purpose of the letter in 1 Timothy 3:15: "I write so that you may know how you ought to conduct yourself in the house of God, which is the church of the living God." Throughout this letter, Paul not only described appropriate conduct for Timothy, but he also described how believers are to conduct themselves.

At the time Paul wrote, Timothy was in Ephesus where he had been sent to correct problems that had emerged there. Ephesus was the premier city in Asia Minor, the site of the temple of Diana. We know from Luke's account of Paul's missionary work there that many in Ephesus had turned to the Lord, abandoning worship of their deity and other well-established occult practices. Paul's letter to the Ephesians, sent some time before Timothy was dispatched there, emphasized the priority of Christ as head of His Church and the lifestyle appropriate for Christians. It's clear from 1 Timothy that many Ephesians had strayed from the focus on Jesus and godly living that Paul urged in his letter. In fact, false teaching had seriously corrupted the church in Ephesus.

In 1 Timothy, Paul is concerned about abandoning sound doctrine in favor of "fables and endless genealogies, which cause disputes rather than godly edification" (1:4). These were promoted by persons "desiring to be teachers of the law" who understood "neither what they say nor the things which they affirm" (1:7). This misinformation had significantly corrupted the way the Ephesian Christians lived (1:9–11).

Paul called for a commitment to "a quiet and peaceable life in all godliness and reverence" (2:2). In chapter 2, Paul focused on three matters that needed to be corrected if this was to be achieved in Ephesus. Men needed to refocus their prayers (2:1–8), women needed to refocus their priorities (2:9, 10), and (certain?) women needed to learn, rather than to teach and domineer (2:11–15).

Paul then reviewed guidelines to teach the church concerning the selection of elders (3:1–7) and deacons and deaconesses (3:8–13). In chapter 4, Paul returned to the problem of false teaching. He identified certain ascetic practices urged by some as "doctrines of demons" (4:1–5). Timothy was to counter by teaching "words of faith and good doctrine" and by rejecting "profane and old wives' fables" (4:6–7). Timothy was not only to "command and teach" (4:11) these things, but was also to be an example of the godly lifestyle which sound doctrine will produce (4:12–16).

In chapter 5, Paul gave guidelines to use when enrolling women in a teaching order of godly widows whose special mission was to instruct younger wives (5:1–16). He encouraged respect for church elders (5:17–22), and suggested a treatment for Timothy's frequent stomach problems (5:23–25). In the last chapter of his letter, Paul again mentioned persons who taught "otherwise" (6:3) and were "obsessed with disputes and arguments over words, from which come envy, strife, reviling, evil suspicions" and whose underlying motive was financial gain (6:1–6).

False teaching was significantly influencing the church in Ephesus. Those who introduced the false teaching were men (see Hymenaeus and Alexander in 1:20 and the reference to the typical false teacher as "he" in 6:4). Yet it would appear from 2 Timothy 3:6 that these false teachers had adopted a strategy of appealing to "gullible women loaded down with sins, led away by various lusts." Strikingly, the women described in 1 Timothy 2 display a superficial interest in their appearance with no concern for "propriety and moderation" (2:9, 10), and also a strident resistance to instruction.

Against this background we can interpret what Paul wrote in 1 Timothy 2:11–15. After rebuking the superficiality of those Ephesian women who were more interested in beauty aids than in good works, the Apostle had this to say:

> Let a woman learn in silence with all submission. And I do not permit a woman to teach or have authority over a man, but to be in silence. For Adam was formed first, then Eve. And Adam was not deceived, but the woman being deceived, fell into transgression. Nevertheless she will be saved in childbearing if they continue in faith, love, and holiness, with self-control.

While Paul's prohibition here seems absolute, on closer examination, several caveats become apparent.

"Let a woman learn" (1 Tim. 2:11). Paul's remarks begin with an imperative: women are told "to learn." As we saw in exploring the view of women reflected in the Gospels, the idea that women should "learn" was decisively rejected in rabbinic Judaism, nor was it a view commonly held in the Roman world. In contrast, Paul *wants* women to learn.

We can speculate why Paul wanted women to learn. One reason clearly is that if they were grounded in good doctrine, false teachers wouldn't easily lead them astray. Another reason is expressed in 1 Timothy 1:3, 5. The teaching of right doctrine produces "love from a pure heart, from a good conscience, and from sincere faith" (1 Tim. 1:3, 5). God's transforming work in the believer requires a grasp of God's truth. We can even speculate further. Only a woman who has learned will later be able to teach— if not men, then surely younger women (see 1 Tim. 5:3–10). Paul himself said that older women were called to be "teachers of good things" (Titus 2:3).

"Learn in silence with all submission" (1 Tim. 2:11). Here Paul indicated how the women he addressed should learn. They should learn:

◆ in silence
◆ with all submission

The word translated "in silence" is *hessychia*, and is better translated "in quietness." This is not a demand for silence, but rather an appeal for a quiet demeanor. This Greek word is found in this same chapter where Paul urged all Christians to lead "a quiet and peaceable life in all godliness and reverence" (2:2). That Paul called on the women to adopt this quiet attitude suggests that, in Ephesus, some women *lacked* this quality and were disruptive. Paul may have had in mind the younger women he mentioned in 5:13 who were "wandering about from house to house, and not only idle but also gossips and busybodies, saying things which they ought not."

The phrase "with all submission" (2:11) also refers to a basic attitude. The false teachers Paul described are proud; obsessed with disputes; and given to envy, strife, and reviling (6:4, 5)—just the opposite of that attitude of gentleness and mutual submission with which Christians are to approach all interpersonal relationships.

We have to conclude that Paul's first exhortation is not intended to muzzle the women of Ephesus but to encourage a quiet and submissive attitude conducive to learning God's truth.

"I do not permit a woman to teach or to have authority over a man, but to be in silence" (1 Tim. 2:12). This verse is the "proof text" most frequently offered as evidence that women are to take a secondary and silent role in the church. If this is what Paul intended us to understand, his other references to women show that he violated his own teaching. For as we have seen, Paul welcomed women as co-workers with him in the gospel. So what can Paul mean?

First, the phrase "to be in silence" is again an unfortunate translation. The word here, as in 2:2 and 2:11, is *hesuchia*, and refers to demeanor or attitude.

Paul was not saying that women are to "shut up," but rather to stop resisting instruction.

Second, there is an intimate link here between "teaching" and "having authority over a man." The word for "teach" is *didaskein*, the most common Greek word for instruction. The word translated "to have authority over" is *authentein*, which may be understood either as "to exercise authority" or "to domineer." These possible meanings of *authentein* have led to several suggestions as to the link between "teaching" and exercising authority over men/domineering over men.

◆ All teaching involves the exercise of an authority denied to women.

◆ Only authoritative teaching [as by church elders] is denied to women.

◆ In the first century, teaching by any woman would appear to be domineering.

◆ The Ephesian women who were not to teach were both unlearned and characterized by a domineering attitude.

It is clearly vital to understand which of the above views is correct. If all teaching by women involved the exercise of an authority denied to women, women should not teach or preach in our churches. If only authoritative teaching is in view, women may teach and preach, but they are not to be elders who are responsible for the governance of the church and to authoritatively interpret Scripture. If this is a matter of how first-century people viewed women teachers, the restriction would apply only to women teaching in that culture. If the problem is the domineering attitude of the Ephesian women, the restriction is situation specific, and not binding on women who approach teaching with the attitude that Paul described in 2 Timothy 2:24, 25.

If we examine these possibilities, we can perhaps eliminate one or more.

(1) **All teaching involves the exercise of an authority denied to women**. This notion does not seem to hold up. Luke portrays Aquila and Priscilla taking Apollos aside where "*they* explained to him the way of God more accurately" (Acts 18:26). Surely this was teaching. In 1 Corinthians 16:19, Paul mentioned the two again with "the church that is in their house." Again a teaching role may be implied. Paul frequently identified women as his "fellow workers," and even says Junia is "of note among the apostles" (Rom. 16:7). Given the evidence that women prophesied, and given Paul's teaching on the Spirit's distribution of spiritual gifts to all members of the Body of Christ (1 Cor. 12:7), this interpretation of our passage is most unlikely. The fact is that women did teach in the early church.

(2) **Only authoritative teaching [as by church elders] is denied to women**. This interpretation makes two assumptions. First, that only men served as elders (*episkopoi, presbuteroi*). This assumption can be supported from 1 Timothy 3, where Paul outlines qualifications for both elders and deacons. While the passage indicates there were women deacons, it assumes that elders are to be men. Second, the interpretation assumes that we can distinguish teaching in general from "authoritative teaching." This may be implied from references made to the "ruling" role of elders (see 1 Tim. 5:7; 1 Pet. 5:2–5), but the distinction is not stated explicitly in Scripture.

(3) **In the first century, teaching by any woman would appear to be domineering**. This option seems attractive at first. As Sigounts and Shank have noted ("Public Roles for Women in the Pauline Church" in the *Journal of the Evangelical Theological Society* 26 (1983): page 289:

> The Greek view of teachers prevented 'respectable' women from occupying that role. Greek education was centered around a master who had a deep, personal, extended relationship with his pupils. ... Because of the authority inherent in the Greek conception of the role, women teachers would have been unacceptably domineering.

While this solution is attractive to those who seek a purely cultural explanation for Paul's words, it is seriously flawed. Teaching in the Christian church was quite different from the cultural model. The few passages that describe church meetings picture believers using their spiritual gifts to minister to each other (see 1 Cor. 14:26; Col. 3:16; Heb. 10:24, 25). We can hardly identify the teaching gift as it was used in the church with the conception of teaching prevalent in the general culture.

(4) **The Ephesian women who were not to teach were both unlearned and characterized by a domineering attitude**. Certainly the situation in Ephesus, as reflected in 1 Timothy, fits this understanding of the verse. The following are all suggestive of a domineering attitude:

◆ Paul's emphasis on the necessity of the women learning

◆ his frequent references to false teaching that had corrupted both doctrine and lifestyle

◆ his call to the Ephesian women to reorder their priorities and show more concern for godliness than for self-beautification

◆ his description of false teachers as "proud, knowing nothing" and characterized by "envy, strife, reviling, and evil suspicions" (1 Tim. 6:4)

While the first and third ways of understanding this verse can be clearly ruled out, the second and fourth interpretations remain possibilities. Neither of them supports the notion that mature, godly, and knowledgeable Christian women should not be permitted to teach in our churches.

"The woman, being deceived, fell into transgression" (1 Tim. 2:13, 14). Some have taken Paul's observation that "Adam was formed first, then Eve" to imply that men are to be the leaders in the church and women the followers. Similarly, the reference to Eve being deceived is taken as support for the notion that women are more susceptible to error than men and should not serve as teachers or leaders.

One problem with this view is that the Genesis 2 creation story to which Paul appealed emphasizes the *equality* of Adam and Eve as possessors together of the divine image, with co-dominion over the creation. That Adam was not deceived when he ate the forbidden fruit hardly exonerates him. In fact, it makes him more responsible: It was Adam's Fall, not Eve's. Whatever reason Paul had for referring to Adam and Eve here, it cannot be to establish a subordinate role for women, or to indicate a weakness of character that would prevent them from teaching.

But what if Paul is developing an analogy between Adam and Eve's experience and the situation in Ephesus rather than basing teaching on a text? Surely there are points of comparison between what happened in Eden and what is taking place in Ephesus. Because Eve was deceived she took the forbidden fruit and gave it to Adam. The *deception of Eve* started the chain of events that led to disaster. In Ephesus, women were also being deceived.

But what does Paul mean by saying Adam was created first, and then Eve? Paul is simply reminding the Ephesians that woman was created to *complete* man. Without Eve, Adam was incomplete. Thus men need women as partners for our race to reach its full potential. If the women in Ephesus are deceived, *this can lead the whole church into spiritual disaster.*

What then must be done in Ephesus? Are the women to be silenced and kept from participating in the ministry and mission of the church? Of course not! The women must learn! The women must be grounded in God's truth, so that they will recognize error when they see it! Only when this has happened will balance be restored. The women of the church in Ephesus will be equipped for that full partnership with the men that results in a whole and complete congregation. For this to happen, the women must adopt a quiet and submissive attitude and become teachable.

How different this attitude is from the competitive, know-it-all, domineering attitude that Paul's letter implies the Ephesian women had adopted. We can hardly doubt that when these women had learned, and their attitudes *had* changed, that they took their place as equals beside the men as Eve did beside Adam in the original creation.

Nevertheless she will be saved in childbearing if they continue in faith, love, and holiness, with self-control (1 Tim. 2:15). This final word from Paul has confused commentators across the ages. Yet if we understand Paul's intent in referring to Adam and Eve to be drawing an analogy with the situation in Ephesus, it makes perfect sense. One of the consequences to Eve of the Fall was "I will greatly multiply your sorrow and your conception; in pain you shall bring forth children" (Gen. 3:16). Christ died to free humankind from the consequences that flowed from Adam's Fall. So Paul encouraged the Ephesian women. God in Christ intends to rescue them from the consequences of sin, and as a sign of ultimate deliverance will bring them "safely through" (save in) childbearing. It has been estimated that 5 percent of first-century women died in childbirth. A safe childbirth was the subject of many recorded prayers of women of this era. It would have been a stunning testimony to God's grace, and evidence to both men and women that in Christ the effects of the curse are lifted, if the Christian women of Ephesus were brought safely through this experience.

But Paul added a caveat. "She [the woman] will be saved...if *they* continue in faith, love, and holiness" [emphasis added]. Paul does not say if *she* continues, but if *they* continue. Who are *they?* They must be the man *and* the woman, Adam's sons and Eve's daughters, who in Christ are called back to innocence, to live simple lives of faith, love, and holiness—together.

In Ephesus the problem was that the women were untaught and unruly. They could not join their men as equals. How fascinating that Paul encouraged equipping women to be partners in the body of Christ that together the life of faith, love, and holiness Jesus encourages might better be achieved today.

TWO INTERPRETATIONS OF 1 TIMOTHY 2:13, 14

The Text	Hierarchical	Egalitarian
Its nature	Theology	Analogy
Adam was formed first, then Eve.	Man is superior, woman inferior.	Men need women as partners to complete them.
Adam was not deceived, but the woman being deceived fell into transgession.	Men must be leaders in the church, for men are not easily deceived.	The fact that the women in Ephesus are untaught and domineering is serious and must be corrected.
She will be saved in childbearing . . .	The child borne by Mary will save women (a forced, debated interpretation).	In Christ, consequences of the Fall are reversed: Paul promises Christian women will see this by surviving the dangers of childbirth.
. . . if they continue in faith, love, and holiness with self-control.	(No interpretation, as this appears to make salvation dependent on works.)	To fully experience the promised reversal of the consequences of the Fall now, men and women must live the Christian life as partners.

Conclusions

We have surveyed Paul's letters to discern his view of women. We have examined three kinds of data found in Paul's letters to first-century churches.

First we examined casual references Paul made to women. These clearly show that the apostle valued women highly as co-workers and church leaders. There is evidence that two women held important offices, Phoebe as a deacon, and Junia as a "notable" apostle.

We then surveyed two "household code" sections in Paul's letters. These show that the apostle, while not challenging the patriarchal structure of first-century society, did promote the radical transformation of husband/wife relationships. Paul's innovation of defining reciprocal duties owed by husbands and wives to each other introduced an equalizing principle that simply did not exist in pagan society.

Third, we looked at three passages that contain specific teaching on women. Many have read a hierarchical structure into these passages that seems to conflict with the data in the Gospels, Acts, and with Paul's own casual references to women. Yet as we looked more closely at each passage, we saw that each can (and should) be understood to support the view that women are to be active participants with men in ministries in the church. Rather than limit women's participation by denying them significant roles, these passages were intended to correct specific situations in Corinth and in Ephesus that prevented women praying, prophesying, and teaching *effectively*.

Yet in all our discussion, we have not mentioned one stunning affirmation found in Galatians 3:26-28. There, Paul wrote:

> For you are all sons of God through faith in Christ Jesus. For as many of you as were baptized into Christ have put on Christ. There is neither Jew nor Greek, there is neither slave nor free, there is neither male nor female; for you are all one in Christ Jesus.

All believers alike are lifted in Christ to the legal position held only by "sons" in Roman law. In the church, all the old barriers are taken down. Whether the barrier is ethnic (Jew vs. Greek), social (slave vs. free), or gender-based (male vs. female), that barrier is irrelevant in the body of Christ. We are to see each other as equals now: as one in Christ Jesus.

Appendix E
Proberbs 31 Woman

In Praise of Wives

If we were to ask whether women were valued as persons in Old Testament times, we could hardly do better than to turn to Proverbs 31. While the description was written after the age of judges, it does provide unique insight into how the women who filled the traditional roles were viewed in that society and into the abilities needed if women were to be successful. While the description portrays a woman in a family who is far wealthier than most of her contemporaries, the advantages she enjoys enrich, rather than diminish, the Old Testament's window into the lives of ordinary women. While the NKJV text treats each verse in isolation, the passage is reproduced below in paragraph format to give a better overview of themes the writer develops.

Who can find a virtuous wife? For her worth is far above rubies. The heart of her husband safely trusts her; so he will have no lack of gain. She does him good and not evil all the days of her life.

She seeks wool and flax, and willingly works with her hands. She is like the merchant ships, she brings her food from afar. She also rises while it is yet night, and provides food for her household, and a portion for her maidservants. She considers a field and buys it; from her profits she plants a vineyard. She girds herself with strength, and strengthens her arms. She perceives that her merchandise is good, and her lamp does not go out by night. She stretches out her hands to the distaff, and her hand holds the spindle.

She extends her hand to the poor, yes, she reaches out her hands to the needy. She is not afraid of snow for her household, for all her household is clothed with scarlet.

She makes tapestry for herself; her clothing is fine linen and purple.

Her husband is known in the gates, when he sits among the elders of the land.

She makes linen garments and sells them, and supplies sashes for the merchants.

Strength and honor are her clothing; she shall rejoice in time to come. She opens her mouth with wisdom, and on her tongue is the law of kindness. She watches over the ways of her household, and does not eat the bread of idleness.

Her children rise up and call her blessed; her husband also, and he praises her: "Many daughters have done well, but you excel them all." Charm is deceitful and beauty is passing, but a woman who fears the LORD, *she shall be praised.*

What does Proverbs 31:10–30 reveal? Let's examine the text.

Her character (vv. 10–12). She is virtuous, trustworthy, and committed to doing good.

Her lifestyle (vv. 13–19). She fulfills all of the traditional household roles performed by women, working hard to care for her family.

Her values (vv. 20,21). She has a deep concern for the needy, as well as for the welfare of her family.

Her sense of self-worth (v. 22). She thinks enough of herself to enjoy the luxuries her hard work makes possible for her.

Her impact (v. 23). She is not simply known as her husband's wife: he is also respected as her husband!

Her enterprise (v. 24). She takes steps to sell any excess produced in her household. Her enterprise is also reflected in verse 16.

Her wisdom (vv. 25–27). The good wife is valued for her wisdom, as well as for her work. She is sensitive to what is happening in her household and offers good counsel in a loving way.

Her reward (vv. 28–30). Her reward is the love and praise of her children and her husband, and the knowledge that what she values is pleasing to the Lord.

A closer look at Proverbs 31:10–20. One of the most important contributions of Proverbs 31 to a biblical view of women is found in an analysis of the traits required to function as a woman in Old Testament society.

In our day, we're familiar with stereotypes that too often are used to determine appropriate male and female roles. We assume a man is more aggressive and better equipped to earn a living in a competitive world. We assume a woman is more nurturing and is the appropriate person to care for children. So men should work outside the home, and women should work at home. We assume a man has a mathematical mind, so men should be engineers and scientists. Women are more verbal, so they make good teachers and social workers. Men see the big picture, so they should be bosses. Women are better at details, so they should be secretaries.

While such stereotypes are debunked today, most in our society still assume that basic differences do exist between men and women, and these differences mean men are better suited for certain jobs and women are better suited for other jobs. The disparity in pay between men and women in the workplace also reflects the persistent notion that somehow men bring more to any job than a woman does. For many Christians, these notions are justified by what they suppose the Bible teaches, even though proof texts are hard to find. So it is important to examine Proverbs 31 and to see what contribution it may make to a truly biblical understanding of this issue.

When we do look closely at the description of the tasks performed by a virtuous wife, we make a number of interesting discoveries. Descriptive phrases we need to consider closely are the following:

- "She seeks wool and flax" (v. 13)
- "She works with her hands" (v. 13)
- "She brings her food from afar" (v. 14)
- She provides "a portion for her maidservants" (v. 15)
- She "considers a field and buys it" (v. 16).
- "From her profits she plants a vineyard" (v. 16)
- "She perceives that her merchandise is good" (v. 18).
- "She extends her hand to the poor" (v. 20).
- "All her household is clothed with scarlet" (v. 21)
- "Her clothing is fine linen and purple" (v. 22).
- "She makes linen garments and sells them" (v. 24)
- She "supplies sashes for the merchants" (v. 24).
- She "watches over the ways of her household" (v. 27).

What Does an Examination of These Phrases Reveal?

"She seeks wool and flax" (v. 13). Wool and flax were the raw materials from which clothing was made. The word "seeks" implies a careful evaluation of the raw materials before they are purchased or used in order to obtain the best. In modern terms, the virtuous wife of Proverbs 31 served as her own purchasing agent and sought out quality goods at the best price for her household enterprises.

"She works with her hands" (v. 13). It is important for anyone who operates an enterprise to know every aspect of production. The virtuous wife described here is no absentee manager: she knows every step in the process of creating garments, and works hands-on in each phase. Her own skill enables her to instruct and teach others, to assign tasks, and to supervise their work.

She provides a "portion for her maidservants" (v. 15). The reference here is not to feeding her staff, as the association with the first half of the verse might suggest. This phrase refers to the virtuous woman's management of her maidservants—her employees.

It's clear that the woman described in Proverbs 31 was not like most other women of her time, in that she was unusually well to do. Few households had maidservants. But a woman who had these advantages was expected to 'manage the maidservants who worked under her. And this meant she was responsible to organize and assign "portions"—tasks. She must plan the work needed to be done each day, select the right persons to accomplish each task, and supervise their efforts.

"She brings her food from afar" (v. 14). While most Israelites subsisted on foodstuffs that they themselves grew, or were locally available, the woman described in Proverbs 31 had more options. She could obtain melons, fruits and nuts, and vegetables grown in other parts of Israel and even beyond. In addition to her other tasks, this woman planned meals and menus carefully, taking care to provide her family and staff with a varied diet that would prove nourishing and tasteful.

She "considers a field and buys it" (v. 16). It's common to picture women in Scripture's patriarchal society as under their husband's thumb. This verse suggests that women had more access to personal wealth than we might suppose and the discretionary power to spend money without consulting their husbands. The virtuous wife of Proverbs 31 used her resources wisely. She "considers a field," determining whether or not it will be a good investment. When she is sure that it is, she buys it.

"From her profits she plants a vineyard" (v. 16). The virtuous woman not only purchases land, she puts it to use. In this case, the woman determines that the land is suitable for a vineyard, so she takes profits from her other household enterprises and invests in planting a vineyard.

Many more factors than the suitability of a plot of land for a crop are involved in making a good investment. Does the crop have a market? Is it a local market or will the produce have to be transported? Planting a vineyard called for serious consideration and a major investment. The land had to be cleared of stones and then walled in. A winepress had to be constructed. Jars had to be obtained in which to store the juice the vines produced. During the summer, boys would have to be hired to sit on raised towers to drive flocks of birds away. The owner of a vineyard would need a local source of labor during the harvest. If the jars of wine were to be shipped to another area or even across the Mediterranean, transport would have to be arranged, and contracts executed with middlemen who would sell the wine.

We cannot doubt that the wife of Proverbs 31 fully understood what was involved in planting a vineyard, had evaluated the market factors, and felt capable of making the necessary arrangements. In modern terms, the wife of Proverbs 31 looked at the economy, did a marketing study, assessed the labor market, and in the end, decided it would be wise to diversify by adding a vineyard to her other enterprises.

"She perceives that her merchandise is good" (v. 18). The chapter makes clear the nature of her primary merchandise. Verse 24 says the virtuous woman "makes linen garments and sells them, and supplies sashes for the merchants." Her maidservants (employees) were producing more cloth than the household could use. So she arranged to sell the excess to merchants. What is more, she made sure the cloth she sold was of the highest quality. In addition to her other tasks, the virtuous woman carefully checked the finished products, exercising quality control.

"She extends her hand to the poor" (v. 20). The wife of Proverbs 31 controlled discretionary funds. She was free to disperse them as she chose, even to give them away to the poor.

"All her household is clothed in scarlet" (v. 21). The reference to scarlet is significant. Untreated wool was a dingy off-white, and was normally dyed whenever possible. As red dyes remained fixed and were less likely to bleach out, crimson and scarlet clothing was more desirable—and more expensive. The virtuous woman of Proverbs 31 is a successful wife and businesswoman. Her enterprises have paid well, and she is able to clothe her household—not just her family but her servants as well—in the more expensive clothes.

The same point is made in describing the good wife as clothed in "linen and purple." Linen was expensive, and purple dye was the most expensive dye of all. This special dye was made from the crushed shells of the murex shellfish. Truly, the virtuous woman of Proverbs 31 was quite capable—and very successful.

What does all this imply? Simply that while the responsibilities of women were in-doors rather than outdoors, to fulfill these responsibilities women needed and exercised similar abilities as men exercised.

We cannot look at the Bible's description of the virtuous woman's activities and imagine for a moment that women were inferior to men by nature or that the gifts and abilities of women went unrecognized in Old Testament times.

Certainly Ruth's capabilities were quickly recognized when she arrived in Judah with her mother-in-law. Ruth was quickly established in the eyes of the community as a quality person. In expressing this view, Boaz, who later married Ruth, used the key word from Proverbs 31 to characterize her: "All the people of my town know that you are a *virtuous* woman" (Ruth 3:11). "Virtue" was not only a moral characteristic, but also a word that clearly identified a woman of proven abilities.

Expository Index

An expository index organizes information by topic and guides the reader to Bible verses and book pages that are critical to understanding the subject. It does not list every verse referred to in the book, but identifies key verses. It also does not list every mention of a topic in the book, but directs the reader to pages where a topic is discussed in some depth. Thus, an expository index helps the reader avoid the frustration of looking up verses in the Bible or the book, only to discover that they contribute in only a small way to one's understanding of the subject.

This expository index organizes references to women by topic, and also by their names. Topics and subtopics are identified in the left-hand column. Key Bible verses and passages are listed in the center column under "Scriptures." The far right column identifies pages in this book where the topic is covered.

Please note that material under subtopics is sometimes organized chronologically by the sequence of appearance in Scripture, and sometimes alphabetically, depending upon which organization will be most helpful in understanding the information.

Women in the Bible – Unnamed

Topic	Scripture	Page
Gifted artisans	Ex. 35:22-29	74
Hebrew widows	Acts 6:1-7	304
Hellenistic widows	Acts 6:1-7	303-304
Hemorrhaging woman	Matt. 9:20-22	87
Jairus's wife and daughter	Matt. 9:18-25	94
Jephthah's daughter	Judg. 10	97
Jeroboam's wife	1 Kin. 14:1-13	100
Jerusalem disciples	Acts 5:14	303
Job's wife	Job 1, 2	104
Lot's wife	Gen. 19	273
Naaman's wife's slave girl	2 Kin. 5:2, 3	146
Noah's wife	Gen. 6–9	147
Notable woman of Shunem	2 Kin. 4:8; 8:1-6	229
Paul's sister	Acts 23:16	307
Persecuted disciples	Acts 8:3	304
Peter's mother in law	Matt. 8:14, 15	148
Pharaoh's daughter	Ex. 2:1-10; Acts 7:21, 22; Heb. 11:24	149
Philip's daughters	Acts 21:9	153
Philippian slave girl	Acts 16:16-19	151
Pilate's wife	Matt. 27:19	156
Potiphar's wife	Gen. 39	157
Praying disciples	Acts 1:14	303
Prominent women	Acts 13:50; 17:4, 12	162
Queen of Sheba	1 Kin. 10; 2 Chron. 9	165
Samaritan Mother	2 Kin. 6:25-33	203
Samaritan woman	John 4:6-42	204
Samaritan women	Acts 8:12	304
Samson's mother	Judg. 13	208
Shunammite woman	2 Kings 4:8-37; 8:1-6	229
Sinful woman	Luke 7:36-50	301
Syro-Phoenecian woman	Matt. 15:21-28	231
Timothy's mother	Acts 16:1	304
Two harlots	1 Kin. 3:16-27	240
Tyrian disciples	Acts 21:5	306
Widow of Nain	Luke 7:11-15	243
Widow of Zarepath	1 Kin. 17; Luke 4:26, 27	245
Widow, poor	Luke 21:1-4	302
Widow with the mite	Mark 12:42-43	242
Widowed wife of a prophet	2 Kin. 4:1-7	245
Widows	Acts 9:39-41	294, 304
Wise woman of Tekoa	2 Sam. 14:2-22	248
Wise woman of the city	2 Sam. 20	248
Witch of En Dor	1 Sam. 28	249
Woman who blessed Jesus' mother	Luke 11:27-28	252
Woman with issue of blood	Matt. 9:20-22	87-88
Women disciples	Acts 1:14	252
Women of Israel	1 Sam. 18:6-8	254
Women witnesses to resurrection	Luke 24	300

Scripture Index

Bible references are in boldface type, followed by the pages on which they appear in this book.

JOSHUA

2, 178; 2:1-24, 177; 2:4, 5, 180; 2:9-11, 178; 6, 178; 6:17-25, 177; 6:26, 178; 9, 192; 11:1-11, 43; 15:13-19, 5; 17:3-5, 255; 17:3-6, 263; 17:11, 249

JUDGES

1:19, 287; 4, 42, 91, 263; 4:4, 44, 45, 91; 4:5, 45, 91; 4:6, 7, 46; 4:8, 9, 46; 4:17, 92; 5, 42, 91, 263; 5:4, 43; 5:24-26, 92; 5:31, 44; 10, 97; 11, 97; 11:31, 97; 11:35, 97; 11:36, 37, 98; 13, 208; 13:2, 209; 13:3, 209; 13:8, 309; 13:9, 309; 13:12, 309; 13:17-23, 209; 13:20, 310; 13:23, 310; 14:3, 210; 14:4, 210; 16, 48

RUTH

1, 265; 1:16, 17, 195; 1:9, 195; 1:9-17, 195; 1:20, 264; 2:11, 197; 2:12, 196; 3:1, 199; 3:11, 198, 326; 4:11, 166, 170; 4:11, 12, 268; 4:18-22, 268

1 SAMUEL

1, 82; 1:5, 83; 1:8, 83; 1:11, 84; 1:12-17, 84; 1:17, 84; 1:23, 83; 1:24-28, 84; 1:28, 98; 2, 82, 85; 2:1, 85; 2:1-10, 84; 2:19, 85; 2:21, 85; 3:20, 85; 14:49, 139; 14:50, 11, 261; 18:6-8, 254; 18:7, 254; 18:17, 290; 18:17-28, 139; 18:20, 290; 18:20-28, 290; 18:21, 290; 19:10-17, 139; 19:11-17, 291; 23:3-42, 1; 25, 261; 25:3-42, 1; 25:18, 31; 25:23-31, 1; 25:25, 2; 25:26, 3; 25:28, 2; 25:28, 2, 3; 25:29, 3; 25:30, 3; 25:32, 3; 25:38, 3; 25:40, 3; 25:42, 3; 25:43, 261; 25:44, 139, 291; 26:6, 267; 27:3, 1, 261; 28:5-25, 249; 28:9, 249; 30:5, 1, 261; 31:11-13, 192

2 SAMUEL

1:26, 268; 2:2, 1; 2:3, 261; 3:2, 1, 261; 3:3, 261, 264; 3:5, 263; 3:7, 191; 3:13, 291; 3:13, 14, 139; 3:13-16, 291; 3:15, 16, 291; 5:13, 290; 6:16-23, 139; 6:20-23, 291; 6:23, 140; 11, 22; 11:1, 21; 11:1-27, 20; 12, 23; 12:1-24, 20; 12:9, 23; 12:13, 23; 12:28-31, 20; 13, 236, 266; 13:1, 236; 13:12, 237; 13:16, 237; 13:17, 237; 13:20, 236, 238; 14:2, 249; 14:2-22, 248; 14:27, 266; 16:1, 31; 16:21-23, 39; 17:25, 261; 20:3, 39; 20:16, 249; 20:16-22, 248; 21:1-14, 191, 192; 21:8, 265; 21:10, 193; 21:1-14, 192; 23:39, 20

1 KINGS

1:2, 25; 1:3, 261; 1:5, 263; 1:15, 261; 1:21, 20; 2, 22, 25; 2:13-25, 20; 2:17, 25; 2:17-22, 261; 3, 22; 3:16-27, 240; 4:11, 267; 4:15, 262; 10:1-10, 165; 10:13, 166; 11:18-20, 266; 12:12, 13, 100; 13, 270; 14:1-13, 100; 14:12, 13, 100; 14:17, 101; 14:21-31, 265; 15:2-13, 264; 16:31,101; 17, 245; 17:10-16, 246; 17:12, 246; 17:12-15, 246; 17:17-24, 246; 17:18, 246; 17:22, 246; 17:24, 246; 18, 103; 18:1-13, 101; 19:1, 2, 101; 19:3, 103; 20:5, 290; 21:1-15, 101; 21:4, 292; 21:7-11, 292; 21:14-16, 292; 21:23, 103; 22:43, 18

2 KINGS

4:1-7, 245; 4:8-37, 229; 4:13, 230; 4:16, 230; 4:28, 230; 5:2, 3, 146; 5:3, 146; 6:25-33, 203; 8:1-6, 229; 8:18, 17; 8:26, 17; 9:1-37, 101; 9:30, 103; 11:1, 17; 11:2, 95; 11:1-20, 17; 11:18, 20, 18; 12:21, 266; 14:9, 268; 15:2, 263; 15:33, 264; 18:2, 261; 21:19, 265; 22:1, 263; 22:13, 14, 90; 23:31, 263; 24:8, 265; 24:18, 263

1 CHRONICLES

1:32, 33, 264; 2:16, 17, 261; 2:19, 263; 2:24, 261; 2:26, 262; 2:29, 261; 2:31, 261-62; 2:46, 263; 2:48, 264; 2:50, 263; 3:1, 1; 3:2, 264; 3:3, 261, 263; 3:5, 22; 4:3, 263; 4:4, 263; 7:15, 16, 264; 7:24, 266; 8:8, 263; 15:25-29, 139

2 CHRONICLES

7:32, 266; 9:1-9; 165; 11:18, 261, 264; 11:20-22, 264; 13:2, 264; 21:8, 139; 22, 17; 22:11, 95; 23, 17; 24:7, 17; 24:26, 266; 25:18, 268; 26:3, 263; 27:1, 264; 34:22, 90

EZRA

8:10, 266

NEHEMIAH

6:14, 265

ESTHER

1:10-17, 62; 1:10-22, 240; 1:13, 241; 1:15-20, 241; 3:8-11, 62; 4:11, 62; 4:14, 60; 4:16, 60, 61; 5:10, 267; 5:14, 267; 6:13, 267; 7:6, 60

Notes

Notes